REGULATION OF NETWORK UTILITIES

Both the international study commissioned before the conference and the 'Regulation of European Network Utilities' conference itself were sponsored by the Commissariat général du Plan (French Planning Office).

Regulation of Network Utilities

The European Experience

Edited by

CLAUDE HENRY
MICHEL MATHEU
ALAIN JEUNEMAÎTRE

OXFORD

UNIVERSITY PRESS

OXFORD
UNIVERSITY PRESS

Great Clarendon Street, Oxford OX2 6DP

Oxford University Press is a department of the University of Oxford.
It furthers the University's objective of excellence in research, scholarship,
and education by publishing worldwide in

Oxford New York

Athens Auckland Bangkok Bogotá Buenos Aires Cape Town
Chennai Dar es Salaam Delhi Florence Hong Kong Istanbul Karachi
Kolkata Kuala Lumpur Madrid Melbourne Mexico City Mumbai Nairobi
Paris São Paulo Shanghai Singapore Taipei Tokyo Toronto Warsaw

with associated companies in Berlin Ibadan

Oxford is a registered trade mark of Oxford University Press
in the UK and in certain other countries

Published in the United States
by Oxford University Press Inc., New York

© Oxford University Press, 2001

British Library Cataloguing in Publication Data
Data available

Library of Congress Cataloging in Publication Data
Regulation of network utilities: the European experience / edited by Claude Henry,
Michel Matheu, Alain Jeunemaître.
p. cm.
Papers presented to a conference.
Includes bibliographical references.
1. Public utilities—Government policy—Europe—Congresses. 2. Telecommunication
policy—Europe—Congresses. 3. Competition—Europe—Congresses. I. Henry, Claude.
II. Matheu, Michel. III. Jeunemaître, Alain.
HD2768.E854 R44 2001   363.6'094—dc21   2001032882
ISBN 0-19-924415-4

1 3 5 7 9 10 8 6 4 2

Typeset by Newgen Imaging Systems Pvt. Ltd, Chennai, India
Printed in Great Britain
on acid-free paper by
T. J. International Ltd., Padstow, Cornwall

Contents

Acknowledgements

Over the past two years, extensive research on regulation of utilities has been commissioned and carried out on behalf of the French 'Commissariat Général du Plan', directly attached to the Prime Minister's Office. The Commissariat is responsible for shaping medium-term economic prospects for France on economic issues and political alternatives. Obviously, regulation of utilities could not be addressed solely from the French perspective. The topic hinges on EU Commission initiatives and is very much influenced by the policies of other European Member States. Therefore, from the outset, the work has encompassed European experiences and most of the Commissariat Général du Plan seminars have invited leading academics and regulators from European countries to give their views. This book is very much indebted to those experts who contributed to the process and provided fresh independent thinking.

In July 2000, the work-in-progress culminated in a two-day conference held in Oxford. We are very grateful to Jean Michel Charpin, Commissaire Général du Plan, who has given financial support and a keynote address and also to Sir Anthony Atkinson, Warden of Nuffield College, and Jean Claude Vatin, then Director of the Maison française d'Oxford, who agreed to host the conference in their respective institutions. Thanks to both for making it an extremely pleasant and lively event and to Stephanie Wright, Claire Stevenson, and Paola Belloni who offered priceless advice and administrative help.

At the conference, additional contributions were selected and each session was organized so that papers were subject to review and comments by discussants from the business community, regulatory agencies, governmental departments, and European universities. These individuals added invaluable input and their contributions led to useful amendments. We are very much indebted to them. For reasons of space, we list them all by name overleaf.

Inevitably there comes a time for orchestration and administration of the editing process. Several individuals have played a major role and deserve special thanks for their energy and efforts. In particular, we would like to thank Katherine and Tim Keyworth, who helped to put some of the papers into more native English, and Gisèle Lefèvre (Commissariat du Plan) and Michèle Breton (CRG) who swiftly dealt with secretariat matters.

Finally, the entire venture would not have been so successful without the diligence and efficiency of Oxford University Press, especially Andrew Schuller, Sue Hughes, and Rebecca Bryant who guaranteed a thorough check of the manuscript and speedy copy-editing. Many thanks to them and their professionalism.

Speakers

Curt Andersson (Post och Telestyrelsen, Sweden[1])
Tony Atkinson (Nuffield College, UK)
Luc Baumstark (Commissariat Général du Plan, France)
Francesco Bavagnoli (Università del Piemonte Orientale, Italy)
Pierre-André Buigues (Direction général de la Concurrence, European Commission)
Dominique Bureau (Ministère de l'Aménagement du territoire et de l'Environnement, France)
Sir Ian Byatt (OFWAT, UK)
Jean-Michel Charpin (Commissariat Général du Plan, France)
François Colas-Belcourt (Agence de l'eau Seine Normandie, France)
Simon Cowan (Worcester College, UK)
Jacques Crémer (Université Toulouse II, France)
Nicolas Curien (CNAM, France)
Hervé Dumez (École Polytechnique, France)
Katharina Gassner (OXERA, UK)
Claude Henry (École Polytechnique, France)
Alain Jeunemaître (Nuffield College, Maison Française d'Oxford, UK and France)
David Kennedy (European Bank for Reconstruction and Development)
Michel Matheu (Commissariat Général du Plan, France)
Pippo Ranci (Autorità per l'Energia Elettrica e il Gas, Italy)
Antonio Jorge Vasconcelos (Entitade Reguladore do Sector Electrico, Portugal)
Peter Vass (University of Bath, UK)

[1] The country indicated is the country of the institution employing the speaker, which may not coincide with his nationality.

Discussants

Douglas Andrew (Civil Aviation Authority, UK)

David Azéma (Eurostar, UK)

Patrick Babin (Lyonnaise des Eaux, France)

Jean-Paul Bouttes (EDF, France)

Alain Bravo (Alcatel, France)

Jean-Marie Chevalier (Université Paris Dauphine, France)

Olivier Coste (Cabinet du Premier Ministre, France)

Hervé Dumez (École Polytechnique, France)

Katharina Gassner (OXERA, UK)

Jean-Michel Glachant (Atom—Université de Paris I, France)

Jeanne Golay (Water UK)

Marc Henry (Columbia University, USA)

Einar Hope (Norwegian School of Economics)

Bruno Lescoeur (London Electricity, UK)

Philip O'Donnell (Strategic Rail Authority, UK)

Steve Thomas (British Telecom, UK)

Catherine Waddams (Warwick Business School, UK)

Contributors

Curt Andersson has been director for public policy of Europolitan AB, one of the three Swedish GSM operators, since the spring 2000. He has served as deputy and acting director general of PTS (the Swedish post office, telecommunications, and radio regulator) and as senior adviser to the Swedish Ministry of Industry, Employment, and Communications. Before joining PTS he was executive board member of the Swedish Professional Telecoms Users Association (NTK) and was responsible for new technologies at the Federation of Swedish Industries.

After receiving his doctorate in transport economics, **Luc Baumstark** joined the department in charge of sectoral studies at the French Planning Office, a public think-tank reporting to the prime minister. He is currently working on the regulation of the public utilities and has written the last report commissioned by the French government about liberalization of network utilities, published in April 2000.

Francesco Bavagnoli, who graduated from Università Luigi Bocconi Milan in 1998 with a degree in economics, is now researching at Università del Piemonte Orientale Amedeo Avogadro, Facoltà di Economia di Novara, with a focus on business topics such as accounting and auditing.

Ulf Böge, Ph.D. (political science), has been president of the Bundeskartellamt in Bonn since the beginning of 2000. Earlier he held positions as director general for economic policy (1998) and director general for energy policy (1997) in the Federal Ministry of Economics. He has a variety of other experience, *inter alia* as a member of the Governing Board of the International Energy Agency (IEA), Paris (1994–8), head of the German Delegation of the European Energy Charter negotiations (1991–4), EU negotiator of the Energy Charter Treaty during the German EU presidency (signed in Lisbon in December 1994).

Dr **Pierre A. Buigues** is head of the Telecommunications, Information Society and Post unit in the Directorate General for Competition of the European Commission since 1999. He was previously head of unit in the Directorate General for Economic and Financial Affairs. His recent work includes books and articles such as *European Policies on Competition, Trade and Industry: Conflicts and Complementaries* (co-edited with A. Jacquemin and A. Sapir)(Cheltenham, Glos., 1995) *and Competitiveness and the Value of Intangible Assets* (co-edited with A. Jacquemin) (Cheltenham, Glos., 2000).

Dominique Bureau is director of the Economic Evaluation Directorate at the French Ministry of Environment. He is also a member of Conseil d'Analyse

Economique, an advisory body to the French prime minister. He teaches at the École Polytechnique in Paris, mainly in the field of applied public economics.

Sir **Ian Byatt** was appointed the first director general of Water Services in 1989. He is an economist and an expert on the regulation of public utilities. His career in the civil service included spells at the Ministry of Housing and Local Government and the Department of Environment, before joining the Treasury in 1972 as under secretary and later as deputy chief economic adviser. He has lectured in economics at both Durham University (1958–62) and the London School of Economics (1964–7).

Simon Cowan is the Wigmore fellow in Economics at Worcester College, Oxford, and a lecturer at the Department of Economics at the University of Oxford. He is the author, with Mark Armstrong and John Vickers, of *Regulatory Reform: Economic Analysis and British Experience* (Cambridge, Mass., 1994). Before taking up his current post he worked in the private sector and acted as a consultant to the UK government on the privatization and regulation of the water industry.

Jacques Crémer received his Ph.D. from MIT in 1978. He has held appointments at the University of Pennsylvania and the Virginia Polytechnic Institute. Since 1991 he has been Director of Research at the CNRS and assigned to the GREMAQ (University of Toulouse). He also teaches at the École Polytechnique and the University of Southampton. He is a fellow of the Econometric Society and member of its executive council.

Nicolas Curien is currently professor at Conservatoire National des Arts et Métiers (CNAM), the French public body in charge of continuing education within the Ministry of Education, in charge of the chair 'Telecommunications Economics and Policy'. Having trained as a telecommunications engineer, he was formerly chief economist at France Telecom and at the Ministry of Defence, before joining the National School for Economical and Statistical Studies (ENSAE), and then the CNAM. He is a member of the French Commission of the Public Service of Post and Telecommunications (CSSPPT), and of the scientific council of the Electricity Regulatory Commission (CRE).

Hervé Dumez is director of research at the CNRS (Centre de Recherche en Gestion de l'École Polytechnique). His main stream of research focuses on regulation, the globalization of markets, and EU integration. Recent publications with Alain Jeunemaître include: 'Les Institutions de la régulation des marchés: étude de quelques modèles de référence', *Revue Internationale de Droit Économique*, 1999/1, and *Understanding and Regulating the Market at a Time of Globalisation* (Basingstoke, Hants., 2000). He teaches on markets and regulation at the university of Paris X Nanterre.

Katharina Gassner is currently working as a consultant with Oxford Economic Research Associates. Previously she occupied a post as teaching assistant at the

University of Lausanne, and has recently submitted her Ph.D. to the London School of Economics. Her work focuses on the liberalization and regulation of energy and telecommunication networks in Europe. In 1998 and 1999 she worked for the French Commissariat Général du Plan, where she provided analysis on the institutional framework underlying the regulatory authorities set up in the newly liberalized European countries.

Olivier Guersent has worked successively in the antitrust authorities in France (1984–91) and since 1992 for the European Commission in Brussels. In the Commission, he was initially employed in the Directorate General for Competition (Merger Task Force, 1992–6) before being appointed in 1996 as adviser to Competition Commissioner Karel Van Miert. In 1999 he became adviser to Regional Policy Commissioner Michel Barnier.

Claude Henry is director of research at the Centre National de la Recherche Scientifique (Paris) and professor of econometrics and political economy at the Université de Lausanne. He is also member of the Council of Economic Advisers of the Prime Minister of France. He has served as co-editor of the *Review of Economic Studies* and of the *Journal of Public Economics*.

Alain Jeunemaître, director of research at CNRS–Maison Française d'Oxford, is affiliated to Nuffield College and the Regulatory Policy Institute (Hertford College), Oxford. His main stream of research focuses on regulation, the globalization of markets, and the EU integration. Publications include *Financial Markets Regulation: a Practitioner Perspective* (Basingstoke, Hants., 1997) and, with Hervé Dumez, *Understanding and Regulating the Market at a Time of Globalisation* (Basingstoke, Hants., 2000). He teaches on markets and regulation at the University of Paris X Nanterre.

Bruno Johannès is in charge of socioeconomic studies of the Seine–Normandy Water Agency. He is an engineer, and a graduate in public management and environmental economics.

David Kennedy is an economist at the European Bank for Reconstruction and Development. He previously worked for the World Bank, and the Centre for the Study of Regulated Industries, and has acted as a consultant to various regulated companies. He completed a Ph.D. in economics at the London School of Economics, and has published widely in the field of infrastructure reform.

Michel Matheu is currently head of the department in charge of sectoral studies at the French Planning Office, a public think-tank reporting to the prime minister. Formerly he worked as a researcher at the Ecole Polytechnique in Paris and as editor of journals published by the French Ministry of Industry. He wrote two of the main reports commissioned by the French government about the liberalization of network utilities in 1995 and 1996.

Jean-François Pons was a high-ranking civil servant in the Treasury and an adviser at the Cabinet of M. Beregovoy, then minister of Economic and Financial Affairs, before joining the European Commission in October 1989 as a director of monetary affairs, Directorate General II, Economic and Financial Affairs. Since May 1994 he has held his current position as deputy director general at DG IV, Competition Policy.

Pippo Ranci is professor of economic policy at the Università Cattolica, Milano and, since November 1996, president of the Autorità per l'energia elettrica e il gas (Italy's regulator for electricity and gas). An economist with degrees from the Università Cattolica of Milan and the University of Michigan, he has published books and articles on monetary economics and on industrial policies. He co-founded and directed the Istituto per la Ricerca Sociale in Milan, and has been an adviser to the Italian government on economic policies.

Pierre-Alain Roche is the executive director of the Seine–Normandy Water Agency (France). He is professor for hydrology at the Ecole Nationale des Ponts et Chaussées (National School for Civil Engineering), and deputy governor of the World Water Council. He is a graduate of Ecole Polytechnique and Ecole Nationale des Ponts et Chaussées.

Nicholas H. Stern is World Bank chief economist and senior vice president, Development Economics. From 1994 until late 1999 he was chief economist at European Bank for Reconstruction and Development, where he was also special counsellor to the president. Before 1994 his career was mostly in academic life. His research and publications have focused on economic development and growth, economic theory, tax reform, public policy and the role of the state, economies in transition, and crime and criminal statistics.

Jorge Vasconcelos is chairman of the Portuguese Electricity Regulatory Commission (which he set up in 1996) and co-founder and first chairman of the Council of European Energy Regulators. He holds a degree from Porto University and a doctorate in engineering from Erlangen-Nuremberg University, Germany. He began his career in charge of a development programme in the electrical networks department of AEG, Frankfurt. From 1989 to 1996 he was deputy secretary general of Eurelectric (European Association of Power Companies). He was also guest professor at the University of Pavia (Italy) in 1990–1.

José María Vázquez Quintana has been with the Telefónica Group since 1957. In 1996 he took over as director of corporate development in OPTEL, an embryonic company which was later to become the second largest telephony operator in Spain. Later that same year he was appointed secretary general of communications at the Ministry of Development. In November 1996 he left that post to become president of the Comisión del Mercado de las Telecomunicaciones, the Spanish regulator, a position that he still holds.

Peter Vass is director of the Centre for the Study of Regulated Industries (CRI), a research centre at the University of Bath School of Management, and senior lecturer in accounting and finance. An economist and accountant, his experience includes the Government Economic Service, many advisory appointments, and international work. His personal research has focused on comparing and generalizing the economic and financial methodologies applied by regulators.

1

New Regulations for Public Services in Competition

CLAUDE HENRY AND MICHEL MATHEU

The history of network utilities reached a new phase in the late 1970s. The first half of the twentieth century witnessed the mass distribution of these services, with the progressive connection of small local or regional networks. Then in the postwar years there was a general move towards national monopolies, which were usually publicly owned. A third period, characterized by liberalization, has emerged over the last two decades of the century. Competition has been introduced on varying scales in all sectors—energy, transport, telecommunications and the postal service—as a result of the impact of structural changes.

Some of these changes were of an economic nature. In particular, some network utilities were essential factors of competitiveness in industrial sectors that were more exposed than previously to international competition—for instance, electricity in the metallurgy sector. Other developments were more technological in nature. In some sectors it became possible to achieve significant gains by developing competitive, innovative procedures; the telecommunications sector is a striking—but far from isolated—example in this respect. Finally, some changes were due to cultural factors. Generations raised in the services society started to demand quality and personalized service for which the organization and the culture of public monopolies were ill prepared. These changes put considerable pressure on the organization of networks, which led to a restriction in scope of the monopoly that had until then prevailed in network utilities. From the late 1970s, and much more markedly since around 1990, all industrialized countries—and a large number of developing countries—have opened up their network utilities to competition.

The major economic aspects of this liberalization are now well known. Much has been written about them. On the other hand, the problems of public regulation are far from being entirely solved, and more recently much consideration has been given to this aspect. The spread of competition has had a profound effect on the way in which the state intervenes in the relevant sectors. Entirely new forms of regulation are emerging. The creation of independent regulators, the use of sophisticated techniques to ensure fair competition, and the implementation of various procedures to guarantee universal service are just some of the most important examples.

In Europe, some pioneering countries have already tested out new forms of public regulation for long enough to be able to draw some preliminary conclusions. Others have started more recently, sometimes following examples already set and sometimes using more innovative methods. The purpose of this book is to assess what has already been learned and to suggest some questions which need to be addressed.

The aim of this introductory chapter is to set the scene. In Section 1.1 we will try to show that, although the forms of regulation we are going to deal with are fairly new, the issues of public utilities regulation were already being addressed as long ago as the nineteenth century (Section 1.1.1). We will then show how they evolved from that period to the last decade (1.1.2 and 1.1.3). In Section 1.2 we will first give an overview of the major reforms that have taken place in some countries in the last two decades of the twentieth century. The main emphasis will be on changes that affect the way in which the public authorities intervene in network sectors (1.2.2). There is a degree of consensus among the experts on determining a coherent framework for government intervention—specialized regulation (1.2.3), which differs from the traditional methods of regulating competition. There has been much—inconclusive— debate over the best institutional framework for implementing this regulation (1.2.4), often—but not always—through an independent regulator (1.2.5). Both the legal procedures and the actual influence of the regulators vary considerably (1.2.6). One of the reasons for these variations is differences between the countries, another is the differences between sectors (1.2.7).

The specific purpose of this book is to examine, in the various detailed studies that are summarized in Section 1.3, Europe's experience in terms of regulating network utilities.

1.1. THE HISTORY OF REGULATORS: AN OVERVIEW

In most European countries the debate about new regulations did not begin from scratch. Although they were invented at very different periods, two references played an important part in the emergence of new concepts: the American model of regulatory commissions, and the British model of independent regulators. Before setting up the frame of the reforms implemented in the 1970s, it is helpful to look into the history of these forefathers of present European regulators.

1.1.1. *Two American traditions*

Sunshine regulation in Massachusetts
Published in 1869, *A Chapter of Erie* confirmed the fame of its author, the journalist Charles Francis Adams. It was at the same time a brilliant satire of

the captains of industry who made their fortune from the railroads at the expense of the public, and a precise analysis of the means they used to do so.

His fellow Bostonians soon placed Adams at the head of the Massachusetts Railroad Commission. In spite of its name, this commission was not like the quasi-judiciary ones so common in the United States today; in fact, it did not have any regulatory power. As the historian A.T. Hadley wrote a few years later, 'It had really no power, except the power to report, but those reports were strong enough to command respect, and even obedience' (Hadley 1885). By exposing the railroad companies' behaviour to public scrutiny, Adams invented the 'sunshine regulation'. He applied it successfully to improve railway safety, which the companies had outrageously neglected, as well as to lower prices, particularly those of rail freight. Anticipating the European Commission, he demanded that reduction in costs be duly reflected in a reduction of prices. Thus, in a letter written in 1871 to the management of the Massachusetts Railroad, Adams observed that the price of locomotives had gone down from $30,000 to $12,000 and inquired what effect that would have on the railroads' rates. Fearing a public campaign that might lead to intervention by the Massachusetts State Legislature, the railroads preferred to sacrifice $500,000 of profits by cutting their rates.

The Bell Telephone Company invents the private monopoly with regulated profits

In 1876 Alexander Graham Bell, a speech professor living in Boston who was trained as a physicist, communicated with the father of one of his students in what historians consider the first telephone connection: a connection at very short distance (a few hundred meters), but undoubtedly a telephone connection, because modulations in speech were converted into modulations in the amplitude of an electric current. Achieving this before several competitors, including the famous Thomas Edison, enabled Graham Bell to file a patent, soon to be followed by many more as technical progress allowed connection over longer and longer distances and the switching of calls from one line to another.

The innovations of Bell and his first associates and collaborators were not only technical, but also organizational. As early as 1890, they had created the basic structure of what would still be the Bell Telephone Company eighty years later:

- A proliferation of local companies affiliated exclusively with the Bell Company, but which it only partially controlled. This decentralization (which would be progressively reduced starting in 1907) allowed the mobilization of local support and capital and hence accelerated substantially the geographic extension of the company, first in Massachusetts and later throughout most of New England and the state of New York.
- A division, 100 per cent controlled by Bell, to finance, construct and exploit a long-distance system. This was the American Telephone and Telegraph

company, AT&T, which made the first link between Boston and New York as soon as 1885.

- Another division, also 100 per cent controlled by Bell, to develop and produce the equipment for long-distance communication and interconnection. Called Western Electric, it was the preferred supplier of Bell and all its affiliated companies.
- A research centre, the famous Bell Labs, which would make important discoveries in physics and, eventually (on a smaller scale), in economics.

Using to its best advantage the American laws, which protected its initial patents for eighteen years, and multiplying its agreements with local affiliates, the Bell Telephone Company grew quickly. By 1885 it had 150,000 subscribers; at the end of the century there were 2 million and the network of AT&T had reached Chicago. Protected by its patents and by the absence of any public regulation, Bell generated a rate of return on the invested capital of 45 per cent, while the general price index actually decreased by 5 per cent during the same time period.

In the local telephone systems, where the technology was particularly simple to imitate, the situation changed radically from 1894, when the first patents filed by Alexander Graham Bell expired. Competitors entered the market by the thousands. Thus began a wild race for local implantation, not only where service was not yet established, but also where affiliates of Bell were already installed. This race was disorderly, both because the equipment of the competing networks in the same area was incompatible,[1] and because none of the protagonists—not even Bell and its affiliates—had an overall strategy for meeting competition. By 1907 the Bell affiliates controlled less than 50 per cent of the phones and the rate of return of the firm on invested capital had fallen to 5 per cent, while the American economy had passed from deflation to a quasi-stability of prices. Time was ripe for changes at Bell: changes in the management, changes in the control of the capital of the company, and changes in strategy.

In 1907 the Morgan Bank took control of the capital of Bell and placed Theodore Vail at the helm of the company. Vail knew the telephone industry, having been one of the principal directors of Bell before 1900. He was also familiar with finance, which he had learned at the school of 'venture capital', and he had an extraordinary sense of strategic anticipation. He first demonstrated this skill between 1907 and 1912 by organizing the extension of the inter-urban telephone system towards the South and especially towards the West. In this area AT&T had remained by far the most active company, and this persuaded competing local companies to affiliate with Bell in order to profit from the long-distance connection. By 1912 this strategy had produced results: the proportion of telephones controlled by Bell had climbed to about

---

[1] Hence the large number of telephones on the desk of every 'boss' in Chicago, or indeed elsewhere, which one can still see in films evoking this era.

70 per cent and profits to 15 per cent. This result is particularly significant considering the rapidity with which Bell had extended its network. However, such success also brought trouble: the threat of an antitrust suit and even, when the United States was on the verge of entry into the First World War, the menace of 'postalization', at that time an American term for nationalization.[2]

In 1917 and 1918, as part of the war effort, Bell was placed under provisionary public administration, following the model of the post office. The quality of service, in particular the quality of customer relations, went down. That, at least, is how the customers perceived the situation, and this greatly helped Theodore Vail to regain control of the company at the end of the war. However, Vail understood that it would not be possible to return to the prewar situation: the public and its political representatives may not have desired nationalization, but they were not prepared to accept the control of the US economy by 'trusts'. Vail suggested a compromise and in doing so started a system that would become the dominant form of American regulation. He proposed that the Bell Company lose the liberty to fix its own rates for the services provided and that it be placed under the obligations of a public service in regard to universal service. In return, Bell would remain a purely private business, quoted on the stock exchange. It would be guaranteed a fair rate of return on its capital, so its rates would not be regulated directly, but would be set so as to guarantee this rate of return. In addition, Congress would subsequently provide Bell with a legal monopoly on the provision of telephone services and even, indirectly, on the provision of telephone equipment[3] (under a right of preferential provision by its Western Electric division, whose prices were not regulated).

In 1919, when Theodore Vail retired, his model of rate-cap regulation of a private company dominating its sector of activity was firmly in place. A year later AT&T established a connection between New York and San Francisco. Up until 1934, the regulator for long-distance services was still the US Congress, while state commissions regulated local telephone service. In 1934, however, a law created the Federal Communications Commission (FCC), whose duty was to regulate long-distance services.

1.1.2. *Institutional innovation in the telecommunications industry: the United Kingdom and Sweden*

The birth of a British model
When the Thatcher government started to privatize British public service industries in 1983, it had to choose a system of regulation. It wanted to avoid

---

[2] In the UK, the private telephone companies were nationalized in 1912 and incorporated into the postal administration. This was discussed extensively in the USA, where, to this day, the postal system is federally administered.

[3] All other activity by Bell was forbidden, which created a real dilemma 50 years later on the eve of the computer revolution. For more on this, see Vietor (1994).

the flaws of the American system, rife with legalism and political intervention, which was often captured by private interests and which gave little incentive for efficient production. Instead, each sector (telecommunications, gas, water, electricity, railroads) was to be regulated by an office headed by a general director. For example, OFTEL would govern telecommunications, OFGAS gas, OFFER electricity, etc. The collegial structure of American commissions had often produced incoherent decisions. Having observed this, the British gave one individual, the 'regulator', full responsibility for decisions coming from the office that he or she directed. The rules clearly define the role of the director, but are also general enough to allow some room for interpretation. Bryan Carsberg, the first director of OFTEL, used this freedom to make a success of his mission. Carsberg was the first of the British regulators, since British Telecom (BT) was the first company to be privatized, and OFTEL was created at the same time as this privatization. He blazed a trail for others to follow. The establishment, in 1985, of the rates of interconnection to the BT network is a good illustration of his method.

The telecommunications law of 1984 authorized two operators, BT and Mercury, to offer public telephone services and develop infrastructure. BT was the incumbent operator, heir of the telecommunications administration and one of the biggest companies in Great Britain. Mercury was the newcomer, the one that was just building its business, in particular needing to construct its network. As a subsidiary of Cable and Wireless, the main supplier of telecommunications equipment in Great Britain, Mercury was well placed to succeed, but it would take time. It started by constructing dense, specialized networks, first in the City of London, and then went on to establish promising interurban connections such as Birmingham–London. With these connections, Mercury was able to compete with BT because its system used the latest advances in telecommunications equipment. However, Mercury could compete with BT only with BT's own cooperation: the majority of communications passing through the Mercury system had to either start or end on the local networks over which BT had a monopoly. These networks constituted an essential facility: without them, Mercury would be unable to provide what the legislation was meant to guarantee, i.e. competition on interurban connections. Thus, Mercury found itself in the fix of having to ask BT for access to one service that would enable it to compete with another one provided by BT. It would not be surprising, under these circumstances, if BT tried to profit from its position as a monopolist.

As provided by law, the two companies negotiated to determine the conditions of interconnection of their networks. The negotiations were long and drawn out because of the demands of BT. The regulator intervened, as the law provides. For three months, BT continued to drag its feet, complicating the discussions with secondary points and pretending to be unable to provide information asked for by the regulator. Finally, Bryan Carsberg had his staff prepare a proposal ('draft determination') that would establish the conditions of interconnection and, in particular, the interconnection rates. This proposal deliberately favoured Mercury by asking it to contribute very little to the fixed costs of the BT local networks. There were two reasons for this. First, favouring the development of Mercury would improve the conditions of competition. Second, this would serve as a tactical manoeuvre to force BT towards manifesting greater transparency.

Nobody could contest the right of the regulator to propose such a decision: it was provided for in the legislation. He was, however, required to give the concerned parties sufficient time to respond and also to take these responses into account in his final decision. In fact, this obligation provided Carsberg with just the edge he needed in dealing with BT. It was now in the interest of BT to reveal the information it had previously hidden. The roles had been reversed; now the regulator was leading the dance and BT had to follow. Carsberg would later have the evidence that he had correctly calculated his proposition. He would learn that heated discussions had taken place within BT about whether he could be cited for abuse of power; those who thought that the risk of this backfiring was too great won the battle. In the end, the decision of the regulator (determination of interconnection) after the consultation period was praised for promoting competition (see Beesley and Laidlaw 1986).

An 'independent' regulator (an inexact qualification in complex societies with interdependent institutions; see Section 1.2.4 below) such as Bryan Carsberg is faced with economic and social problems that often require rapid action. The nature and complexity of these problems demand that decisions be made not only on a legal basis, but also with the regulator's discretion. He must be free to consider cause and effect, the roles of the different participants and their interactions, and the consequences of any actions he might recommend. According to Sir Christopher Foster the regulator, like a businessman or a general at the head of his troops, must 'be able to make up his mind in the absence of all the relevant facts yet in a way that still, in effect, accounts for them' (Foster 1992: 283).[4] Rather than being a prisoner of judicial formalism, the regulator follows rules of conduct which at the same time preserve his independence (Carsberg had very formal relationships with the directors of the companies in the sector he was regulating, in contrast with the familiarity that could exist between these directors and government officials or politicians) and assure all parties involved an appropriate level of participation. It is, in Foster's terms, a 'natural equity' which is correctly organized, and neither a legal equity nor an assurance of equal division of profits. It would not be an exaggeration to conclude that the regulator is called to use his

---

[4] In this work, Foster presents an extensive analysis of regulation in the USA and the UK founded on his experience as an economics professor at Oxford and the London School of Economics, his work at the Ministry of Industry, as a senior partner at Coopers and Lybrand, and as counsellor to the Minister of Transport for the privatization of British Rail.

'political judgment' in the sense that Isaiah Berlin gives to this concept in his famous essay, 'Political Judgment':

The gift we mean entails, above all, a capacity for integrating a vast amalgam of constantly changing, multicolored, evanescent, perpetually overlapping data, too many, too swift, too intermingled to be caught and pinned down and labeled like so many individual butterflies. To integrate in this sense is to see data (those identified by scientific knowledge as well as by direct perception) as elements in a single pattern, with their implications, to see them as symptoms of past and future possibilities, to see them pragmatically—that is, in terms of what you or others can or will do to them, and what they can or will do to others or to you. To seize a situation in this sense one needs to see, to be given a kind of direct, almost sensuous contact with the relevant data, and not merely to recognize their general characteristics, to classify them or reason about them, or analyze them, or reach conclusions and formulate theories about them. (Berlin 1997: 46)

The first American tradition reinvented in Sweden

The independence of the Swedish regulator of the Post Office and Telecommunications (Post och Telestyrelsen) is just as assured as that of his British colleague (who does not have the additional responsibility of the post office). It is guaranteed by a statute that dates back to the innovations introduced in the fifteenth century by King Gustave I, first of the Vasa dynasty. The modern form of this regulation, by what is called a specialized government agency, is defined in the current Swedish Constitution. The specialized government agency's job is to apply the laws in its area of competence. Its general director, appointed by the government for a six-year term[5] is independent in the sense that no government minister or civil servant can intervene in the decisions he makes as regulator. A dissatisfied minister or civil servant, or indeed any Swedish citizen or institution, may ask an administrative court to examine a decision's conformity with the law the regulator must follow. If the decision is confirmed as legal and the government does not agree, it can always request that the Parliament change the laws.

What can the regulator, who can unilaterally decide on so few issues, make of this independence when deciding on an issue so important for competition as setting interconnection rates? He can lead an inquiry, give opinions and intervene as a mediator. In his own terms, 'two years of negotiations, involving two formal interventions through mediation, have lowered the rates of interconnection by a third and soon by one-half'. However, the negotiations were too long and risked getting blocked, so the regulator's decision was given the power of law in the case of a stalemate. Still, preference is to be given to persuasion and mediation whenever possible.

A good illustration of the method is found in a closer examination of how the regulator treated the interconnection rates, in particular in a case dealing with

---

[5] While the legislature sits only a three-year term.

the interconnection of internet users. It happened that Tele-2, the leading competitor for landline telephones in Sweden against the older (and public) firm Telia, had more success as an internet service provider than did Telia. However, access to the net via Tele-2 required, for most users, use of the local lines of Telia. Not having predicted this sort of use of its local connections, Telia found itself forced to apply its usual interconnection rates. These rates had been conceived to apply to rather short communications—or, in any case, connections a great deal shorter than connections to the internet. Now, Telia wished to diversify its rates, increasing those paid for longer communications. The changes did not seem unreasonable, and the regulator might have approved them before competition for the internet began, but now that Tele-2 had largely conquered the market, it looked like a deliberate effort on the part of Telia to hamper its competitor. The regulator at the time did not have the power to forbid the changes requested by Telia, but he did have the power to explain publicly why he disapproved. This was sufficient to prevent Telia from making the change.

The method of the Swedish regulator of the Post Office and Tele-communications is thus a method of convincing, when necessary, by presenting his arguments to the public. It is regulation by casting light on what is really happening, or a *sunshine regulation*, to use the American terminology.

1.1.3. *The European Commission enters the ring (1988–98)*

In 1988, when the European authorities[6] were making their first efforts to coordinate and open to competition various national public services, the directive Telecommunications Terminals caused a great sensation. It stated that the maintenance of a commercial monopoly on telephone equipment by a national administration was not necessary for the provision of good telephone service (Article 90 of the Treaty of Rome) and, in consequence, should be banned. Several member states, among them Germany and France, immediately appealed to the European Court of Justice, contesting the right of the Commission even to make such a decision. The Court quickly denied their appeal, declaring firmly that 'article 90, paragraph 3, of the Treaty grants the Commission the power to define in a general fashion, through its directives, the obligations that follow from paragraph 1 of this article'. The terminals are certainly not the key element in the telecommunications revolution, but what a contrast between this first step in breaking the monopolies over ten years ago and the teeming activity of the market of today!

Other directives for opening markets have been contested over the last decade and have been similarly upheld. However, it is not these alone that

---

[6] This involved not only the European Commission, but also the Council of Ministers, the European Parliament, and the European Court of Justice.

are important, but rather the parallel development of liberalization and harmonization. It would be a caricature of the record of the European authorities regarding commercial and industrial public services to reduce it to mere liberalization. In contrast to what has happened in the United States, they have made a coordinated effort to harmonize through regulation and to liberalize through the opening to competition. The directives on harmonization—of technical norms, of regulations, of accompanying taxes—are no less important than those on liberalization. It would not be exaggerating to say that the European authorities began regulating—in a spirit obviously different from that of traditional regulations—as soon as they started to dismantle those regulations in order to liberalize trade.

1.2. A NEW REGULATION SYSTEM FOR PUBLIC UTILITIES

The new framework created by pioneering countries like the United Kingdom and Sweden had been made necessary, more than a century after the first American experience, by far-reaching changes that marked the beginning of a new era in the history of public utilities.

1.2.1. *Far-reaching reorganization*

Generally speaking, the major change introduced by the reforms has been to reduce the monopoly's area of involvement. The underlying idea was to restrict the monopoly to activities where a monopoly may be considered 'natural' in the sense of the term as used by economists: when returns are increasing and therefore one large firm is more efficient than several small ones. In the network sectors, a natural monopoly generally involves the infrastructure (railways, electrical cables, etc.) as opposed to the service *per se* (transport of goods or people, supplying electricity, and so on).

In practice, the reforms do not involve restricting the monopoly across the board to infrastructure and opening up all services to competition. In some cases, such as telecommunications, it may be considered that there are so many gains—particularly in terms of technical and commercial innovation—to be expected from competition that it may be extended to infrastructure with positive results. In other cases, the close technical links between infrastructure and services or—on another level entirely—a reluctance on the part of the operators' employees mean that competition is introduced only partially or very gradually.

Furthermore, introducing competition is not a question of all or nothing. It may, on the contrary, be introduced under many different guises. For instance, this could mean restricting competition to certain kinds of services (such as rail freight) or certain types of customers (the largest, on the basis of a consumption threshold, as is often the case in the energy sector), restricting the number of operators (in mobile telephony), choosing between competition within a given service (many operators offering the same service simultaneously) and competition for providing the service (awarding a single operator a concession after an invitation to tender), and so forth.

One of the major practical difficulties that the public authorities face when introducing competition is that the activities carried out under a monopoly and those open to competition coexist within the same company. Prior to liberalization, most monopolies responsible for public services were integrated: they owned the infrastructure and offered a range of services. If the infrastructure, or the infrastructure and part of the output of services, remain under a monopoly while all or some of the services are opened up to competition, the monopoly is faced with a temptation that is hard to resist: using the profits it generates on the monopoly segment to offer artificially low prices in the competitive activity.

This is why another important aspect of the reforms undertaken is to dissociate the monopolistic activities from the competitive activities. In some countries or some sectors it may be deemed necessary to separate them completely, that is to prohibit a company that has a monopoly—or its subsidiaries—from carrying out any competitive activity allied to the monopoly. In most cases there is a less severe form of dissociation: the obligation to spin off competitive activities, or simply to keep separate accounts for each of them. When these changes occur, the ownership of all or part of the units spun off may change: the capital of public operators may be opened up or sold in its entirety to private investors.

A large variety of reforms are therefore possible. In fact, the countries that were the first to implement reforms—in the late 1970s—tested out various systems. The results were deemed sufficiently positive for their example to be widely followed in Europe, using a variety of procedures. The European directives of the late 1980s, and especially the 1990s, have undoubtedly resulted in a certain degree of coordination between the reforms implemented by the member states. But there is no question of harmonization in the strict sense of the term, since these directives generally set the minimum thresholds for opening up the market and fairly general organizational principles. The member states are free to go beyond these thresholds and to use the available margins of subsidiarity. As a result, the European public services environment is far from homogeneous.

1.2.2. *New forms of regulation*

Contrary to a widely held belief, the liberalization of network utilities does not imply deregulation. In fact, the introduction of competition involves setting up new regulations that differ from those that existed previously. This entails a profound change in the ways in which the state intervenes, so profound that we may even speak of new forms of public regulation.

When networks were based on a monopoly, the essential role of the state was to control these monopolies. It made sure that their prices were not excessive, that their economic performance was satisfactory, and that public service obligations were fulfilled.

Once competition is introduced, the way in which the state intervenes inevitably becomes more complex. The public authorities certainly have to abolish many regulations—those that grant operators exclusive or special rights, such as a monopoly on all or some of their activities. They also continue to perform existing duties; in particular, they must still exercise control over the segments of activity that remain under a monopoly. But first and foremost, they have to take on new duties.

In the first instance, the national and European authorities must ensure technical harmonization of the sectors and inter-operability of the networks. The greater the number of operators owing to competition, the more necessary it becomes to ensure that their technical systems are compatible.

But the most important new task lies elsewhere: the state must also guarantee that competition is introduced fairly and that public service obligations are fulfilled. This is why it is necessary to set up regulations that differ qualitatively from those that applied previously (Box 1.1).

The objective of fair competition involves high stakes and calls for complex control mechanisms. This means creating a competitive field from scratch in a sector that has to date been monopolistic. Newcomers need to access existing networks and must be able to do so on fair terms. Scarce resources have to be allocated impartially. Licences for operating services have to be granted. Newcomers' chances of success depend on the authorities performing these different tasks effectively.

The most obvious example is no doubt that of infrastructure access charges, which inevitably provoke strong controversy. When a company retains the monopoly over an infrastructure and carries out competitive service activities, fair competition can only be achieved subject to two conditions. First, the tariffs offered to competing operators must be the same as those the company uses itself. Second, these tariffs must not be established or structured so as to make them a barrier to competitors entering the field. The task of public regulation is to ensure that the conditions for fair competition are in place.

The objective of safeguarding public interest also requires setting up elaborate mechanisms. It is not acceptable for citizens to be deprived of access to services that are essential to the social fabric and the exercise of fundamental rights. If spontaneous market forces seem to threaten such access, it is essential to set up corrective mechanisms, while creating the fewest distortions possible in the competitive field.

Thus, public interest dictates that final tariffs be affordable, or even equal, for all domestic users. This inevitably results in discrepancies between price and cost structures. If we are not careful, the new competitors will skim off the market; that is, they will take positions only in the sectors of activity where

Box 1.1. *Competition, public service, and regulation*

To liberalize is to open to competition. Which competition? Contrary to what is often implied by its supporters, competition is many-sided, beneficial in some circumstances and harmful in others. According to Joseph Schumpeter, economic development results from the carrying out of new combinations which, by the play of competition, lead to the elimination of old combinations (Schumpeter 1934: 66 and 67). This competition of innovation, of selection, of radical transformation of the productive apparatus, is clearly at work in the telecommunications industry, and the European authorities have encouraged it.

Still, in the absence of truly significant innovations that give it a decisive advantage, competition can produce some bad surprises. In the first place, it can multiply fixed costs and reduce productivity if there are increasing returns to scale, as is often the case in industrial and commercial public services. Too many producers, often excessively optimistic, enter a limited market and will make great efforts to stay there. These are situations in which the negative external effects of reciprocal eviction outweigh the positive effects of enlarging the market and selecting the most efficient producers (see Vickers 1995; Ponssard 1995). To this waste is added the temptation to trespass the 'rules of the game', whose respect, whether or not legally enforced, serves the public interest. Such was the case when bus companies operating in provincial Britain manipulated the conditions of service and degraded the product of their competitors,[a] or again when road transport companies and certain airlines have transgressed safety and labour laws. When this happens, competition destroys the very basis on which it is supposed to operate.

Obviously, competition cannot have the hoped-for advantages without appropriate forms of regulation, appropriate to the following three great objectives:

1. the definition and assessment of policies and of public service goals;
2. the control of prices and quality for the benefit of captive users;
3. the control of the conditions of competition and their link with the public service goals.[b]

The definition of public service policies and goals is entrusted to Parliament and the government. However, as the British, Swedish, and Italian experiences show, it is thanks to well-armed regulators, as independent of the private interests they controlled (at the very least[c]) as of political and administrative pressures, that the new entrants in the telecommunications market could have a fair shake[d] with the big operators that were *already in place*.

[a] 'Most of the new entrants adopt the same competitive strategy. The attack usually centres on the busiest routes in urban corridors ... It is not unusual that the rivalry "on the road" leads the bus drivers to "hanging on" at busy stops or along routes to pick up passengers or racing to stops which are known to be busy. The former practice can lead to bunching of buses and congestion in high streets and the latter is potentially dangerous' (Transport Committee, House of Commons, *The Consequences of Bus Deregulation*, November 1995: xviii).

[b] According to the report by R. Denoix de Saint Marc to the French Prime Minister, the classification of public service missions can be characterized as follows: They contribute to two types of fundamental goals:

- goals contributing to economic and social cohesion, in particular to the fight against exclusion;
- goals promoting an efficient and balanced use—in space and in time—of territory and a society of common resources at the regional, national or European level.

[c] But far from being always assured; the captive regulator is not only a theoretical invention.

[d] Without underestimating the role of technical progress and the rigidity of the incumbent firms.

prices are higher than costs. It is therefore necessary for the state to intervene, by taking two kinds of measures. First, it must require that one or more operators supply service to everyone at a regulated price; and second, if necessary it must require that those operators who try to skim off the market bear part of the corresponding burden of costs. This can be ensured through procedures of varying degrees of complexity which transfer costs from advantaged operators to disadvantaged operators. As far as missions of public interest are concerned, operators must play or pay.

The scope of these new tasks is wide and constitutes a new regulatory role for the state. It is clear that, should some of the companies within the liberalized sector remain public, the state needs to draw a clear distinction between its role as a shareholder in certain operators on the one hand, and as a designer and monitor of the rules of the competitive game in which these operators are involved on the other hand. One may not be simultaneously team owner and referee.

The main challenge is to draft and set up the best institutional and procedural framework to ensure the success of the new regulations. The success of the reforms depends on the way in which they are implemented. Competition can be introduced with varying degrees of speed and effectiveness, depending on each specific situation. The very momentum of the sector is at stake. The opening up of one sector enables new industrial strategies to be deployed. Previously unexploited synergies can trigger a trend of horizontal or vertical integration: this is illustrated by the emergence of multi-energy companies or multi-service distributors (water, energy, or telecommunications).

Against this backdrop, we can assess how important it is that institutions and procedures responsible for introducing and regulating competition in network industries be well thought out.

1.2.3. *The outlines of specialized regulation*

Traditionally, the term 'specialized regulation' in network utilities refers to all the duties discussed above, excluding harmonization but including control over monopolies. To give a more synthetic definition,[7] this involves all aspects of intervention on the part of the public authorities, aimed at establishing competition in a sector where it did not previously exist or existed only to a very limited extent, and reconciling the fair exercise of such competition with the duties in the public interest that are incumbent upon network utilities.

From this definition, it can be seen that two limits have to be set to define the scope of specialized regulation. On the one hand, a certain number of tasks clearly have to be defined through democratic debate prior to the exercise of

---

[7] What follows is based on the recent ideas set out in the following report: CGP, French Planning Office (working party led by J. Bergougnoux), *Services publics: perspectives de concurrence et régulation* (Public services: outlook for competition and regulation), la Documentation française, 2000.

regulation. In particular, it is unanimously recognized that it is the legislator's responsibility to define the public service obligations in each sector. It is less clear how detailed the provisions of the regulatory framework, and thus the degree of genuine autonomy enjoyed by the entities responsible for regulation, should be. For instance, the French regulatory bodies do not have rule-making powers—they merely interpret the principles set out in laws and decrees. In contrast, UK regulators have considerable rule-making powers. There is thus a certain grey area between the scope of regulation on the one hand and the powers of the legislative and ruling bodies on the other. For each sector, each country opts for the limits it deems most appropriate.

Another limit that has to be defined is that which separates regulation from the enforcement of competition law. On the one hand, these two aspects of public policy may appear to be very different. The enforcement of competition law essentially involves maintaining equilibrium in a sector where competition has always been present, preventing cartels and any abuse of a dominant position. Regulating a public service network involves boosting competition where it did not previously exist. Another specific feature is that it must also reconcile competition with the fulfilment of duties in the public interest. But there is also a real continuity between the two. The first paragraph—subject to any exceptions given in the following paragraphs—of Article 86 of the Treaty of Rome[8] stipulates that competition law applies to public services. Often the reasoning applied by regulators when competition is first introduced is similar to that followed by the authorities responsible for competition. Against this backdrop, the borderline between the enforcement of competition law and specialized regulation also appears to be rather unclear.

These are practical issues rather than theoretical considerations. Depending on the view of the respective roles of the executive and legislative bodies and the way in which the two boundaries of specialized regulation are drawn, the ensuing measures may differ considerably, thereby leading to the relevant sectors being handled differently. The examples discussed in the document provide clear evidence of the variety of solutions used.

1.2.4. *The quest for the best possible institutional framework*

In theory it is possible to envisage many permutations of the institutional framework, representing contrasting political views of the regulation of network utilities.[9]

Three of these options do not require the creation of a specialized public authority. In the first instance, it could be considered that state intervention

---

[8] Numbering as modified by the Maastricht Treaty.

[9] The following is based on the analyses of M.-A. Frison-Roche. See 'La régulation: monisme ou pluralisme? Equilibres dans le secteur des services publics concurrentiels, Actes du colloque de la DGCCRF du 26 mars 1998', *Petites affiches: La Loi*, 10 July 1998.

brings national interests into play and that it is therefore of a political nature. Then it is only logical for specialized regulation to be undertaken by a state body. This institutional approach does in fact exist, and we will come back to it later. It applies particularly to sectors where only very partial competition has been introduced.

A second view is that, on the contrary, network sectors can be considered as being broadly similar to other sectors, and that the distinction between specialized regulation and regulation of competition is tenuous. Under this view, it is logical to make the competition body responsible for all regulation, even if this means creating a special court. This does sometimes happen.

However, some analysts draw different conclusions from the same type of analysis. In their view, the crucial question in regulation when competition is introduced is that of price equity. They consider that it is easier to assess this *ex post* than *ex ante* or, to be more precise, that it is easier to say in retrospect whether a price is unfair than it is to set the best price in advance. Under this third viewpoint, it would seem only natural to refer disputes to the court for settlement. Only New Zealand has tried this method, which seems to give rise to many practical difficulties.

On the other hand, there are two views that advocate the establishment of a specialized authority. They agree that going from monopoly to a competitive situation is a very special task, requiring an *ad hoc* structure. The competition authority is not suitable, since its duties are very different; nor is a body under the auspices of the executive, since it would lack the continuity of action and independence *vis-à-vis* the former monopolies.

The disagreement focuses on whether or not specialized regulation should be temporary. Some consider that it is possible to achieve a competitive market fairly close to that of other sectors within a reasonable deadline. At the end of this period, it would be logical to abolish the specialized regulatory body and hand over responsibility to the competition body. Some UK analysts think that the telecommunications sector in their country is nearing this stage. For others, duties in the public interest and the continued existence of natural monopolies will mean maintaining a lasting, deep-reaching difference between network sectors and other economic areas, so that the regulatory body will be necessary over an extended period. It is of course too early to know whether either of these views will be adopted on a large scale.

Whatever the case may be, the establishment of specialized regulators has been one of the major innovations under the new regulations, and it is an issue that has provoked much debate.

1.2.5. *What type of specialized regulator?*

In fact, in most countries the most debated question has not been whether it is necessary to create a specialized regulator, but rather whether it is necessary to set up an independent regulator. In general, the pioneering countries that have set up specialized regulatory bodies have established them as bodies that are not entirely under the control of the executive power. They are commonly referred to as *independent regulators*. This is a rather unfortunate term, since it suggests that these bodies are independent of the public authorities, and that they thus have excessive powers which might be exercised arbitrarily.

This view is misleading on two accounts. On the one hand, the regulators are at best independent from the *executive power*. They are still subject to controls by the legislator that set them up and by the courts, which can challenge some of their decisions. Furthermore, absolute independence clearly does not exist: there are many examples of situations where the independent regulatory body is guided to a considerable extent by government policy, including cases in which it disagrees with this policy. Even in countries where they hold considerable powers and jealously guard their prerogatives, specialized regulators have been seen to bow to government opinion when industrial restructuring occurs. Nevertheless, comparative—if not full—criteria of independence do exist. These include the fact that members of the body cannot be dismissed before the end of their term of office, and that there are fair appeal procedures before the courts or the competition body, a sound budget which is protected from cuts, and a large number of qualified staff. Once these conditions are in place, we cannot speak of absolute independence, but the impartiality of decisions is certainly protected.

Why grant limited but substantial independence to a specialized regulatory body? There are many arguments in favour of this.

First and foremost, it provides a suitable response to the dilemma posed by the state as shareholder and judge. If the rules of the game are applied, or stipulated, by an independent body, this conflict of interests can be managed openly. True, this does not arise if former monopolies are privatized. But even here, many analysts consider that an independent regulator would be better placed to arbitrate between the interests of the former monopoly and the interests of newcomers to the market. In particular, owing to the fact that it is an 'outsider', it can be more transparent and can justify its decisions more clearly. Not only is the independent regulator legally bound against arbitrary decisions, but also, such decisions go against the interests of the independent regulator, as they would undermine its legitimacy and could jeopardize its existence.

Some observers also consider that it is more difficult for the dominant operator in a sector to 'capture' an independent regulator than for a body under government control. This is obviously difficult to prove, but on the other hand it is true that in many countries government bodies have become accustomed to identifying themselves with former public monopolies and to depending on their expertise and skills.

Finally, very pragmatic reasons are often put forward. Only an independent body bringing together various skills and working without government interference would be able to investigate complicated disputes efficiently and

rapidly. It also seems to be difficult for public authorities to recruit and remu-
nerate suitable experts, who must have very specialized knowledge. In addition,
the courts or even the competition bodies take a very long time to settle disputes,
while the dynamics of introducing competition call for very quick reactions.

When a choice in principle is made in favour of specialized regulation, a
decision must still be made as to *how many* regulators are required. Creating
a single regulator for all sectors is probably not to be recommended. This
would be tantamount to denying the specific features of each sector and would
make competence-sharing with the competition body extremely difficult. On
the other hand, there is the question of knowing to what extent linked sectors
should be grouped together. Technological developments tend to blur the
distinction between sectors that previously appeared to be entirely separate.
For instance, gas and electricity can now be more easily interchanged, and gas
can be used to generate electricity; postal and telecommunications services are
in competition, and technological convergence is bringing telecommunications
and audio-visual services closer together. Some experts think it desirable to
merge the regulatory bodies responsible for related sectors, either when liberalization is first introduced or after a transition period. Others are of the opinion that related problems can be solved by adequate coordination between the
specialized regulators. In the specific case of telecommunications and broadcasting services, the wide range of public service obligations in the broadcasting
sector in many countries further complicates the debate.

There is also a geographical aspect involved in the question as to *how many
regulators* there should be. Although networks were generally built on a
national basis, international markets are emerging in most sectors: worldwide
in telecommunications, continental in energy and, to a lesser extent, railways.
Some regulatory tasks involve these markets as a whole rather than in a single
country. Some chapters of this book will show that there is already a type of
de facto European regulation, either in the form of legal rulings issued by
the Community authorities, or through cooperation between national regulators
in the manner of informal clubs. At the other extreme, some countries with
a federal or decentralized system make regional or local bodies responsible for
some regulatory tasks.

1.2.6. *From legal prerogatives to real powers*

If an independent regulator is established, the next step is to define the extent of
its powers. This depends on the choices made in terms of the boundaries of
regulation. In the first place, the extent of the powers granted to the regulator
may vary. This involves the three traditional powers.

In some instances the independent regulator may have virtual legislative
powers, as is the case in the United States. This applies if the regulator has the
power to lay down organizational principles that are so wide-ranging that in
other fields in the same country they could come within the realm of the law.

In addition, the regulator may have a varying degree of power to lay down regulations. In some countries, such as France or Italy, the constitution prohibits a non-executive body from holding real ruling powers; thus, in principle the regulators can only interpret general provisions which are clearly defined by the executive. In many other countries, the independent bodies may hold substantial ruling powers. The regulator may also have a varying degree of responsibility for monitoring the mechanics of the system, such as special tariffs or adjustment funds, which make it possible to reconcile the exercise of competition with public interest.

Finally, some regulators are granted powers of investigation, the power to settle disputes, and the power to impose penalties, which make them virtual judges, whereas others can only instigate procedures which are then handled by the competent bodies: the former thus have some legal power, whereas the latter do not. To sum up, a regulator with significant powers acquires the status of a new kind of administrative body, straddling the three powers, while others only have one or two of the three powers.

The boundary between an independent regulator and a competition body, which as we have seen is theoretically blurred, can also be adjusted. It is possible for the same dispute to be brought before both bodies. Generally, the competition body retains its usual prerogatives over network utilities. But sometimes the independent regulator is given some of the tasks of enforcing competition law, owing to the fact that these are close to the regulatory duties. This was the course taken in the UK regulation reform.

In very concrete terms, depending on the extent of the powers invested in the independent regulator, the latter can have a varying influence on the economic performance of the sector. A regulator carries more weight if it can actually set infrastructure access charges rather than only proposing them, or if it can grant or renew licences rather than merely overseeing the decision. In some cases powers may have appeared excessive. For instance, some observers considered that, in view of its power in setting price ceilings, the UK electricity regulator interfered unduly in matters related to the stock market; in 1994 its interventions did indeed trigger very significant fluctuations in distributors' share prices.

Nevertheless, the theoretical powers of a regulator do not entirely determine its actual influence.[10] In some cases this influence can be much more extensive than might have been expected.

First, independent regulators that duly justify their decisions can have an influence that goes well beyond the theoretical limits of their powers. In many countries the regulators take care to ensure a large degree of consistency and

[10] The analyses that follow in this section and the next are based on an unpublished conference paper by C. Henry, 'Régulateurs sectoriels et autorités de concurrence en France et en Europe' (Market-sector regulators and competition bodies in France and Europe), Conférences Jules Dupuit, 19 May 1999.

gradually set up a clear doctrine, after consultation with the competition body and the appeal courts. As a result, it becomes increasingly difficult to challenge their views, even if they are only able to make recommendations to the executive. Similarly, involving consumers and communicating with the general public reinforces the independent regulators.

This effect may subsequently be reinforced by the effect of public debate: this is known as *sunshine regulation*. In the nineteenth century some American regulatory bodies in the rail sector were able to increase the impact of their advice and reports just because these were made public. By publicly condemning excessive tariffs, it was possible to get them lowered without resorting to legal action. The same effect has been seen in Europe recently—for instance in Sweden.

The regulators' impact on their sector also depends on the skill with which they manage to acquire information that it would be in the interests of regulated companies to withhold from them. To succeed, they have to confront many pieces of information, analyse the impact of their involvement, and test their assumptions. It seems that the regulation of telecommunications in the UK was especially effective from the outset, precisely because the information revelation tactics proved particularly effective.

1.2.7. *Market-sector or national models?*

All the above may have given the reader the impression of an excessively wide range of possibilities. Do we actually see the full choice available in terms of institutions and procedures, or is the diversity mitigated by some regularities? In theory, two causal patterns could play a determining role; either the specific technical and economic techniques of each sector influence the options for regulation, or the legal practices and cultural traditions in the various countries form the basis for national schemes of regulation.

A comparison between the various European countries does in fact reveal a certain degree of convergence at market-sector level. Table 1.1 gives an idea of the European range. Judging from the European experience, it would

Table 1.1. *Dominant Regulatory Patterns in Europe*

Sector	Regulators
Energy	Generally an independent regulator, at least for electricity (in exceptional cases, regulation by the competition body)
Railways	Generally administrative regulation (in exceptional cases, an independent regulator)
Postal service	Often administrative regulation (some independent regulators, perhaps linked with telecoms)
Telecommunications	Independent regulators

appear that an independent regulator is seen as a necessity in the sectors that have been opened up to a high level of competition (telecommunications and, to a lesser extent, electricity). However, sectors in which competition is introduced only very gradually are often regulated by a government body. This is the argument put forward by many governments for the railways. They raise objections to the creation of a new body, seen as unnecessary to regulate competition that concerns only a very minor part of the market. The reasons are less clear in the case of postal services. They are probably more closely related to the political significance involved in having post offices in rural areas: governments are loath to hand such a sensitive issue over to an independent body.

Given the above, can we speak of national models, or should we think in terms of the economic or political features of each sector as being more of a determining factor? A detailed look at the powers of regulators highlights differences between various countries that have apparently opted for the same formula. Table 1.2 compares the powers and practices of energy regulators— or, rather, electricity, since gas is not subject to independent regulation everywhere—in some countries. As can be seen, the decision-making powers, and also the consultation mechanisms, of the various regulators in one sector can be very different. If we extend a comparison of this kind to all sectors,[11] it is possible to distinguish certain homogeneous features at national level, which are detailed in several chapters of this book.

The clearest case is that of the United Kingdom, which used a single model to set up regulators in all sectors. They are individual rather than collegiate bodies, which sets them apart from the rest of Europe. Their independence is guaranteed and they have extensive powers, covering the three major powers. The appeal procedure, involving the competition body, is also a particular feature.

The French and Spanish regulators have rather less extensive powers than most of their counterparts in other countries. A specific feature in France is the very minor role of consumers and the presence of a government representative at meetings of the electricity regulator. But there is no question of a 'Latin' model, since Italy set up powerful bodies fairly early on. Italian legal experts gave much consideration to the counterweight, or fourth power, provided by independent authorities.

The tradition of sunshine regulation is probably most visible in Sweden. Initially, the post and telecommunications regulator had virtually no power, which did not however prevent it from obtaining significant tariff reductions on the part of the dominant operator. Its powers have in the meantime increased, but it continues to act in line with a system of conviction and mediation.

It would be premature to look for an overall scheme to account for specific national features. Various determining factors probably play a role. In some

[11] Here it was possible to make a fairly full comparison only for energy.

Table 1.2. *Comparison between the Bodies of Several European Countries*

Country	France (electricity only)	UK	Italy	Spain
Resources	Budgetary	Paid by the profession at a level set by an annual vote	Paid by the profession at a level set by law, which can be changed by the government	Paid by the profession according to the activity of the sector
Awarding or renewal of licences	Consulted	Awards (the general terms and conditions are set by the government)	Joint decision (the Authority makes a proposal, but only the chairman of the Council may reject the second proposal, on serious grounds)	Makes proposals
Setting tariffs or price ceilings	Makes a recommendation	Sets	Sets	Makes a recommendation
Consultation of consumers	Informal	Regional consumer councils, national council	Mandatory periodic meetings with associations	Consultative council must be consulted under various procedures
Appeal	Paris Court of Appeal, administrative court for certain types of decision	Competition body (and the courts in the event of failure to comply with the body's rulings)	Administrative Court of Milan, then Council of State	Ministry of Industry, administrative court for certain types of decision

Sources: Ofgem, 'Autorità per l'energia elettrica e il gas'; and chapters of this book.

cases, the major explanatory factors may be legal tradition and political philosophy: this is probably true for France and perhaps for the UK. But other factors may also play a role. For instance, the rapid increase in the number of independent regulators in Italy no doubt stems from the fact that the traditional public bodies in Italy have generally been discredited since the 1970s.

Readers can form their own opinion by taking a more detailed look at the various countries studied. The next section presents a brief overview of the various contributions that follow.

1.3. A SHORT SUMMARY OF THE BOOK

1.3.1. *The reforms of the pioneer countries*

The first part of this book examines the 'pioneer' countries, that is to say those that reformed their public service networks several years before the introduction of Community legislation.

In most European countries the United Kingdom is inevitably taken as a model, whether it be as a shining example or one to be avoided at all costs. With an independent regulator in each sector, this country is a genuine testing ground for regulatory methods. Thus, the book opens with three contributions that assess the theoretical and experimental work carried out in the United Kingdom.

Professor *Simon Cowan*'s text assesses the developments of economic theory applied by the UK regulators. He divides them into two main categories. The first relates to the problems arising from price regulation. First and foremost, economists have explored the classic issue of the trade-off between limiting profits and attempting to maximize efficiency. The regulator cannot achieve both these aims; that is to say, it cannot request that the operator reduce its costs and at the same time prevent it from retaining part of the profits. Economic theory has also helped to determine fair infrastructure access tariffs, by inventing and then by transcending the efficient component pricing rule established in the 1980s. Finally, this theory helped the regulator to perfect the operating rules of the Anglo-Welsh electrical pool, thereby putting restraint on the long-standing collusion between major operators.

The second series of economic issues relates to monitoring the industrial structure of regulated sectors. Governments must make several choices in the light of economic theory: whether to separate the monopolistic segments of activity from competitive segments, whether to divide ex-monopolies on the basis of activities or on the basis of geographical considerations, whether temporarily to accept oligopolies or to rapidly grant access to numerous new entrants, etc.

To conclude, Simon Cowan identifies three major goals for the future: to combat operators' tendency to underinvest, to focus more on relative prices within each sector, and to attempt to eliminate the risks of collusion on markets where there are few competitors covering a wide range of services.

In Chapter 3, Professor *Peter Vass* attempts to define the main features of the UK regulatory model. One of the original aspects of this model is that it is applied mainly to firms belonging to the private sector, as the government had privatized former monopolies at a very early stage. The chosen institutional model creates independent regulators and two clear-cut separations. First, is 'horizontal separation': social justice problems are the responsibility of the elected authorities, whereas monitoring monopolies and correcting external effects come within the remit of the regulators. Second, is 'vertical separation': it is the government's duty to establish basic guidelines, while it is the regulators' responsibility to advise the government and to actually apply the rules. Naturally, the regulatory purview is not limited to regulators and ministries but also includes consultative bodies, in particular consumer associations, self-regulatory practices in certain domains, and appeal and auditing procedures. Each body is in charge of specific tasks and objectives.

The main aim of UK regulation is to protect consumers, in particular to ensure that they pay the lowest possible price for a given quality. Regularly assessed price caps are the main instruments used to achieve this goal. In practice, regulators find it difficult to reconcile economic concepts with the empirical data that accounting intermediate technology (IT) systems produce. To help deal with this difficulty, Peter Vass developed a truncated cash flow model, which is steadily being improved to take into account long-term investments, retail price trends, etc. He concludes that polishing the tools is the key to achieving a subtle balance in regulation: if coherent, well defined goals are required, one needs none the less some flexibility in current decision-making.

In Chapter 4 *Ian Byatt*, Director-General of Water Services (1989–2000), cites the water sector a singular instance of UK regulation. In some ways it is an extreme case, as in other countries there is no national regulator of this utility at a local level. Furthermore, the privatization of water was in the UK one of the few such privatizations not to have been backed by public opinion from the start. The reform clearly separated operating aspects from regulatory ones, whereas previously the water authorities carried out both aspects, as well as the economic regulation of environmental policies.

After ten years of the new system, the regulator's assessment is positive. Private operators have become more efficient. This is borne out by facts and figures. Several of the top foreign operators have penetrated the UK market, and prices have risen much less than one might have feared with increasingly strict regulation. There is an incentive for companies to perform as regulation governs prices and no longer profits. The regulator is a genuinely independent authority which acts transparently and communicates with consumers. Admittedly, distribution companies have a geographical monopoly, but it is possible to provide incentives through yardstick competition. According to Ian Byatt, the difficulty for the regulator in the next few years will be to find a fair compromise between the two extremes: that is to say, between banning mergers that may lead to an oligopoly which is liable to prevent yardstick competition from being applied correctly, and allowing mergers and acquisitions that can often result in industry becoming more dynamic.

The second pioneer country in question, Sweden, is in turn discussed by an academic and a regulator according to the general structure of the book. The most striking feature of the Swedish model is the gradual but far-reaching nature of the reforms, without ideological bias, and in a way often reminiscent of the former US sunshine regulation.

The reform of the Swedish railways, analysed in Chapter 5 by *Luc Baumstark*, an expert at the French Planning Office, is typical in this respect. Its objectives were clear: to streamline public spending in the sector and to promote rail travel. To achieve this, it was decided to concentrate government spending on invest-ment, to gradually introduce competition on services, and to decentralize many decisions at a local level. A state body, Banverket, was put in charge of infra-structure, and it made large-scale investments over a long catch-up period. Competition was introduced on services, starting with the unprofitable ones, and was subsequently extended to freight. The results were noteworthy: there was an increase in traffic, and real competition on all segments except freight, where the ex-monopoly SJ retains 90 per cent of the market.

There is no independent regulator. Regulatory duties are shared between the competition authority and a new entity, Rikstrafiken, whose role has not been fully defined, which is in charge of promoting multi-modal traffic for con-sumers and regional development. As is often the case in Sweden, this body does not have wide-reaching formal powers but its influence is increasing. Luc Baumstark concludes that the future will determine whether this system is sufficient to meet the challenges of the second phase of reforms: to remove SJ's monopoly on rolling stock, minimize abuse of its dominant position (railway staff sometimes refuse to cooperate with SJ's competitors), and define more clearly and coherently the scope of the monopoly. It will probably be necessary to make a choice between two organizational models: marginal competition, which would spur SJ, and a competitive market, which would make room for powerful competitors. The second option would probably require a truly independent regulator.

Following this, in Chapter 6 *Curt Andersson*, a former telecommunications regulator, first discusses the start of telecommunications regulation in Sweden. The earliest laws governing the liberalization of the sector date back to 1993. The only uncertainties related to threats on the staff of the established operator Televerket, now Telia. The national context was favourable on the whole, in so far as, since 1990, the idea of minimal and transparent government regulation for all economic and social sectors has existed in Sweden. The concept of an independent regulator did not encounter much resistance, as some government bodies were already almost independent.

The powers of the regulator were fairly limited in the first few years. To wield its authority, it had to play the role of mediator, and threaten to undertake procedures that could be brought before the courts and result in high fines, rather than directly exercise formal prerogatives. Even today, with the enhanced powers it has had since 1997, the regulator makes greater use of mediation rather than coercion. Finally, the introduction of competition and the pressures on Telia have steadily mounted, and now there is a genuine free market. In 2000, only the portability of numbers remained to be implemented. Will specialized regulation have to be imposed for some time to come, or will general competition law take its place? According to Curt Andersson, there are still several problems that do not come under competition law, such as allocating frequencies, but there are only few of these, so that specialized regulation must be seen as a temporary system.

1.3.2. *Second-wave countries*

Many European countries undertook reforms only a few years ago. Therefore they cannot enjoy as much retrospection as the pioneer countries. Their choices were influenced by those of their precursors; some, however, have innovated in relation to their legal system or cultural heritage. In the second part of this book, we will consider four of these countries: France, Italy, Spain and Germany.

In Chapter 7 *Dominique Bureau*, of the Prime Minister's Council of Economic Analysis, and Professor *Nicolas Curien* analyse the new regulations in the French telecommunications and electricity sectors, established by laws voted in 1996 and 2000. These two sectors share similar features, such as a powerful public operator holding major facilities, but they also display differences, above all in the scope of the natural monopoly or in the pace of developments of markets and techniques. The government decided to step up the implementation of far-reaching measures aimed at establishing competition in the telecommunications sector.

However, even in this sector, the rate of liberalization was not as fast as it could have been. The terms and conditions for allocating frequencies for the new-generation mobile phones and the opening of the local loop sparked heated debates. France stands out, as it offsets the additional costs associated with providing a universal service, while several countries believe that the appointed operator has more benefits than additional costs. In the electricity sector France has applied only the minimum requirements of the European directive: the opening up of the market is as tight as authorized and the established operator remains in place, even though the transmission network manager enjoys some degree of autonomy. Furthermore, the government partially privatized France Telecom, while EDF remains entirely public.

In both sectors, independent regulators operate under the constraints of French constitutional law, which does not allow total delegation of regulatory power to a single independent body. They have the power to prepare and to propose decisions rather than to pass them. This particularly applies to the electricity regulator. Dominique Bureau and Nicolas Curien's assessment of the reforms is somewhat mixed: their view of the telecommunications regulator's involvement is favourable, despite the restrictions imposed on it, but they do express reservations about the financing of public interest missions in the telecommunications sector and concern over possible conflicts of interest within the government *vis-à-vis* the electricity sector.

Pierre-Alain Roche and *Bruno Johannès*, who are respectively the director and economist at the Seine-Normandie Water Agency, which is the largest in France, discuss regulations concerning the water sector in Chapter 8. Unlike the major energy, transport and communication networks, which have been in the hands of state monopolies for many years, the water sector in France is dominated by a private oligopoly. Public regulation is applied at various levels according to its nature: at national level for environmental regulation; at regional level, through the water agencies, for financial reallocation (from polluters to economic agents who invest in cleanup operations); at local community level for the regulation of the services. Even though some municipalities, especially small and medium-sized ones, choose to manage the water supply, most large towns delegate it to one of the companies in the oligopoly.

This delegation system has been criticized. It is accused of providing excessively asymmetric information to large private groups and towns, of renewing concessions too easily (in over 90 per cent of the cases), and of insufficiently monitoring the fulfilment of contracts. Even though two recent laws have improved the situation, several innovations are still necessary: to provide greater incentives through the delegation contracts, to improve the skills of local government, and to compare price and quality levels between different municipalities. Moreover, renewing infrastructure will soon become a crucial issue. The authors conclude that, even though it is the towns' responsibility to maintain existing infrastructure stocks and develop them in the short term, long-term investments required to protect the environment are dependent on the water agencies' reallocation system.

In Chapter 9 Professor *Francesco Bavagnoli* examines the rapid emergence of independent regulators in Italy. For many years Italy, like France, had subscribed to the State monopoly model, which seemed to be justified on the basis of the required level of investments, the difficulty for a relatively weak state to monitor private monopolies, and the interventionist economic environment of the postwar period. Recently confidence in politicians and cumbersome public interventions has waned, technical advances have given rise to new possibilities, and the Italian approach has radically changed: competition has been introduced and a model of regulation by independent administrative authorities has been established. Such authorities already existed in Italy, for instance the Central Bank and the Council of State. Consequently, the changes to Italian institutional law brought about by the establishment of institutions in the UK common law tradition did not come as too much of a surprise to the Italians.

The necessary waivers to the Constitution, which, as in France, basically prohibits delegating regulatory power, have been or will be found.

The new regulators are genuinely independent, and their prerogatives span legislative, executive, and judicial powers. It is still difficult to assess their structural impact on regulated sectors. Francesco Bavagnoli concludes that this impact will probably depend on three decisive criteria: (1) direct government intervention in network sectors is not desirable, (2) the regulator should act transparently and be effectively monitored, and (3) assessments should be made in tandem with the Competition Authority.

Professor *Pippo Ranci* contributes the following chapter in the light of his experience as chairman of the Italian Energy Regulation Authority. This body was founded in 1995 in a favourable environment, as few embraced the former system of state supervision, which was chaotic and poorly applied. Major changes were introduced requiring a real cultural change: the creation of incentive-based regulations, the implementation of tariffs reflecting costs (inevitably, much more complex than beforehand), support for environmentally friendly production methods, and a strict monitoring of the quality of provision of electricity. The role of the regulator has become increasingly important in the light of the implementation of European liberalization of the electricity and gas sectors since 1999, and of the privatization process of the major public operators.

With the advent of the integrated European market, it is important that the regulation of the various EU member states be consistent. It would be ideal for the market to be equally open in all countries, but the directives do not require this: failing that, reciprocity clauses make it easier for markets to operate in a reasonably fair manner. The informal coordination of regulators is also important: in particular, it should make it possible to deal with the delicate issue of pricing cross-border transport. Pippo Ranci sees the building of a fair and competition-based continental market as one of the major challenges that the national regulators will have to meet.

The third model, which differs considerably from the first two, which are themselves very different, proves that a 'Latin' model does not exist as such. In Chapter 11 Professor *Nicolas Curien* and *Michel Matheu*, head of department at the French Planning Office, outline the paradoxical situation in Spain where politicians express a desire for liberalization but where quasi-monopolies or oligopolies persist.

The electricity sector in Spain is dominated by two recently privatized companies which control a substantial part of production and distribution. The government planned to open the market rapidly and established an independent regulatory body, but in practice competition remains underdeveloped, for two main reasons: first, as a result of insufficient interconnection, the Iberian Peninsula is not in a position to import competition from continental Europe; second, the regulator and the Competition Authority, despite being independent, are constrained by limited budgets and powers.

In the telecommunications sector, the operator Telefónica, whose capital has always been mainly private, even though the state held a golden share, occupies a dominant position. Even in this case, the budgetary resources of the regulator seem limited, and its results are at times disappointing, particularly in terms of obtaining sufficient transparency in the accounts of the company. Questions raised regarding the opening of the local loop have intensified since 1999. The portability of numbers, on the other hand, is at a more advanced stage than in the rest of Europe. Spanish regulators finally appear to have reached a crossroads: practices do not correspond to the highly liberal aspirations of the government, but the law has established the conditions for greater competition.

The telecommunications regulator *José Maria Vasquez Quintana* completes the presentation of Spain in Chapter 12. He observes that liberalization of the telecommunications sector in his country was stepped up greatly in relation to initial plans, as it was successfully completed by 1998 while the deadline set for Spain was 2003. The law established a regulatory body which may be considered more independent than the Competition Authority. In principle, the government establishes the rules and the regulator applies them. In reality, the government has broader powers in certain areas, such as allocating the scant resources, monitoring Telefónica's retail prices and authorizing new services. Within the government, the preparation of laws concerning the sector and price regulation come within the remit of the various ministries.

Like the previous authors, José María Vásquez Quintana emphasizes the fact that Spain is ahead of schedule as regards portability of numbers and preselection. He adds that new entrants have found price and service niches, and that offers of cheap national calls abound. Nevertheless, at the end of 1999 Telefónica was still holding over 94 per cent of fixed vocal telephony (90 per cent of national calls) and 63 per cent of mobile telephony.

In Chapter 13 *Katharina Gassner*, an expert at Oxera, presents Germany's case, which differs from most of the others. The country's federal tradition led to the adoption of more decentralized regulatory structures, which hampered the development of independent regulators.

The electricity sector is highly fragmented in terms of distribution, with the coexistence of eighty regional companies (which also ensure a certain level of production) as well as 850 local companies. The 1998 law, opening the sector in accordance with the European directive, is unusual in two respects. On the one hand, the government granted the sector the right to self-regulation in the area of transport; and on the other, it did not create a specialized regulator: the Competition Authority (Bundeskartellamt) oversees the regulation of the sector. Competitive offers emerged, even for domestic consumers, but the fierce competition has also prompted operators to merge, threatening to generate an oligopoly, even though Germany is very well connected to the rest of Europe and sets a great deal of store on competition.

Similarly, even though the Deutsche Bahn group (DB) possesses the infrastructure and manages the bulk of long-distance rail transport, there have always been local operators. The reform of 1994 removed railway debt, entrusted management of infrastructure and service to different entities within the DB, and delegated the organization of regional transport to the *Länder*. At a federal level, the regulatory body comes within the sway of the Minister of Transport. Without holding a very substantial market share, many companies entered freight and regional transport activities.

Finally, the telecommunications sector was entirely liberalized between 1996 and 1998 in accordance with the European directive. It is the only one of the three sectors under review to be regulated by the usual independent sector authority, which also oversees the Post Office. Deutsche Telekom is less dominant today than most European ex-monopolies, and prices have fallen significantly.

Dr *Ulf Böge*, chairman of the German competition authority, the Bundes-kartellamt (BKA), sheds a light on this German idiosyncrasy in Chapter 14. He analyses the German policy in the energy sector, where no independent reg-ulator was created. While the situation of the gas industry is still relatively disappointing, the results in the electricity industry are very significant. Germany witnessed a drastic decrease in prices to industrial consumers. Although no authoritarian measures were taken by government, several suc-cessive agreements were reached between producers and consumers as to the implementation of third-party access and network use charges. The process of opening up the market was accelerated by decisions made by the BKA in a few cases of litigation. The next step will be to strengthen competition on the market for private customers, a market that seems to be hampered by high transmission tariffs and unfair switching charges.

Dr Böge is convinced that entrusting the BKA with the task of regulation in the energy sector was a relevant choice. From his point of view, the energy sector should not be compared with the telecommunications industry, where a sector-specific regulator was created. There were already many companies operating on the market when the law liberalizing the sector was passed, and therefore no need to organize the transition from monopoly to competition. There is evidence that implementation of competition legislation by the BKA will provide enough incentives to create fairly rapidly a competitive market.

1.3.3. *New regulatory issues in Europe and beyond*

The third part of the book tackles a number of cross-border issues, starting with four chapters on questions of European regulation. A number of problems exceeding the national framework are examined, and consideration is given to how these issues are being dealt with, either by the EU institutions or in other ways.

Two chapters by *Pierre-André Buigues*, head of section at the Directorate General for Competition at the European Commission, *Olivier Guersent*, adviser to the Commissioner Michel Barnier, and *Jean-François Pons*, deputy director-general of the Directorate General for Competition at the European Commission, examine the role of the European authorities.

Chapter 15 examines the current functions of these bodies and their relationship with member-state institutions. It should be borne in mind that the European Union intervenes in public network services, with a view to either liberalization, as per Article 86,[12] or harmonization, as per Article 95. This intervention is conducted through regulations, which are directly applicable, or through a directive, which must be transposed into national law, or through recommendations, which are not mandatory but whose publication is much quicker. Recently the 'soft law' approach has been increasingly emphasized: a more widespread use of recommendations, or even incentives for self-regulation.

In terms of implementation, government authorities hold most of the powers. This should become increasingly clear. Member states may organize the allocation of scant resources as they wish, provided that the procedures are not discriminatory. Furthermore, in the sectors that are already open to competition, regulation will increasingly consist in imposing temporary measures (i.e. measures that should gradually disappear as competition becomes more fierce) on businesses holding a large market share. This would be implemented mainly at a national level. To provide another example, the European Commission ceases its inquiries regarding anti-competition cases at a national level when they are being properly dealt with by the national authorities. In brief, the more competition there is, the more the principle of subsidiarity prevails.

Chapter 16, by the same three authors, outlines European regulatory models for the future. The national regulatory systems of the different countries and the regulatory structure in the various sectors both differ at present, even though the main principles are generally the same. This is not very surprising, in that the treaties explicitly provide for trade-offs between objectives aimed at economic efficiency and objectives in the public interest: the latter can be assessed differently on a country-by-country basis. Currently, the role of the Commission is not to ensure that these models are uniform, but to ensure a degree of homogeneity. In particular, it attempts to ensure that any infringements of the competition law remain proportionate to the issues related to public interest that provoked them in the first place.

This model may gradually change as more competition is introduced into utility sectors. The authors examine three possible scenarios. Under the first one, the current model would be maintained, but it would be made more flexible, through closer cooperation between the Commission and the national regulators, and through informal partnerships between the national regulators in the same sector. In the second scenario, the authors assume that governments would become more aware of disparities between member-states and of

---

[12] The articles from European treaties are identified according to the new numbering system (after the Treaty of Maastricht).

the issues with implications at the European level. Centralized regulation at a European level could also be envisaged. The authors believe that this scenario has one major drawback: European regulation would lack political legitimacy. Under the third scenario, sector-based regulation would gradually disappear with the rise of general competition regulation, which would considerably simplify issues related to subsidiarity. The authors conclude that, even though a general development of this nature is plausible, the fact remains that certain tasks will require specialized regulation for some time to come, so that for the near future the first scenario is the most convincing.

The question of cooperation between the European regulators is dealt with in greater depth in Chapter 17 by *Jorge Vasconcelos*, the Portuguese energy regulator. He observes that, for a start, the energy sector is subject to different regulations in each country. On the one hand, not all countries have opted for the same degree of openness to competition. On the other hand, two countries stand out on an institutional level: Germany, which has not created a sector-based regulatory body, and the Netherlands, which has created an autonomous body within the Competition Authority.

The regulators of the different countries have two good reasons for cooperation: to share their experiences, and to exchange data. In particular, they wish to monitor multinational operators and compare the performance levels of operators in their respective countries. Specifically, they have established a place of discussion, the Florence Forum, which has been meeting regularly since 1998 and brings together regulators, national governments, and the European Commission. This body formulated concrete proposals for harmonizing national practices and the European market, particularly in terms of access conditions and tariffs of transmission infrastructures. In the wake of the Forum, network operators and market operators also formed a European association, while the regulators meet at the Council of European Energy Regulators (CEER). Jorge Vasconcelos concludes that this cooperative scheme is the start of a new form of European regulation. Contrary to the model provided by the US federal commissions, no supranational body regulates European networks.

The problems of cooperation in Europe regarding air traffic have finally been analysed in Chapter 18 by *Hervé Dumez* and *Alain Jeunemaître*, both research directors at the Ecole Polytechnique in Paris. Air traffic control services display certain characteristics of a natural monopoly, although it is not easy to separate a segment of activity functioning as a monopoly from a segment of services provided in a competitive market. At present, they are organized as monopolies by geographical areas. These monopolies are not highly regulated, and furthermore rush hours are managed by a system of queues and not by a price system reflecting the shortage of slots.

The problem in Europe is not a new one. In the 1960s attempts were made to transfer air traffic control to a European agency, Eurocontrol. The experiment failed, as only four European countries agreed that their work should be delegated to the new organization. Eurocontrol was not scrapped, but its role is now almost entirely consultative. Air traffic control management then experienced more and more difficulties as a result of the rapid increase in air traffic, and various informal cooperation schemes proved inconclusive. At present the sector is not formally regulated, but it is monitored by a specific organization, the Performance Review Commission (PRC), whose practices are similar to those of the sunshine regulation. Reports drawn up by the PRC provide an accurate analysis of air traffic control.

In the light of their findings, Hervé Dumez and Alain Jeunemaître advocate a harmonized, incentive-based system of tariffs for services, in order to reduce delays and improve the efficiency of air traffic control. Nevertheless, air traffic finally shows signs of being an original sector at a crossroads: it should change from a state monopoly to a more competition-based management system, and the European Commission is likely to intervene more forcefully by demanding a clear distinction between the operator and the regulator, or even by introducing directives to increase efficiency, from which the hybrid status of Eurocontrol should evolve.

In the book's penultimate chapter, *David Kennedy*, economist at the European Bank for Reconstruction and Development (EBRD), and Professor *Nick Stern* present the state of reforms in countries of central and eastern Europe, and in the Baltic states. All sectors in these countries have experienced the same problems as in the communist period: excessively low tariffs leading to wastage, cross-subsidies from major consumers to individuals, and indifference to environmental problems. The reasons for the reforms are similar in all countries: efficiency gains through competition and privatization, and also imitation of the dominant European model to facilitate EU membership.

For all that, the situation is not identical in all sectors. In the electricity sector, half of the countries are undertaking major reforms, including the implementation of incentive-based regulations. There has not been widespread privatization, even though there are new private entrants, and the regulators in general are not independent. The telecommunications sector is being privatized more rapidly: this already applies, or will soon apply, to three-quarters of the countries examined. However, regulation is not independent. Competition is stiffer in mobile telephony than in fixed-line telephony, in which only three countries have operators other than the ex-monopolist. In the water sector, management and regulation, which were often nationally run in the communist era, are now carried out at a district level. The private sector is emerging, but regulation is hardly incentive-based. In the case of railways there have been few changes, apart from the fact that several countries have transformed their operator from government departments into businesses.

Hungary appears to be a pioneer in most sectors, while Albania and the ex-Yugoslavian republics are making little headway. The authors conclude that, all things considered, the transformation of operators into businesses has progressed greatly, as has the introduction of the private sector. Further liberalization is required, especially in electricity and telecommunications, as is the implementation of a regulatory framework with a lesser degree of government involvement.

The final chapter, by Professor *Jacques Crémer*, examines regulation of a new sector in which national criteria do not necessarily apply: that of the internet. In one way, the regulatory problems raised by internet are similar to those posed by the telecommunications sector, as the same networks are used. However, in many respects the questions are more complex and new. In particular, access providers and backbones constitute a two-tier hierarchy of networks, of which only the higher level communicates. In the absence of strict competition regulations, there is no guarantee that operators will provide a good quality of interconnection between the backbones.

At the same time, the world-wide standardization required for efficient interconnection is very difficult to organize. International organizations currently provide for this. Their procedures seem to be voluntary agreements in which consumers' interests are not formally represented. Another, more centralized, international organization also oversees the standardization of the web, and raises the same type of question: should we entrust the management of procedures that have such a considerable impact on society to a private body? In Jacques Crémer's view, one thing is certain: these organizations have an almost monopolistic power and therefore should be strictly monitored by organizations with a democratic legitimacy.

A public debate concerning the concept of a universal service is underway *vis-à-vis* another aspect of regulation: should we extend the universal nature of telephony to more advanced services such as internet? Jacques Crémer considers the question of a universal access to services for schools, but in general there would seem to be no reason to subsidize services to individuals.

REFERENCES

Beesley, M. and Laidlaw, B. (1986). *The British Telecom Mercury Interconnect Determination: An Exposition and Commentary*, London: Spicer and Pleger.

Berlin, I. (1997). *The Sense of Reality*. New York: Farrar, Straus & Giroux.

CGP (French Planning Agency), Working Party led by J. Bergougnoux (2000). *Services publics: perspectives de concurrence et régulation* (Public services: outlook for competition and regulation), Paris: la Documentation française.

DGCCRF (1998). 'La Régulation: monisme ou pluralisme? Equilibres dans secteur des services publics concurrentiels, Actes du colloque de la DGCCRF du 26 mars 1998', *Petites affiches*, 10 July.

Foster, C. (1992). *Privatization, Public Ownership and the Regulation of Natural Monopoly*, Oxford: Basil Blackwell.

Hadley, A.-T. (1985). *Railroad Transportation: Its History and its Laws*, New York: Putman.

Henry, C. (1999). 'Régulateurs sectoriels et autorités de concurrence en France et en Europe' (Market-sector regulators and competition bodies in France and Europe), paper presented at the Jules Dupuit conference, 19 May 1999.

Ponssard, J.-P. (1995). 'Concurrence stratégique et réglementation de la concurrence dans un oligopole naturel', *Revue d'économie industrielle*, Special Issue, 385–401.

Schumpeter, J. (1934). *The Theory of Economic Development*, Cambridge, Mass.: Harvard University Press.

Transport Committee, House of Commons (1995). 'The Consequences of Bus Deregulation', November, p. *xviii*.

Vickers, J. (1995). 'Entry and Competitive Selection', unpublished paper, Institute of Economics and Statistics, Oxford University.

Vietor, R. (1994). *Contrived Competition*, Cambridge, Mass.: Belknap Press.

PART I

TWO PIONEER COUNTRIES

2

Developments in Regulatory Principles: The UK Experience

SIMON COWAN

2.1. INTRODUCTION

The UK, along with Chile, was the pioneer of privatization of state-owned utilities in the 1980s, and has served as a model for subsequent privatizations and new forms of regulation elsewhere in the world. As experience has been gained and practical lessons have been learned, the theory of regulation has also developed. In this paper I assess some recent theoretical developments in regulation in the light of UK experience. The choice of topics is motivated by UK practice, but the purpose is not to claim that there is a tight mapping between observed features of actual regulation and the theory.[1] Instead I present some key ideas using, for the most part, a unified modelling framework. Armstrong *et al.* (1994) and Laffont and Tirole (1993) present more detailed surveys of regulation theory.

For analytical purposes, a useful distinction is made between the regulation of conduct and the regulation of industry structure (see Kay and Vickers 1988). The paper is divided into three main sections. Section 2.2 examines the regulation of conduct. The focus is on the regulation of the prices of natural monopolies, but the design of rules for competitive spot markets is also addressed. The recent literature on access pricing is covered in some detail. Section 2.3 discusses the role of industry structure in regulation. Section 2.4 covers the role of commitment in regulation, and Section 2.5 concludes.

2.2. REGULATION OF PRICES

2.2.1. *Setting price levels for natural monopolies*

Price-cap regulation is now the standard method of regulating utilities in the UK, and the model developed here has been copied in many countries. Professor Stephen Littlechild was asked by the Department of Industry to

---

[1] For an interesting discussion of the role of economists in policymaking see Faulhaber and Baumol (1988).

examine possible schemes for the regulation of the profitability of British Telecommunications (BT) when its privatization was planned. In his report Professor Littlechild argued that the focus of regulation should be on prices and not profits, and that US-style rate-of-return regulation generated poor incentives for cost efficiency and encouraged regulatory capture (Littlechild 1983). He recommended RPI − X regulation for prices in the markets where BT faced no competition. An index of prices is allowed to grow by at most the rate of growth of the retail price index (RPI), which is the main measure of consumer price inflation, less a predetermined X factor initially set at 3 per cent for BT. Thus, real prices had to fall by at least 3 per cent each year. The X factor remained fixed and was independent of observed costs and profits during the five-year period before the cap was reviewed.

Price caps in practice are characterized by: (i) relatively long periods between formal price reviews; (ii) a commitment by the regulatory agency to avoid resetting the price cap during the lag between reviews in spite of new information being available during that period; (iii) some flexibility to choose relative prices as long as the price index satisfies the RPI − X constraint. The intention is to provide incentives for the firm to cut its costs before the next price review occurs. These incentives exist because cost-cutting does not entail immediate price reductions.

The main insight of the theory behind price caps and related incentive mechanisms is that, when the firm has more information about its own costs than the regulator, it will act efficiently only if it is given incentives to do so. In general, though, the provision of incentives for cost reduction requires that the firm be allowed to earn supernormal profits. If the regulator requires the firm to cut prices whenever it reduces costs, then excess profits can be minimized, but costs will be higher than otherwise. The regulator determines how observed costs should be reflected in prices to trade off the objectives of cost minimization and profit (or rent) elimination.

The model that follows is an adapted version of the model of Laffont and Tirole (1986, 1993).[2] The consumer has a unit demand for the product and always purchases. Consumer surplus is $V = U - p$ where U is gross utility and p is the price. The cost function has two elements. The first is the accounting cost, $c = \theta - e$, where θ is an exogenous cost parameter and e is cost-reducing effort. The regulator observes c but not its individual components. The distribution of θ is common knowledge and the highest possible value of θ is $\bar{\theta}$, while the expected value is $E(\theta)$.[3] The second part of the cost function is the cost of effort, $F(e)$, where $F(0) = 0$, $F' > 0$ and $F'' > 0$. The regulator maximizes

---

[2] An alternative model involves a trade-off between providing incentives to the firm and providing insurance. Armstrong et al. (1994: ch. 2) explore this model, which has similar results to those presented here.

[3] Since we are restricting attention to linear incentive schemes, the only characteristics of the distribution function of θ that must be known are the highest possible value of θ and the expected value.

a weighted sum of consumer surplus and profits, $W = U - p + \alpha[p - c - F(e)]$ where α, the weight on profits, satisfies $0 < \alpha \le 1$. Subtracting and adding total costs gives

$$W = U - c - F(e) - (1 - \alpha)[p - c - F(e)]. \tag{1}$$

Equation (1) shows that the regulator wants to minimize total cost, $c + F(e)$, and, when $\alpha < 1$, to eliminate the rents that the firm earns. With full information, the firm is ordered to set the level of e that minimizes $c + F(e)$ and receives a price that just covers total costs, so both objectives are achieved. But with asymmetric information about θ and e there is usually a trade-off.

The regulatory instrument is a function relating the price to observed operating cost: $p(c)$. For simplicity I restrict attention to linear functions, so $p = k + \beta c$, where β is the cost pass-through coefficient. A pure price cap is a special case where $\beta = 0$, while rate-of-return regulation is characterized by $k = 0$ and $\beta = 1$. Two constraints must be satisfied. First, the regulator must take account of the way the firm optimizes. Profits are $\Pi = k + (\beta - 1)(\theta - e) - F(e)$, so the firm's choice of e is characterized by the first-order condition $1 - \beta = F'(e^*)$. This determines an effort function $e^*(\beta)$, with $de^*(\beta)/d\beta = -1/F'' < 0$. Greater cost pass-through reduces effort.

The second constraint is that the firm must be willing to participate whatever the value of θ that is realized. This implies that profits should be at least zero when the exogenous cost parameter takes on its highest feasible value, $\bar{\theta}$. Profits in this case are $\Pi(\bar{\theta}) = k - (1 - \beta)(\bar{\theta} - e^*) - F(e^*)$. Since the regulator doesn't want to leave unnecessary rents, k is chosen to ensure that $\Pi(\bar{\theta}) = 0$. Using the implied value of k, the general expression for profits is $\Pi(\theta) = (1 - \beta)(\bar{\theta} - \theta)$ and $E(\Pi) = (1 - \beta)(\bar{\theta} - E(\theta))$, so the regulator has to set $\beta \le 1$. As β rises, the firm puts in less effort and costs rise, but expected rents fall.

We now characterize the solution to the regulator's trade-off between cost efficiency and rent extraction. Expected total costs are $E(\theta) - e^*(\beta) + F(e^*(\beta))$ and the cost to the regulator of the expected rents is $(1 - \alpha)(1 - \beta)(\bar{\theta} - E(\theta))$. Choosing β to minimize the sum of these two terms, and noting that $1 - \beta = F'(e)$, we find the optimal value of β to be

$$\beta^* = (1 - \alpha)(\bar{\theta} - E(\theta))F''(e^*(\beta)). \tag{2}$$

If the value defined in (2) is greater than 1, then the regulator sets $\beta^* = 1$. Three factors determine the optimal value of the pass-through coefficient. First, the closer α is to 1, the less is the regulatory concern about rents and the lower β^* can be. Second, if the range of uncertainty about θ rises, i.e. if $\bar{\theta} - E(\theta)$ increases, the regulator wants to set a higher value of β^* to reduce rents. Third, if the marginal cost of effort increases sharply (if F'' is high), the cost of providing incentives for cost efficiency increases and the regulator raises β^*. Price-cap regulation is a special case that applies when $\alpha = 1$, so the regulator is indifferent to rents and can concentrate on offering full incentives for cost minimization. Rate-of-return regulation is a special case where $\beta^* = 1$, so the firm has no incentive to reduce costs, but rents are minimized. In the more general intermediate case there is some degree of cost pass-through. In the UK some cost pass-through (within the regulatory period) was allowed in the formulae by which the gas, electricity, and water industries were regulated. Of course, at the time of the formal price review price levels are adjusted to take account of realized and anticipated cost changes, so no price cap scheme is ever 'pure' in practice.

What options does a regulator have to improve the trade-off between the promotion of cost efficiency and the minimization of rents? Two standard answers are yardstick competition and franchising. *Yardstick competition* is feasible when there are several similar regionally separated firms. In the UK the regional water companies and the electricity distribution companies have been regulated using versions of yardstick competition. The report by Stephen Littlechild (1986) on the regulation of privatized water companies recommended the use of yardstick competition, and the subsequent Water Industry Act 1991 established a formal role for the use of comparative information by the regulator.

The classic statement of the theory of yardstick competition is by Shleifer (1985). The essence of the Shleifer model can be shown in our framework. Suppose there are two separate firms, 1 and 2, and that their cost parameters, θ_1 and θ_2, are perfectly correlated. The regulator then immediately improves its information position relative to the case where the cost shocks are independent. If $c_2 > c_1$, the regulator knows that firm 2 has chosen a lower effort level than 1, and 2 can be penalized for this. The regulator should relate the allowed price for one firm to the other firm's accounting cost. For firm 1 the price is $p_1 = F(e^{**}) + c_2$, which gives it the incentive to invest in the first-best effort level, defined by $1 = F'(e^{**})$, since it cannot influence its own price. Effort costs are just covered. Firm 1's profits are $\Pi_1 = F(e^{**}) + \theta_2 - e_2 - \theta_1 + e_1 - F(e_1) = 0$ since $e_1 = e_2 = e^{**}$ and $\theta_1 = \theta_2$. Thus, yardstick competition ensures that costs are minimized and rents are eliminated in spite of the information asymmetry. More generally, if the cost shocks are not perfectly correlated the regulator can set the price as a linear function of the two accounting cost levels, and the trade-off between rent extraction and cost reduction is partially improved.

The second way to improve the trade-off is to use competition for the market, or *franchising*. Auctioning the right to supply monopoly services has been used for the train operating services in the UK, for the water sector in France, and for infrastructure projects in many developing countries. The key point is that in an auction of an incentive contract the regulator is offering a prize with potential rents attached. Firms compete to earn those rents, and competition will dissipate the excess profitability. In a Chadwick–Demsetz auction potential suppliers compete over the price that they are prepared to charge customers (and perhaps also over quality). Suppose for simplicity that each firm knows the values of both its own and the other firm's θ variable and that $\theta_2 > \theta_1$. The regulator fixes a value of β in advance and the optimal choice of effort for the winning firm is e^*. The winning firm is the one that offers the lower fixed part of the price function, k.

Firm 2's lowest possible offer is $k_2 = (1 - \beta)(\theta_2 - e^*) + F(e^*)$. Firm 1 wins the contract by setting k_1 just below this level. Its rent is $\Pi_1 = (1 - \beta)(\theta_2 - \theta_1)$. The equivalent rent in the case where firm 1 was regulated without an auction would be $(1 - \beta)(\bar{\theta} - \theta_1) \geq (1 - \beta)(\theta_2 - \theta_1)$. Auctioning the contract achieves the same level of efficiency but lower rents—the trade-off is improved. An implication is that the greater the number of firms, the better the outcome for the regulator, since the likely gap between the top two θ levels will be smaller. Similarly, the more correlated are θ_1 and θ_2, the smaller the expected gap between them and thus the smaller the rent for the winner. As the correlation tends towards unity, the regulator will reduce β towards zero (which induces productive efficiency) and rents will be eliminated. The identical outcome would occur if neither firm knows its rival's value of θ and the auction is awarded on a second-price sealed-bid basis. In practice, in the UK the role of franchising has been relatively small, probably because the investment requirements of the firms that have been privatized have been very large, and franchising is easier to apply to the management of assets than to their expansion.

2.2.2. *Relative prices and multiproduct issues*

Many regulated utilities produce more than one distinct product or serve multiple markets. What is the optimal price structure for a multiproduct firm that will remain a monopoly? In telecommunications the balance between line rentals, long-distance call prices, and local call prices is important; in railways it is crucial that the relative price of peak and off-peak services is appropriate; while in the energy industries the geographical structure of prices is important. The theoretical answer is that Ramsey–Boiteux prices, which maximize consumer surplus subject to a profit constraint, are optimal. Suppose that there are two products and that consumer surplus is $V(P_1, P_2)$, where P_i is the price of product i. The derivative of consumer surplus with respect to P_i is $-Q_i$, i.e. -1 times the quantity demanded of i. Denoting profits by $\Pi(P_1, P_2)$, the optimal prices are characterized by the tangency condition,

$$\frac{\partial V/\partial P_1}{\partial V/\partial P_2} = \frac{Q_1}{Q_2} = \frac{\partial \Pi/\partial P_1}{\partial \Pi/\partial P_2}, \tag{3}$$

and the profit constraint. Can the firm be given incentives to choose the Ramsey–Boiteux prices? If the regulator knows the consumer surplus function, then the answer is 'yes'. The firm would choose prices to maximize profits subject to the constraint that $V(P_1, P_2)$ equals a target level, which generates prices that satisfy (3).

In practice, the regulator is unlikely to be able to compute consumer surplus. Vogelsang and Finsinger (1979) recommended an ingenious mechanism which ensures that the firm eventually sets Ramsey–Boiteux prices in spite of the regulator's lack of information about costs and demands. Using a second subscript to denote the time period, the period t constraint is

$$\sum_{i=1}^{2} P_{i,t} Q_{i,t-1} \leq C_{t-1}, \tag{4}$$

which means that the cost to the consumer of buying the previous period's quantities at the new prices must be no greater than the firm's total cost in the last period. In the limit, the repeated application of constraint (4) drives profits to zero, and Vogelsang and Finsinger show that equation (3) is satisfied, so Ramsey–Boiteux prices are achieved. The model does depend crucially, however, on the firm ignoring the effect that its current decisions have on the level of future constraints. Sappington (1980) shows that a firm acting strategically might choose to inflate costs early on in the process in order to increase rents in the future, and that the welfare effects of this behaviour can be very severe.

The main reason why the Vogelsang–Finsinger mechanism has problems is that actual costs are mentioned in the constraint. The price constraints that are applied to BT and to the water companies in England and Wales are of the form

$$\sum_{i=1}^{n} P_{i,t} Q_{i,t-1} \leq (1 + RPI - X) \sum_{i=1}^{n} P_{i,t-1} Q_{i,t-1},$$

where RPI is the percentage growth in the retail price index. A Laspeyres index of prices is capped, and because the firm cannot affect either RPI or X it has no incentive to manipulate its costs. Vogelsang (1989) shows that in the limit this type of Laspeyres constraint leads to Ramsey–Boiteux prices, though the rents will be extracted from the firm only if X is set appropriately.

In a recent paper, Armstrong and Vickers (2000) use mechanism design techniques to analyse multiproduct regulation when there is asymmetric information about costs and demand. They assume that the regulator has no information on realized demands so schemes such as the Vogelsang–Finsinger one defined in (4) are not feasible. When there is uncertainty about costs, it is optimal to give discretion over relative prices to the firm (since both the firm and the regulator want prices to reflect realized costs); however, with uncertainty over demand, there should be no discretion if demand shocks are multiplicative (these do not alter elasticities, so Ramsey–Boiteux prices can be implemented without decentralized decision-making by the firm), but some discretion if uncertainty about demand is additive.

A final point to note is that contestable markets theory provides guidance on the regulation of prices when an incumbent monopolist is threatened by entry (see Baumol *et al*. 1982, and Vickers 1997). In particular, regarding the price for a particular product line, the price should lie in between an incremental cost floor and a stand-alone cost ceiling if both predatory pricing and cross-subsidy are to be prevented. This issue has been particularly important in the telecommunications market in the UK, where entry is free but where BT still has a dominant position in many market segments.

2.2.3. *Access pricing*

The access pricing issue arises when a firm N, which operates the network as a natural monopoly, also offers services over the network that may be subject to potential competition. Competitors at the retail stage need access to the natural monopoly services of N in order to sell to final customers, and the question is: what is the correct price for these services? Early cases where this was an issue were (i) the electricity industry before privatization, where independent power producers were allowed to supply electricity to the transmission company, which itself owned most generating capacity and was unwilling to buy the rival power at a reasonable price, and (ii) interconnection between the new long-distance rival, Mercury, and the incumbent, BT, in the telecommunications market, where the initial determination allowed Mercury to complete calls via BT's network at a price close to marginal cost. Interconnection remains a critical issue for telecommunications, and will become important in the water industry as competition via common carriage develops there. The electricity, gas, and rail industries have been subjected to vertical separation, which changes the access pricing issue. There is no incentive for a separate network firm to favour one supplier over another, and the issue instead is how to recover the fixed costs of the network from charges for the use of the network.

The access pricing issue can be thought of as a special case of multiproduct pricing, where N has two types of customer: final consumers, and intermediate goods producers, i.e. the rival retailers and its own retail division. Here we present a version of the model of Armstrong *et al.*(1996). Suppose initially that N is a vertically integrated firm and has no competition downstream. The marginal cost to N of a unit of network services is b and its marginal cost in the downstream (retailing) sector is c. The regulator has full demand and cost information and, in the absence of public subsidies or two-part tariffs, sets the retail price equal to average cost: $\overline{P} = b + c + F/Q(\overline{P})$ where $Q(\overline{P})$ is retail demand at price $\overline{P}$ and F is the fixed cost in the network sector. Now a competitive supplier enters the retail sector. The competitor produces an identical product, acts as a price-taker, and has marginal cost in the retail sector of $MC(s)$ which is increasing in its supply, s, and satisfies $MC(0) < c < MC(Q(\overline{P}))$. The latter condition implies that it is socially efficient to have the competitor doing some (but not all) of the retailing.

The competitor chooses its output level, s, where its marginal retail cost plus the access charge paid to the network firm, a, equals the retail price, $\overline{P}$.

So

$$MC(s) = \overline{P} - a \tag{5}$$

The competitor's supply is increasing in its margin $\overline{P} - a$ since the marginal retail cost rises with the quantity supplied. Suppose the regulator leaves the retail price at $\overline{P}$ and fixes the access charge. Since consumers pay $\overline{P}$ whoever supplies them, they are unaffected by competition and the optimal access price is the one that minimizes total retail costs. Cost minimization requires that the marginal retail costs of the rival and of N are equal:

$$MC(s) = c. \tag{6}$$

Equations (5) and (6) jointly imply that the optimal access charge is

$$a^* = \overline{P} - c. \tag{7}$$

This is the Efficient Component Pricing Rule (ECPR) of Baumol (1983) and Willig (1979). It has been applied in the New Zealand telecommunications industry, and one interpretation of the access price regime applied to BT from 1992 to 1997 (known as the Access Deficit Contributions scheme) was that it was based on the ECPR (Laffont and Tirole 1996). A useful way to think of the ECPR is that the marginal cost to N of providing a unit of access is the direct marginal cost, b, plus the opportunity cost of the lost profit on the retail sales, $\overline{P} - b - c$. Adding these gives a^*. Because N is fully compensated for its lost retail profits, it still breaks even. Indeed, because $\overline{P}$ was originally set to cover average costs, the amount by which a^* exceeds b is exactly the average fixed cost $F/Q(\overline{P})$. Note that the same outcome holds if N is split into (i) a network firm and (ii) a retailer facing the same access charge as the rival and a fixed retail price of $\overline{P}$. Now the regulator sets a to cover N's average costs, so $a^* = b + F/Q(\overline{P})$.

If N is not regulated, will it have the incentive to choose a^*? In general the answer is no. N chooses a to maximize its profits from access. The revenue from selling access is as and the variable cost is bs. In addition, the network firm loses retail profits of $(\overline{P} - b - c)s$. So the net profit from access is $[a - (\overline{P} - c)]s(\overline{P} - a)$. Clearly, N wants to set a above the ECPR level, $(\overline{P} - c)$. The social cost of such profit maximization is that the marginal sales that the network firm makes are produced with less efficiency than marginal sales of the rival. Indeed, if N and the rival retailer were allowed to merge there would be productive efficiency, as the merged firm would maximize its profits by allocating retail sales to minimize costs.

The analysis that justified the ECPR assumed that the retail price must remain fixed at $\overline{P}$. We now assess the consequence of relaxing this assumption. The firm has two types of customer, and standard second-best arguments imply that the distortions that are necessary to generate revenue to fund the network's fixed costs should be spread across the two markets, and not all concentrated on final customers. The Ramsey–Boiteux pricing structure is characterized by an access charge *exceeding* the ECPR level defined in (7), while P is below $\bar{P}$. The firm is able to cut the retail price using the extra profits generated from its access customers. Thus, the Ramsey–Boiteux price structure has the network part of N more than covering its costs, while the retail side operates at a slight loss. Naturally, if the network and retail businesses of N are separated, the Ramsey–Boiteux structure is not sustainable. In practice, however, regulators, while acknowledging the theoretical arguments in favour of Ramsey–Boiteux prices, have not sought to apply them in practice because the informational requirements are excessive.

The analysis so far has assumed that N and the rival produce perfect substitutes. If instead they sell products that are imperfect substitutes in demand, then there is a case for reducing the access charge *below* the ECPR level. Suppose, for example, that the demand for a new telecommunications service is completely independent of local call demand, but the new service needs access to N's local lines. In this case N loses no profit from offering access (as long as there is no congestion on the local lines) and the optimal value of a is b, the marginal cost of providing the network services. In general, the more independent in demand the products are, the closer the optimal access charge is to marginal cost, b.

Finally, a recent development in the theory of access pricing has been the analysis of reciprocal access, which applies to telecommunications networks that need jointly to interconnect with each other because of network externalities (see Laffont *et al.* 1998; Armstrong 1998). How should the access charge be set in this case? An important insight of this literature is that, if the firms are free to negotiate an access charge, this will be above the socially efficient level. Suppose there is symmetry, so that the sum firm 1 pays to firm 2 for call completion is the same as the revenue it receives from 2. At first sight one might imagine that firm 1 is indifferent between all access prices. But the access charge is a component of marginal costs, and the higher is the symmetric access price, the more each firm will want to raise its final price to customers. In the end, the firms could achieve a collusive outcome simply through the use of the access price. The socially optimal access charge will be below the ECPR level in this case to offset the positive mark-ups that oligopolists set, and could even be below the marginal cost of providing the network service, b.

2.2.4. *Establishing upstream spot markets*

Spot markets have been created in the electricity and gas sectors in the UK. California, Chile, and Norway have undertaken similar reforms. Markets for instant delivery are necessary to ensure that energy systems balance. Particularly in electricity, there is a need for minute-to-minute coordination between the transmission company and the power generators. The first example of such a spot market in the UK was the Electricity Pool, a centralized arrangement run by the transmission company to determine which generators are called on to run. Rival generators announce their capacities and prices for each period of the next day, and the Pool constructs a supply curve. The price paid to all generators is the price of the marginal producer. In addition, generators receive 'capacity payments' which are higher the more likely it is that there will be a power failure and the higher the estimated cost that customers bear in the event of such a failure. If the market for generation were competitive, one would expect this system to generate efficient outcomes, with price in the daily auction equal to marginal cost and the capacity payments providing long-run incentives for investment.

In practice, the Pool has worked less efficiently. Standard game theory would suggest that when there are only a few bidders, each with a portfolio of plants with different marginal costs, they will be tempted to restrict capacity or to raise the price of their marginal plants. This will reduce the likelihood that the marginal plants are called on to generate, but will enhance the profits of those of their plants with lower marginal costs that are almost certain to be called on. In an early analysis of the operation of the Pool, Green and Newbery (1992) modelled the game as one where the competing generators offered supply functions, and they showed that the duopolistic structure of the generating market was likely to lead to inefficient outcomes.

Recently the regulatory authorities have moved to promote new trading arrangements in electricity (and gas trading has been reformed). The new trading arrangements are designed to promote more flexibility by allowing trading to take place outside the Pool, by encouraging the growth of futures and forward markets, and by allowing demand-side bidding, while maintaining a short-run balancing market. In the balancing market bidders will receive the amount of their bid rather than the price of the marginal bidder. Wolfram (1999) uses the auction theory to assess the introduction of discriminatory pricing. Changing the rules of the game will alter bidding behaviour, and the hope of the regulator is that collusion will be less feasible than under the current system. The point to note here is that the theory of mechanism design can help regulators to establish rules of such spot markets which ensure that the participants have incentives to behave in ways that enhance the objectives of regulators.

2.3. REGULATION OF INDUSTRY STRUCTURE AND ENTRY CONDITIONS

2.3.1. *Industry structure*

It is commonly argued that regulation is easier when the natural monopoly parts of a firm are separated from the competitive parts. In the usual case the natural monopoly business is a network that rivals must use in order to reach final customers, as in the access pricing case considered in Section 2.2, so vertical separation is called for. BT and the water companies were not restructured at privatization, but the electricity and railway industries have been vertically separated, and the incumbent in the gas market broke itself up a decade after privatization. If information is symmetric, however, it is difficult to see why vertical separation would help. We saw in Section 2.2 that, with the retail price fixed at $\overline{P}$, vertical separation generates exactly the same outcome as allowing vertical integration while using the ECPR (equation (7)) to determine the access price.

When an incumbent is vertically integrated, it is likely that the regulator will find it difficult to determine the optimal access price, since cost information is likely to be noisy, and the incumbent has the incentive to allocate as many costs as possible to the network part of the business. Suppose that the regulator can observe $b + c$ when the firm is integrated, but cannot split this cost up into the network component, b, and the retail part, c. The firm reports its value of c (and thus of b). Let this cost report be $\hat{c}$ while the true value is c. The regulator sets the retail price on average cost pricing principles, so $\overline{P} = b + c + F/Q(\overline{P})$, and the access charge is determined using the ECPR, so $a = \overline{P} - \hat{c}$. If the firm announces the correct value of c, then it earns profits of zero. By announcing $\hat{c} < c$ the firm does not alter the retail price, but it pushes up the access charge and thus increases its profits. The asymmetry of information allows the firm to set the profit-maximizing access price, thus generating productive inefficiency in retailing. If vertical separation allows the regulator to observe both b and c, then he sets $P = a + c$ and $a = b + F/Q(P)$. Productive efficiency in retailing is achieved (and rents are minimized), so both the market share of rivals and the level of welfare are higher than in the vertically integrated case. If the costs of break-up are smaller than the welfare gain from the improvement in the regulator's information caused by separation, then it is worthwhile.

Two other aspects of industry structure have also been of concern to regulators. In the electricity industry, the UK government decided to alter the *horizontal* structure at the generation stage. The Central Electricity Generating Board was split into three companies, a nuclear company with 20 per cent of capacity, and two fossil-fuel generators with 50 and 30 per cent of capacity. The nuclear company played no role in determining prices in the Electricity Pool, since it bid zero to ensure that its plants always ran, so effectively creating a duopoly. The conditions for collusion could hardly have been better. The theory of non-cooperative collusion suggests that it is sustainable when the number of players is low, there is a homogeneous product, frequent purchases are made by customers, and the firms have spare capacities so that prices can be driven down in the punishment phase (Tirole 1988; Shapiro 1989). Even if the firms are acting non-cooperatively, standard theory suggests that price–cost margins are inversely related to the degree of concentration in the industry. Green and Newbery (1992) suggest that welfare would have been significantly higher if five competing generators had been created at the outset.

The ability to apply yardstick competition is dependent on a *regional separation* of firms. In the water and electricity distribution industries, this regional separation existed even before privatization. There might be a trade-off between keeping firms regionally separated to provide comparative information and allowing them to merge to gain the benefits of economies of scale and scope. In the water industry all nontrivial mergers have to be referred to the Competition Commission, which must take account of the impact of a proposed merger on the regulator's ability to make comparisons.

2.3.2. *Liberalization of entry conditions*

The final aspect of structural regulation is the licensing policy of the regulatory authorities. When competition is feasible, the question is: should the regulator free all entry, or should the rate of entry be controlled? Initially, in telecommunications UK regulators opted for slow liberalization. Only one competitor, Mercury, was licensed to compete with BT, and simple resale of capacity leased from BT at wholesale rates was not allowed. Following a review of the duopoly policy in 1991, entry was fully liberalized. In electricity and gas, entry into the market for supply to large customers was liberalized early on in the process but was not effective initially because of the lack of attention to access prices and conditions.

One argument for allowing limited entry is that entry can lead to excessive duplication of fixed costs when the firms sell homogeneous products. Mankiw and Whinston (1986) present the theoretical argument for this. Entry of a new firm benefits consumers through a reduction of prices but harms existing firms as the entrant steals some of their profitable business. At the margin, when there are sunk costs, so that price exceeds marginal cost in free entry equilibrium, it is better to have slightly fewer firms. This result is not robust, however, to changes in the assumptions. Restricting entry might facilitate collusion. New firms might introduce different products that provide extra consumer benefits. Entrants might be more efficient than the incumbent in utility markets. The alternative view—that entry should be fully liberalized—has dominated since the end of the duopoly policy for telecommunications. Apart from the non-robustness of the Mankiw–Whinston result, a free entry policy can be justified on the basis of contestability theory, or from an Austrian standpoint that competition *per se* is best.

A new entrant in a utility supply market has to offer a significant price discount relative to the incumbent because consumers face switching costs. The ability to take a competitive supply might require the customer to install new equipment, such as a new telephone or a meter, to use a new telephone number, to remain at home in order to have the meter read when the switch takes place, or to key in extra digits to access a new provider. If the incumbent uses complicated and frequently changing nonlinear tariffs, then the customer faces another switching cost because price comparison is more difficult. Entrants will have to offer significant price discounts to attract customers. Evaluation of the effectiveness of competition should allow for the switching costs that are incurred. In addition, new entrants have to spend heavily on advertising to make customers aware of their existence and to persuade them to switch. Advertising is an endogenous sunk cost in the sense of Sutton (1991), and equilibrium market structures might not be characterized by large numbers of competitors. The more advertising is necessary to win and to retain customers, and the greater the degree of price competition that is expected between the rivals, the more concentrated the market structure is likely to be.

2.4. REGULATORY COMMITMENT

When regulators cannot commit to future prices, there is a hold-up problem—firms might not invest optimally. Utilities' assets have long lives and few alternative uses, and it is tempting for politicians to adjust previous agreements. We can show the problem with a simple variation of the model of Section 2.1. Suppose now that there is no asymmetry of information (both sides know θ and e) so there is no incentive constraint. The first-best solution has the firm choosing e^{**}, which minimizes total costs, and the regulator setting the price equal to $\theta - e^{**} + F(e^{**})$ to cover all costs. In the new game the firm chooses its effort level and incurs the costs of effort *before* the regulator sets the price. The problem is that in a one-shot game the regulator takes the sunk costs, $F(e^{**})$, as given. Once the effort costs have been sunk, the firm will participate as long as operating costs, $c = \theta - e$, are covered. The regulator's objective is to choose p to maximize $W = U - p + \alpha(p - c) - \alpha F(e)$ subject to $p \geq c$. For $\alpha < 1$ the solution is $p = c$ and the sunk costs are not covered. Anticipating this outcome, the firm chooses not to invest in any effort at the first stage and costs are excessively high. This underinvestment problem is caused by the inability of the regulator to commit to a price level in advance of the firm choosing its sunk costs.

There are two solutions to the underinvestment problem. First, even if it is impossible for the regulator to commit to a price schedule, it might be in its interests to avoid expropriation if the game lasts indefinitely. Salant and Woroch (1992) have a model in which the regulator allows the firm to recover both the operating costs and the incremental sunk costs incurred in that period. The firm in turn increases its effort level (or capital stock) to approach the optimal level (e^{**}) asymptotically. The fact that the firm always has further investment in effort that it can undertake prevents the regulator from wanting to renege on the price agreement, because the firm will refuse to do any more investment if the regulator has cheated. Salant and Woroch show that the equilibrium of this game can be approximately efficient.

The second solution is to develop institutions that effectively create commitment. Levy and Spiller (1996) discuss the importance of the institutional endowment of a country in determining the degree of commitment. At a minimum, the regulatory agency needs to act independently of the government (though there must be some accountability), so the agency should not simply be part of a government ministry. The parallel with the argument for an independent central bank should be clear. Levy and Spiller point out that it is also important that the politicians are not able to change the rules of the game arbitrarily, so the way the legislature works, the degree of independence of the judiciary, and the availability of appeal mechanisms are also important. It can be argued that the UK is relatively fortunate, since its institutional endowment is sufficiently strong that the danger of underinvestment is low.

2.5. CONCLUSION

In this paper I have presented a selected review of regulatory principles and related them to UK experience. Where are regulation and the theory of regulation likely to go from here? There are at least three issues on which there is a need for more work. First, while price-cap regulation seems to provide good incentives for operating cost efficiency, it is not clear that it provides optimal investment incentives for utilities. Developing robust mechanisms for investment without encouraging gold-plating will be important. Second, more attention is likely to be paid to relative prices in the network parts of the utilities than to price levels, which in many cases have been reduced significantly because of the incentives provided by price-cap regulation. Third, regulators are already coping with the issue of managing competition in retail markets while protecting existing customers of incumbents from excessive pricing. If equilibrium market structures are going to be characterized by a small number of competitors, perhaps supplying multiple utility services, regulators will also have to be aware of the dangers of collusion.

REFERENCES

Armstrong, M. (1998). 'Network Interconnection in Telecommunications', *Economic Journal*, 108: 545–64.

——and Vickers, J. (2000). 'Multiproduct Price Regulation under Asymmetric Information', *Journal of Industrial Economics*, 48: 137–60.

——Cowan, S., and Vickers, J. (1994). *Regulatory Reform: Economic Analysis and British Experience*, Cambridge, Mass.: MIT Press.

——Doyle, C., and Vickers, J. (1996). 'The Access Pricing Problem: A Synthesis', *Journal of Industrial Economics*, 44: 131–50.

Baumol, W. (1983). 'Some Subtle Issues in Railway Regulation', *International Journal of Transport Economics*, 10: 341–55.

——Panzar, J., and Willig, R. (1982). *Contestable Markets and the Theory of Industrial Structure*, New York: Harcourt Brace Jovanovich.

Faulhaber, G. R. and Baumol, W. J. (1988). 'Economists as Innovators: Practical Products of Theoretical Research', *Journal of Economic Literature*, 26: 577–600.

Green, R. and Newbery, D. (1992). 'Competition in the British Electricity Spot Market', *Journal of Political Economy*, 100: 1089–99.

Kay, J. and Vickers, J. (1988). 'Regulatory Reform in Britain', *Economic Policy*, 7: 285–343.

Laffont, J.-J. and Tirole, J. (1986). 'Using Cost Information to Regulate Firms', *Journal of Political Economy*, 94: 614–41.

——and Tirole, J.(1993). *A Theory of Incentives in Procurement and Regulation*, Cambridge, Mass.: MIT Press.

——and Tirole, J. (1996). 'Creating Competition through Interconnection: Theory and Practice', *Journal of Regulatory Economics*, 10: 227–56.

Laffont, J-J., Rey, P., and Tirole, J. (1998). 'Network Competition: I. Overview and Nondiscriminatory Pricing'; II. Discriminatory Pricing', *RAND Journal of Economics*, 29: 1–37; 38–56.

Levy, B. and Spiller, P. T. (1996). 'A Framework for Resolving the Regulatory Problem', in B. Levy and P. T. Spiller (eds.), *Regulation, Institutions and Commitment*, Cambridge: Cambridge University Press.

Littlechild S. C. (1983). *Regulation of British Telecommunications' Profitability*. London: Department of Industry, HMSO.

——(1986). *Economic Regulation of Privatised Water Authorities*. London: HMSO.

Mankiw, G. and Whinston, M. (1986). 'Free Entry and Social Efficiency', *RAND Journal of Economics*, 17: 48–58.

Salant, D. and Woroch, G. (1992). 'Trigger Price Regulation', *RAND Journal of Economics*, 23: 29–51.

Sappington, D. (1980). 'Strategic Firm Behavior under a Dynamic Regulatory Adjustment Process', *Bell Journal of Economics*, 11: 360–72.

Shapiro, C. (1989). 'Theories of Oligopoly Behaviour', in R. Schmalensee and R. Willig (eds.), *Handbook of Industrial Organization*, Vol. 1, Amsterdam: North-Holland.

Shleifer A. (1985). 'A Theory of Yardstick Competition', *RAND Journal of Economics*, 16: 319–17.

Sutton, J. (1991). *Sunk Costs and Market Structure*, Cambridge, Mass.: MIT Press.

Tirole, J. (1988). *The Theory of Industrial Organization*, Cambridge, Mass.: MIT Press.

Vickers, J. S. (1997). 'Regulation, Competition and the Structure of Prices', *Oxford Review of Economic Policy*, 13: 15–26.

Vogelsang, I. (1989). 'Price Cap Regulation of Telecommunications Services: A Long-Run Approach', in M. A. Crew (ed.), *Deregulation and Diversification of Utilities*, Boston: Kluwer.

——and Finsinger, J. (1979). 'A Regulatory Adjustment Process for Optimal Pricing by Multiproduct Monopoly Firms', *Bell Journal of Economics*, 10: 157–71.

Willig, R. (1979). 'The Theory of Network Access Pricing', in H. M. Trebing (ed.), *Issues in Public Utility Regulation*, East Lansing, Mich.: Michigan State University Public Utilities Papers.

Wolfram, C. D. (1999). 'Electricity Markets: Should the Rest of the World Adopt the UK Reforms?' University of California Energy Institute POWER Working Paper No. 69, http:\\www.ucei.berkeley.edu/ucei.

3

The UK Model

PETER VASS

3.1. INTRODUCTION

The UK model of regulation for 'network industries' (water, energy, transport, and communications) reflects, I suggest, a balance; a balance of pragmatic evolution informed, and constrained, by a coherent policy framework and 'institutional' roles and responsibilities designed to address the *objectives* of regulation. The UK system therefore combines experience and practical adaptation with consistency, and discretion with accountability; firm foundations for a rational regulatory policy which seeks to maintain public confidence and achieve an outcome in the best long-term interests of all.

This chapter starts with an overview of the reasons for regulation and the principles of good regulation which have been used to develop the institutional structure and regulatory roles in the UK. It is argued that the UK regulatory framework has evolved to address, separately, the three main types of market—or 'conduct'—failure. The model of *incentive regulation*, with its presumption in favour of competition, is then reviewed, with a focus on the financial and accounting models adopted. It ends with reflections on regulatory policy and the recent development of the proposal for 'mutual' ownership as the end-game for natural monopoly, essential service infrastructure.

3.2. THE REGULATORY CONTEXT

The UK model can be considered and evaluated in terms of four key questions that should be addressed to regulatory policy-makers, if there is to be public confidence and consent to the system of regulation. This is particularly important for network utilities that provide public services—public not necessarily in the sense of ownership, but in terms of their essential contribution to the well-being of the country and its citizens. The four questions are:

1. Why regulation? Regulation is a means to an end, not an end in itself, and so the *objectives* of regulation must be clearly understood.

2. What is regulation? A clear definition of regulatory activities is required, running from legitimacy and empowerment (authority for policy) through the processes of administering regulation and monitoring conduct to the enforcement of outcomes.
3. Who does what and why? The institutional structure for regulation, the appropriateness and efficiency of the regulatory methodologies and instruments used, and the checks and balances in the system all contribute to the effectiveness of regulatory policy.
4. How accountable and transparent is regulation?

Important regulatory choices include such things as economic regulators focusing on output performance rather than inputs utilized (such as the amount of capital spend); the use of market instruments, such as tradable permits, rather than command and control systems, in pollution control; and whether or not social objectives (public service and universal service obligations) should be met by regulated companies through cross-subsidy and exclusive rights, by a social fund levy on all players in a competitive market, or by direct support to the disadvantaged from government, financed by taxation.

To bring all this together inevitably means complexity, and complexity, when regulating essential services—particularly if it involves judgements and trade-offs—will occasion vigorous public debate. The UK has had its fair share of regulatory controversies since BT became the first of the regulated industries to be privatized in 1984, but the controversies have been positive in the sense that they have contributed to the evolution of the regulatory system, while not undermining the basic framework of incentive regulation adopted for successive privatizations. Regulators have been accused of inconsistency and arbitrary decision-making.[1] Government has been criticized for setting weak price controls at privatization, in particular for water and electricity, which were seen as having led to excess profits and excessive rewards for directors.[2] The criticism reached its peak at the ill-fated AGM of British Gas in London's Docklands in 1996, when its chief executive Cedric Brown was publicly vilified and dubbed 'Cedric the Pig'.[3] Such criticism provided a basis for improved public understanding and created regulatory focus.

The strength of the underlying framework in the UK regulatory system has been demonstrated, however, by the continuity of policy between the Conservative administrations over 1979–97 and the new Labour government, elected in May 1997. The bare facts on the progress of privatization are set out in Table 3.1, listing privatizations that have seen the transfer of virtually all of

---

[1] C. Veljanovski, 'The Regulation Game', in C. Veljanovski (ed.), *Regulators and the Market* (London: IEA, 1991).
[2] National Consumer Council (NCC), *Paying the Price: A Consumer View of Water, Gas, Electricity and Telephone Regulation* (London: HMSO, 1993).
[3] Employment Committee, *The Remuneration of Directors and Chief Executives of Privatized Utilities*, HC 159, Session 1994–5, Third Report, (London: HMSO, 1995).

Table 3.1. *History of Privatization*

Company	Year
British Telecom	1984
British Gas	1986
British Airports Authority (BAA)	1987
Water and Sewerage Authorities in England and Wales (RWAs)	1989
UK Electricity Industry	1990–6
British Rail	1996–7

the traditionally nationalized public service industries.[4] The last two of these were significantly restructured at privatization in order to facilitate competition.

The present Labour government continues to consider the privatization of air traffic control and, although often using words such as 'liberalization' or 'commercialization', rather than 'privatization', has incorporated the Post Office. In Scotland and Northern Ireland the water service remains publicly owned, albeit with access now to private-sector funding through the Private Finance Initiative (PFI). The canal network, publicly owned by the British Waterways Board, is another exception (which may prove to be the basis for a national water grid). The London Underground is to be partially privatized through a public–private partnership (PPP).

3.2.1. *Why regulate?*

Economists have usually dominated the discussion of this question. Government has a role—in short—to correct for 'market failures'. Without market failures, there would be no need for government, an argument that echoes the 'invisible hand' of Adam Smith. One observation of his is ample illustration of why there can be market failure:

People of the same trade seldom meet together, even for merriment and diversion but the conversation ends in a conspiracy against the public or in some contrivance to raise prices. (Adam Smith, *The Wealth of Nations, 1776*)

The objective of regulation, therefore, is to correct for market failures. Implicit in this, of course, is the baseline of the market—the outcome of free choice by consumers and producers of goods and services. Regulation should be 'targeted' on the market failure to be addressed and 'proportionate' in the means adopted. These principles have been adopted as objectives of UK regulatory conduct

---

[4] D. Marsh, 'Privatization under Mrs Thatcher: A Review of the Literature', *Public Administration*, 69 (Winter 1991).

and are codified in statements from bodies such as the government's Better Regulation Task Force (see, for example, their *Principles of Good Regulation*, published in January 1998) and the OECD on Regulatory Reforms.[5]

The reference point of the free market is an important context in understanding the development of the UK regulatory model. Liberalization, not ownership, therefore takes precedence in the regulatory scheme, a priority that has created tensions with the traditional focus on public service industries, and the understanding that these should be publicly owned. Privatization, rather than liberalization with public ownership, has remained the preferred option, however, because it avoids the potential conflicts of interest arising from being both owner and regulator. We have, however, reached a stage where the idea of public services, privately provided does not now appear to be a contradiction, and where regulation should be seen as a surrogate for competition wherever there is either 'natural monopoly' or a 'transitional period' until effective competition can be achieved.[6]

Overall, the regulatory presumption has been to introduce competition wherever possible. Competition has, however, to be broadly defined and can incorporate:

- competition in the market;
- competition for the market (franchises and concessions);
- competition for corporate control (takeovers through the capital market);
- comparative administered competition (yardstick).

All of these approaches to regulation have been developed in the UK, with the consequential restructuring of the traditional, vertically integrated industries, in particular to separate the potentially competitive businesses from the network (transport) infrastructure. This restructuring has taken place after privatization as much as at privatization, proving the point that, where the underlying regulatory objective is consumer protection through competition, then the 'settlement' at privatization can, and will, be unwound, where this is necessary to facilitate competition. British Gas learned this lesson through successive Monopolies and Mergers Commission (MMC) inquiries and a notably acrimonious relationship with the first gas regulator, Jim McKinnon. Separation of network infrastructure from competitive supply has led to a regulatory focus on access pricing and common carriage, and the appropriate incremental and activity-based long-run cost measures to support it.[7] The appropriate methodologies are not clear-cut.[8]

---

[5] Organization for Economic Co-operation and Development (OECD), *The OECD Report on Regulatory Reform*, June 1997, 'Synthesis Report', Vol. 1, 'Sectoral Studies', and Vol. 2, 'Thematic studies' (Paris: OECD, 1997).

[6] S. Littlechild, *Regulation of British Telecommunications' Profitability* (London: DTI, 1983).

[7] British Telecommunications (BT), *Long Run Incremental Cost Methodology* and *Long Run Incremental Cost Model: Relationships and Parameters* (two parts) (London: BT, November 1997).

[8] Office of Telecommunications (OFTEL), *Reconciliation of the Top Down and Bottom Up Incremental Cost Models: Final Report* (London: OFTEL, December 1996).

3.2.2. The three 'conduct' failures

The concept of market failures, while technically appropriate, is semantically a problem for many of the 'stakeholders' in the regulatory debate. Competition for markets may have a pejorative sense for commentators on the environmental and social impacts of the provision of essential services. The words themselves convey an 'econo-centric' view which is judged wanting in these, clearly, non-economic areas of human endeavour and community to which different value systems should apply.

While it can be argued that the concept of market failures, like cost–benefit analysis, is an all-inclusive evaluative system, it is of little help if the argument falls on deaf ears. To engage all parties, a common, and acceptable, terminology needs to be found, from which the argument and rationalizations can proceed. Given the important role of regulatory process in securing legitimacy, the term 'conduct failures' will be used to describe the inclusive and synthesizing aspect (between regulatory objectives and process) of what would otherwise be properly termed 'market failures'.

A three-way split of conduct failures is useful; two are immediately recognizable as traditional market failures, the last less so, in part because economists often divide allocative and technical efficiency from distributive equity in the discussions of public policy and finance. Distributive outcomes from a market economy that do not meet the tests of political acceptability, given a democratic system, should be seen as a form of market (i.e. conduct) failure, and the mechanisms for addressing that unacceptable outcome as regulation.

The three types of conduct failure are:

1. the abuse of monopoly power and anti-competitive behaviour;
2. 'external' effects not reflected in private costs and benefits (externalities and 'public' goods);
3. social exclusion and inequity (discriminatory outcomes).

This classification is reflected in the institutional structures for regulation in the UK model.

In passing, we should note the continuing semantic problems that regulatory debate encounters. If we focus our regulatory prescription on each of the three types of conduct failure, then we find that regulation of the abuse of monopoly power will have cost-reflective tariffs as a policy objective. In this context, cross-subsidies are discriminatory and cost-reflective tariffs, non-discriminatory. For regulators and commentators in the field of social exclusion and equity, however, the purpose of a public service obligation is to discriminate in favour of particular outcomes (e.g. prices the same everywhere, as with the price of a stamp). In this context cost-reflective tariffs would be discriminatory. There are many occasions in which regulatory debate in the UK has been touched by a certain 'Alice in Wonderland' quality of semantic danger and misinterpretation.

3.3. THE INSTITUTIONAL FRAMEWORK

3.3.1. *The division of roles*

The good regulatory principle of 'targeting' has evolved in the institutional framework for regulation in the UK.[9] The 'horizontal' division of regulatory roles and responsibilities is designed to focus on each particular type of 'conduct' failure. This can be commended for reasons of efficiency and effectiveness, transparency and accountability. In this context it can quite properly be said that regulators of the abuse of monopoly power—the so-called 'economic regulators'—are not agents of social justice.

The horizontal division of responsibility for addressing 'conduct' failures cannot be divorced from the 'vertical' hierarchy of responsibility for the three levels of regulatory activity (setting policy and rules, monitoring, and enforcement) which runs from direct government responsibility through to various levels of devolved responsibility. In particular, where (macro) decisions need to be made on behalf of the public or all consumers and involve major questions of safety or health (e.g. standards for the quality of drinking water), then those decisions need to be vested in government and its ministers, reflecting the legitimacy of the democratic mandate. This equally applies to the imposition of positive discrimination and regulation to achieve social inclusion and equity. 'Executive' implementation of competition policy and regulation of the abuse of monopoly power can properly be devolved to 'economic' regulators. Some public good standards, such as security of supply, may remain with the economic regulators.

The institutional structure can therefore be summarized as a two-way framework in Figure 3.1. The economic context for regulating all three conduct failures is apparent, however, and can be summarized as follows.

1. *Monopoly power* Economic regulation should control the abuse of monopoly power by encouraging competition where appropriate and by long-term periodic price control of natural monopoly businesses, implying cost-reflective tariffs and a regulatory role as a competition authority.
2. *Public goods and externalities* Environmental standards should be set by government but should incorporate a cost–benefit test to ensure that in principle the standards so set are at a level where the incremental (or marginal) cost is equal to the incremental benefit.
3. *Where the 'uncorrected' distribution of income and access to essential services is 'politically' unacceptable* Government and income support agencies should specify the means by which a politically acceptable outcome can be achieved, subject to the economic test that the means used should minimize any economic and financial distortions.

---

[9] Better Regulation Task Force, *The Better Regulation Guide* (see also *The Guide to Better European Regulation*) (London: Regulatory Impact Unit, Cabinet Office, 1998).

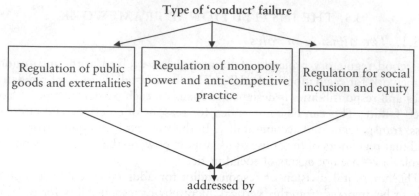

Type of 'conduct' failure

| Regulation of public goods and externalities | Regulation of monopoly power and anti-competitive practice | Regulation for social inclusion and equity |

addressed by

**the hierarchy of responsibilities:
policy to enforcement**

Institution	Role
Government and its departments	**Regulatory policy** *Set standards and rules* • incorporating EU legislation into UK law • issuing licences and permissions *or* delegating responsibility to NDPBs
Non-ministerial and non-departmental public bodies (NDPBs)	*Advise government on policy* setting some regulatory policy/standards and permissions (delegated authority) ↓ **Executive implementation of regulation** *Monitor* regulated providers/clients *Enforce* regulation

Figure 3.1. *Two-way-tri-partite model*

Note: This figure was developed as part of a CRI research project on the regulatory framework, funded by EDEXCEL (forthcoming).

The European context of the vertical hierarchy of responsibility and the role of advisory bodies can be illustrated by waste water regulation.

Setting standards versus monitoring and enforcement Directives on water discharge standards in the European Union are set by the European Commission, following consultation with the European Parliament and ratification by the member states' Council of Ministers. The UK minister will have been advised by, among others, the Environment Agency. The government is required to incorporate a waste water directive into UK law (taking account of any derogations or definitional criteria over which there is a member state discretion). The Environment Agency is responsible for monitoring and enforcing compliance with the directive by the licensed water and sewerage companies.

The overlap of regulatory roles and responsibilities in practice can also be usefully illustrated by the water sector.

OFWAT and the three 'conduct' failures OFWAT (i.e. the Director General) is an economic regulator, and one of its main functions is the control of the abuse of monopoly power. However, the Director General is also responsible for setting certain levels of service standards on behalf of all consumers in an area or region, including pressure, leakage, and reliability (security) of supply. The Director General also has statutory duties to have regard to the needs of special interest groups, such as the elderly, the disabled, and rural customers (and the metered water bills for certain classes of disadvantaged customer are now capped by law). OFWAT, in practice, therefore, could be entered into each of the three classifications of conduct failure. Consumer representation (the ten regional Customer Service Committees) is also part of OFWAT.

3.3.2. *The wider context*

Figure 3.2 sets the basic framework in the wider regulatory context, identifying in particular the role of cross-sectoral and sectoral institutions, and the relationship between the latter and self-regulatory arrangements (collective self-regulation). This relationship has recently been referred to as 'co-regulation' by OFTEL, which places the responsibility on the regulated industry, but with appropriate public oversight. The split between consumer 'representation' and consumer 'advocacy' is also identified, where consumer representation on behalf of all consumers is seen as part of each economic regulator's role, and consumer advocacy relates to lobbying on behalf of particular 'interest' groups. This distinction is particularly important in relation to the current policy in the Utilities Bill of setting up an 'independent' energy consumers council, while at the same time giving the regulator a primary duty of consumer protection.[10] The government intends to apply this policy to all sectors.

The policy is contradictory, and we will have to wait and see whether the bureaucracy of the arrangements can be reasonably managed through memorandums of agreement or whether it provokes conflict to an extent that might undermine confidence in the regulatory system. Note too the important

---

[10] R. Brooke, *The Consumer's-Eye View of Utilities* (London: Local Government Association, 2000).

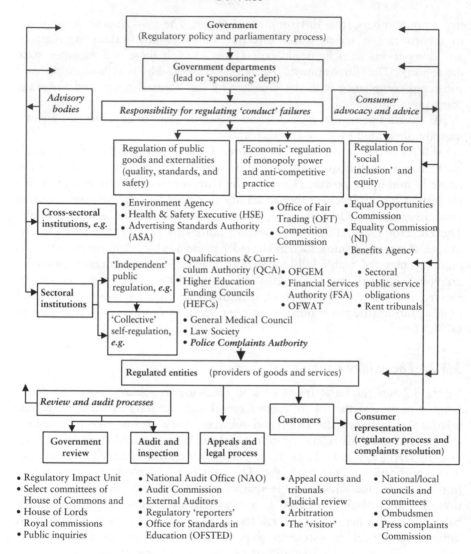

Figure 3.2. *The Regulatory Framework*

Note: This figure was developed as part of a CRI research project on the regulatory framework, funded by EDEXCEL (forthcoming).

role of audit, regulatory review, and appeal mechanisms, including the Competition Commission and judicial review.[11] The National Audit Office has progressively developed its 'value for money' studies of the regulatory

[11] Monopolies and Mergers Commission (MMC), *Northern Ireland Electricity plc: A Report on a Reference under Article 15 of the Electricity (Northern Ireland) Order 1992* (London: Stationery Office, 1997).

offices.[12] These are then reviewed by the Committee of Public Accounts (PAC).[13] Parliamentary scrutiny is also well developed through the select committees.[14]

3.3.3. *The economic regulators*

The economic regulators represent a distinctive 'unbundling' of state institutions, which is reflected in their being called 'independent'. This has had definite advantages in developing transparency (see, for instance, the development of the 'cost of quality' debate in water), accountability (consider, in particular, the fact that the powers are vested in the individual Director General and not the 'office'—which is a non-ministerial public body), and regulatory focus with appropriate discretion (as evidenced by the limitations placed on ministerial advice to regulators and the refusal of the then gas regulator, Clare Spottiswoode, to take on the responsibility for levying environmental taxes through price controls). However, there has been a vigorous debate about whether 'technocratic' appointments to non-departmental public bodies (NDPBs) represents a democratic deficit.[15]

However, unbundling, with the consequential increase in formal, public interchanges between the various regulatory institutions of government, has allowed outsiders to listen in to government 'talking to itself'—something that previously would have taken place behind closed doors. The 'due process' of consultation, and regulators giving reasons for decisions, has also improved dramatically—something that was both necessary for, and has underpinned the legitimacy of, the 'independent' regulators.

The present position is given in Table 3.2. The Post Office will be subject, in a similar way, to arm's-length regulation by the Postal Services Commission (PostComm) from 2001. The government has announced the replacement for the retiring water regulator, Ian Byatt; Philip Fletcher is, untypically, a career

---

[12] National Audit Office (NAO), *The Work of the Directors General of Telecommunications, Gas Supply, Water Service and Electricity Supply: Report by the Controller and Auditor General*, HC 645, Session 1995–6, (London: Stationery Office, 1996); J. Marshall, 'Value for Money and Money for Value', in P. Vass (ed.), *CRI Regulatory Review 1998/99* (Bath: CRI/University of Bath, 1999).

[13] Committee of Public Accounts (PAC), *Office of Telecommunications: Licence Compliance and Consumer Protection, Sixth Report*, House of Commons, no. 123 (London: HMSO, 1993); *The Work of the Directors General of Telecommunications, Gas Supply, Water Services and Electricity Supply: Sixteenth Report*, House of Commons, Session 1996-7, no. 89 (London: Stationery Office, 1997).

[14] Trade and Industry Committee, *Energy Regulation*, HC 50-1, Session 1996–7, First Report (London: Stationery Office, 1997); Trade and Industry Committee, *Telecommunications Regulation*, HC 254, Session 1996–7, Third Report (London: Stationery Office, 1997).

[15] G. Majone, 'The Rise of the Regulatory State in Europe', *Western European Politics*, 17/3, July 1994; 'Paradoxes of Privatization and Deregulation', *Journal of European Public Policy*, 1/1 (June 1994); *Independence versus Accountability? Non-majoritarian Institutions and Democratic Government in Europe*, Working Paper no. 94/3 (Florence: European University Institute, 1994).

Table 3.2. *Economic regulators*

Acronym	Full Title	Director General
OFTEL	Office of Telecommunications	David Edmonds
OFGAS	Office of Gas Supply	Callum McCarthy
OFFER	Office of Electricity Regulation	Callum McCarthy
Now OFGAS and OFFER are combined to be:		
OFGEM	Office of Gas and Electricity Markets	
OFREG	Office of Regulation of Electricity and Gas (Northern Ireland)	Douglas McIldoon
OFWAT	Office of Water Services	Ian Byatt
CAA	Civil Aviation Authority (economic regulation)	Douglas Andrew
ORR	Office of the Rail Regulator	Tom Winsor
OPRAF	Office of Passenger Rail Franchising (now part of the Strategic Rail Authority)	Mike Grant

civil servant. PostComm and Ofgem will regulate by a board, rather than an individual director general; the latter will be entitled the Gas and Electricity Markets Authority (GEMA).

3.3.4. *The purpose of economic regulation*

There has been much criticism of the statutory duties of the economic regulators, although it is understandable that at privatization the emphasis of the legislation should have been on investor confidence (hence the primary duty to ensure that the regulated business can finance itself) and continuity of supply of these essential services (hence the primary duty to ensure that all reasonable demands for supply will be met). The division into primary and secondary duties (of which consumer protection was often cited as a secondary duty) did not, however, alter the fundamental regulatory objective and conduct of the regulator, which was to secure consumer protection. This emphasis has been clearly recorded in the regulators' annual reports.

The statement of the regulatory objective, and the constraints to which it is subject, might best be set out as in Table 3.3. The Government's Utilities Bill, which sought, before water and telecommunications were withdrawn, to harmonize the statutory duties, would have reflected this by placing a primary duty of consumer protection on all of the regulators.

Table 3.3. *The Regulatory objective*

Primary objective	Subject to constraints such as:
Consumer protection with a focus on achieving the lowest possible prices for a given, or required, quality of service by price control or by promoting competition	• Ensuring that the business can finance itself (minimum required return for an efficient company) • Specified environmental and service standards • Non-discriminatory tariffs based on cost • Specified public service obligations

3.3.5. *Incentive regulation*

The theory of 'incentive' regulation, based on the periodic resetting of maximum allowed prices rather than profit control (often referred to as 'rate of return' regulation), has been well, and repeatedly, articulated, not least in the consultation documents from the regulators which accompany each periodic review. The price controls are defined as an allowable increase or decrease on the previous year's tariffs, indexed for inflation; hence the general description $RPI - X$. The overall price control can be a weighted average of prices (a basket), which allows a re-balancing of tariffs, but with supplementary price caps on particular elements as required. Quality standards have been set (with guaranteed compensation payments to customers for various individual service failures) to ensure that a lowering of standards is not an option to increase profits. Incentive regulation with maximum price controls is seen as:

• controlling the abuse of monopoly power (i.e. prices no higher than the prevailing long-run cost of supply—suitably defined);
• promoting technical efficiency, productivity improvements, and innovation, which reduces the long-run cost of supply through the ability of management to earn *economic profit* (profit over and above that necessary to earn a normal rate in return, i.e. the cost of capital);
• achieving an 'equitable' bargain between consumers and producers (shareholders and management) as the improved cost structure revealed by the out-performance that generates the economic profits is passed on to consumers by way of even lower prices, or even higher standards, at the next periodic review.

This regulatory bargain is shown schematically in Figure 3.3, and can be summed up as follows:

High profits today are the quid pro quo for lower prices tomorrow.

The degree of out-performance is affected by the choice of the length of the review period and the extent to which the management is incentivized by their remuneration. Performance bonuses and share options are both ways in which shareholders can improve their return at the price of sharing some of the improved return with managers.

P. Vass

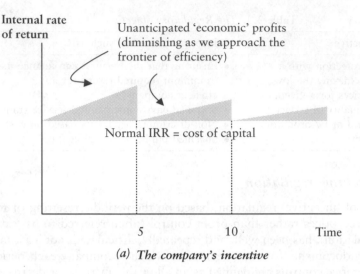

(a) **The company's incentive**

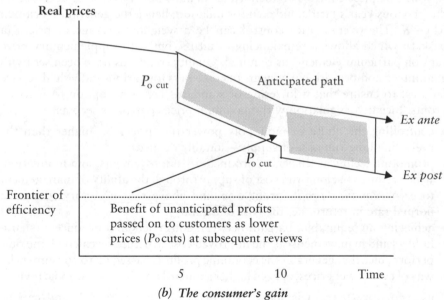

(b) **The consumer's gain**

Figure 3.3. *Surrogate competition: shareholder and consumer gain*

The 'equitable' share has been an on-going debate in regulation, and a five-year review period has settled down as the typical balance between incentives, equity, and the risk associated with longer review periods.[16] Typical calculations

---

[16] Monopolies and Mergers Commission (MMC), *Manchester Airport plc: A Report on the Economic Regulation of Manchester Airport plc* (London: Stationery Office, 1997).

show that in a steady state the majority of benefits go to consumers, but these do not answer the important questions about the relationships between reward and performance, and the other determinants of performance.[17] For example, a £1 annual saving made at the start of a review period would yield

$$\frac{\text{Present value of £1 for 5 years @ 7\%}}{\text{Present value of a £1 perpetuity @ 7\%}} = \frac{4.1}{14.29} = 28.7\%.$$

That is, 71 per cent of the unanticipated gain is passed to customers and 29 per cent is retained by shareholders.

It is interesting to note that in one sense the distribution of rewards is just that, and so public policy and support should be focused on achieving efficiency and productivity improvements, whoever gains, while in practice the public debate has rarely had a good word to say for economic profits. In part this seems to arise from the difficulty of accepting, or distinguishing, good from bad profit, where good profits arise from efficiency and bad profits from the abuse of monopoly power. Too often, 'utilities profit' has been a term used purely in a pejorative sense.

The system of maximum price controls with annual out-performance will mean that prices are greater than the long run cost of supply for a period, but the deadweight loss of allocative efficiency is, for the most part, judged to be significantly outweighed by the gain in technical efficiency.

3.4. FINANCIAL AND ACCOUNTING INTERFACE

The well understood economic theory has not been so well matched by an understanding of the accounting theory and its application.[18] This has been an important omission which has caused much unnecessary confusion about regulatory methodology and practice, resulted in inconsistent and, at times, erroneous practice, and missed a good opportunity for effective reporting of the financial and performance outcomes of incentive regulation.[19] It is important because, in practice, price controls are set by a financial methodology that integrates economic cash flow modelling (i.e. future cash flows) with accounting numbers which reflect both accumulated balances from the past (the opening regulatory book value) and balances at the end of the review period which are attributable to subsequent periods. The economic and accounting measures are brought together in the *truncated cash flow model*.[20]

---

[17] I. Viehoff, '*Evaluating RPI − X*', *Topics*, 17 (London: National Economic Research Associates, 1995).

[18] M. Board *et al.*, *Accounting Requirements for Regulated Industries*, CRI Research Report 9 (Bath: CRI/University of Bath, 1998).

[19] D. Newbery, 'Determining the Regulatory Asset Base for Utility Price Regulation', *Utilities Policy*, 6/1 (1997).

[20] P. Vass, 'The Methodology for Resetting *X*', in P. Vass (ed.), *CRI Regulatory Review 1997* (Bath: CRI/University of Bath, 1997).

The truncated cash flow model provides a frame of reference for analysing many of the key problems of economic regulation and provides insights into the explanation for past regulatory 'mistakes' and developments. The model is derived from the basic regulatory equation for allowed revenue through price controls, i.e.

Allowed Revenue should equal the forecast cost for the review period.

More precisely, the forecast present value of revenue (PVR^F) should equal the forecast present value of costs (PVC^F), which is the fundamental regulatory equation:

$PVR^F = PVC^F$, or
Forecast net present value $(NPV^F) = 0$.

The present value of costs is derived from discounting a forecast cost series for the review period by the cost of capital (taking account of the weighting of debt and equity and the pre- and post-tax position appropriately). The future cash flows will include operating expenditure (OPEX) and capital expenditure (CAPEX), and, since many capital expenditures will have a life that goes beyond the end of the current review period, it would not be appropriate to charge current consumers with the full cost of acquiring those capital assets in this period. The cash flow model will therefore be truncated at the end of the period with the inclusion of a notional receipt, reflecting the value of the assets to be transferred to subsequent periods and charged to consumers in those periods. The closing regulatory book value will be calculated by attributing a cost for the use of the capital assets, i.e. capital consumption, to this period's consumers. Accountants measure this as depreciation.

The opening regulatory book value can be based on known, i.e. actual, figures (the rolled-forward capital acquisitions and provision for depreciation), and therefore would not be a forecast like the rest. However, in order to maintain both OPEX and CAPEX incentives to efficiency through each review period, the practice has emerged, particularly in OFWAT, of maintaining the original forecast for at least five years before it is replaced by the actual expenditure. Conversely, however, the approach of maintaining higher incentives over successive review periods through a 'glide' path of convergence of the current, above-normal rate of return to the cost of capital over, say, ten years has disappeared in favour of the *instant convergence* truncated cash flow model.[21]

Schematically, the model looks like Figure 3.4, where the opening regulatory book value is (RBV_o) and the closing regulatory book value is (RBV_c). CAPEX and OPEX will be based on forecast costs for an efficient company, and the

---

[21] Monopolies and Mergers Commission (MMC), *South West Water Services Ltd: A Report on the Determination of Adjustment Factors and Infrastructure Charges* (London: HMSO, 1995).

	1_0	1	2	3	4	5	6_0
Opening regulatory book value	X						
OPEX (cash flows)		X	X	X	X	X	
CAPEX (cash flows)		X	X	X	X	X	
Closing regulatory book value							(X)
Undiscounted 'cost' series	X	X	X	X	X	X	(X)

Figure 3.4. *The truncated cash flow model*

relationship between the RBV_o and RBV_c is simply

$$RBV_c = RBV_o + \text{total CAPEX}$$
$$- \text{attributable depreciation provision for the period.}$$

The hitherto undiscounted cost series is discounted at the cost of capital to derive the single regulatory number, the present value of costs. The above formula demonstrates why the foundations of regulatory finance are to allow investors a *return on* investment until the *return of* investment by way of depreciation. Immediately we can see that, if allowed revenue is set equal to the forecast present value of costs, then this will ensure that the regulator is meeting the statutory duty (or equivalent) to ensure that the regulated business can finance itself, but based only on the *minimum* necessary cost of capital (given the risk of the firm) and for an *efficient* company (reflected in OPEX and CAPEX forecasts).

Also, we can see that the profile of annual allowed revenue can vary to meet regulatory objectives as long as the present value over the whole period is the same. The 'natural' method of profiling is to calculate annual allowed revenue such that the forecast regulatory accounts for each year would show a normal rate of return (i.e., allowed revenue equals OPEX, depreciation, plus the cost of capital on the regulatory book value). This well reflects the regulator's duty to allow the regulated company to finance itself, and also facilitates comparison with the 'out-turn' for the year when judging performance. A P_o cut at the beginning of each regulatory period, assuming there is out-performance to be passed on, is the normal consequence of this approach to profiling. A P_o cut reinforces the underlying benefits for consumers of the incentive on the regulated companies to out-perform.

However, other profiles have been chosen, or argued for, to meet presentational objectives. This can occur particularly where rising quality standards are expected to increase prices later in the period.

Finally, we can see that, in relation to previous periods, prices may rise or fall, depending on the balance between efficiency and productivity improvements and increasing OPEX and CAPEX requirements to meet higher quality and safety and security standards. For this reason, the CAPEX forecasts in practice often distinguish between replacement expenditure (i.e. that necessary to maintain a steady-state or going concern) and new—or enhancement—expenditure. For this reason, some regulatory presentations—notably OFWAT—distinguish the efficiency factor (X) from the quality driver (Q) in the price control formula (K); i.e.,

$$Q - X = K.$$

3.4.1. *Economic profit, variance analysis, and reporting*

Economic profit is the difference between the discounted forecast revenue and cost series (NPV^F) and the 'out-turn' revenue and cost series (NPV^A). Other things being equal, the out-turn closing regulatory book value would become the opening regulatory book value for the next period. The difference between the forecast and out-turn regulatory accounts reflects 'economic' profit, and disaggregation through variance analysis helps identify the causes of these variations. Typically, these have been divided into management-driven efficiencies and productivity improvements, windfalls and illegitimate 'gaming' profits. The first should clearly be retained by shareholders, and the last clawed back. Windfalls should probably be retained, but future formulae developed to include *error correction mechanisms* which eliminate the windfall or the artificial incentive to expand sales.

The introduction by OFFER and OFGAS in the energy sector of fixed-cost drivers, rather than simple volume drivers, is an example of such a development. In rail, cost analysis and its relationship with traffic volume has become a particularly important issue for calculating track access charges. This is because the high fixed-cost charges (and the consequential low marginal cost charges) on the train operating companies (TOCs) gives them a strong incentive to expand passenger services up to capacity (with resulting congestion), but there is little incentive on Railtrack to invest in new capacity to overcome bottlenecks.

Variance analysis could also provide a foundation for 'profit-sharing' as one way of bringing forward the benefit of out-performance to the consumers, but such a policy has not generally found favour, not least because to maintain the overall level of incentives the economic value of the profit-shared element would need to be rolled forward and added to allowed revenue in subsequent periods.[22]

Presentation would be facilitated by distinguishing between the following elements of allowed revenue:

- allowed revenue equal to the forecast PVC;
- carry-overs to maintain incentives;
- clawbacks reflecting 'gamed' profits.

---

[22] P. Vass, 'Profit Sharing and Incentive Regulation', in P. Vass (ed.), *Regulatory Review 1996* (Bath: CRI/University of Bath, 1996).

Harmonization of reporting practice across sectors might be helped by establishing a professional 'context' for regulatory accounting standards.[23]

3.4.2. *Indexing and the three models*

The truncated cash flow model takes account of changes in relative and general prices by indexing. Changes in the general level of prices need to be taken into account because investors want a return that reflects any decline in the value of money; i.e., they want to maintain the value of their investment in real terms. This is an accepted regulatory principle. Indexing the model by the retail price index (RPI) allows this to be achieved, and financial capital maintenance (FCM) has become the benchmark for periodic price controls in practice.[24] Given the annual accounted cost structure set out in the profiling of annual revenue above, then each year's allowed revenue, and hence cost components, are increased by RPI; i.e.,

(OPEX × RPI) + (Depreciation × RPI)
+(Regulatory book value × RPI × Real cost of capital)
= (Initial allowed revenue for the year × RPI).

The interesting point that comes out of this is that the regulatory scheme incorporates an indexed asset base to which is applied the real cost capital. Since debt is often denominated in historical cost terms, with nominal interest rates incorporating the inflation premium, it suggests that indexed bonds might be a very suitable form of finance for utilities. It also shows that the traditional shorthand for the UK incentive regulatory system, RPI − X, is well grounded.

3.4.3. *The three models*

Indexing plays an important role, however, well beyond the simple application of financial capital maintenance. Relative prices change over time so that the replacement cost of assets diverges from the financial capital maintenance of accumulated past investments. Also, acquisition cost has often differed markedly from the replacement cost of assets acquired (the so-called discount at privatization). Taken together, this represents a regulatory dilemma, since on the one hand the regulator would wish to set prices that reflect the appropriate cost—or replacement cost—of assets so that consumers have the right signals when making their purchasing decisions, but on the other hand he would not wish to see shareholders making windfall gains purely from changes in the

---

[23] P. Vass (ed.), *Accounting for Regulation: A Comparative Assessment*, Proceedings 25, CRI Conference September 1999 (Bath: CRI/University of Bath, 2000).

[24] G. Whittington, 'The Role of Current (Replacement) Cost Accounting for Regulated Businesses', in P. Vass (ed.), *The Financial Methodology of Incentive Regulation: Reconciling Accounting and Economics*, Proceedings 23, CRI Conference (Bath: CRI/University of Bath, 1998).

value of money relative to the cost of inputs, or from overlooking the discount at privatization.

Different approaches have been taken by the regulators, as well as by the MMC (as it was before the Competition Commission came into force), although a comprehensive accounting model can encompass them all.[25] Different terminologies, as well as different models, have also muddied the waters. The three main models that have been applied meet different regulatory objectives, although this has not always been explicitly recognized.[26] Each of them is based, however, on an approach that eliminates the windfall gains to shareholders, although in the case of gas this was achieved only after correcting the methodology used by the MMC in its 1993 report when it came to its 1997 report on Transco's periodic review by OFGAS (now OFGEM).[27]

The three main models are:

1. *financial capital maintenance*: this is based on retail-price-indexed acquisition cost;
2. *replacement cost with an abatement of the regulatory book value* (the 'regulatory hybrid'): this charges consumers replacement cost depreciation but offsets any excess over retail-price-indexed acquisition cost by reducing the regulatory book value and retaining the difference in the balance sheet as an undistributable reserve representing the consumers' (rather than the shareholders') interest;
3. *renewals provisions*: this divides the truncated cash flow model into two parts: future cash flows, for which a long-term annual repair and renewal provision is made, and the original investment (acquisition cost) at privatization, on which a return is allowed for the indefinite future. No depreciation charges are involved as the assets are expected to be maintained in perpetuity through the renewals provision.

Each of these models results in a different profile of allowed revenue across review periods. Most notably, with a significant discount at privatization, the financial capital maintenance (FCM) model results in lower prices today and higher prices tomorrow in order to fund higher replacement expenditures when the depreciation provision has been only in respect of the discounted acquisition cost of assets. The regulatory hybrid, based on immediate replacement depreciation, leads to more level prices over time, starting immediately. Renewals provisions are based on the timing of future cash flows, and, because

---

[25] Monopolies and Mergers Commission (MMC), *Gas*, vol. 1, (Cm. 2314) and *British Gas plc*, vol. 1 (Cm. 2315); vol. 2, *Reports under the Gas and Fair Trading Acts* (Cm. 2316); vol. 3, *Reports* (Cm. 2317) (London: Stationery Office, 1993).

[26] P. Vass, 'Accounting for Regulation', in P. Vass (ed.), *CRI Regulatory Review 1998/99* (Bath: CRI/University of Bath, 1999).

[27] Monopolies and Mergers Commission (MMC), *BG plc: A Report under the Gas Act 1996 on the Restriction of Prices for Gas Transportation and Storage Services* (London: Stationery Office, 1997).

they involve no depreciation charge on the acquisition costs of assets at privatization, in general lead to the lowest long-run prices, assuming going concern. Models can be combined, as OFWAT has done, using infrastructure renewals to account for 'underground' assets and the regulatory hybrid (replacement cost) for 'overground' assets.

It is interesting to note that the FCM model is simply a special case of the replacement cost regulatory hybrid model, where the discount at privatization is progressively written off in the former through abated depreciation charges to the profit and loss account (and hence to consumers); i.e.,

> Replacement cost provision for depreciation
> = Depreciation charge to profit and loss account based on acquisition cost + Depreciation charge on revalued element from acquisition cost to replacement cost, debited (i.e. written off) to the revaluation reserve.

The MMC's method, which is broadly equivalent, was to abate the current replacement cost depreciation charge by the market-to-asset ratio (MAR), on the same basis that it reflected the discount at privatization. At the same time, the cost of capital was also abated by the MAR. In the MMC's method the MAR would change and tend to 1 as discounted acquisition assets were replaced at full value.

The annual allowed revenue under the hybrid model is therefore:

> OPEX + Replacement cost depreciation + [Replacement book value
> − Discount at privatization = Regulatory book value X cost of capital].

Complications have arisen, however, where, at each periodic review, 'market' uplifts to the regulatory asset base have been made to achieve other regulatory objectives. These include uplift on the privatization value to either the end of first-day trading value or an average of the next 100–200-day values, as well as other one-off revaluations to increase allowed revenue, either to maintain the absolute value of the earnings stream for shareholders where the cost of capital has fallen (which may have occurred in order to honour some implicit 'promise' to investors at privatization) or to maintain confidence for future investment. Contrary to popular understanding, it was the methodological error associated with 'uplift' at the first electricity distribution price review which led to the public demand that the review be reopened by OFFER and the Director General, Professor Littlechild, rather than what had, or had not, been revealed by the proposed takeover of Northern Electricity by Trafalgar House.

3.5. POLICY REFLECTIONS

We can discern distinct periods in the development of regulatory debate and practice, but the Labour Party's election to government in May 1997 is particularly important, in that the outcome has been a continuity, and in some respects an acceleration, of past policies, contrary to a widespread expectation that there would be radical reform.[28] The debate was well represented by left-of-centre organizations, arguing for tougher regulation and social intervention.[29] However, it was counterbalanced on the right, arguing for limitations on regulatory discretion and the continuation of a market orientation.[30] There were also independent, academic contributions[31] and a major report from the Consumers' Association.[32]

The initial review of utility regulation began in a reforming spirit, but in practice the outcomes have been competition-orientated. New regulators have been appointed, but ministerial involvement in 'independent' economic regulation remains constrained. 'Authorities' will be introduced to replace Director Generals, but not across the board (see water) and, even so, the benefits of the direct accountability of an individual regulator will probably prove to have been so useful that it will have to be maintained by developing the role of the chairman (as a surrogate for the DG). The important adversarial nature of the relationship between the regulator and the regulated has also been recognized as a benefit, and not a failure, of regulation, and social action plans will not upset, in any material way, the original division of responsibilities for addressing the three main types of market failure because of the overall presumption in favour of competition. Combining regulators in broad sectors will continue, as it has done in energy, where relevant, and is expected to occur in telecommunications and broadcasting to reflect the technical convergence of the two (to be called OFCOM?).

Convergence of practice between regulators has, in any event, taken place. An important catalyst has been industrial restructuring resulting from takeovers (which has put competitive pressure on even natural monopoly

[28] Department of Trade and Industry (DTI), *A Fair Deal for Consumers: Modernising the Framework for Utility Regulation*, Cm. 3898, March 1998 (London: Stationery Office, 1998); *A Fair Deal for Consumers: The Response to Consultation* (London: DTI, 1998).

[29] M. Waterson, *Regulation and Ownership of the Major Utilities*, Fabian Society Discussion Paper no. 5 (London: Fabian Society, 1991);. P. Hain, *Regulating for the Common Good*, GMB discussion pamphlet (London: GMB, 1994); D. Corry, D. Souter and M. Waterson, (eds.), *Regulating our Utilities* (London: Institute of Public Policy Research, 1994); D. Corry (ed.), *Regulating in the Public Interest: Looking to the Future* (London: IPPR, 1995); J. Dickie, *Earth, Wind and Fire: Utility Regulation under New Labour*, Fabian Society Discussion Paper no. 28 (London: Fabian Society, 1996).

[30] E. Butler *et al. But Who Will Regulate the Regulators?* (London: Adam Smith Institute, 1993); C. Veljanovski, *The Future of Industry Regulation in the UK* (London: European Policy Forum, 1993); Confederation of British Industry (CBI), *Regulating the Regulators*, CBI Discussion Paper (London: CBI, 1996).

[31] R. Baldwin (ed.), *Regulation in Question: The Growing Agenda* (London: London School of Economics, 1995); J. Flemming, *The Report of the Commission on the Regulation of Privatized Utilities* (London: European Policy Forum, 1997).

[32] Consumers' Association, *Utilities in Transition: A Consumer Perspective*, Policy Report (London: Consumers' Association, 1997).

businesses to improve their efficiency) and the development of multi-utilities to take an advantage of economies of scale and scope. Regulators have 'ring-fenced' the licensed regulated business to ensure that the necessary information and resources are made available, and have set strict transfer pricing rules to avoid cross-subsidy.[33] The government has supported industrial restructuring by removing its initial 'golden shares', which has allowed foreign ownership, particularly by US companies in the electricity sector, although water-to-water mergers have been discouraged in order to ensure that sufficient 'comparators' are available to the regulator for judging efficiency at each periodic review. Vertical reintegration in the energy sector has been allowed, given the introduction of supply competition.

Introducing competition has remained at the heart of regulation.[34] European competition rules have been adopted to prohibit cartels and abuse of a dominant position,[35] and, uniquely, competition has been introduced into domestic gas and electricity supply during 1996–8. It remains a moot point whether the benefits will outweigh the costs of achieving it. Similarly, the benefits of introducing the new electricity trading arrangements (NETA), which will replace the 'Pool', may be undermined if competition problems with the bilateral contracts market (which will account for the vast majority of the trading) simply reflect the current failure of the 'contracts for differences' market to unwind the main fluctuations of the marginal pool price, which is the initial basis for settlement. Energy trading reforms have been complemented by the introduction of market mechanisms in infrastructure services, such as auctions for capacity in gas. Bidding by airlines for scarce airport slots is another example, but this reform is complicated by established 'grandfather' rights and international agreements.

Competition has led to the progressive removal of retail price controls, but sectoral regulators have retained a role as competition authorities, having concurrent powers with the Office of Fair Trading. This joint responsibility may be seen as an unnecessary regulatory burden. The water sector is the last to develop competition, and although the Competition Act 1998 can secure common carriage rights for new entrant suppliers to complement the existing 'inset' appointments, it may be that a franchising of operations will prove to be the most practical way of developing competition, given that water resources are not yet tradable, and many domestic water customers are not metered.[36]

[33] Regulatory Offices Joint Paper, *Regulatory Issues associated with Multi-Utilities* Joint Consultation Paper, May 1998 (London, Birmingham, and Belfast: OFFER, OFGAS, OFTEL, OFWAT, OFREG, 1998).
[34] D. Helm and T. Jenkinson, (eds.) *Competition in Regulated Industries* (Oxford: Oxford University Press, 1998).
[35] D. Parker, *Reforming Competition Law in the UK: The Competition Act 1998*, CRI Occasional Paper no. 14 (Bath: CRI/University of Bath, 2000).
[36] Department of the Environment, Transport, and the Regions (DETR), *Competition in the Water Industry in England and Wales: a Consultation Document* (London: DETR, 2000).

Environmental policy and market instruments have been exhaustively analysed, but progress remains slow because of the difficult redistributive impacts, which government has yet to tackle confidently.[37] The mild energy tax, rather than a strong carbon tax focused on the issues of global warming, is one example; water metering is another. At present we have the rather unsatisfactory position of a clear incentive for all to move to metering (with benefits for water conservation) but an 'unwillingness' on the part of the government to publicize it pro-actively—given that there would be pronounced redistributive effects.[38]

It could be that energy and water are seen as being both 'essential' and 'luxury' goods at the margin, depending on the level of consumption involved. This has led to much debate on tariff structures, with rising block tariffs an important means by which the essential–luxury split could be taken into account. More appropriate, perhaps, would be to define long-run marginal cost (LRMC) to include external costs, so that tariffs reflected cost, leaving any issue of affordability to be dealt with in a targeted way through direct government subsidy and income support, funded by taxation.

3.6. MUTUALS

The UK model of outright privatization with 'incentive' regulation has improved efficiency and quality of service in many areas. Funding for major capital investment has also been forthcoming, which might have been denied under macroeconomic constraints imposed by governments on the public-sector borrowing requirement (PSBR). However, a question remains about the prospects for equity-based ownership when the frontier for further efficiency improvement (real or supposed) has been reached. The recent announcements in the water industry (notably Hyder and Kelda) about the sale of water service assets to mutual ownership (in the case of Kelda, a registered community asset mutual—RCAM) expose the issues behind one version of the end-game.[39]

Given three areas of cost—(1) OPEX, (2) CAPEX, capital consumption (depreciation), and (3) CAPEX, capital finance (cost of capital)—the equity-based model provides strong incentives on management to improve efficiency. The higher cost of equity capital brings a price, however: a higher weighted cost of capital than would be the case with a debt-financed, nationalized industry. Once the frontier of OPEX and CAPEX efficiency has been reached, however, the main remaining area of cost improvement by which the regulated company can out-perform is the cost of capital. This could be achieved by increasing the

---

[37] Royal Commission on Environmental Pollution, *Energy: The Changing Climate*, 22nd Report, Cm. 4749 (London: HMSO, 2000).

[38] P. Vass, 'The Impact of Water Metering on Council Tax Based Charges', in Guy Palmer (ed.), *Water Charging and Social Justice: Why Politicians Must Act* (London: New Policy Institute, 2000).

[39] Office of Water Services (OFWAT), *The Proposed Restructuring of the Kelda Group: A Consultation Paper by the Director General of Water Services* (Birmingham: OFWAT, 2000).

debt level above that assumed by the regulator (subject to investor confidence).

The problem is that in a group structure the capital-intensive nature of the regulated infrastructure subsidiary might unacceptably distort the group-weighted cost of capital if it were 100 per cent debt-financed, and so drive up the cost of capital, thereby prejudicing the overall commercial development of the other non-regulated subsidiaries. Selling off the assets to a mutual, and then contracting with that mutual to operate the assets for it—albeit prospectively, with competitive tendering—would seem to bring many advantages to the regulated company. The restructured industry might look as depicted in Figure 3.5.

The three key regulatory problems are, however:

1. Would the new arrangement simply become 'cost pass through' to customers, who would now bear much of the risk?
2. Would concentration by merger and takeover of the operations management companies quickly develop into a 'managed' contract market which undermined competition?
3. Should the mutual owner purchase the assets at the rolled-forward regulatory book value (RBV), or only at a significant discount where current share prices are below the RBV?

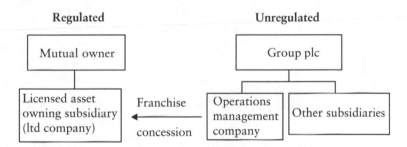

Figure 3.5. *Mutual ownership with franchised management*

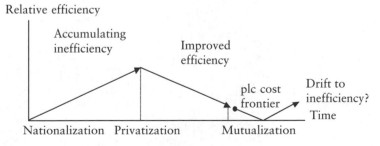

Figure 3.6. *Industry life-cycle?*

Depending on the answers to these questions, a schematic life-cycle diagram of the relative efficiency of network services provision, based on UK experience, might look something like Figure 3.6.

3.7. CONCLUSION

Regulation of utilities and network industries in the UK can offer three general lessons.

First, the regulatory objectives must be clear, and if so targeted solutions can result, using the most efficient instruments for the job. This includes 'independent' economic regulators. Second, accountability and transparency has been significantly enhanced from the 'unbundling' of the state, so that different institutions address the different 'conduct' failures. And third, regulation needs to be 'consistent' within the general framework of objectives to be achieved, but flexible and discretionary in application so that regulation can evolve, and thereby retain legitimacy and public support. Consistent principles thereby complement, and constrain, discretionary application within a transparent and accountable 'due process' of regulation.

But directors of regulated companies have to play their part, too.[40]

[40] J. Kay and A. Silberston, 'Corporate Governance', *National Institute Economic Review*, 3/95 (August 1995).

4

The Water Regulation Regime in England and Wales

IAN BYATT

4.1. THE ECONOMIC AND POLITICAL CONTEXT

Privatization arose from the economic and political difficulties of Britain in the 1970s. Solutions had to be found to high inflation, growing microeconomic inflexibility, and ineffective attempts by government to manage the economy. Macroeconomic policy seemed unable to control inflation and to generate employment. Microeconomic intervention was propping up inefficient companies and reducing the ability of the economy to adjust to new challenges.

Privatization was only one element in the reforms of the 1980s. The control of inflation, the reform of the tax system, the greater flexibility of the labour market, including a shift of power away from the unions, and tighter control of public spending were all necessary to restore the health of the economy and to revive the liberal basis of economic life essential to economic success. But privatization was a crucial element.

For the utilities, privatization started in a hesitant way. The initial approach of the government that came to power in 1979 was to seek a more liberal approach to the financing of nationalized industry investment, especially in telecommunications. It proved, however, impossible to do this within the constraints necessarily put on public borrowing to deliver the government's anti-inflation policy.

Following the failure of the 'Busby Bonds',[1] the government then made the bold decision to privatize British Telecom. As it was at that time a monopoly, a regulatory regime was set up to control its prices. Following the pioneering work of Professor Stephen Littlechild[2] (1986), the government decided on arm's-length control by a specialist regulator on an RPI − X basis. Price control was seen as temporary, pending the development of competition.

---

[1] The government spent some time considering how BT might be able to borrow on specific bonds while remaining a public corporation.

[2] S.C. Littlechild, *Economic Regulation of Privatised Water Authorities: A Report Submitted to the Department of the Environment*, London: HMSO, January 1986.

4.2. THE WATER INDUSTRY AND THE NEED FOR REGULATION

Plans for further privatization of other utilities followed the success of the flotation of British Telecom. Of the privatizations in the 1980s, the water industry was the most controversial. How could public service be provided by a private monopoly, and, moreover, one where the prospects for competition seemed remote?

On the other hand, the water industry was in need of capital to meet the European Community obligations resulting from previous and new directives. It was also argued by the water authorities that their assets needed substantial renewal as a result of constraints on public expenditure, especially those resulting from the conditions imposed on the UK in 1976 for support by the International Monetary Fund.

A first, and major, step towards privatization was taken by the then secretary of state, Nicholas Ridley, when in 1988 he began to separate out the regulatory functions of the regional water authorities from their service functions. The management of river basins, in particular the policing of the discharge of waste water to rivers, estuaries, and coastal water, was put into the hands of a new National Rivers Authority (NRA). (Subsequently the NRA was incorporated into the Environment Agency, EA.) This removed from the water authorities their ability to set their own environmental objectives and standards. These objectives could now be set by a body remaining in the public sector, so that privatized water companies would have clear, externally imposed, environmental objectives.

The process went a step further with the establishment of the Drinking Water Inspectorate (DWI), initially within the Department of the Environment, to police standards of drinking water. In due course the DWI would become a free-standing body, within the public sector.

4.3. ECONOMIC REGULATION

The architecture for regulation was completed by establishing an economic regulator to control the prices that the privatized companies could charge. This price control was to be of the form RPI $\pm$ K, where K was a factor that would take account of a company's capital investment programme as well as its prospective increase in efficiency.

It was expected, at privatization, that RPI $\pm$ K would protect customers, yet give companies scope to use business methods to increase efficiency. The K factor would be set only periodically—in the case of water, every five or ten years.

The new regime was intended:

1. to improve water quality (both supplies of drinking water and discharge of waste water) to meet EU, and national, objectives;

2. to protect customers by limiting the prices they could be charged (and to avoid deterioration in customer service);
3. to mobilize business skills to provide services to customers and to the environment efficiently and economically;
4. to develop a framework that utilized comparative competition to the benefit of customers; and
5. to enable market competition to develop.

In setting price limits, the regulator has to act in the manner that he considers is best calculated to ensure that the companies properly carry out their functions and can finance them. Subject to that he must protect customers, promote efficiency and economy, and facilitate competition between existing and potential suppliers.

It was originally envisaged that price reviews would take place every ten years to reflect the long-term nature of the industry. Meanwhile, companies would be able to apply for adjustments to their price limits to reflect specified changes in circumstances such as a new legally enforceable water quality obligation. Provision was made also for five-year reviews; in practice, five-year reviews have become the norm.

The regulator, the Director General of Water Services (DGWS), is appointed by ministers but acts independently from them in carrying out his statutory duties. He is appointed for a term of up to five years and thus has sufficient security of tenure to take an independent position. He remains, however, subject to challenge in the courts if he exceeds his powers. His decisions on price limits are subject to appeal to the Competition Commission (previously the Monopolies & Mergers Commission).

The DGWS is financed, through licence fees paid by the companies, to appoint an office (OFWAT) to assist him in the discharge of his statutory duties. To help him in his task of protecting customers, he appoints customer service committees (CSCs). Each company is allocated to a CSC, which acts as an informed customer champion. The chairmen of the CSCs come together in the OFWAT National Customer Council.

4.4. THE BIRTH PANGS AND THE HEALTHY BABY

The privatization itself was risky. Nowhere in the world did a fully privatized water and sewerage business exist. Many were sceptical, particularly about one of the water authorities which had a record of weakness. Political uncertainty about the result of the impending General Election in 1992 added to the risks.

Inevitably, the flotation price was low. While initially the taxpayer may have lost, the customer has gained, as the asset valuation used for regulating purposes is based on the flotation price plus subsequent net investment, all indexed to today's price level. The taxpayer's losses were recouped by the windfall (utility) tax levied in 1997 by the incoming Labour government.

Shareholders have had a good return, amounting to between 11 and 16 per cent annually in real terms, over the period since privatization before payment of the utility tax. They have been compensated for the risks involved in the flotation of the water companies.

4.5. ACHIEVEMENTS OF THE LAST TEN YEARS

What has been achieved over the last ten years? What has gone well?
    There have been spectacular successes, stemming from two factors:

1. privatization of the companies, i.e. those ultimately responsible for delivery of services to customers and to the environment;
2. a system of incentive regulation managed by an appointed regulator who acts at arm's length from ministers.

This success has shown itself in a number of ways.

• Prices to customers, after rising considerably in the five years after privatization, have now fallen, back towards the pre-privatization level.
• There is much greater efficiency. This is well documented and covers operations, capital maintenance, quality enhancement, and the raising of finance. Moreover, the companies have indicated that they can increase their efficiency even further.
• As a result of a doubling of investment, compared with the days of nationalization, the delivery of service to customers and to the environment has improved dramatically. This is also well documented. There are, however, issues about the cost effectiveness of some of the expenditure involved.

4.6. DRIVERS OF THE BILLS

In the early years of privatization, bills were driven upwards by obligations, mainly for higher standards of drinking water quality and for better protection of the environment. Higher efficiency has been a growing countervailing force. As Table 4.1 shows, over the fifteen years since privatization the annual average household bill will have risen by some €61. Quality improvements will have accounted for an increase of €158, while other improvements and the growth of supply will have accounted for an increase of €35. Offsetting these increases, efficiency improvements will have accounted for a decrease of €133.
    The position has varied in each of the three five-year periods. The increase driven by quality improvements is much the same for all three—around €48 per household customer. These figures do not, however, take account of the growing efficiency achieved by the companies in delivering the quality improvements. Allowing for this, the quality programmes have become bigger; that is, outputs have increased in each of the five-year periods.

Table 4.1 *Changes in Annual Household Water Rates, 1990–2005*

	Constant prices (€)			
	1990–5	1995–2000	2000–5	1990–2005
Quality improvements	58	54	46	158
Other improvements and growth in supply	29	5	2	35
Greater efficiency	−8	−29	−96	−133
Total change	78	30	−48	61

The effect on the bills of other improvements and the growth of supply has become smaller, period by period. This reflects the slower growth in demand for water, the regulator's view that such growth should be self-financing, and the ability of the companies to improve customer service without explicit allowance in price limits.

The changes in efficiency are dramatic. At privatization in 1989, ministers assumed that companies could become more efficient, but, following the experience of nationalization, not by very much. In practice, the companies did better than was assumed. In *Future Charges for Water and Sewerage Services*[3] OFWAT set price limits on the basis that efficiency could improve at a faster rate. Again the companies out-performed. In *Final Determinations*[4] OFWAT was able to assume a much bigger increase in efficiency, taking account of past out-performance as well as assuming further efficiency savings in the future.

In 1989 it was assumed that quality improvements would push the bill up much more than efficiency improvements would pull it down. By 1994 the gap was much smaller. Bills would have gone down significantly had it not been for the scale of improvements to water quality and to the environment. By 1999, the scale of the efficiency achieved by the water companies was such that a large quality programme could be carried out and bills could still fall.

It might be more difficult in the future to combine reductions in bills with a large quality programme. The growth in efficiency may slow down. (In setting price limits, we assumed a slower growth in efficiency in 2000–5 than took place in 1995–2000.) The cost of capital has fallen, but by 2005 companies may have limited scope to increase gearing further. The scale of quality investment may, however, be smaller to reflect the view of the Chairman of the EA that 'by 2005 most of the environmental damage of the past 200 years will have been repaired'.

It is crucial to make rational decisions about the scale of new quality obligations. The EA should develop environmental trade-offs—e.g. between air

[3] Office of Water Services, *Future Charges for Water and Sewerage Services: The Outcome of the Periodic Review*, Birmingham, July 1994.
[4] Office of Water Services, *Final Determinations: Future Water and Sewerage Charges 2000–05*, Birmingham, November 1999.

and water pollution—as well as progressing its analysis in water. Some of the quality projects have shown poor value for money. Customers increasingly expect more careful attention to be given to assessments of benefit as set against costs.

4.7. DELIVERY OF OUTCOMES

The regulators will monitor the delivery of the service provided by the water companies to customers and to the environment. The quality regulators will act if timed obligations are not met. OFWAT will ensure that there is no deterioration in standards of service.

Exactly how companies meet their obligations should depend on how efficient and innovative they can be. We allow for what we regard as reasonable levels of expenditure in setting price limits. But no one in OFWAT insists that any particular levels of expenditure be met. If companies can do the job more economically, their shareholders deserve a reward. Equally, if companies spend more than is allowed for in price limits, this should be at the expense of shareholders.

4.8. THE QUALITY DEBATE

Because of the importance, to the investment programme and to prices to customers, of improvements in water and environmental quality, I sought to stage a debate on those matters in *The cost of quality*,[5] which set out two quality scenarios and showed how they would affect customers' bills. This exercise in transparency has led to the publication of much more information in the cost of improving quality. Unfortunately, work on estimating benefits has lagged behind.

Nevertheless, we have, at both the 1994 and 1999 price reviews, sent an open letter to ministers,[6] setting out our views of the costs of the water quality and environmental programmes being considered. In both reviews, ministers have replied in public,[7] setting out their position on the water quality and

[5] Office of Water Services, *The Cost of Quality: A Strategic Assessment of the Prospects for Future Water Bills*, Birmingham, August 1992.

[6] Office of Water Services, *Paying for Quality: The Political Perspective*, Birmingham, July 1993; *Setting the Quality Framework: An Open Letter to the Secretary of State for the Environment, Transport and the Regions and the Secretary of State for Wales*, Birmingham, April 1998; *informing the Final Decisions on 'Raising the Quality': An Open Letter to the Secretary of State for the Environment, Transport and the Regions and the Secretary of State for Wales*, Birmingham, January 1999.

[7] Department of the Environment, Welsh Office, *Water Charges: The Quality Framework*, London: Department of the Environment, October 1993; Department of the Environment, Transport and the Regions, Welsh Office, *Raising the Quality: Guidance to the Director General of Water Services on the Environmental and Quality Objectives to be Achieved by the Water Industry in England and Wales 2000–05*, London: Department of the Environment, Transport and the Regions, September 1998; *Maintaining Public Water Supplies: Ministerial Guidance to the Director General of Water Services on Issues Arising in Preparation of Water Resources Plans by*

environmental obligations which, knowing the costs, they wish to impose on water companies during the period of the price limits.

As meeting these obligations will be part of the functions of a water company, the regulator can allow for the costs of (economical) discharge of these obligations in price limits.

4.9. THE STRUCTURE OF THE WATER COMPANIES

The water industry is highly capital-intensive with high investment relative to turnover. There are ten water and sewerage companies (WaSCs) and fourteen water-only companies (WoCs). The WoCs had never been nationalized, but had been subject to dividend control for many years.

There are 22 million water customers and 21 million sewerage customers.[8] Household customers account for 80 per cent of customers: 99.6 per cent of households are connected to the public water supply and 95.5 per cent to the public sewerage system. Water companies also serve business customers and are major contributors to draining highways and other surface areas.

While the water companies are regional monopolies, they must provide services to all customers and they must also comply with rising quality obligations. If companies fail to meet their obligations they face prosecution and enforcement action by regulators, which ultimately could lead to the loss of a company's licence.

The demand for water is broadly constant. Household demand accounts for 70 per cent of water delivered.[9] This continues to rise as the number of households increase. Water delivered to business customers, on the other hand, especially to large customers, is falling.

The combined turnover of the companies is €11 billion.[10] They have a regulatory capital value of €42 billion. Since privatization they have invested about €52 billion; annual investment is expected to continue to run at €5 billion.

The companies vary greatly in size. The turnover of the WaSCs varies from €2 billion (Thames Water Utilitics) to €0.4 billion (Wessex Water Services). The turnover of the WoCs varies from €224 million (Three Valleys) to €24 million (Cambridge).

The water industry is part of the global market. French companies (Vivendi, Suez Lyonnaise des Eaux, and Saur) own one WaSC (Northumbrian) and six

---

the *Water Companies of England and Wales*, London: Department of the Environment, Transport and the Regions, January 1999.

[8] Office of Water Services, *Report on Tariff Structure and Charges*, published annually since 1995.

[9] Office of Water Services, *Report on Leakage and Water Efficiency*, published annually since 1997.

[10] Office of Water Services, *Report on Financial Performance and Expenditure of the Water Companies in England and Wales*, published annually since 1991; *Report on Company Performance*, published annually since 1992.

WoCs. The US Enron Corporation owns a WaSC (Wessex). Scottish Power owns another WaSC (Southern Water). Union Fenosa (Spain) recently bought Cambridge Water Company. Towards the end of 2000, RWE (Germany) took over Thames Water. All companies are subject to takeover. If overseas companies can improve the effectiveness and efficiency of the water industry in England and Wales, they are welcomed. The playing field is level, irrespective of nationality.

4.10. THE SCOPE FOR COMPARATIVE COMPETITION

The scope for market competition has been limited, but the water industry has offered more scope for comparative competition than perhaps any of the other utilities.

Not only did we inherit a range of companies operating in different parts of the country, but Parliament decided that, in order to protect the regulator's ability to compare the costs and performance of water companies, any merger above a relatively small scale should be referred to the Competition Commission.[11] The Commission has to decide on the scale of any detriment to the regulator's ability to make comparisons, judge whether any other benefit that could arise only from the merger might outweigh any such detriment, and make a recommendation to ministers who make the final decisions on whether or not the merger can proceed. The Commission might recommend that the merger is not against the public interest, that it should proceed only subject to a remedy to counter any detriment, or that it is against the public interest and should not be allowed to proceed.

The Commission has heard several cases, notably the formation of the Three Valleys Company (Vivendi) in North London,[12] the takeover of Northumbrian Water by Suez Lyonnaise,[13] the proposed takeover of South West Water by either Wessex Water or Severn Trent Water,[14] and the takeover of Mid Kent Water by a joint venture consisting of Vivendi and Saur.[15] The first of these cases (Three Valleys) was allowed to proceed subject to a 10 per cent reduction in prices over a period of six years. The second (Northumbrian) was allowed to

---

[11] SI 1994/73, *The Water Enterprises (Merger) (Modification) Regulations, 1994*, London: HMSO, 1994.

[12] Monopolies and Mergers Commission, *General Utilities, The Colne Valley Company and Rickmansworth Water Company: A Report on the Proposed Merger*, Cm. 1029, London: HMSO, April 1990.

[13] Monopolies and Mergers Commission, *Lyonnaise des Eaux SA and Northumbria Water Group plc: A Report on the Merger Situation*, Cm. 2936, London: HMSO, July 1995.

[14] Monopolies and Mergers Commission, *Wessex Water plc and South West Water plc: A Report on the Proposed Merger*, Cm. 3430, London: Stationery Office, October 1996; *Severn Trent Water plc and South West Water plc: A Report on the Proposed Merger*, Cm. 3429, London: Stationery Office, October 1996.

[15] Monopolies and Mergers Commission, *Mid Kent Holdings plc and General Utilities plc and Saur plc: A Report on the Proposed Merger*, Cm. 3514, London: Stationery Office, January 1997.

proceed subject to a price reduction (for water only) of 15 per cent over a period of six years. The other two proposals were blocked.

I have consistently argued that loss of comparators[16] constitutes a detriment to all customers nationally, because the existence of comparators helps the regulator to set tight price limits and encourages companies to improve customer service. But I have not taken a rigid position. There have been a number of small mergers; the number of licences has fallen from thirty-nine to twenty-four. Where a merger could provide benefits to customers, as in the case of Three Valleys and Northumbrian, it has been allowed to proceed subject to price reductions.

4.11. THE POLITICAL DIMENSION

The regime was put in place by a Conservative government whose objective was to roll back the frontiers of the state. It believed that the government of business was not the business of government. It also believed that, where markets were not able to achieve a good solution on their own, for example because there was significant monopoly power, privatization plus regulation was preferable to state ownership.

The New Labour government elected in 1997 has a different philosophical approach to further privatization. It has, however, set its face against any re-nationalization and affirmed its commitment to arm's-length regulation. It believes that $RPI - X$ should be retained as the fundamental system of price regulation, so long as regulators continue to judge that this is best for customers. It has gone further than its Conservative predecessor in pushing for more competition in the UK economy. The Chancellor of the Exchequer has emphasized the importance of competition to benefit customers, especially by reducing prices. In 1998 Parliament passed the Competition Act.[17] This Act gives considerable power to sector regulators acting concurrently with the Director General of Fair Trading to punish abuse of a dominant market position within the UK.

Despite this clear position, there remain siren calls for more involvement by ministers in matters that are the province of regulators. Taken to extremes, they could involve the nationalization of regulation while the companies remained privatized. I advise ministers to read Homer and follow the example of Odysseus, who asked his crew to plug his ears and tie him to the mast. While the interest of ministers in social and environmental matters is to be welcomed, they should not blur responsibilities, or, worse still, the arm's length relationship, by using social and environmental concerns to intrude into economic regulation.

Our liberal civil society, a community of citizens, benefits from a plurality of institutions. Utility regulators are a recent but a significant addition. They

[16] Ibid.   [17] *Competition Act 1998*, London: Stationery Office, November 1998.

can take their place alongside other non-ministerial decision-making bodies. They take their authority from their statutory duties, establishing their credibility through openness, integrity, and fairness.

4.12. THE REGULATORY AGENDA

As the first director general, I have had considerable scope in setting the agenda and responding to events.

I made my first statement, published in the privatization prospectus,[18] shortly after my appointment in August 1989. Most of it has been put into operation. But the agenda has developed; we have been part of an historical process. Adapting to this, and seizing opportunities when they arise, is a major part of the regulator's trade.

The position of the regulator has been even more exposed than I had expected. I knew utilities would always be in the public eye, and that greater transparency would expose issues previously kept under wraps. I could see the conflicts inherent in concerns for the environment and concerns for bills. But I had not expected the scale of the conflicts and degree of the antagonisms.

Paradoxically, perhaps, the independence of the regulator from ministers has made it easier to chart a steady course and to balance conflicting interests. Government ministers usually have a short term of office and are subject to constant pressures to satisfy interest groups. Their turnover is rapid; in eleven years I have worked with twelve different secretaries of state (six English and six Welsh)[19] and six different ministers for the environment.

I needed regulatory stability to establish good systems for regulating monopoly utilities:

- *good process*, allowing wide consultation with interested parties, proper relationships with companies, and opportunities for the paying customers to register their views. We needed to devise practical ways of establishing our integrity and building up the confidence of diverse groups;
- *an accepted methodology*. We started with RPI − X as the brain-child of Stephen Littlechild. It has evolved over the years into a sophisticated medium-term approach, increasingly finely tuned but retaining powerful incentives to greater efficiency. This has involved careful analysis of costs and performance across all the companies and extensive work on the cost of capital;
- *sound information*, collected on a comparative basis, on the costs, levels of service, environmental improvements, and efficiency of water companies. This information has been widely disseminated, in accessible form,[20] to

[18]*The Water Shares Offer: Prospectus. Offers for Sale on Behalf of the Secretary of State for the Environment and the Secretary of State for Wales*, London: Schroders, 1989.

[19] I include, since the establishment of a Welsh Assembly, two first secretaries.

[20]*Maintaining Public Water Supplies*, 1999; *Report on Tariff Structure*, 1995, Report on Leakage, 1997; Office of Water Services, *Report on Cost of Water Delivered and Sewage Collected*, published annually, 1992–6.

reach a wide range of interested parties. The basic data *July Returns*[21] is available through our Library.

Transparency of process and content are desirable in order to develop good policy. Experience has taught me that it is a great strength to independent regulators. It is not possible to please everyone, but in a mature society, wide knowledge of what regulators are doing, and why, helps those who have to make, or live with, difficult decisions.

4.13. THE SUCCESSES OF REGULATION

Regulation has, I believe, produced a good deal for customers and a good deal for the environment. It has done this for the following reasons.

- We regulate by outcomes, not by expenditure; by outputs, not inputs. State-owned regional water authorities did not have clear quality, environmental, and service objectives: privatized water companies do. Their performance is widely monitored and they are held to account for failure.
- We have adjusted price limits to allow companies to finance ambitious investment programmes to improve water quality and to protect the environment.

Incentives work. We allow companies to make money by reducing costs (but not by cutting corners). At price reviews we transfer the benefit of a lower cost base to customers.

- We provide incentives for good outcomes. Companies performing well are rewarded at price reviews; companies performing badly are penalized. Companies who share benefits with customers between price reviews have this recognized in future price limits.
- We have maintained, and stimulated, comparative competition to the benefit of customers. We have published comparisons of levels of service[22] and pushed the laggards to catch up with the leaders. We have examined costs comparatively. While expecting everyone to do better, we have assumed that the less efficient would catch up with the more efficient. Companies do not like to be left behind, and shareholders do not like to have failures in their portfolios. Incentives work.
- As the original dual product companies have diversified, we have strengthened the ring-fencing of the core water business to avoid cross-subsidy or putting the appointed business at risk from other operations.
- We are creating a level playing field for market competition to develop.

---

[21] Office of Water Services, *Water Company July Returns*, submitted annually since 1990.
[22] Office of Water Services, *Report on Levels of Services for the Water Industry in England and Wales*, published annually since 1990.

We live in a global market; protection is not good for sound business. We benefit from the presence of French, Scottish, American, Spanish, and German companies in the water business in England and Wales. If our companies do well at home, they should be able to compete in world markets—and vice-versa.

Water companies are subject to takeover, thus keeping up pressure on management. To balance this with the maintenance of comparative competition, water–water mergers have to show a positive benefit to customers, while non-water–water mergers are allowed to proceed unless there is a detriment to customers.

4.14. WORKING WITH OTHER REGULATORS

Regulators do not work in isolation. We cooperate both with the quality regulators and with the other utility regulators. We work closely with the DWI and the EA on the details of the quality programme to be allowed for in price limits. We monitor the performance of the companies in tandem.

Work with the other utility regulators has involved debate on regulatory strategy, exchange of experience on particular issues, and day to day cooperation. We have a joint work programme[23] and report publicly on its progress.

4.15. LEARNING FROM EXPERIENCE

I have enjoyed the way my role, and that of OFWAT, has developed in the last ten years. We started with an Act of Parliament, the Water Act,[24] a licence for water companies,[25] and a clean sheet on process, methodology, information and publicity. We have built up an efficient and effective office, with excellent staff at all levels. We have developed a comprehensive system for reporting on company performance, including financial performance, their costs and efficiency, and the prices they charge.[26]

We keep a systematic, and sometimes beady, eye on outcomes and take action where things are going wrong. In 1996 the first €64 million 'fine' was levied on Yorkshire Water following an investigation of its performance during the drought of 1995.[27]

---

[23] Office of Water Services, *Statement by Oftel, Ofgem, ORR and Ofreg on Joint Working*, Birmingham, October 1999.

[24] *Water Act 1989*, London: HMSO, 1989.

[25] *Instrument(s) of Appointment of the Water and Sewerage Companies*, 1989.

[26] *Report on Financial Performance*, 1991; *Report on Cost of Water Delivered*, 1992–6; Office of Water Services, *Report on Water and Sewerage Service Unit Costs and Relative Efficiency*; published annually since 1997; *Report on Tariff Structure*, 1995.

[27] Office of Water Services, *Report on Conclusions from Ofwat's Enquiry into the Performance of Yorkshire Water Services Ltd*, Birmingham, June 1996.

We tell the world what is going on, through:

- my annual report[28] and those of the Customer Service Committees (CSCs) and the OFWAT National Customer Council (ONCC),[29] and
- our regular publications on companies—on their financial performance, levels of service, on efficiency and tariffs.[30]

I like to think of this as a model for other services still in the public sector.

I am proud that we have been able to do this within a modest budget. Including regulation and customer representation, we spend €18 million a year, equivalent to £0.60 for every customer.

4.16. CUSTOMER REPRESENTATION

CSCs are making sure that services meet the needs of citizens. Each regional committee has built up its own network using practical skills and local knowledge. They deal with complaints that customers have not been able to resolve with their companies. They monitor the quality of companies' customer service, using independent audits. They have lobbied for the appointment of non-executive directors, with skills in customer service, to utility boards; in a number of cases such directors have come from their ranks. CSCs have been involved in the arrangements for the market research conducted by companies.

As the water industry has a strong regional dimension, the CSCs naturally have different views, often reflecting, quite rightly, the preoccupations of the area. A striking example is provided by the debate I encouraged on *Paying for Water*[31] in the early years of regulation. The differing views on metering were well expressed by the CSCs: half favoured metering and half opposed it.

The chairmen meet together about six times a year in the ONCC (originally the Chairmen's Group). This gives them an opportunity to exchange their different regional experiences and to talk to the regulator. I have always found it useful to listen to chairmen; we have done much useful work together. Where there has been consistency of view, the ONCC has formulated a national position.

[28] Office of Water Services, *Director General's Annual Report*, published annually since 1990, London: HMSO/ Stationery Office.

[29] OFWAT National Customer Council, OFWAT Customer Service Committees, *Representing Water Customers: The Annual Report of the OFWAT National Customer Council and the Ten Regional Customer Service Committees*, published annually since 1997; individual OFWAT Customer Service Committee annual reports, published annually 1991–6.

[30] *Report on Tariff Structure*, 1995; *Report on Financial Performance*, 1991; *Report on Cost of Water Delivered*, 1992–6; *Report on Levels of Service*, 1990; *Report on Water and Sewerage Service Unit Cost*, 1997.

[31] Office of Water Services, *Paying for Water: A Time for Decisions. A Consultation Paper issued by the Director General of Water Services on Future Charging Policy for Water and Sewerage Services*, Birmingham, November 1990.

4.17. PAYING FOR WATER

We in OFWAT have also been concerned with water services as a market.

The use of a tax basis (1971 rateable values) for charging restricts consumer choice and hampers the normal working of supply and demand. Hence we consulted at an early stage on *Paying for Water*. Following this consultation, we adopted policies for selective rather than universal metering.

Progress has varied, having been much more rapid in East Anglia than in Wales. Penetration of meters is now, however, rising steadily and may be stimulated by the recent Water Industry Act,[32] which gives all households a right to a meter free of charge for installation. Under that Act, OFWAT has to approve companies' charges schemes before they can lawfully collect money from most customers. We will use these powers to ensure that charges for particular services and for particular groups of customers properly reflect economic costs.

4.18. MARKET COMPETITION

The scope for competition in water is less than in telecoms, gas, or electricity. But the agenda is now opening up. The Competition Act 1998 is a milestone. Companies have already set out principles for access to their networks and we have asked them to translate these into access codes governing 'common carriage' of an entrant's water. Ministers have agreed to reduce the threshold for inset appointments,[33] and I hope they will legislate to liberalize trading in abstraction licences.[34]

At present competition is concentrated on large users, but the right to optional metering and the installation of meters in new properties and, indeed, when occupancy changes could open up competition for household customers, particularly in conjunction with the development of common carriage.

Our objective is to create a level playing field, i.e. to provide opportunities for competition to flourish,[35] by giving competitors access to the monopoly inherent in the water and sewerage networks. This access would be on fair terms and include access to abstraction rights not allocated through a market process. It would not be our intention to force competition or to stipulate dates for achieving specific goals. Rather, we aim to create a framework to allow competition to develop where customers can benefit.

---

[32] *Water Industry Act 1999*, London: Stationery Office, July 1999.

[33] Department of the Environment, Transport and the Regions, National Assembly for Wales, *Competition in the Water Industry in England and Wales*, London: Department of the Environment, Transport and the Regions, April 2000.

[34] Department of the Environment, Transport and the Regions, *Economic Instruments in Relation to Water Abstraction: A Consultation Paper*, London: Department of the Environment, Transport and the Regions, April 2000.

[35] Office of Fair Trading, *Competition Act 1998: Application in the Water and Sewerage Sectors*, London: Office of Fair Trading, January 2000.

4.19. CONCLUSION

Four years ago I said that RPI − X was alive and well and living in the water industry, but that it was an adolescent, vigorous, but sometimes gauche and with much to learn.[36] Since then it has matured—while retaining its vigour.

Good process has been established with wide consultation. There is an accepted methodology. Sound information is collected and widely disseminated. The RPI − X arrangements have developed, within a reasonable budget, into medium-term incentive regulation with a mechanism for transferring the benefits of a reduced cost base to customers at successive price reviews. These should continue along present lines to provide incentives for companies to improve performance.

CSCs are making sure that services meet the needs of citizens. Each regional committee has built up its own network, using local knowledge and expertise to represent customers and deal with unresolved complaints. The meetings of their chairmen in the ONCC enable them to exchange information, talk to the regulator, and formulate a collective national voice. Any changes in institutional arrangements should respect this good practice.

Arm's-length working of regulators and ministers has been effective in achieving results while reducing costs. Regulators work together within a statutory framework. They are well placed to take a medium-term view and to resist specific pressures from interest groups. Siren calls to nationalize regulation should be resisted. Where ministers wish to implement social or environmental measures they should use specific legal provisions, and the costs should be clear to those paying the bills.

Finally, the time is ripe for more competition in the water industry. The Competition Act 1998 has shifted the legal balance. The job of the regulator is to create a level playing field so that market competition can develop. To facilitate competition further, the scope for inset arrangements should be widened and abstraction licences opened up to trading. Market competition will inevitably take time to mature, however, and until then we should preserve the conditions where comparative competition can flourish. Any further reduction in the number and range of comparators should—and will—be examined by the Competition Commission and approved only if there are positive benefits to remedy the detriment to comparative competition.

[36] Ian Byatt, *Price Control Review: Letter to Clare Spottiswoode, Director General, Office of Gas Supply*, Birmingham, August 1995.

5

The Pioneering Swedish
Experiment in Railway Regulation

LUC BAUMSTARK

5.1. INTRODUCTION

Sweden's railway reform is arousing interest in Europe. Initiated well before the European directive of 1991, it constitutes an ideal observatory for other countries facing the same problems. Held up as a success by numerous observers and presented as an alternative to the British reform, from which it differs in numerous respects, this experiment shows how deregulation of the railway industry can take a very different path. In Sweden, while the reform has been very gradual in nature, it appears to reflect a strong commitment. The decisions made to open the sector to competition have occurred without great discontinuity, as part of a transport policy whose main characteristics are the decentralization of decisions and a massive renewal of investment in railways.

Openness to competition has not led to withdrawal by the state. Instead, it has been accompanied by profound institutional changes that have gradually created a new framework for public intervention that this paper proposes to analyse.

5.2. VERY GRADUAL DEREGULATION OF THE RAIL SERVICES MARKET

The remarks made in the literature on the subject often reduce the Swedish railway reform to simply the institutional separation of infrastructure and

I would like to thank all those who helped me one way or another to carry out this investigation on railway reform in Sweden: Hakan Jacobsson, Rikstrafiken, Bertil Hylèn; Swedish National Road and Transport Research Institute; Dag Fagring, Secretary General, Bus and Coach Federation; Roger Pyddoke and Lennart Thörn, Sika Institute; Lennart Göranson, Deputy Director General, Lars-Göran Hansson, and Per-Arne Sundbom, Konkurrensverket; Märta-Lena Schwaiger, Managing Director, Swedish Public Transport Association; Lars Hallsten, Federation of Swedish Industries; Kersti Karlsson, Deputy Director, Ministry of Industry, Employment and Communications; Bertrand Furno and Olivier Foulonneau, Poste d'Expansion Economique, Ambassade de France; Mikael Prenler, Transport Policy Section Banverket; and particularly Gunnard Alexandersson, Stockholm School of Economics. However I am alone responsible for the contents of this paper.

operations imposed by public authorities. It is true that at the time such a separation was a revolutionary step in this industry, which was heavily integrated from its conception. But the railway reform that has been implemented in Sweden over the past fifteen years cannot be so easily summarized. The creation of Banverket, the authority in charge of the network, is a decision that reflects a broader reform of the transport system, whose main goal is to stimulate and enhance the efficiency of rail transport.

5.2.1. A rail reform policy in the context of an ambitious transport policy

The rail reform primarily reflects the overall transformation of Swedish society. This partly accounts for the political consensus that enabled the public authorities to take a whole series of decisive steps affecting public transportation. The modernization of public services has been sustained by the challenge to the Swedish economic model that began in the late 1980s and is reflected mainly in the desire to improve public finances, decentralize administration, and rationalize services by adapting them to needs.

These general considerations can easily be applied to transport. The government proposed a policy of sustainable transport development whose main principles were clearly stated: to strengthen and improve the socioeconomic valuation of investments to be used as the basis for public choices, making all players aware of the costs of transportation by incorporating the social costs in the price of transport, while ensuring that the mobility requirements of economic players, citizens, and industry are met.

In this general context, succeeding governments across the whole of the political spectrum all demonstrated the same desire to develop the railway sector. They all felt that the vitality of this form of transportation was essential to ensure the efficiency and performance of the transportation system as a whole. Rail transport was viewed as, on the one hand, a strategic tool, underpinning the country's ability to export to Europe, and on the other a way of avoiding the substantial economic cost of a log-jam or the rationing of the system as a result of massive congestion or environmental constraints.

This political will was very clearly displayed at the same time that the railway industry was in evident decline, as in all European countries: annual deficits of the public operator, which were already very large, were getting worse; vital investments in maintenance were being neglected; the services offered were not adapted to mobility needs, while the competition from other forms of transport, both road and marine, was becoming much more serious.

The public authorities had essentially three goals: to stem the deficits posted by the public operator and make rail economically viable; to renew investment in the sector to give it the resources to grow; and, finally, to find a way to finance the unprofitable routes whose closing posed insoluble political problems.

The underlying idea, very clearly set out in numerous official publications, was that railway transportation had to be on the same level as the road system. The government would take charge of rail infrastructure as it did for roads (valuation methods for all forms of transport had to be consistent) and would force the railway operator to become a commercial enterprise. Infrastructure construction and maintenance, financing, and the infrastructure pricing system would be based as much on political decisions as they are for roads, while the supply of services would be based on the free initiative of agents.

The public authorities were thus conducting three reforms simultaneously: they were (1) significantly renewing investments; (2) placing the established public operator in a much more incentive-based system by gradually introducing competition; and (3) involving regional authorities in the definition and financing of local transport services.

5.2.2. *Massive renewal of investment*

Without going into the details of the investment policy, there are certain elements specific to the context of the Swedish reform that should be noted.

First of all, the Swedish rail system in 1999 had nearly 15,000 km of track. Although its length puts it well behind France and Germany, it nevertheless represents a major European network. It accounted for just over 6.5 per cent of the railway system operated in the European Community in 1991. It is operated with a rather small work-force (in 1995 only 1.5 per cent of the total rail work-force of the European Community) but carried 8.4 per cent of the kilometre-tons transported in the EU. These numbers illustrate the relative efficiency of the system.[1]

In spite of this rather exceptional position, on the eve of the reform, the system was in a state of substantial underinvestment. As Figure 5.1 indicates, the reform represents a spectacular break from the prior trend, with annual investment in this sector quintupling between 1988 and 1995. This investment programme represents no less than 40 billion Swedish kronor (SEK), the most this industry has ever experienced in its whole history. The amount of new investment over the 1988–2007 period may well reach 100 billion SEK.

Furthermore, the renovation of the rail system, based on a socioeconomic analysis for each project, has not been concentrated on just a few very expensive projects. Having opted for commuter technology, Sweden created the high-speed network that is indispensable for the development of rail transport by rebuilding existing lines. This choice made it possible to raise sufficient resources to reinforce the main lines and invest significantly in the

---

[1] For the issue of the efficiency of rail systems, see the study conducted by the Laboratoire d'Economie des Transports de l'Université Lyon 2 on behalf of the Commissariat Général du Plan, *Performance des entreprises de réseaux ferroviaires en Europe*, December 1999.

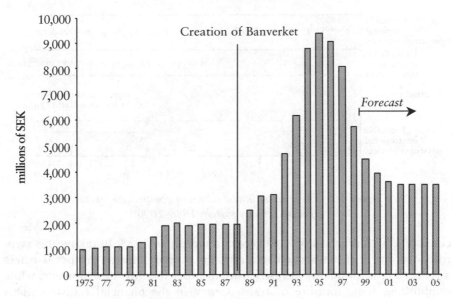

Figure 5.1. *The renewal of investment in the railway system*
Source: Banverket.

freight system.[2] The exceptional pace of investment in that period has now slackened. The next programme seeks to consolidate the system and protect the environment. The ten-year plan for 1998–2007 calls for nearly 36 billion SEK, which implies annual investment levels much higher than those before reform. In 1999 Banverket invested 5.6 billion SEK, of which 85 per cent was new investment and 70 per cent investment for activities included in the investment programme (representing an order of magnitude of some 50 per cent of revenues of SJ, the public operator).

Furthermore in Sweden this massive infrastructure reconstruction policy has been accompanied by very low user charges.[3] The rates,[4] initially set to be

[2] These investments include programmes for creating detours around urban areas, for double-tracking where there had been only single track, for increasing the speed of trains, for strengthening lines to accommodate heavier trains, etc.

[3] On this point, see specifically the conclusions of theoretical investigations and recommendations made by the European Conference of Ministers of Transport (ECMT) on the rates for rail infrastructure, *User Charges for Railway Infrastructure*, Round Table 107, 1998; the applied studies of Centre d'économie industrielle de l'Ecole Nationale Sujchiema des Mines de Paris (CERNA) on Swedish, British, and German reforms; Manuel Baritaud, and François Lévêque, *Péages d'infrastructures ferroviaires en Europe: arrangement de réglementation et droit d'accès au sillon*, May 2000.

[4] The rates reflect a social marginal cost approach (variable share divided into different components based on the costs directly chargeable to the user of the infrastructure, including external costs and a fixed share paid according to weight class and by axle for the locomotives).

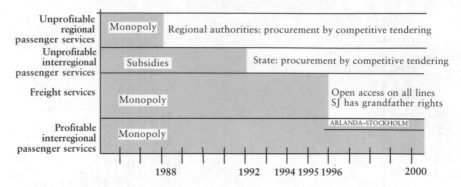

Figure 5.2. *The gradual introduction of competition in the Swedish railway system 1986–2000*

consistent with road tax policy, were cut sharply in 1998. In taking this step, the government demonstrated its desire to support railway traffic. It offers a reduced cost for quality infrastructure in order to allow development, while establishing some measure of transparency in the financial transfers. This strategy constitutes one of the components of the regulatory framework that is now being established.

5.2.3. *Gradual and methodical deregulation*

Without going into the details of a multi-step reform,[5] which is not yet completed, a number of key elements deserve more detailed discussion to appreciate how the current regulatory framework has been gradually created. It has occurred as the system moved from an organizational model focused on a public monopoly to a model in which competition becomes increasingly fierce, as shown in Figure 5.2.

The issue of railway reform has been around since the early 1970s. As in other European countries, Swedish national authorities looked for ways of reducing the industry deficit to a level commensurate with marginal cost rates and hoped in this way to create conditions that would enable the public operator to be more efficient. These concerns found an initial response in the Transport Policy Act of 1979. By creating a new local and regional institution, the County Public Transport Authorities (CPTA),[6] this legislation transferred

---

The coverage of maintenance costs is very low, especially since the 1999 reform, which led to a reduction in the amount of revenue from 1.045 million SEK to 275 million SEK. The remainder is covered by the government budget.

[5] See on this matter the work of Nilsson (1995), Hylén (1996), and the very detailed studies of Alexandersson, and Hultén (1999, 2000), on which the following discussion is substantially based.

[6] Sweden is divided into 24 counties. In each of these, the responsibility for local public transport is exercised by a limited liability company (County Public Transport Authorities, CPTA), owned jointly by the regional councils and the municipalities.

responsibility for organizing local public transport to the regional level. This applied to bus services as well as to certain local rail services threatened with closure. Some regions responded by using government grants to reorganize these services, and a large number of lines were in fact closed and replaced by bus lines. Other rail lines were maintained after contract negotiations with the local authorities responsible for their operation.

Realizing, in the 1980s, that the financial situation of the railway company was getting worse and the market share of rail transport was declining further, the political authorities looked to a much more radical reform. They decided, with the 1988 Transport Policy Act, to strengthen the role of the regional authorities in regional traffic and to reduce the activity of the public operator to operating the rail services, with all of the infrastructure being entrusted to an administration established for this purpose: Banverket (the National Rail Administration). This separation of infrastructure and rail services was described, quite appropriately, as a revolution. In fact, it was only an additional step in a process already initiated. The Railway Act of 1985 had already introduced a thoroughgoing change of organization by requiring separate accounting for the infrastructure and freight and passenger services and introducing a commercial relationship between these services, based on payment of royalties for the use of the infrastructure. Nevertheless, the institutional separation that took place three years later more clearly defined the respective responsibilities of the government and the public operator. The government took charge of the infrastructure, and the operator concentrated on running its business on purely commercial logic. To that end, the public operator was given complete freedom in setting rates, schedules, salaries, and organization. The operator made commitments in terms of financial results and paid a royalty based on the social marginal cost, which was assumed to be the way to make optimum use of the infrastructure.

The clarification between the government and the public railway company did not stop there. The reform then separated the so-called main lines from regional or county lines, used only for local and regional traffic. Moreover, the government transferred to the regional authorities responsibility for regional services as well as the equipment and financial resources for financing these services. By authorizing the regions to contract with the supplier of their choice through open bidding, as had already been done with the bus services, the Swedish Parliament introduced real competition and dismantled the company's monopoly. While this option was not compulsory, it was used by some regions as early as 1990, and today nearly all county lines have been included in the calls for tender. However, at this early stage of the reform there was still very limited opportunity for competition, because the public operator, SJ, had exclusive rights to freight services and the whole mainline service. All non-profitable lines operated on this system by SJ were subsidized by the public authorities, which in return required productivity gains from SJ.

The public authorities, aware of the risks facing the whole system because of the dominant position of the public operator, decided to continue deregulation of the sector further upstream. In 1992 the reform intensified and entered a new phase: the public authorities, seeing the advantages that the counties had obtained from the tendering process, decided to extend it to the inter-regional lines for which SJ wanted subsidies. In 1994, the Conservative Party then in power decided to deregulate the whole sector. A bill was adopted by Parliament in 1994, and it took a change of government to reverse this decision.

However, although the new Social Democratic majority stated its opposition to total deregulation of the railway industry, it did not stop the deregulation process already underway. In 1996 the government deregulated freight subject to an undertaking not to challenge existing SJ traffic. It expanded the separa-tion of management of infrastructure and operations by transferring respon-sibility for slot allocation and traffic control, functions that SJ had managed to retain in 1988, to Banverket. This was a decisive step in the opening of the railway market. Furthermore, by expanding the jurisdiction of the CPTAs to services affecting several counties, even if they used the main-line system, the public authorities increased the number of services available for bidding.

The government pushed the reform further in 1998 by proposing a new transportation policy, endorsed by Parliament in June 1998. The most notable of these decisions was the spectacular cut in tolls for the use of the railway system and the change in environmental taxation. In fact, on the occasion of this law, the government tried to resolve points that had caused real problems for new entrants to this market. Accordingly, it arranged a whole series of technical provisions that further shaped the industry's regulatory framework. These included non-discriminatory access to key infrastructures and facili-ties, including the stations and terminals, and to the passenger information system, which was transferred from SJ to Banverket. This series of measures should not detract from the creation of a new institution, Rikstrafiken, to promote a coordinated mass transport system, thus demonstrating how much ground has been covered since 1990 and the reality of industry dereg-ulation (see Section 5.3.4).

In early 2000, SJ had a legal monopoly only on the interregional passenger services it operated without subsidies, many new operators having entered the market.

5.2.4. The main effects of reform

What are the effects of this reform? Initially, the government hoped to improve the financial situation of the established operator and improve the market share of rail traffic. Now, although it is too soon to judge, we can see that SJ earnings, which had improved until 1995, worsened again from 1996. Revenues, which had risen from 10.9 billion SEK in 1992 to 12 billion SEK in 1995, then stagnated at 11.3 billion SEK. Operating earnings went back into

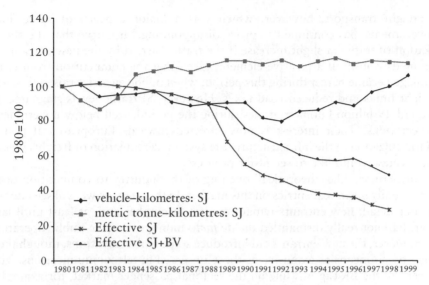

Figure 5.3. *Traffic and personnel of the public operator*

Note: 1996–9 figures are projected.

Source: SIKA.

the red in 1996. Nevertheless, substantial productivity gains were achieved, thereby establishing SJ as a champion compared with other major European operators. Over ten years, as Figure 5.3 illustrates, the company cut its staff by more than half, from 25,638 in 1989 to 11,308 in 1998. (There were 45,316 employees in 1970.) These reductions were obtained by transferring more than 8,000 people to Banverket, which at the start of the reform (in 1988) took over system maintenance and in 1996 was given responsibility for managing traffic. Another portion of the staff was directed to SJ group activities, some of which have since been sold off.[7] Others were recruited by the new entrants to this market.

In terms of traffic, the results vary according to the different categories. For passenger traffic there has clearly been a very significant improvement. Figure 5.3 reflects only traffic carried by SJ, and the figures shown for the past few years should be increased to allow for traffic carried by the other operators. Thus, although it is always difficult to establish a cause-and-effect relationship, the improvement observed since 1996 may be broadly explained by the introduction of competition to the industry and the involvement of the counties in the organization of regional transport.

[7] At the request of the government, SJ has withdrawn from Swebus and ASG, the respective leaders in bus and road freight transport in Sweden.

Freight transport, however, which was a major concern of succeeding governments, has continued to prove disappointing.[8] It is true that the stabilization of traffic (a slight increase if the traffic carried by the new entrants is counted) is in itself a positive element, given that the competition from road haulage became fiercer during this period, when public agencies raised the axle weight limits and reduced road taxes. However, SJ traffic levels stagnated at around 19 billion kilometre-tones during the period, well below government expectations. Their interest is now directed towards European rail policy (harmonization of the infrastructure rate system, deregulation of freight) where the Swedes would like to see faster progress.

Furthermore, the 'theoretical' opening of the industry to competition does not actually mean real entries on this market. In this area, as we will see later in greater detail, new entrants remain modest in number and, at least until last year, had not really dismantled the *de facto* monopoly of the public operator.

However, the new entrants did introduce some real innovations, though they were by no means as extensive as those observed in telecommunications. The advent of the BKTag bus line on the regional passenger market, for example, was accompanied by significant changes in terms of both technical aspects of equipment and maintenance and, more seriously, work rules. The train driver has become responsible not only for travel but also for successful completion of the trip. These changes, which SJ was unable to obtain from its staff, were then disseminated throughout the industry, including the public operator.[9]

Ultimately, some very significant cost reductions were obtained. The subsidies requested by the operators in their bids provide a very accurate indication of this. Cuts have been estimated to average nearly 20–25 per cent. Cost reductions for freight are less visible but just as real. In fact, as a result of pressure from new entrants, the freight sector saw the price of some contracts drop very significantly. Reductions mentioned by the Ministry of Transport are in the order of 10–15 per cent.

We now look at the regulatory framework introduced in these years in greater detail.

5.3. GRADUALLY INSTITUTED REGULATORY FRAMEWORK

The reform, by introducing competition, complicated the rules of the game for the players and changed how the government intervened. The current

[8] As part of the renewed investment, the public operator estimated that it would be possible to reverse the trends for passenger travel and freight. At the time, they spoke of doubling passenger traffic by the year 2000 and increasing freight traffic by 50 per cent.

[9] It should be noted that the reform disrupted practices that the unions were very attached to, such as that requiring drivers to alternate on different types of traffic (urban, long distance, passenger, freight). Such practices represented very severe constraints on personnel management. SJ estimates that they were the source of the loss of a number of markets.

regulatory framework has brought in new players, whose role has or will become decisive in the future. As they gain in experience, the countries will exert increasing pressure on operators, while the organization of various functions of Banverket, the infrastructure manager, which has already significantly changed, will doubtless continue to evolve in the future, to concentrate even more on system management tasks. The interventions by competition authorities will doubtless be more numerous as competition intensifies and new entrants organize. The recent desire to structure certain general interest services around a new agency, Rikstrafiken, may be a sign that a real industry regulatory agency is on the way.

5.3.1. *The role of the regions grows*

As the brief historical review has indicated, the decentralization of the organization of local passenger transport is one of the major features of the Swedish rail reform. This decentralization is based on the broadly shared conviction that the region is the appropriate level at which to define and organize local transport services. More importantly, however, the involvement of counties in regulation has changed the balance of power between public authorities and the public operator. It almost seems as if the Swedish government has been using the counties as a lever to redesign the whole rail system. The changes made have spread and have had an impact on the whole rail industry.

The county authorities, the true organizers of local transport, have an exclusive right to franchise county lines and were in fact behind a large number of changes. Initially they were able to pressure SJ as a contractor into acceding to their wishes, since they directly paid for the services and could ultimately decide to develop alternative bus services. The pressure on SJ became stronger when the counties were allowed to contract with the operator of their choice, which they did not fail to do. This ensured the entry of new operators into the rail market.

The counties have extensive power, which has strengthened over the years of their experience. They define the service and decide on the length of the contract and when to call for tenders. They generally have rolling stock available, set the rates, and collect them. The counties have invested heavily in the sector: they have increased the number of departures, opened new services by better harmonizing rail and bus services, etc. In a number of areas, the increases in traffic have been very significant and generally have been accompanied by noticeable declines in cost per passenger.

However, it must not be overlooked that these changes were obtained when the counties that had invested in the sector enjoyed substantial subsidies from the government, which were offered in exchange for the transfer of responsibility. These subsidies, covered by contract until the end of 1999, are now under review. This signals the start of a difficult period between the counties and the government, since the government has no intention of systematically renewing these subsidies. Even though the costs of rail services have declined throughout this period, owing to the call-for-tender procedures, it is nevertheless true that withdrawal of subsidies by the government will force the counties to invest more to avoid the closure of certain lines. That was one of the objectives of the reform, but some of its effects were postponed. The reform will thus move into a decisive phase.

5.3.2. The central role of Banverket, a multi-purpose agency

Established in 1988, Banverket is the heart of the Swedish railway system. This new institution has become the agency with overall responsibility for decisions concerning the development and organization of the railway system and it has been entrusted with several functions. The first is network operational services, including all technical competence and infrastructure maintenance services; the second covers the administrative duties necessary for the operational tasks to be properly performed; finally, a third function concerns the regulatory tasks which the agency executes in four more or less autonomous departments.

The first of these departments looks after issues associated with national defence. The second, which purchases unprofitable services on the main national lines for the government—and whose importance increased when Parliament authorized it, under a restrictive procedure, to compete with SJ for unprofitable interregional passenger services—has just become a new Rikstrafiken responsibility. The third department, the Railway Inspectorate (29 employees), awards licences, defines safety rules[10] and ensures their application, and has the power to investigate in the event of incidents or accidents. This department is also responsible for publishing and explaining the rules so that they do not become obstacles to access to the system; a handbook is regularly published for this purpose. Finally, the fourth department, the Rail Traffic Administration, whose head is appointed by the government (1,044 employees in 1999), has taken over the regulatory and traffic control tasks that were transferred belatedly from SJ to Banverket. This department is being closely watched, because it is in charge of slot allocation for new operators, traffic control, and the organization of the traffic plan. The power of this department challenges the special relationships that some CPTAs had established with SJ.

The relations between this new agency, SJ, and the administration are not as simple as the organization chart might suggest. First of all, Banverket is an independent agency. It is supervised by the Minister of Transport and its activity is financed directly through funds voted in the government budget. Banverket does not collect the tolls paid by the railway operators for the use of the infrastructure. While there is no question of its independence, it is

---

[10] These rules include driver training.

nevertheless very closely linked to the government, if only because its directors are appointed by the government and Parliament participates in defining the capital investment programmes[11] and tolls. While Banverket is in charge of evaluating and executing investments on the main lines, local network investments depend on the requirements of local communities, which organize and finance local policy for all transportation for which government financing is possible.

Relations between Banverket and SJ have evolved over time. The process of splitting up infrastructure and operations occurred in several stages, with implications for the regulation of the sector. The division of responsibilities between SJ and Banverket testifies to the problems inherent in implementing the separation between infrastructure and rail services. The 1988 reform did not complete the separation since, for example, the established operator SJ, having been dispossessed of the rails, was nevertheless still the owner of the ground and still owned all the terminal installations (nearly 2,300 km of track[12]). While Banverket effectively obtained control of the platforms, marshalling yards, and signals, SJ kept the stations and in practice remained responsible for slot allocation and traffic control. In 1996 this structure was again reformed. The jurisdiction of Banverket was expanded with the creation of a division in charge of slot allocation and traffic management, accompanied by the transfer to Banverket of a large number of SJ employees. This decision by Parliament meant that a further decisive stage of the reform had been reached.

The Rail Traffic Administration within Banverket, which is in charge of slot allocation and defines annual timetable planning, represents the core of the system. It allocates access to infrastructure, controls traffic (daily traffic control), and plans investments. Any operator with a licence (approved by the Rail Inspectorate) can apply for access to the infrastructure from this department. The transport authorities may opt to apply for access to certain infrastructures directly.[13]

It is important to distinguish carefully between the functions of allocating slots and daily traffic control, provided by several centres. The former determines the operator access to the system. It is the basic element in the regulation of the rail market and therefore should be isolated from all those who seek access to the system (including the manager of the system when using the system for maintenance), while the latter, which organizes the physical routing of the trains on a daily basis (and therefore represents one of the fundamental

[11] Every 4 years Banverket renews a capital investment plan spread over 10 years in cooperation with the counties, transport operators, and industry. This plan is based on a cost–benefit analysis integrating environmental considerations and the effects of transportation on health.

[12] It should be noted that in 1998 Banverket took over nearly 700 km (or 5 per cent of the system) of secondary track, strategic for freight traffic, that SJ still had under its control. In spite of that, in 1999 Banverket controlled only 80 per cent of the system, with 10 per cent of the secondary system still out of its grasp and 9 per cent of the system belonging to the municipalities and certain private operators (such as A-trains providing access to the airport).

[13] To date, no end-users such as the major freight shippers have applied for slots.

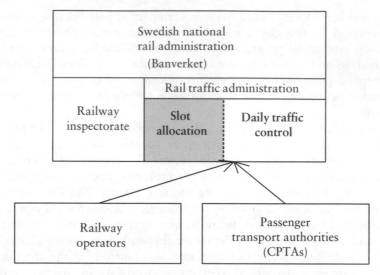

Figure 5.4. *Regulatory functions entrusted to Banverket*

tasks of the system manager), implements the adjustment arising from the traffic plan. Fewer regulatory problems occur in this area, except for managing delays or disruptions. These priority roles, which require the greatest transparency, need to be controlled. In the current organization, these two functions are not dissociated.

Slot allocation, on which the traffic plan is based, implements three main rules in practice. The first is that international traffic has priority over national traffic. The second refers to grandfather rights, under which an operator with a slot one year may request to keep it the following year even if it is claimed by a new operator. The third involves regional services. Local authorities in charge of organizing local transport may obtain slots for a protracted period.

As part of this general framework, the effective allocation of slots is based on an economic logic determined by the value of time. System access is allocated primarily to transport services for which gaining time is most important. Rail traffic is then organized on the basis of this particular schedule.

While disputes occasionally occur between various freight operators or between intercity and local traffic,[14] 'congestion' on the system is limited to the outskirts of the main cities and a few system nodes. In practice, disputes are resolved using a consensus-based, constructive approach, known as the *reasoning process*. Operators are urged to settle their potential disputes before

---

[14] Several lines are used for various services by different operators. An example is the case of the Stockholm–Märsta/Arlanda–Uppsala line, on which the profitable main line services are provided by SJ, county services are financed by various CPTAs and operated by different operators, airport service is provided by private-operator A-train, and the inter-county services to Norrland are contracted by the government and supplied by Tagkompaniet.

turning to the authorities in charge of the traffic plan. This attitude seeks to introduce the greatest possible flexibility while avoiding regulatory intervention. Finally, when there are disruptions on the system and priorities must be assigned between different trains to restore the desired traffic pattern, the general rule is that a train that is on time has priority over a train that is late.

To conclude, the current slots are not now allocated using an economic mechanism, although the authorities are looking for ways to introduce more flexibility in system use. However, while slots are not yet being auctioned, economic mechanisms of this type seem to be under consideration only for sharing slot allocation between different trains, not for arbitrating conflicts between different operators. This is the area in which arbitrage currently plays the largest role.

5.3.3. *The still limited role of the Konkurrensverket*

Since 1 July 1992, Sweden has had competition law based largely on the rules in the Treaty of Rome and the Single Act. This law is based on two major principles: prohibition of commercial practices that distort competition, and prohibition of the abuse of a dominant position.

This law created a specific executive and judiciary arrangement to ensure that the rules are applied. The Swedish Competition Authority (Konkurrensverket), which is the first component of this arrangement, has appropriate power.[15] The Act authorizes the agency to propose regulatory changes. For example, it can suggest changes to rules that it considers create obstacles to real competition in both the private and public sectors. The law also authorizes the agency to apply sanctions and impose fines commensurate with the seriousness of the violations. Finally, the law establishes a court procedure for recourse, through the Stockholm City Court, or by appeal to the Market Court.

The experts at the Konkurrensverket remain critical of the reality of competition in the railways, since public operator SJ can use its monopoly power on the main lines, and more broadly its dominant position on the whole sector, to prevent other operators from entering the market. Those in charge willingly admit that this sector remains quite special. Cooperation with Banverket appears fairly limited, and until quite recently competition remained quite marginal. Unlike such sectors as telecommunications, where competition appears obvious, the railway sector seems relatively impervious. One of the essential issues remains how to introduce more competition into the sector. On this point, the competition authority may have its own views and

---

[15] This agency has five operational departments: three for specific industry groups (agriculture; building, energy, and transport; and finance, post, and telecommunications), which monitor violations of the competition rules and deal with exemptions; another that monitors mergers and acquisitions; and a third that deals with competition policy. Added to these are the administrative services, secretariats for legal affairs, economics and European affairs which should be added to the above. The agency has a total staff of about 120.

may openly say what should and what shouldn't be done, but its impact still seems quite limited.

However, the competition authority has not been inactive throughout this period. When the regional and interregional lines were opened in 1992, the government was counting on the appearance of new entrants, especially since SJ had lost a few secondary lines, mainly to BKTag, during the first round of bidding. When these contracts came up for renewal, SJ nevertheless succeeded in winning back markets it had lost during the first round. BKTag then complained to the competition agency, claiming that SJ had won these operating contracts by offering prices that were below their costs. After an investigation, the competition authority finally began proceedings in 1996 and found against SJ. The public operator then appealed this decision, which was nevertheless confirmed two years later by the Stockholm Court (December 1998). Although mitigating circumstances were considered, SJ will have to pay a fine to BKTag, which may sue SJ for damages.

The Swedish competition agency, although it has not had to deal with other matters in this industry, played a decisive role in its deregulation. By its intervention, it symbolically marked the entrance of the industry in the competitive world, affirming that the new constraints applied to all and that they should be respected in the future.

5.3.4. *Drafting a forum for consultation*

In June 1998, on the basis of several reports, the government decided to create a new agency: Rikstrafiken. This small agency (staff of eight), which advises the Minister of Transport and reports to him directly, was accompanied by the elimination of the division of Banverket that until then had been responsible for franchising unprofitable interregional lines.

The main mission of this independent agency, which became operational on 1 July 1999, is to promote coordinated long-distance mass transit, in the interest of passengers and regional development. Behind these words, the lawmakers were targeting problems with transfers, harmonizing ticketing systems, managing passenger information from several operators, etc. This agency also has to make sure that those with special needs have access to transport and that there is equal access to long-distance transport. For this, the agency must make an inventory of the sector's shortcomings, maintain a minimum level of cooperation between the various players in the industry (railway operators, administrative bodies, local public authorities and occupational associations), and establish permanent contact with travellers. This is done indirectly, through market studies and surveys of satisfaction, but also more directly, through various user groups, a list of which Rikstrafiken has just prepared. Cooperation with these user groups is still inadequate, however, and the agency is currently studying other ways of providing a platform for voicing the concerns of public transport users. Its internet site is one of its first results. Although modest, it already offers complete information and a user-friendly interface for accessing the rail services offered by various providers.

This achievement is the result of new cooperation between Rikstrafiken and Samtrafiken, a company jointly owned by the rail operators and the regional transport authorities. Thus, operators who may in fact be competing with each other, as well as public authorities, are active and working together to simplify access to timetables and the fare systems, facilitate searches for routes that involve several stations, require other forms of transport, etc.[16]

Another important aspect is that Rikstrafiken is an intermodal agency, responsible for all long-distance public transport. This means that it organizes air, boat, and even intermodal services (train + bus). The total cost of these services is currently in the order of 800 million SEK. It is planned that this agency's funds will not be allocated to a specific mode but will finance long-distance transport services on the basis of socioeconomic evaluations, selecting the best suited form.

The role of Rikstrafiken is still quite modest. But, as recent events indicate quite clearly, it shows every likelihood of becoming stronger in future. It fulfils a particular function that seeks to assert in a competitive context the necessity of defining service missions of general public interest and to ensure that the competition in which the various operators engage does not undermine them. It is very likely that this new agency, along with the competition agency, will constitute the future regulatory framework for the railway industry, which, as we will see, remains quite fragile.

5.4. MAKING THE REFORM CREDIBLE BY LOWERING THE BARRIERS TO ENTRY

The market has only marginally been opened, even though, since early 2000, the SJ monopoly has experienced some significant reverses. The activities of the new entrants remain quite modest in terms of both volume and sales. This does not mean that the reform has had no effect on the behaviour of SJ. The fact that certain markets are in the process of being challenged—which is all the more credible, given the actual loss of certain services, including some important ones, at the end of the period—has led the public operator to reduce its costs more quickly than it would have done without such competitive pressure. However, the regulatory framework is still fragile, and the Swedish reform today faces a number of very important and real problems whose resolution poses a real challenge for the public authorities.

5.4.1. *The weakness of new entrants on the Swedish market*

In the view of many experts and commissions, the Swedish market in its present form is still largely controlled by SJ, whose monopoly has not really been

---

[16] See the www.samtrafiken.se internet site [2000].

dismantled. While the reform enabled a dozen or so new entrants to appear, until very recently they had not managed to capture a significant share of the market. Their success is difficult to assess, since the statistical system has not yet been adjusted to the new situation. Projections such as those in Table 5.1 give at least a rough idea of how the sector is evolving. As the main percentages in this table show, the SJ market share losses vary according to the sectors, and a comparison of the situation with that of the previous year reflects very sharp changes.

The freight situation remains totally under the control of SJ, which handles virtually all traffic (90 per cent). The market structure is somewhat unusual in that many operators (more than ten) have entered this sector, some of which have already gone bankrupt. In most cases these new independent players, whose activity mainly involves diverting traffic towards SJ, pose no direct

Table 5.1. *Market Shares of Different Segments of the Swedish Railway Market, 2000 (Forecast)[a]*

Train operator	Passenger services procured by CPTAs (%)	Passenger services procured by the state (%)	All procured passenger services (%)	All passenger services (%)	All freight services (%)	All railway services (%)
SJ	11.5	28.1	20.2	65.6	90.3	78.7
Citypendeln/ Sydvästen	69.1	16.7	41.5	17.9	—	8.4
A-train	—	25.2	13.3	5.7	—	2.7
Tågkompaniet	1.3	25.0	13.2	5.7	—	2.7
BKTåg/BSM Järnväg	5.6	5.0	5.3	2.2	1.2	1.7
CGEA (Connex/ Linjebuss)	12.4	—	5.9	2.5	—	1.2
LKAB (MTAB)	—	—	—	—	8.0	4.3
Other freight operators	—	—	—	—	0.5	0.3
All private firms	88.5	71.9	79.8	34.4	1.7	17.1

[a]These market shares are calculated on the basis of estimates of sales, subject to numerous assumptions that cannot be specified here. What should be noted is that the figures for operations by CGEA do not reflect the operations of the Stockholm subway and tram services. Thus, the market share shown here does not express the importance the company has acquired in providing urban public transport services in the capital since taking a 60 per cent stake in the capital of *Linjebus*. It should be noted that substantial suburban traffic is the responsibility of Citypendeln (VIAGTI and BKTag).

Source: compiled by Gunnar Alexandersson, Stockholm School of Economics, 2000.

threat to the public authority, which has control of long-distance trains. However, the existence of the sub-contractors does demonstrate that it is possible to organize free access to the infrastructure. However, the situation of the freight sector is not fully expressed in this diverted traffic. Besides these small operators, there are two special operators. The first, LKAB, a mining company, obtained the right to have its own trains travel on the tracks as soon as the freight sector was opened in 1992. This company, benefiting from its improved position, was able to renegotiate its contracts with SJ. A few years later, the sector saw the appearance of a new rail operator, MTAB, a consortium of the mining company, SJ, and the Norwegian public authority, NSB. While the public monopoly still retains a stake in the company, it does not have a majority interest. Thus, on this strategic route (Iron Ore line), the mining company has succeeded in circumventing the SJ monopoly, thereby achieving significant cuts in costs. It now appears, with an 8 per cent market share, as one of the heavyweight operators in the freight sector. The second very active operator, surprisingly enough, is BKTag, better known for its flamboyant entry into the passenger sector. Its presence in the freight market reflects a very different approach from that of the mining company. This operator has found that, as entry into the freight market was much easier, this provided an opportunity to use the sector as a base for entering the passenger market at lower risk. The strategy has paid off: BKTag, which is incidentally allied to powerful foreign groups, is now SJ's main competitor.

In passenger transport the situation looks very different. In this case it is important to distinguish between the specific situation of regional transport, the first to be opened to competition, and that of interregional transport.

In regional transport, SJ has lost a large number of contracts. Even when it has been able to hang on to some, the competition has been sufficiently strong that it was possible only by sharply reducing its prices. It was not unusual, in fact, to find three or even four or five bidders in some calls for tenders. These new entrants are in some cases urban public transit companies or operators of long-distance buses. That is the case for BKTag, Linjebuss, ViaGTI with Go-Ahead, and BKTag and even Swebus,[17] the subsidiary of the SJ group which the company had to sell to the British Stagecoach Company.(So far, Swebus has not won any contracts.) Others have appeared directly from the rail sector. One was Sydtag, whose passenger business was taken over by BKTag after it went bankrupt in 1997; it was a sub-contractor to SJ in the freight sector. This was also true of BSM, which entered both the freight and passenger transport

[17] Swebus is one of the very first Swedish bus operators on the interregional lines that were opened to competition early in 1999. By forcing SJ to sell this operator in 1996, the public authorities clearly separated the development of interregional bus services from the deregulation of the problematic railway sectors, which SJ was using to close down the bus lines. By doing so, the public authorities heightened the competitive pressure on SJ rail services. This pressure has been exercised not only by the long-distance bus line services, but also by the fact that Swebus became a serious potential competitor for regional rail lines.

markets; it initially worked for Banverket on the renovation and maintenance of the rail system. Finally, there was Tagkompaniet, a brand-new company created by three former executives of SJ with the help of financiers. These operators, except for the foreign ones, are too small in size to challenge the public monopoly on its own terrain. However, the appearance of international operators on the market has profoundly changed the balance of power. The alliance founded at the end of this period (BKTag with Go-Ahead and VIAGTI (SNCF)), as well as the purchase of Linjebuss by CGEA (Vivendi)), mark a decisive step. Gradually, the market share of SJ is being eroded. It accounted for only 55 per cent of this segment in 1998 and has dropped below 12 per cent with the loss of Stockholm commuter traffic.[18]

The situation of the interregional lines is totally different. First, the decision by the public authorities to arrange calls for tender on unprofitable inter-regional lines that the government had been financing by covering SJ deficits came much later, in 1992. And, although SJ had to face real competition, it wasn't until 1998 that three of the ten subsidized interregional lines were lost to other operators. With the loss of the interregional line serving Nâssjö-Skövde to BSM Jarnavag AB, the service between the country's second and third largest cities (Gothenburg and Malmö) to Sydvästen, and the night train service to Tagkompaniet (north of Sweden), SJ saw its monopoly crumble in early 2000. When the traffic between Stockholm and Arlanda airport,[19] provided by the private consortium, is added, the loss is significant, with the SJ market share for all passenger transport dropping to about 65 per cent.

However, as we shall see, this statistic does not give an accurate idea of the problems facing new entrants as a result of the behaviour of SJ. These events pose some fundamental issues regarding the current regulatory framework.

5.4.2. Insufficiently stabilized regulatory framework

At the time of the reform, concerns focused on the consequences of separating the infrastructure from rail services with respect to service growth and safety. In fact, these problems did not really arise. The main sensitive points that were sources of potential conflict or dysfunction were resolved by an informal consultation procedure between SJ and Banverket which, according to the

---

[18] This contract was won by a private consortium (VIAGTI, Go-Ahead, and BKTag) for a 5-year period with the possibility of extending the contract for 10 years if all parties are satisfied.

[19] The rail services linking Stockholm and the Arlanda airport, no longer under SJ, are a very special case. The Arlanda Link consortium, led by GEC–Alsthom, won a call for tenders in 1994 for the construction and operation of this line. This contract, which the Social Democratic opposition fiercely challenged at the time, was amended when the party returned to power. The amendment provides that the infrastructure must be open to third parties in return for a toll paid to the private operator (A-train), and operating rights are to be renegotiated in 10 years. The A-train rates are not covered by regulation, with the government considering competition from buses sufficiently strong to avoid abuse by the private operator.

experts, works rather well. It is in this framework, for example, that decisions were made on the division of jurisdictions, responsibilities, and ownership of certain elements of the infrastructure between the operator and manager. There is a consensus on the positive effects of this separation:[20] it allows a more precise division of labour, improved planning, etc. The real issue for public authorities today is to stabilize the regulatory framework of the sector and implement procedures that allow competition to play out properly, without jeopardizing the growth of the sector.

The gradual deregulation of the railway industry that is increasingly reshaping the market is now encountering new resistance, which the public authorities will have to resolve actively or see the reform grind to a halt. These market structures remain quite fragile, and the institutional framework necessary for the rail services market to operate smoothly will require strengthening and protection. This means intervening in the structures of this emerging market to quickly lower persistent barriers to entry and then disciplining the public operator, which must gradually become one of several operators.

Access to essential functions

There are still too many barriers to entry. An analysis of the problems encountered by new operators highlights several points.

Access to rolling stock is one of the first points to note. This constitutes a key feature of deregulation, to the extent that acquisition of this essential production factor poses significant problems to new entrants, especially because for the most part they have only very short-term contracts. That is why, when the reform began, the government transferred the necessary equipment to the counties; in so doing, it facilitated the entry of new operators on the regional markets. For interregional services that the government submits for bids, the situation is quite different. In this case, the new entrants must have the equipment necessary to provide the service. They thus have no choice but to lease the equipment from SJ, and this is a very effective barrier to entry. There are not many alternatives. The accounting solution, which would involve requiring that SJ charge for its equipment according to cost and verify that the costs charged are correct, has little credibility. Buying the equipment exposes the operators, who are modest in size and whose business may vary substantially from one period to the next, to substantial risks. The regions, for other reasons, (replacement of equipment) and the new entrants (to avoid the SJ monopoly) are interested in seeing the emergence of a rolling stock leasing

---

[20] 'In our experience, the division of functions ... works excellently and we believe that total separation between the infrastructure provider and transport operators creates the best conditions for the achievement of effective services and sound competition. In our assessment, without this division it would not have been possible to bring about swift changes as have actually taken place in the Swedish rail sector', (Swedish Government Offices, *The Reasons underlying Sweden's Stance on the EU Railway Package*, 1998, p. 4).

market.[21] The British solution, based on the establishment of leasing companies, seems difficult to plan for a single country. It is on the other hand possible that this problem could be solved at a European level,[22] especially if SJ's competitors are foreign operators who develop an equipment strategy that reflects a much larger market than just Sweden.

Other aspects that could be studied more closely include the traveller information and reservation systems that will become potential elements in distorting competition, as they have been in the airline sector. These problems were already apparent in 1999 on the West Coast Line when SJ refused to allow competitors to use its ticketing system, which it considered a strategic element. This attitude led the private operators to develop their own system. In itself, there is nothing wrong with this refusal. However, the new entrants, especially because of the terms of the agreements, which may be for only one year, cannot afford to write off such investments over a long period. Some have therefore levelled charges of unfair conduct by the dominant operator. Furthermore, these multiple systems, by making reservations for trips requiring the services of several operators more complex, are detrimental to the quality of the rail service. Forcing SJ to open its reservation system in return for financial compensation has proved unfeasible. One of the missions of Rikstrafiken in fact is to encourage cooperation and resolve situations of this kind.

The same problem arises for other essential facilities to which SJ must allow access in a non-discriminatory way (stations, maintenance shops, emergency equipment, energy supplies, ferry terminals, etc.). There are many examples of the problems involved in implementing this principle. The CPTAs, for example, believe that SJ tends to charge them more for access to its essential facilities when they have used an operator other than SJ. These disputed practices, which are difficult to prove, have led some experts to propose breaking up SJ to isolate its functions. Others consider that, on the contrary, maintaining these essential functions within SJ is necessary for the efficiency of the overall structure, and that it is preferable to leave them within the dominant operator, with the threat of legal action against the operator providing a deterrent against abuse. Clearly, these issues must undergo more substantial review. This implies adequate resources in order to verify that neutral and non-discriminatory access is in fact available.

What makes these problems especially acute is the length of the contracts, which in some cases is much too short. However, it seems that we may be seeing an increase in the length of contracts. The problem seems less crucial for the regional contracts, which generally run for periods of three to five years and have much lower costs of market entry because the regions have rolling stock

---

[21] During 1999 the CPTAs created a company to coordinate their equipment needs in time, in order to put downward pressure on delivery periods. This company could form the basis for a future leasing market.

[22] Tagkompaniet, which now operates the night services between Stockholm and northern Sweden, imported equipment.

and can apply all their weight to SJ in the event of a dispute. The major Stockholm commuter train contract is for five years, with the possibility of renewal for an additional fifteen years. On the other hand, the problem seems much more sensitive for the interregional services because the length of the contracts proposed by the government is in the order of one to two years. This practice clearly gives an advantage to the dominant operator, since market entry costs are much higher. Recent events, to be discussed below, have convinced Rikstrafiken that the government calls for tender must be made for five-year periods, in order to offer a safer framework for new entries.

The learning curve and transaction costs

Entering a market with SJ is not easy. The cost of entry is high and implies a minimum amount of expertise, including preparing bids. There is thus an interest in seeing the regulatory framework become stable. In this case the cost would go down and competition would be facilitated. It should be noted that over the last ten years the number of bidders has tended to increase. This experimental phase is important, but it is also the most risky for operators since they don't know if the institutional environment is sufficiently credible to warrant investment in the sector. The first successes, and the application of sanctions in response to abuses by the dominant operator, may ultimately attract more powerful operators, better equipped to respond to the more complex calls for tenders out of the reach of the smaller operators. The last two calls for tenders for rail services in the Stockholm region were in fact won by companies that had powerful groups of foreign investors operating in almost all European countries. There is to a certain extent a virtuous circle, in which the effectiveness of competition simulates competition. But this mechanism can also reverse quickly. If the regulatory framework appears flexible and gives the impression that it can be influenced by the public operator, potential new entrants will no longer venture on this market.

The labour market

Heightened competition has also produced tensions in the labour market for railway personnel, especially for drivers.

When BKTag won the first call for tenders, in 1990, it did not encounter any particular difficulty in hiring personnel, and the private operator was in fact able to form motivated teams. This played a decisive role in the results obtained by the new entrant, because its efficiency was based in part on work rules quite different from those used at SJ. Moreover, a rather innovative project led by three former SJ executives was behind the formation of Tagkompaniet; this company, which won new contracts in December 1999 and January 2000, operates the whole range of passenger services and has proved to be a serious competitor.

However, while some people voluntarily left SJ to join the competition, posing a major threat to the SJ monopoly, real tensions were now starting to appear. The new entrants were facing uncooperative or even openly hostile behaviour. This was already the case, for example, when SJ lost its first calls for tenders. Station employees were then visibly unenthusiastic about providing competitors with services. That was fairly marginal, but with the loss of the commuter service in the capital, personnel problems grew considerably.

The arrival of the private consortium called Citypendeln led to numerous demonstrations that disrupted service, causing delays and cancellations of trains. The staff decided at the last minute not to join the new operator. This hardening of attitude, which is considered by some to have been orchestrated by SJ and the unions, forced the operator, with its back to the wall, to renegotiate working conditions and salaries, thereby raising the costs on which it had based its bid. Five months after the service began, the situation had still not stabilized, with Citypendeln having even been forced to sub-contract a portion of the service to SJ. This obviously had financial consequences, with the consortium having to pay fines to the Stockholm transport authority. Furthermore, the poor quality of service was damaging the image of the company and doing greater harm to the reform, and the seriousness of the situation was starting to worry the political authorities.

5.4.3. *The reform is at a turning point*

The start of the year 2000 was widely described as a historic moment for the Swedish rail industry, with the public operator losing its *de facto* monopoly over the main passenger lines which the government had regularly put up for bids since 1992. The paradox is that the start of the year was characterized more by the abrupt halt to the operation of one of these lines by the private consortium (Sydvasten: ViaGTI, Go-Ahead, and BKTag). This event and the previous conflict between SJ and BKTag [23] constitute the most serious incidents in the reform process and may block the Swedish reform. Without going into the details of a complex case, it is nevertheless worth examining some of the issues involved, since it very clearly demonstrates the main weaknesses of the current regulatory structure.

The line between Malmö and Gothenburg was opened by the government for bids in 1998 for a one-year period. This was contrary to the rule that inter-regional lines could be put up for tender only when SJ declared them unprofitable. Parliament effectively circumvented this rule, which protected the monopoly of commercial services, deciding that the situation on this line raised serious concerns. SJ was losing money on this line but refused to declare it as unprofitable, claiming that the situation could be improved in a cost-cutting programme. Furthermore, the deregulation of bus services introduced at the

---

[23] This is the conflict that led BKTag to instigate proceedings against SJ before the competition authorities, which ruled in its favour. The SJ appeal was rejected but BKTag is still waiting to be compensated.

same time suggested that, without some response by the rail operator, the bus companies, which had an excellent highway infrastructure between these two cities, would be able to compete very seriously with the rail service and to threaten its very existence.

The result of the call for tender generated real surprise, because the winner of the bidding felt they could operate this line with no subsidy. SJ then complained to the government, explaining that this decision threatened an international liaison project linking these two cities with Norway.

The agency in charge of interregional links, Rikstrafiken, had in 1999 asked the government for authorization to extend the contracts of three new entrants until 2002 without renewing the calls for tender. The government gave a favourable response except for the contract with Sydvasten; for this contract, it declared instead that the service on this line would be awarded to SJ without a tender in 2001, so that it could develop an international service establishing a link between Oslo, Gothenburg, Malmö, and Copenhagen in cooperation with NSB, the Norwegian public operator. This was a service for which SJ again requested no subsidy. This decision, coming three days after the service had been started by Sydvasten, had the effect of pouring cold water over the latter service. The owners of the private consortium then tried unsuccessfully to negotiate with the government in order to change the rule that allowed SJ to keep a monopoly on profitable inter-county lines. This decision radically changed the outlook and the development prospects of the company, which had invested in the hope of being at least able to renew its bid. The company then found itself in financial difficulty when increases in traffic did not generate the hoped-for revenues and it was confronted with personnel problems, as some employees began to look for other work. It then decided to stop operating the line. The company filed for bankruptcy and withdrew, and the operation of the line returned to SJ.

These decisions raise up a number of points. First of all, the rule defining the limits of the monopoly of the public authority raises some serious questions.[24] This rule, surprisingly, gives the monopoly company exorbitant power to define the limits of its own monopoly, since a line can be subject to tendering and be awarded to another company only if SJ declares that it is not profitable. This episode shows very clearly that this approach is not tenable, and the decision by Parliament to override it in 1998 is quite clear in this respect. By taking this decision, Parliament sought to defend the railway service. To some extent, it suspected that the dominant operator, facing the loss of a major market, was ready to assume losses on a strategic service and to offset them from its other revenue for the sole purpose of preventing competitors from entering the market. This suspicion is all the stronger since it has a monopoly and there is no way of verifying costs on each individual line.

---

[24] Rikstrafiken had raised several questions during the fourth quarter of 1999, suggesting that there were some ambiguities in the way the monopoly of SJ had been defined.

This rule also raises a basic problem. It is quite surprising that a service that the authorities wish to maintain in the public interest should be open to competition at the best price, entrusted to the most efficient operator, and then withdrawn from that very same operator when, as a result of its extreme efficiency, it no longer requests a subsidy. The rule, established initially to deal appropriately with unprofitable lines threatened with closure, has ultimately proved to be unsuited to the purpose for which it was established, i.e. to develop services in the public interest. Applying this rule to the letter would encourage efficient operators to do the minimum required. What the Sydvasten proposal clearly demonstrates, even if this company was not able to carry it out in practice, was that the profitability of a line cannot be determined independently of its operator. A number of experts therefore propose that the rule should be changed. The government should entrust lines that interest a number of operators for a given period to the bidder that offers the most. This rule, which has the merit of being clear, would allow operations to be entrusted to the operator that proposes the most attractive services and would also generate revenues that could be reinvested in the rail service, thereby improving services of interest to all operators which they could not pay for on their own.

From the standpoint of the regulatory procedures, the current situation seems quite unstable and it may in fact harm the reform. It should be noted that the government made a decision contrary to the recommendations of Rikstrafiken, which had suggested that the services of new entrants be contracted for a more extended period. This was a risky decision. It shows that the regulatory function providing for competition is not being sufficiently asserted. Furthermore, the competition authorities seem to have been poorly equipped to deal with a problem of this nature.

The risk is that this decision may discredit a gradual reform which until now was based on very clear objectives, and could distort the signals sent to the other players. On this point, the withdrawal of British operator Go Ahead is rather disturbing for the rest of the industry,[25] because the strategy of the small entrants is based on alliances that will enable them to avoid the barriers to entry that they cannot overcome alone.

Finally, it was not by chance that this incident occurred when the competition had taken a very important part of its market away from SJ. The rail reform is in fact at a crossroads. Either the government wants to retain a highly monopolistic structure, using competition at the margin to obtain substantial efficiency gains from the public monopoly, or it wants to take another step by

---

[25] This company stated in a press release dated 19 May that it was terminating its development project in Sweden to refocus on the British market. It noted that, with its partners, it had to close the service on the West Coast Line because it was unable to continue operations. It also announced that, because of unforeseen problems encountered in operating Stockholm suburban transport services, together with disagreements with the Swedish authorities, the group had reversed its decision to operate in Sweden and had transferred its rights to ViaGTI. The company concluded that entry to the Swedish market was more difficult than anticipated.

organizing a real market in which SJ remains the principal operator but must deal with powerful competitors backed by large foreign groups. The relative consensus of recent years, shared by supporters of both approaches, is collapsing just as SJ, losing a major market share, is becoming more fragile. Some commentators believe that SJ's earnings will be decisive in determining which option is ultimately chosen.

5.5. CONCLUSION

Under either of the above scenarios, it is necessary to strengthen the regulatory function. In the past, this was accomplished by the complex interplay of different parties: Banverket, Parliament, the competition authorities, new entrants. The major issues facing the public authorities in the future therefore clearly emerge.

The first is the status of the SJ and its monopoly over commercial lines. (Many wish it to become a corporation and work under the same business conditions as its competitors.) The second involves the withdrawal of Banverket from the sovereign regulatory functions it performs today, with the Rail Inspectorate division becoming responsible for security matters and the Rail Traffic Administration for the management of system access. Regarding the latter point, in 1995 the government had already considered transferring jurisdiction over slot allocation and traffic control from SJ to a separate agency with no link to either SJ or Banverket. This is an essential matter, especially if there should be more situations in which a single line is operated by different operators.

Rikstrafiken may well absorb these functions in the near future and become a true independent regulator with increased powers. As K. Dahlström, executive director of Rikstrafiken, stated on 3 September 1999, 'all competition must take place on equal terms; otherwise deregulation of rail services is meaningless'. Equality of access assumes the establishment of asymmetrical regulation, to protect new entrants as long as SJ can influence the production costs of its competitors. The inherent difficulty in such an exercise clearly emerges, together with the need to entrust regulation of this industry to a regulator that is truly independent from the operators.

REFERENCES

Alexandersson, G. and Hultén, S. (1999). 'Sweden', chapter 3 in D. M. Van de Velde (ed.), *Changing Trains: Railway Reform and the Role of Competition. The Experience of Six Countries*, Ashgate, Aldershot, Hants., UK.

—— and —— (2000). 'Competitive Tendering of Railway Services in Sweden: Extent and Effects 1989–1999', paper presented to the International Conference on Regulatory Reforms in the Railway Sector, June.

Banverket (1996, 1999). *Annual Reports.*

—— (2000). 'Swedish Experience in Rail Policy Developments in Sweden since 1988', meeting with Commissioner Ms. Loyola de Palacio, Brussels, 4 April 2000.

Baritaud, M. and Lévêque, F. (2000). 'Les Péages d'infrastructures ferroviaires en Europe: options de réglementation et Droits d'Accès au Sillon', final report, www.cerna.ensmp.fr [2000, 97pp.]

Bylund, B. (2000). 'Europe Needs a Railway Reform', *European Railway Review*, 6/1.

ECMT, (1998). *User Charges for Railway Infrastructure*, OECD Round Table 107.

Foulonneau, O. (1999). 'Bilan des réformes ferroviaires en Suède', PEE, Ambassade de France.

Hylén, B. (1996). 'L'Expérience suédoise', in *La Séparation infrastructure/exploitation dans les services ferroviaires*, CEMT, OECD Round Table, 103: 103–46.

Johannesson, D. (2000). 'Railway Deregulation: Europe's ECU 40 Billion Prize', *European Railway Review*, 6/1.

Konkurrentsverket (Swedish Competition Authority) (1996). *Competition on Deregulated Markets, Stockholm.*

—— (1997, 1999). *Annual Reports.*

—— (1998). 'Competition Rules in Sweden', Stockholm.

Nilsson, J.-E. (1995). *Swedish Railways Case Study*, CTS Working Paper 1995: 2 (reprint of ch. 8 in R. Kopicki, and L. S. Thompson, (eds.), *Best Methods of Railway Restructuring*, CFS Discussion Paper Series, no. 111, Washington: World Bank.

Nordenlöw, L. and Alexandersson, G. (2000). 'Standing in the Shadow of the Giants: Conditions for Entry and Survival of Small Businesses on the Deregulated Bus and Railway Industries in Sweden', Stockholm School of Economics, 3rd KFB Research Conference Stockholm, 13–14, June 2000.

Permanent Representation of Sweden to the European Union (1999). 'Authorised Applicants in the Rail Freight Sector', Brussels: EU, February 1999.

Rikstrafiken (2000). *Rikstrafiken Co-ordinates Long Distance Travel*, Stockholm: National Public Transport Agency.

Swedish Government Offices (1998). *The Reasons underlying Sweden's Stance on the EU Railway Package, Stockholm.*

Transport Public (1999). 'Transport public: les français exportent leur savoir-faire', *Transport Public*, May, pp. 18–36.

6

Sweden: A Case of Lighter or Tighter Telecommunications Regulation?

CURT ANDERSSON

6.1. INTRODUCTION

Sweden was one of the early countries to introduce new telecommunications (telecoms) regulation, opening up to competition formally in 1993. This transition had a history of more than a decade during which business users, politicians, and the internal EEC debate played the roles of change agents. Business users were partly looking at the low US tariffs in comparison with practices elsewhere; but there was also an emerging need within multinational firms to take more detailed control of their telecoms systems. This was the case not least in the automotive industry, where electronic trading and just-in-time delivery of parts were becoming crucial to the main business. In consequence, Volvo was one of the most active advocates of a more flexible system. Through the European Round Table of Industrialists, liberalization became a key issue also in discussions with the European Commission, which in its 1987 Green Paper drew up a framework for telecommunications as a competitive industry. The political interest in Sweden turned out to be spread across the field from conservatives and liberals to the social democrats, who were in power at the time when reforms were first envisaged. The UK duopoly also provided analytical evidence of how public safeguards could be combined with partial competition, although the case remained to be fully proved in practice at that time.

The main concerns were rather among the work-force of the incumbent, Televerket, and its labour unions, concerns that were addressed in a very open manner within the incumbent. The technology shifts of the preceding decade in microelectronics, digitization, optic fibres, etc., were professionally analysed, all pointing to emerging competition, either outright or implicit depending on the regulatory environment. Only by being first in competition could the incumbent maintain leadership and retain a large proportion of its work-force. As we shall see, however, there is a large step from analysis and conclusion to fully understanding the implications of such a transition.

The telecoms manufacturing industry held a much lower public profile in spite of making much the same analysis as leading operators. The obvious reason for this was that the telecoms equipment market in most countries was still dominated by domestic monopolists, most of whom were not ready for the dramatic changes ahead. One way to promote liberalization nevertheless was to act as advisers to OECD through the BIAC (Business and Industry Advisory Committee) and the ICC (International Chamber of Commerce), since the OECD was one of the first bodies to observe the new economic potential of telecommunications.

From the end-user viewpoint, it was obviously difficult for residential customers to vizualize and/or appreciate the possible change. Business users, however, organized themselves early, both domestically (NTK—Näringslivets Telekommitte) and world-wide (INTUG—International Telecommunications User Group), to be able to make use of the new opportunities as soon as possible. NTK in 1987 published a Swedish discussion paper on why telecommunications must be liberalized and how it could be done.

6.2. AN ENVIRONMENT CONDUCIVE TO LIGHT REGULATION

The reasons why Sweden was so early to reregulate were thus part of a long-term process, but were also due to certain special circumstances of the Swedish telecoms and general regulatory environments.

6.2.1. *Balanced political risks*

While the advantageous potential of competition in telecommunications was obvious to industry experts and many politicians in the early 1980s in many OECD countries, it involved considerable political risk-taking, in that it entailed changing what the electorate considered to be a public good. Especially in Scandinavia, where domestic tariffs were low and provision good, there was limited residential end-user demand for change. As residential international traffic grew, however, so did complaints about high international tariffs.

Even so, the overall political risks were probably smaller in Sweden than elsewhere. There was already practically total fixed penetration of households. Price baskets for business and residential users were among the cheapest within the OECD. Most citizens were frequent telephone users. They were open to new applications like facsimile transmission (fax), and the incumbent provider had started its broad rationalization programme anticipating competition, which included promoting new telecoms services like analogue mobile NMT 450/900. In addition, competition was already partially in place: terminal markets had been opened in 1985 and the PABX market opened fully in 1989. Since 1981 there had been a competing mobile analogue 450 MHz private operator (Comvik), and large users were renting and running their own networks over leased lines. In Sweden there had never been any formal requirement restricting such networks to 'closed user groups'. A new government agency, the State Telecoms Council (Statens Telenämnd), was set up in 1989 to handle terminal issues. Another important factor was that the new—to Sweden—cable TV was very lightly regulated, in essence only requiring that the three public channels be transmitted plus another 'open channel' if possible. However, it took another decade for cable TV to play a part in the telecoms revolution.

Very competent domestic equipment and systems suppliers and modern telecoms and radio training facilities seemed set to provide good opportunities for the industry to compete at home and, over time, abroad, if markets were opened. Altogether, this was a tempting export opportunity to both politicians and industry.

In summary, it seemed that, with relatively limited intervention such as price caps, universal service obligations, and interconnection rules, as demonstrated in the UK, the general public would not have to fear a telecoms breakdown or price rush under the change to a new liberal regime. In addition, both equipment and services export markets could be expected to grow with oncoming international deregulation. The political risk-taking seemed worthwhile to consecutive governments of shifting political colour.

6.2.2. *Revision of public regulation principles*

Since the 1970s, the Swedish regulatory framework in general had been the subject of scrutiny and revision. Regulation emanating from the Second World War and the immediate postwar era was found increasingly to be counter-productively detailed, foremost examples being agriculture and housing sub-sidy schemes as well as currency controls. Special legislation starting in the late 1970s demanded that new laws should be analysed to determine how they were likely to affect the overall economic efficiency. At the same time, old legislation was readdressed. Farming subsidies were hence dismantled under considerable controversy, and the total change of the fiscal system in 1991 was the major case of renewal. There was therefore around 1990 a clear tendency to favour minimal and transparent regulation in all sectors of society. Once it had been decided to liberalize telecommunications around 1990, there was consequently no obstacle to minimal and transparent new telecoms regulation. The problem was rather that such regulation had thus far been very limited, close to non-existent; nor was it quite obvious what Parliament had set as telecoms objectives, to be met by the incumbent, and what was only normal provision by an efficient operator.

The paradox of freeing markets by regulating more was addressed by a light telecoms regulation approach, supported by the new Competition and Consumer Protection Acts which also covered telecommunications. In this the

Swedish 1993 Telecommunications Act was very much along the lines of the principles discussed in the EU 99 Telecommunications Review, resorting as much as possible to horizontal rather than sector regulation. Only the very basic services were regulated, i.e. voice, mobile communications, and leased line provision. In consequence, pure data services were not subject to telecoms licensing. There were no telecoms restrictions on building infrastructure, apart from what would follow from radio frequency scarcity. At the same time, radio regulations were reversed so that frequencies should be assigned if there were no reasons for not granting a licence. The preceding legislation had rather tended to ration the assignment of frequencies.

Setting the 'new' objectives entailed a combination of adopting existing availability criteria of the incumbent and formalizing the universal service, emergency forwarding, and similar requirements so that in principle they would apply to all operators. The requirements were set sufficiently low so as to make business possible for new entrants, the assumption being that competition for customers would provide higher standards than were formally required. A definite change was that defence and adaptation for the handicapped would be procured in competition and paid for via the ordinary government budget rather than via levies imposed on the operators. One reason for this was that the standard was to be set in relation to overall defence and handicap ambitions and not by how much money could be generated within telecommunications to finance the adaptation.

It was also intended that the application of telecoms legislation should be independent of the government, as the government was sole owner of the incumbent. (It is worth noting that there has not until recently been a parliamentary majority in favour of privatizing the major part of Telia, in spite of its being one of the more efficient and hence highly valued operators.) This was more easily accomplished than in some other countries, as Swedish government agencies ordinarily apply adopted legislation independently of the government; it is a constitutional offence for a minister to decide on a case individually unless so specified by Parliament. Should the Telecommunications Act turn out to be applied in a way that is perceived to be against government policy, the government must come back to Parliament with a bill to amend the Act. (In cases relating to illegal breaches of telecoms confidentiality, etc., the government remains the instrument to enforce the Act, but this is an exception, and should be of little importance to the competitive conditions on the telecoms markets.)

The right of appeal against application of the Act is also to be handled by the administrative courts, again to assert its autonomy.

6.2.3. Recent development

Three major regulatory changes took place in the first part of the year 2000. Since 1 May 2000, existing mobile operators have been compelled to negotiate access to excess mobile capacity with registered operators at 'market prices', with any resulting disputes to be settled in a court of civil law. It has further been decided that mobile national roaming will be introduced for up to seven years in existing networks, with a five-year exemption time for new networks. This amendment of the Telecommunications Act came into force on 1 July 2000, but no new mobile licences were scheduled before the UMTS licensing procedure (autumn 2000). Disputes here too are to be settled in a civil court. Finally, the national regulator PTS has ruled that Telia, holding 'significant market power', should decrease its interconnection termination rates to mobiles originally by 40 per cent, backed by an administrative fine of SEK 200 million. (The percentage has since been reduced in response to a voluntary decrease during the process.) Telia has appealed against the PTS decision, and the Administrative Court has declared the ruling 'pending' awaiting the court's decision.

Another change, with effects similar to those of regulatory intervention, is that Telia is going forward with voluntary local loop unbundling and the sale of its cable TV operation, in spite of the fact that the Telia–Telenor merger is not going to take place. The termination vote case is being taken to the Appeal Court (May 2001) and unbundling is mandated by the EU.

6.3. PROGRESS OF THE LIGHT TELECOMS REGULATORY FRAMEWORK

In contrast to the situation in some EEC member states, the re-regulation of the telecoms industry did not present a consitutional problem in Sweden. Nor were the employees of the incumbent civil servants, with the exception of a small number who had chosen to maintain their civil service status when Televerket was turned into the limited company Telia AB. The difficulties lay rather in the detail—what needed regulation, and what existing rules could be disposed of?

Few modern frameworks had been adopted by 1992, and thus there existed hardly any blueprint regulation apart from in the UK, where the duopoly had been dismantled not long before. The UK regulation, however, retained a number of safeguard rules from 1984 that could not be easily introduced in Swedish law. There was a clear political aim in Sweden not to over-regulate from the start, i.e. not to introduce costs that might turn out to be unnecessary in practice. On the other hand, it was recognized that expanding legal demands over time could be detrimental to operators and especially to entrants. The Act should preferably be right to begin with, or at least 'right' enough to last for a number of years.

The principles behind the new legislation could be summarized as follows.

- Regulation should be just sufficient to achieve political objectives.
- Regulation should be foreseeable, but application should also be swift and flexible in relation to the speed of change in the industry itself.

- Procedures of appeal must in consequence be swift.
- Public undertakings like defence adaptation, etc., should be procured by competition funded by the government; universal service obligation could be compensated for.
- The decisive criterion when applying the legislation should be the estimated effects on the end-users.
- Competition should be regarded as the main instrument to achieve efficiency.
- As competition over time can be expected to meet the political objectives, it should be considered whether the legislation as generally applicable is sufficient, or whether sector-specific rules should be introduced.

6.3.1. *Re-regulation takes time*

The application of the new regulation was entrusted to a new regulator, Telestyrelsen (since 1994, PTS—Post-och telestyrelsen). Although established in 1992, a year before the new Telecommunications Act was adopted, PTS was at a major disadvantage in coming to grips with the costing of the telecoms production process. Regarding new operators and the building of new networks, this could be remedied through recruitment and training at PTS; PTS staff were performing the same analysis as the new operators at the same time, and the production process was relatively simple and transparent. In the case of the incumbent, Televerket/Telia AB, however, a full understanding of all that was involved turned out to entail a lengthy period of analysis. Televerket had early adopted the accounting principles necessary for the limited company Telia AB, but those principles were not aimed at disclosing either interconnection costs or a universal service deficit. In addition, Telia was utilizing equipment that had been acquired over time and was sometimes used for both regulated and non-regulated telecoms tasks such as data traffic. Moreover, underlying the public accounts, since around 1989–90 there had been a corporate specific cost allocation system; this was used as input in constructing PTS own-pricing models. Acquiring a complete grasp of the costing system in place for Televerket/Telia was therefore going to take years rather than months, partly because of necessary changes in Telia's accounting and underlying costing models to produce telecoms regulatory, rather than purely accounting, information.

This lengthy learning process was of course particularly problematic regarding interconnection. Entrants to the fixed market soon became extremely dependent on correct interconnection prices; after starting to exploit the arbitrage potential of international accounting rates and corresponding domestic long distance tariffs, where initial margins were so high that imperfect interconnection rates were bearable, entrants were compelled to address the local market to act as full service providers, and in this market the interconnection rates had to be accurate.

Agreement on interconnection rates was basically considered a commercial process, subject only to a broad framework similar to the cost orientation for voice. PTS main instruments were mediation and the monitoring of inter-connection agreements; but as it was not entitled to decide on interconnection prices or conditions, PTS probably could not reach truly cost-orientated levels until after three or four years. (PTS could however decide on the definition of interconnection components, etc., and could eventually propose to the government that the Act should be amended.) On the other hand, markets for the most profitable indirectly accessed services, such as international or long distance telephony, were fast established within a year at interconnection prices somewhere between historic levels and cost orientation. Presumably the mediation mechanism operated by PTS was faster than PTS decisions and subsequent court appeals would have been, considering the initial lack of hard figures.

It is however evident in retrospect that interconnection traffic was most probably significantly overpriced. It is difficult to explain the interconnection price decrease over 1993–8 of 80 per cent by productivity gains alone, although it must be remembered that the net interconnection cost between operators tends to diminish as traffic flows become balanced. Thus, the different approaches between operators to handling the booming internet in 1994/5 may have had similar effects on Telia policy as PTS interventions. It is also clear that after a couple of years the Telia in-house perception of interconnection changed from 'unfair conditions' to a 'profitable business opportunity', which provided a better starting point for negotiations between operators.

Economically, interconnection was of course the major issue of disagreement. But other regulatory burdens were also disputed by the incumbent, not least the net cost of universal service. In this PTS was fortunate, as both the EU and the UK, among others, had hired consultants to estimate the scope of the alleged burden. The same model was applied to Sweden and, as the net cost was estimated at 1 per cent of the telephony turnover, compensation was—and is still—not paid. Relying on consultants for a central regulatory issue like USO was initially disputed by the incumbent. However, the use of consultants, rather than relying wholly on developing all competence within PTS, was from the start planned to speed up the Swedish liberalization process. This was also practised for market surveys, etc., where it would have been difficult to recruit and keep very qualified permanent staff.

6.3.2. *Powers to speed up market access*

Contrary to UK legislation, in Sweden the playing field was not initially tilted in favour of entrants. However, the regulator was instructed to promote 'sound competition' and, although the instruments were fewer than elsewhere, they were quite far-reaching in practice, both formally, e.g. by using administrative fines, or informally, by discussion.

Many of the *de facto* powers of the regulator in the beginning probably resulted from exploiting Telia's reluctance to incur adverse publicity as a new and dominant company. The ambition of the Telia executive management was clearly to keep in line, and 'monopolistic' tendencies in day-to-day operations were usually corrected if they were addressed by either competitors or PTS. In spite of this, the problem of giving preference to incumbent 'old boys' should not be underestimated. As said, the new regulation was perceived by many within Telia to be unfair, and most end-users were not asking for competition: they were asking for a fast service at a good price. Informal intra-corporate contacts could well be the easy way to supply this. Competitors quite frequently complained about such behaviour but were reluctant to file formal complaints, not wanting to embarrass end-users who could be their next customers. To the extent that such uncontrolled practices did exist, it is likely that they decreased as Telia was thoroughly reorganized (twice since 1993) and the old intra-corporate networks were broken up.

Also, because the regulator could issue orders backed by administrative fines to be upheld in court (except for interconnection prices and conditions), it might prove costly not to comply, if the regulator were to win the court case. Such fines are to be set so as to make non-compliance unprofitable. The highest fines proposed have been 50–100 million SEK, and they could be repeated if non-compliance were maintained. To this date no major fines have been paid: either—in most cases—compliance was achieved or the courts have not supported the PTS fine. Equally important, however, a dispute including a high fine might easily engender 'underdog publicity'—with competitors and the regulator being seen as underdogs to the incumbent. Such publicity might also arouse the interest of the EU's DG IV Competition, and DG IV was continuously being updated by Swedish new entrants.

While use of the formal instruments has demanded a sound knowledge of the legal system, successful use of informal ones is of course also conditional on the regulator being perceived as a person of both integrity and determination, 'rough but fair'. In both cases certain measures have been taken to make the regulator staff fully comprehend the responsibility inherent in applying instruments that could have a deep impact not only on entrants but also on the incumbent. This was felt even more necessary in that the staff, for various reasons—there were few 'telecoms regulators' to recruit—although mostly well educated, were young and relatively unexperienced.

6.3.3. Regulation differed by country

While price and access disputes, etc., were initially time consuming for all, greater problems of principle were experienced by foreign operators, who failed to appreciate the differences between UK, US, and Swedish legislation.

Swedish legislation, as mentioned, was not tilted in favour of entrants. The only support offered was that PTS should encourage sound competition. Thus, 'model products' from the UK might not be profitable for an operator in

Sweden. This was further underlined by the traditionally low retail prices, and thus low margins, for indirect access—even today, Swedish price baskets are only two-thirds of UK ones for both residential and business users. Some services/products might have come faster to the Swedish market had they been more tailored to take account of Swedish domestic facts than to fit a 'global blueprint of regulatory similarity'.

In some cases it proved difficult to scale down international experience to the 9 million population spread over an area only slightly smaller than France or Spain in Europe. When PTS employed consultants to devise a licensing procedure for GSM/DCS 1800, the consultants were very reluctant even to extend the number of licences from two to three, for fear that unprofitable business operations would result. (Eventually four licences were given out.) Also, foreign investment banks showed concern about the 'short' length of licence periods: the Swedish approach is to award a maximum of ten years with the possibility of extension if there are no fundamental objections.

Another difference from some countries was that the new Swedish Competition Act, and also the Consumer Protection Act, could be both applied in parallel with the Telecommunications Act and that application was entrusted to separate agencies. In practice, this probably did not cause problems to operators, as Swedish government agencies are instructed to cooperate to minimize the burden on those regulated. The three agencies—the Competition and Consumer Protection Boards and PTS—from the start met regularly to ensure a common understanding of market developments. Since then PTS has formally been given the responsibility to coordinate these contacts. This cooperation however raised the question of PTS credibility. In order to handle, say, interconnection, PTS had access to highly confidential information, the disclosure of which could be very harmful to operators. So that information should not be perceived as 'leaking' from PTS, it was agreed that the Competition Board should ask operators if they would agree to sharing information with PTS, although the Board could have demanded access directly from PTS. A special case of confidentiality related to information treated in mediation, which later in 1997 became even more sensitive when PTS was given the task both to mediate and eventually to arbitrate on interconnection.

A more direct major problem was that it proved difficult to apply the Swedish Competition Act to some telecoms cases. It could be said that the Competition Act tends to uphold efficient competition rather than to promote it from scratch. For instance, a large operator may still not be defined as dominant, which is a requisite for rules about abuse to be imposed. Many cases arising from Competition Act complaints were in fact not resolved, or not resolved in time. The players on the market, however, learnt very quickly to apply for PTS decisions and to file complaints with the Competition Board at the same time—thereafter using the cases as bilateral negotiating material, dropping charges as the parties agreed.

6.4. HOW FAST IS COMPETITION EVOLVING?

A major factor for governments and regulators when measuring success or failure of new telecoms regulation is how fast competition is likely to develop. Judging from the first five years for which market data are available, 1993–8, clear differences appear.

- Using only indirect access has not proved a good basis for competing in local voice, but has been quite successful for international and long distance calling with high initial margins.
- Mobile competition is working on a fast expanding market, but with oligopolistic pricing tendencies.
- The practice of internationally high terminal subsidies contributes to higher traffic rates.
- Early starters (before 1993) have stayed firmly established.
- Newcomers have been successful in niche applications.
- New services are developing, looking successful.
- Major completely new services, like the internet, show a more normal competition market sharing than plain fixed voice and have helped entrants into steady profit.
- Cable television networks are only slowly providing other services.
- Radio access is so far limited.

Whether these developments, with more than 150 registered and licensed operators at the end of 1999, could be judged successful competition is a question that has not yet been analytically answered, with Telia still holding more than 75 per cent of the combined fixed and mobile telecoms market.

6.4.1. *New arbitration tasks and continued mediation*

The Telecommunications Act was amended in 1997 to give PTS decisive rights on interconnection prices and obliging players with significant power (SMP being approximately in excess of 25 per cent of the relevant market) to accommodate all reasonable interconnection demands. Such operators with more than twenty-five per cent of the interconnection market also bear the burden of proof on cost orientation. These amendments were however the result of alignments with EU directives rather than resulting from an analysis of Swedish competition. The requirements to accommodate all reasonable interconnection demands and give burden of proof, however, gave rise to the first opportunity of a tilted playing field in Sweden. A couple of cases have been filed with PTS since, regarding copper/ADSL access and pricing as well as access to mobile networks.

In 1998 PTS decided that mandatory access to mobile networks did not constitute 'reasonable interconnection' and ruled against mandatory fixed access. Nor was the ADSL case deemed an interconnection matter. In both cases however PTS statements refer to the specific applications made. On the other hand, PTS has proposed to the government that the Act should be further amended to provide mandatory access to mobile networks at 'market prices'. The proposal created opposition as well as support from both operators and other parties, and had to be analysed within the Ministry of Industry following public consultation. PTS has also proposed mandatory fixed unbundling for SMP operators.

Between 1997 and 2000 PTS has made no formal interconnection price ruling[1], but the new instrument, to decide on prices, has been displayed in mediation. Mediation has been an important, although not excessively used, instrument. The total number of formal mediations over six years was less than ten, one of which had been called for by the incumbent. In addition, a number of informal discussions with players have assisted in solving disputes. Recently, however, the number of mediations has increased, mostly owing to carrier preselection/number portability, but also to 'hubbing' or 'bouncing' calls to mobiles to make use of lower international accounting rates (lower than domestic mobile termination payments).

Mediation in interconnection cases is quite different from PTS rulings. In mediation the whole of a business agreement can be addressed in order to facilitate an interconnection agreement. Thus, what players discuss during mediations should not be held against them, should a subsequent PTS ruling be needed on an interconnection issue. After 1997, when PTS was given decisive interconnection powers, mediation has been handled by selected PTS staff, which will not take part in a possible PTS ruling. Mediation information is not to be used in the ordinary PTS monitoring or ruling process. This of course requires that PTS staff are perceived as having high personal integrity, and so far that has not been put into question. As a whole, much effort has been made to maintain the confidentiality of business data within PTS. 'All business info will eventually leak, but it should be less likely if the source is PTS.' Unless players are confident about this, it would be very difficult to mediate.

Whether arbitration and mediation by PTS have accelerated competition, compared with a process handled in a civil court, can of course be questioned. It is not unlikely, however, that the PTS- specific telecoms expertise contributed to faster decisions initially. Today more doubts are being expressed. The number of arbitration/mediation requests has led to very long handling time within PTS. Disputes are also increasingly related to 'market prices', i.e. to normal business disputes that are traditionally—and possibly better—handled by civil courts. In addition, telecoms expertise is now widely available for hire, should the court or the parties need it. Furthermore, it should be noted that some of the cases referred to PTS might lead to considerable delay. Handling times of PTS, and of up to three administrative court levels for appeal, could

---

[1] In August 2000 PTS published a number of interconnection rulings, most of which are being appealed.

be increased still more if the case, or part of it, is thereafter brought before a civil court.

6.4.2. *Carrier preselection boosting competition*

In addition to the EU-initiated amendments of the Act in 1997 on the decisive powers of PTS and on significant operators, two other EU interventions seem to be boosting competition: the introduction of operator number portability, and setting a date for carrier preselection. The latter has resulted in an unforeseen array of operators offering fixed telephony at very competitive tariffs. By September 1999 around 10 per cent of former Telia customers had chosen another preselected fixed operator. One reason is probably the coincidence in time between the preselection reform and a booming interest in internet/multimedia/broad-band operations. Most prospective ISP/broad-band operators realized that, for the purpose of being seen by customers and to (cheaply) interest them in other services, offering telephony was a good marketing measure when preselection was much publicized by the regulator and the existing telephone companies.

Apart from the above, the lessons of preselection could be summarized by saying that market players have matters to resolve when many are involved and their individual interests are conflicting. PTS tried for rather too long to promote a market solution which in the end—and quite hastily—had to be replaced by a PTS ruling. Whether this was due to preselection being a very non-market phenomenon or to a more general case of market failure remains to be analysed.

6.5. MAINTAINING REGULATION—FOR HOW LONG, USING WHAT INSTRUMENTS?

As in other EU member states, there is in Sweden a set of telecoms objectives and instruments implementing EU directives within the framework of subsidiarity and proportionality. Objectives range from '112 forwarding' to 'efficient telecommunications'. The former should be met by all at all times, and compliance is easy to monitor; 'efficient telecommunications', however, must be broken down into measurable goals in order to decide whether or not the objective is fulfilled. And 'efficient telecommunications' will of course remain a moving target.

6.5.1 *Risks of regulation*

While objectives like '112' do not raise many problems and incur only a small cost, measures such as mandatory access, cost orientation, and price caps are costly and may result in adverse side-effects over time, apart from promoting the transition from monopoly to competition. The same would apply to USO if the scope is expanded, for example to 'broad-band' or even only to ISDN from 2.4 kilobits per second. Regulated prices and restrictions in using own networks imply obvious risks of false signals for infrastructure investments. Product/ services based on prices set by regulators also lead a dangerous life. Set prices may change drastically if they are based on fixed definitions, such as 25 per cent of the relevant market, making the difference between an EU 'significant' or a 'normal' operator. Regulator decisions could also be overruled in court; this may entail a lengthy process of uncertainty—in some Competition Act cases of up to a year or more. Also, in spite of an increasing supply of benchmark information, there remains much uncertainty about 'true cost' to serve as a basis to set prices. There are signals in Sweden for example pointing to the fact that the price cap on fixed subscription has been set too low, thus preventing investment in competing infrastructure. Raising the price cap, on the other hand, might strengthen the incumbent faster than entrants could expand[2].

There is also a risk element in part of the legislation where objectives and goals were rather loosely defined. This was understandable, and presumably necessary, to create a light regulatory environment in 1993. The main thrust was aimed at, and regulation only applicable to, the incumbent. After nearly ten years under the new regime, however, more operators are approaching levels where transitional measures might apply to their operations, although transition from monopoly is not a relevant policy objective for them. It could also be argued that amended legislation in some cases has been modelled on monopoly transition in spite of there being no initial monopoly; legislation about mandatory access to mobile networks is one such example. If spectrum is still available for more competing networks, access could be gained by building a new one. If this is not understood, important competitive elements are likely to be lost in favour of exploiting regulatory, rather than business, opportunities.

6.5.2. *Dealing with regulatory adverse effects*

Ways to deal with long-term adverse effects might include 'forbearance schemes', as practised in Canada in a somewhat discretionary system. In the EU, however, where forbearance would be applied to differing domestic markets, it is likely that the framework would have to be quite formal, i.e. defining performance criteria to monitor compliance with objectives. If the criteria are met, then not all—perhaps none—of the sector-specific regulatory instruments will be applied on that member state market. The industry would then increasingly be subject only to generally applicable law such as the Competition or Consumer Protection Act. The challenge of defining objectives and developing simple and stable critera should not be underestimated. Similarly, principles concerning whether and how to reapply sector rules need analysing. However, forbearance might still be the most interesting way of not impeding telecommunications by obsolete rules within the whole of EU when accommodating also the last implementers.

---

[2] The price cap was dismantled in 2000.

It would obviously be worthwhile to analyse an approach of this kind as part of the 99 Review of EU telecoms regulation. Several member states have had detailed regulation for more than ten years and adverse effects are not unlikely. Other member states are still in early transition, but the speed of change may be great, demanding adaptive regulation in those cases too. The accession states may or may not have a better position. They certainly have the opportunity to devise a modern and adaptive legislation by 2003, not having to tie in with existing EU rules; but they may have to tie in with holders of special rights and with too little purchasing power for some citizens.

The Swedish industry itself favours adaptive legislation in principle, but opinions differ when it comes to the competitive performance criteria that will need to be met. The balancing of short-term advantages and long-term detrimental regulatory intervention is still not being addressed in depth by many operators. One reason can be that most operators are still young; another that the uncertainty over five to ten years is perceived as too great to expand analysis above short-term interest. In addition, shareholder value is becoming increasingly important internationally, again to fend off hostile takeovers. And shareholder value seems to have short shelf-life, not being based mainly on regulatory long-term insight.

6.5.3. *Unbundling the local loop—the last major transitory change*[3]*?*

Indirect local access as well as equal access/portability have for long been issues of controversy. The latter was addressed by legislation in 1999, while unbundling seems to be taking a voluntary route, at least regarding the incumbent Telia, although the proposed tariffs have not seemed generally attractive. Both cases include the short–long-term balance perspective. A number of operators that from the start would have been beneficiaries of mandatory access are now approaching SMP status and could find themselves on the 'giving' side, depending on how relevant markets are defined. If, for instance, international traffic is considered as a market on its own, Telia is already below a 60 per cent market share.

The formal unbundling discussion contains a wide spread of argument; for instance, did the macroeconomic model by OVUM not fully recommend unbundling in Sweden? On the other hand, a large number of entrants supported it, as did eventually PTS. Since then objections have been put forward that mandatory unbundling might conflict with the Swedish freedom of speech legislation. In the meantime, Telia has voluntarily put unbundling, along with selling off its cable TV network, as a proposition to the European Commission, provided the Commission agrees to the proposed Telia–Telenor merger.

---

[3] Unbundling has been mandated by the EU since 2001.

In parallel with the fixed copper discussion, mobile operators are providing fixed/mobile converging solutions to businesses and are expanding them for residential use. Use of the electricity grid for telecommunications has been working well, but expansion seems to be pending. Clearly expanding are upgraded cable TV and fixed wireless solutions. The main unbundling interest is likely to centre on ADSL access rather than traditional voice.

Unbundling is thus a much more long-term and complex issue than carrier preselection. Carrier preselection is certainly weakening incumbents in telephony. The regulation is more than marginally interfering, but in a traditional service. Unbundling centres on the new competition based on new infrastructure. If ADSL turns out to be an efficient broad-band service, regulating access to the copper network is likely to have a profound impact also on the other competing technologies. The fundamental issue will be the pricing principles. In most cases, cost-orientated—or partially cost-orientated—access would probably be very competitive in the short term and would block other technologies without additional features such as mobility or much higher capacity. If ADSL does not meet the broad-band expectations, a time gap in alternatives is an obvious risk, as price-regulated copper access is likely to have slowed down investment in 'better' technologies. It could be argued that the question about regulating unbundling really goes back to the philosophy of whether the technology shifts make parallel investment efficient—or whether it is still a case of making the best use of the existing infrastructure.

Parallel *v.* single infrastructure however is still an open issue. While the regulation of ADSL is being discussed, cable TV networks are being upgraded to broad-band capacity. Upgrading GSM to packet-switched GPRS could provide more than 100 kilobytes per second, good for many internet applications. Next is EDGE with 384 kb per second and eventually UMTS with 2Mbps (stationary) for moving pictures. Smaller access networks are upgraded with fibre–coax to the home. Radio access with capacities of tens of megabits per second is being tried out, as is downloading via terrestrial and satellite digital TV.

So, is there a need still to regulate, and if so, how ?

6.6. LIGHTER OR TIGHTER?

In connection with the EU 99 Telecommunications Review, the European Commission is raising a number of pertinent regulatory issues:

- Is there a need to maintain telecoms regulation, and if so for how long?
- Is there radio frequency scarcity, and if so how could it be handled?
- How should broadcasting contents and provision be handled when converging with telecommunications?
- What sort of rules and security do we need on the internet?
- Is there a case for specific IT consumer protection and privacy?

From a Swedish perspective, some observations might be made.

6.6.1. *Telecommunications*

Once competition is working, there are still matters that require orderly behaviour, such as numbering and (perhaps) internet addressing. The internet is proving to be a challenging alternative to government intervention as issues of order are handled by a set of private organizations. Numbering is probably more difficult to handle than in the internet model, as it involves a long time investment, costly capacity expansion, and individual numbers that are perceived to have both business and personal value. Not least, problems of carrier preselection in Sweden point to a case for continued public responsibility.

The matter of directories is more complex, especially as more and more residential (fixed and mobile) users choose not to list, while businesses are eager to be listed.

Another area relates to USO and especially to handicap access and emergency issues. Affordable traditional universal service is hardly likely to disappear once established, as long as non-financial benefits are greater than costs to the provider. The case is probably different if handicap adaptation is not properly financed. The same applies to non-USO defence adaptation, in excess of the operator's own needs. In both instances, the Swedish public procurement model seems to be satisfactory to the end-users as well as cost-efficient for the Treasury. The forwarding of '112' is probably considered by most to be so much a part of state responsibility that government control is preferred. The cost is usually small in countries with high penetration.

Whether interconnection disputes need sector resolution, or could rely on competition legislation only, is another aspect that could be discussed. There is obviously a great span between a 25 per cent significant operator and a dominant one liable to abuse its position, but is telecommunications distinctly different from other industries operating without the 25 per cent criterion? It is more clear that consumer issues are likely to be of general character also in telecommunications, as no competitor is liable to provide service below present minimum availability or coverage requirements.

In short, most of the telecoms regulation is probably a transitional phenomenon.

6.6.2. *Scarcities—of what?*

The only case for limiting the number of telecoms operators in the EU is if resources are scarce. Radio frequencies and numbers are the two examples mentioned in this regard.

The case of frequencies is fundamental. On the one hand, radio is playing an increasingly important part in competitive telecoms; thus, frequency demand is likely to increase. On the other hand, improved spectrum efficiency, software radio, lower scales of economy in equipment manufacture, and more efficient coding/IP technology will contribute to a lower demand for frequencies for certain applications. It is also clear that scarcity varies within the EU.

Spectrum auctioning is proposed as one instrument to address scarcity, short licence periods and upgrading the efficiency of networks as others. It is necessary that these issues are analysed in the near future, so that services are not hampered by tradition or by pan-European blueprints blocking other use in member states with better spectrum opportunities than the most crowded ones.

It should also be observed that both operators and manufacturing industries are trying out the use of common spectrum bands to increase usage efficiency. Such a system would look for available frequencies over a whole band and not only in sub-bands licensed for one operator. If these approaches work well, they imply very different and less regulating systems to handle radio frequencies. In the meantime, increasing pressure will be put on the administrative models to allocate enough spectrum for new and spectrum-efficient applications.

6.6.3. *Convergence and broadcasting*

Broadcasting—in the format of digital TV—is only just at the point of becoming a case for telecoms regulation. That is, it has been planned to provide interactive services as part of digital terrestrial broadcasting; as this requires access to the radio spectrum, there could be a case for limiting the number of telecoms operators. It must then be clarified whether the selection process for the traditional TV part of the broadcasting licence could also be described as such an open and transparent procedure as is required by telecoms regulation. A problem of this kind could of course be avoided if contents and infrastructure regulations were kept separate. What remains, however, is to allocate frequencies for preferred use. With the interest that most governments show, broadcasting is likely to remain regulated.

6.6.4. *The internet*

The internet is probably the most different telecoms service from a legal standpoint, in that it is not based on domestic *or* international government regulation—in fact, not even on traditional standards—but rather on its own set of rules, even if some aspects of the net, such as the Internet Protocol (IP), are fast encroaching on traditional standardization. Many of the regulatory concerns do not in fact relate to the internet as such but rather to services or practices on the net, such as e-commerce rules, consumer protection, or individual privacy. Directly attributable to the net however are addresses/domains and the IP architecture, which could jeopardize security both in telecommunications itself and within user networks. The latter in particular seems to be requiring an increasing government responsibility to safeguard the functioning of the domestic networks. However, the government task is likely to be mostly monitoring, similar to Y2K preparations, as the prime interest lies with the operators, who alone can deal with hacker attacks quickly and flexibly enough.

Recognizing the transport capacity and global character of the net, it is also becoming evident that matters such as encryption or legal tapping as well as cross-border criminal offences on the net will require the attention of sovereign states. It is equally evident that this can be handled only multilaterally. In cases of slanderous or abusive material on the net, most ISPs so far seem to be quite ready to ban such material—in the extreme, even if this should fly in the face of the traditional freedom of information rights as regards printed material.

6.6.5. *IT consumer protection*

Closely related to internet issues are IT consumer and privacy protection. These of course apply not only to internet communication but also to 'traditional' telecommunications. These cases involve detailed regulation about, for example, procedures to disconnect customers on non-payment. The reason for such detail is that there were no alternatives to fixed-line connections. This is still the basic case on most markets, but the alternatives to basic communication, such as prepaid SIM-cards for less expensive mobile telephones, should not be discarded. Such a solution could look more costly, but if, for instance, it is used mainly for access to emergency services or to receive incoming calls, it would give good value compared with fixed costs. An alternative to detailed consumer regulation—as long as it is perceived to be needed—could be industry codes of practice, which in Sweden are often agreed between the Consumer Board and different industrial groupings (usually referred to as 'soft law').

A soft law approach strikes a balance between the general consumer legislation and a temporary (?) need for telecoms detail with maintained flexibility. The step from traditional telecommunications to the internet, including e-commerce, etc., adds another dimension by being truly transborder. What consumer protection would be applicable in cross-border business? This could of course be handled multilaterally, but perhaps the fast route is provided by the industry itself in the shape of 'Good Business Practice' seals, guaranteeing fair trading and a refusal to disclose customer information to others unless authorized by the customer to do so.

The ownership of the information about personal behaviour is crucial in most IT applications, but some are specific to telecoms services. One is the positioning of records which, with varying degrees of precision, is possible via automatic tellers, mobile handsets, or anti-theft devices in cars. To the extent that this information is collected by the telecoms operating systems, the safeguarding of confidentiality might be most efficiently supervised by national telecoms regulators, but the cross-border issues remain to be addressed.

6.7. REFINEMENT AND PERPETUATION

Whether regulation is likely to be even lighter or tighter is a very timely debate. The initial EU 99 Telecommunications Review layout points rather to lighter regulation in the form of adaptive sector-specific rules giving way to generally applicable legislation once, say, competition performance criteria are met. On the other hand, as regulators become more experienced, they will be the first to detect shortcomings of sector legislation that need to be addressed. Sometimes however they will also be among the last to see that major regulatory elements are becoming obsolete. The refinement and perpetuation of rules are among the greatest threats to a well functioning market.

REFERENCES

Information about Swedish Telecoms legislation could be found at www.pts.se. The Acts are translated into English, but amending procedures, analytical reports, etc., are mainly in Swedish only.

Information about the EU 99 Telecommunications Review can be found at www.ispo.cec.be/infosoc/telecompolicy/review99.

PART II

SECOND-WAVE COUNTRIES

7

Establishing Independent Regulators in France

DOMINIQUE BUREAU AND NICOLAS CURIEN

7.1. INTRODUCTION

The telecommunications and electricity sectors are not the only ones in France for which the state has gradually delegated regulatory responsibility to independent authorities. The Broadcasting Council (CSA) and the Stockmarket Regulatory Body (COB) also hold such powers. However, they operate on established markets where public operators are no longer dominant and do not control essential facilities.

Among network industries, again, telecommunications and electricity are not the only sectors affected by liberalization and market-oriented EU directives. For example, regional air transport has evolved very rapidly towards a competitive framework with a regulation based only on common law. On the other hand, the liberalization of the postal and rail services in France has been postponed to date.

Given the two criteria of opening to competition and maintaining a public operator in a dominant position in at least some market segments, with control over access to essential facilities, telecommunications and electricity appear to be the two exemplary sectors for studying the emergence of independent regulatory authorities in France. Both sectors also stand out because of their considerable economic force, and because the two public-sector companies involved, France Télécom and EdF, were deemed to be efficient and potentially able to withstand international competition.

7.2. THE NEW MARKET ORGANIZATION

Both sectors can be examined simultaneously, as the organizational structure that has been chosen for both markets is extremely similar (Table 7.1). The main characteristics of this structure can be summarized as follows.

1. The vertical integration of the incumbent firm has been preserved.
2. Market liberalization is based on a regulated third-party access to the network.

Table 7.1. *Overall market organization*

	Telecommunications (LRT)	Electricity (LMDSPE)
Access: third-party access regulation	**L34-8-1** – Subject to objective and non-discriminatory terms, the operators agree to requests for interconnection, given that the ART[a] is empowered, further to consultation with the Competition Council, to order changes in the contractual agreements.	**Art. 23** – A right of access to transport and distribution networks is guaranteed in order to ensure compliance with the terms of the contractual agreements with eligible clients.
		Art. 2 – EdF manages the public transport network. In terms of management, the corresponding service is autonomous (art. 12).
	L36 – A Telecommunications Regulatory Authority is to be established in order to define the rules governing the technical and financial aspects of interconnection (L36-6) . . .	**Art. 28** – Establishment of the CRE, which sets the network user charges (Art. 4), and settles disputes over access (Art. 36).
	. . . in order to settle disputes on interconnection (L36-8)	
Interconnection charges	**L34-8-2** – Interconnection charges remunerate the effective use of the transport and distribution network and reflect the attendant costs	**Art. 4** – The user charges for the public transport and distribution networks are calculated on a non-discriminatory basis based on the overall cost of these networks.

Regulation of retail prices	L35-2-1 – The specifications for an operator entrusted with providing the universal service set the terms on which its charges and the quality of its service are monitored. L36-7 – ART issues a ruling on charges and guidelines for prices over the longer term related to the universal service. This also applies to charges for services for which there is no competition. The latter require approval by the Ministers for Telecommunications and Economy.	Art. 4 – Charges to non-eligible clients are regulated (reference to s. 2, art. 1 of the 1986 decree on competition). The CRE[b] issues a ruling on these charges.
Public-service duties; separation between transport and funding of the universal service	L35-3-1 – A universal service fund is to be established. The amount of net contributions is submitted by ART to the minister for approval. Once the imbalance arising from the current scale of charges has been absorbed, additional compensation over and above compensation for interconnection will be terminated.	Art. 5 – Charges arising from public service duties are allocated as follows: • to the operators, based on the CRE's proposal related to excess costs of production (public service Fund for Electricity production); • to the distribution bodies (Electricity adjustment Fund)

[a]Telecommunications Regulatory Authority.
[b]Electricity Regulation Committee.

3. The role of sectoral regulators focuses on network access conditions and on the assessment of the net costs of public service obligations reimbursed to the incumbent operator, who remains the exclusive provider of universal service.
4. The role of competition authorities is confirmed, as the sectoral regulators' ability to regulate disputes between operators is focused on network access conditions. In order to ensure the consistency of decisions made by the competition authorities and the sectoral regulators, the same Court of Appeal is used.
5. Retail price regulation remains a matter of government responsibility, as the role of the regulatory authority in this respect goes no further than reviewing individual cases and making recommendations.

The organizational structure settled in both sectors has not been based on a general pre-established model, however. The need for independent sector authorities has been recognized only gradually as the appropriate solution, following a process of liberalization which was accepted rather than actively sought after. The two sectors have been treated as specific cases, and they still differ in the advancement of the liberalization process.

The telecommunications market has been completely opened up to competition since 1 January 1998, and the change-over was carried out within the European Community deadline: the new law on regulation (LRT) was endorsed in July 1996 and the Telecommunications Regulatory Authority (ART) was established in January 1997. In contrast, while the directive on electricity has been in force since February 1999, the bill on the modernization and development of the electricity public service (LMDSPE), establishing the Electricity Regulation Committee (CRE), was adopted only on 10 February 2000, and a great deal of uncertainty remains concerning the future operation of the electricity market and the role of its regulator.

In both sectors, the regulation has to solve similar problems which are encountered in all network industries opening to competition: how to prevent the incumbent operator from establishing its access to network conditions for the purposes of maintaining and abusing its dominant position in markets where competition should prevail. For that purpose, the simplest solution would be to dissociate the natural monopoly sectors from those open to competition, by disintegrating the historical operator's vertical structure. It was with this aim in mind that ATT was initially broken up and the railway reforms in continental Europe were implemented.

The boundaries between the monopolistic and competitive segments, however, frequently proved difficult to establish, and this separation of activities could lead to high transaction or coordination costs, especially if the network infrastructure does not show structural excess supply. It has therefore frequently appeared preferable to maintain some degree of technical integration, combined with a formal regulation of network access conditions or essential services, based on the principles of transparency and non-discrimination.

7.2.1 *Telecommunications*

The issue of network access in the telecommunications sector consists in allowing the interconnection to the established operator's network for alternative networks used by incoming operators, or for service providers who themselves do not operate their own network. A group of economic experts lead by Paul Champsaur, managing director of INSEE (National Institute for Statistics and Economic Studies), was asked to make recommendations on both interconnection and universal service; in April 1996, before submission of the proposed bill on telecommunications regulation, this body clearly opted for a separation of the two aspects. While the charges for interconnection must aim at making the use of infrastructure resources shared between several operators cost-effective, financing the universal service must be effective in terms of social distribution, ensuring that everyone can afford the access to the telephone service. These two objectives require two different systems: on the one hand, an access pricing system which sets the *input* price of interconnection for new operators; on the other hand, a compensation fund to which all operators contribute in order to finance telephone service provision for those who would not have access if market forces alone prevailed. In the first case, it is a matter of regulating the market for an intermediate good; in the second, it is a question of implementing a corrective system to offset the rationing in end-user market that would be caused by free competition.

In terms of interconnection, the telecommunications regulation law of 27 July 1996 (LRT) requires operators of networks that are open to the public to fulfil the requests of telephone service providers under objective, transparent, and non-discriminatory conditions, whether these providers themselves operate their own network or not. Contractual interconnection agreements between the parties involved stipulate the technical and financial conditions for interconnection; these should be conveyed to the Telecommunications Regulatory Authority (ART) which may require amendments to existing agreements. Furthermore, the major operators, i.e. those that hold at least 25 per cent of the relevant market (in practice only two such companies, i.e. France Telecom and SFR for mobile telephony), are required to publish a catalogue outlining their technical services and terms for interconnection, subject to prior approval by the ART.

The requirement for objectivity implies that interconnection charges are cost-based, and the need for transparency implies that the operator duly separate the costs of interconnection services from those of other services, using appropriate cost accounting. Finally, non-discrimination requires that candidates for interconnection be treated in the same way, provided that they hold the same type of licence. However, it allows network operators (holders of L33-1 licences) to enjoy more favourable prices than non-network based telephone service providers (holders of L34-1 licences), in order to encourage the development of alternative infrastructures. The principle of non-discrimination applies first and foremost to the established operator, which should not provide interconnection for itself at an internal transfer rate below the external rate; this is subject to control through accounting transparency.

The lawmaker's aim to regulate interconnection, rather than allowing market forces to rule, is based on the imbalances arising from the initial phase of market liberalization, in which the established operator holds a dominant position; this position could be abused by offering unfavourable or discriminatory interconnection terms, i.e. failing to apply the principle of equal access. In a context of strong market growth, it is possible that after the *economic* regulation written into the current law will come a phase of *behavioural* regulation, in which supervision will be carried out *ex post* rather than *ex ante*, with the regulatory authority and/or the Competition Council intervening only to mediate in disputes and to settle claims. This development would be a response to the sector's increasing liberalization. However, the aim is not to replace the initial market failures with a cumbersome and stringent regulatory system in the transition phase.

Economic interconnection regulation has a two-fold objective:

1. *Ensuring efficiency of market entry.* It is important to ensure that the technology of operators entering the market is at least as efficient as that of the incumbent operator and to discourage market entry by inefficient operators as a result of over-attractive terms for interconnection. On the other hand, it is vital to ensure that the established operator does not *trap* candidates for entry through a *scissor* effect, by implementing interconnection rates that are too close to retail prices, thus eliminating profit margins. Finally, it is vital to encourage the construction of alternative infrastructures, while avoiding inefficient duplication of essential facilities.
2. *Guaranteeing efficient management of existing monopolized infrastructures* that are open to interconnection. Return on interconnection should be sufficient to prevent the incumbent operator transferring a large part of its productivity and quality efforts from infrastructures that remain temporarily sheltered into activities that are directly exposed to competition. Furthermore, pricing should promote an incentive for cost reduction and technical progress in the area that remains a monopoly.

The interconnection pricing principles that should be adopted vary depending on which of these two aims takes priority. Indeed, the price signal that ensures efficient entry is not generally the one that produces the best interconnection resource allocation.

Entry efficiency
If the most important consideration is entry efficiency, then the appropriate pricing rule is that suggested by the economists W. Baumol and G. Sidak. According to this rule, known as the Efficient Component Pricing Rule (ECPR),

the interconnection price is set equal to the opportunity cost of interconnected traffic for the incumbent operator, i.e. the retail price per minute minus the cost per minute of conveying the call over the network component that is subject to competition. In fact, if a new entrant sets its retail price just below that of the established operator (in order to actually enter the market) and pays the interconnection at the opportunity cost of the latter, then the profit margin of this company is equal to its cost advantage on the competitive component of the network. Therefore, only competitors with an efficient technology can break into the market.

In theory, the ECPR rule would seem to bring several benefits. In addition to filtering out inefficient candidates, it is also relatively undemanding in terms of information. On the one hand, the retail price is clearly identified, although structural variations in prices and various pricing options mean that the regulator must define an average price index; on the other hand, the cost of the competitive element is quite readily observable, owing to the technological rivalry that accompanies the introduction of competition. Furthermore, assuming the somewhat unlikely scenario that the situation prior to competition was efficient in terms of maximizing consumers' surplus while maintaining budget balance for the incumbent, the situation would be further improved after market entry; the incumbent would maintain budget balance, while the ECPR regulation would offset its forgone profits on the end-user market, with new entrants and their customers sharing the advantages of cost reduction as a result of technological advances.

In practice, however, several pitfalls emerge. First, the ECPR rule does not actually set an interconnection rate: rather, it imposes a link between the intermediate price and the retail price. Implementing the rule forges a direct link between regulation of the intermediate interconnection market and the end-user market. This may be a problem when the government rather than the regulatory authorities is responsible for controlling end-user prices, as stipulated by the LRT in France, for example. In contrast with Baumol's assumption (as seems much more likely), if the initial situation involves a monopoly with substantial profits, it will be entirely preserved by the ECPR regulation. Finally, this rule hardly encourages the incumbent to implement anti-competitive management practices. It is in the incumbent's interest to raise profits from interconnection by avoiding wherever possible price cuts on the end-user market, for example by generating competition over quality rather than prices. The incumbent also benefits from increasing the reduction in the costs of the service subject to competition at the risk of damaging the operation of the resources used for interconnection, for example by moving productivity investments from one area to another. Following unsuccessful experiments in the UK and New Zealand, the ECPR rule is now considered an inefficient regulatory instrument, given its implementation difficulties and its adverse effects on the incumbent's productivity.

Resource allocation efficiency

When the main concern of the regulator is the efficient use of the monopolized infrastructure that provides interconnection, a problem of cost allocation arises: how can we find a non-discriminatory way of sharing infrastructure costs which does not lead to cross-subsidies or encourage new entrants to resort to bypassing the essential facilities, and which gives an incentive to efficient management while responding to the requests made? There is no procedure that fulfils all these criteria. The theory of cooperative games applied to cost allocation shows that the existence of subsidy-free charges is not guaranteed and that, if such charges do exist, they are usually discriminatory and do not yield an optimal social surplus. Furthermore, Ramsey–Boiteux prices, which achieve this maximal surplus, are discriminatory and may indeed generate cross-subsidies. This problem arises because a second-best pricing rate is sought in order to recover the total infrastructure costs; this however, sends out a biased signal to potential entrants into the market, as the price is greater than that of first-best, which is equal to the long-term marginal cost—or, rather, to the long-term incremental average cost (CMILT), given the indivisibility of entry. In order to resolve the question pragmatically, French lawmakers have decided to take a mixed approach, bringing interconnection rates into line with CMILTs in the long run, while temporarily providing additional compensation, designed to take into account the financial viability of the incumbent.

The decree of the LRT legislation of May 1997 established an interconnection committee, which brings together the various operators under the supervision of the ART. There have been tough discussions within this committee over CMILT calculation methods. The face-off involves two schools of thought. On the one hand, there is an analytical top-down method, which establishes CMILTs by adding those costs directly linked to interconnection to a quota of fixed and common charges, calculated using accounting allocation drivers. On the other hand, there is a constructivist bottom-up method, which involves simulating interconnection through a piecewise modelling of the network including the latest available technology and then deducting the CMILT from aggregating the elementary costs of the constitutive pieces of the model. Clearly, the first method, leading to *maximalist* costs which are historical rather than long-term, is more favoured by the existing operator, while the second method, which provides *minimalist* CMILTs, is favoured by incoming operators. The ART, which is responsible for approving the method that will eventually be used, is hoping for a convergence of the top-down and bottom-up procedures or, at least, for an explanation of the causes of divergence.

Interconnection conditions

Interconnection price catalogues were published by the major operator, France Télécom, and were approved by the ART, for years 1998 to 2001. In accordance with the terms of the catalogue, interconnection is supplied at three distinct levels on the France Télécom network; at the local subscriber switch

(CAA) and, moving towards the core of the network, at the first-level tandem switch (CT1) or the second-level tandem switch (CT2). The prices in Table 7.2 relate to peak time, a 30 per cent reduction being applied during off-peak time. Telephone service providers that are not network operators but use a third-party operator (L34-1 licences) direct their traffic through a first-level tandem switch and pay higher rates (shown in parentheses in the table).

We can see that the rates fell substantially in the three years following the opening of the market and by 1999 were very close to rates in the United Kingdom; this is hardly surprising, given that these were the benchmark rates used for setting of French rates, owing to the lack of an adequately tested method for calculating interconnection costs. Charges that are proportional to the capacity requested are added to charges based on the volume of traffic; the former are expressed in digital primary blocks (BPN), with one block corresponding to a bit rate of 2 Mbits/sec, i.e. equivalent to 30 telephone circuits. In 1999 the BPN was invoiced at FrF 30,740 or FrF 43,360 for the local switch level (CAA) or the tandem switch levels (CT1 and CT2), respectively. For an *average* operator, conveying 60 per cent of its traffic at peak time and totalling 2.4 million minutes per BPN per year, the average price per minute stands at 4.7 centimes, 10.1 centimes, and 14.2 centimes respectively, depending on the level of interconnection (estimate made by the ART in its decision of December 1998). Finally, interconnection also incorporates the physical link between the point where the operator's services are terminated (point of presence) and the France Télécom network. Charges for this link, when it exceeds one kilometre, fell 40 per cent in 1999 compared with 1998; this facilitated tandem interconnection, given that a significant number of subscriber switches were still not technically open to interconnection.

In France, interconnection currently stops at the subscriber switch level. France Télécom's competitors (in a similar position to that of France Télécom in the international arena, where it is an incoming operator) claim for the unbundling of the local loop beyond the CAA, in order to reach customers representing their primary sales target without having to pay for the network components that are not directly related to this purpose. The incumbent operator, which fears an aggressive cream-skimming of its most profitable market segments, does not consider unbundling as an urgency. Furthermore, it is not particularly inclined to fasten the pace of technical innovations into the

Table 7.2. *Interconnection rates in France, 1998 to 2001 (centimes/minute)*

	1998	1999	2000	2001	Evolution 2000/2001	Evolution 3 years
CAA	6.09	4.64	4.37	4.04	− 7,55%	− 33,66%
CT1	12.78	10.08	8.89	8.21	− 7,65%	− 35,76%
CT2	17.57	14.19	12.58	11.51	− 8,51%	− 34,49%
Average	11.44	8.99	7.99	7.38	− 7,63%	− 35,49%

local network, such as ADSL technology, which allows the upgrading of copper links in order to provide access to internet multimedia services, as it is concerned about the risk of expropriation of its infrastructure investments in the event that the regulatory authorities would eventually decide on the unbundling, which they effectively did in the course of the year 2000.

This concern is further heightened by the situation inherited from the national Cable Plan initiated in the 1980s. As a result of this plan, France Télécom today happens to be the owner of a large number of loss-making networks used by cable companies which are currently becoming its competitors for internet access and local telephone services. Regulatory uncertainty over local network unbundling is also detrimental to newcomers to long distance telephone services, whose prospects of striking a balance between interconnection and the use of alternative local infrastructures could change considerably following unbundling. More transparency should prevail by the end of 2001, the deadline imposed on France Télécom for implementing unbundling.

7.2.2 *Electricity*

In comparison with telecommunications, the electricity sector has several distinctive features. First, the transport and distribution networks can be considered as natural monopolies. Unlike the telecommunications sector, where a gradual *symmetrization* of the market is contemplated, with the various operators investing in the infrastructure in such a way that interconnection will tend to become reciprocal, a more traditional organization is being retained in the electricity sector, where only the upstream market is open to competition while the network infrastructure remains a public monopoly. Electricity transport has also two specific features: on the one hand, an instant balancing of the network, without any possibility of stocking to smooth out the gaps; on the other hand, the separation of physical supply and sales contracts. Real-time imbalances between supply and demand cannot simply be offset, given the speed of the electric stream; this requires particular attention to short-term network equilibrium, which should follow both safety rules and use in priority power plants with the lowest fuel costs.

Opening up the production of electricity to competition will probably lead to a restructuring of the market rather than a change in its scale, with two geographical dimensions: national and supranational. On a national scale, we should expect to see the traditional effects of liberalization: diversification of available services; greater price discipline, especially for eligible consumers; pressure on the operators to be efficient. These effects are largely a result of the diversification of production plants that now exists, with an increasing use of gas and multiple energy sources, and possibly renewable energy sources. However, given the durable excess supply that is a particular feature of the French electricity sector, it is rather the threat of entry that will lead to lower prices and better quality of services. New entries on a large-scale market may be socially ineffective in the short term.

Furthermore, we can expect electricity markets for the largest consumers to emerge, extending beyond the established national frameworks. Eligible consumers are mainly those firms that are highly exposed to international competition, and for which electricity prices can be a decisive location factor. Such companies should therefore be able to enjoy better prices on the French market, given that the European markets now suffer from substantial over-capacity, relating to the compartmentalization of national markets despite their technical interconnection, especially at the continental level. By favouring the restructuring of the electricity sector to the benefit of the most successful firms, unification of the European market would therefore represent a competitive advantage for European industry.

It has also been recognized that EdF should take its place in this competition, which is gradually being established at the European level. However, while the liberalization of the telecommunications sector took place at a time when a consensus on the benefits of competition was emerging, the desirable degree of liberalization of the electricity sector has remained subject to debate in France. Liberalization has been limited, as only the largest consumers are eligible; thresholds have been set in order to fulfil *à minima* the EU directive (25 per cent, rising to 30 per cent in 2003). The choice of a regulated third-party access solution was late, and was accepted only because the alternative solution, implying a centralized exchange-based market, would have required the vertical disintegration of EdF and the building of a new transport network management system.

There are nevertheless technical and economic reasons for maintaining such a technical vertical integration between production and transport. For example, wholesale markets, such as the English Pool and the Scandinavian Nordpool, operate on a day-to-day basis, with price equilibrium achieved on the basis of forecasts for the following day. But real-time equilibrium is still carried out, technically through dispatching by carriers such as NGC in the United Kingdom, Statnett in Norway, Svenska Krafnät in Sweden. The initial single-buyer proposal, put forward by France when the directive was being established, aimed to facilitate overall optimization of available equipment by putting producers in competition, then centrally managing the system balance on a real-time basis. The British Pool system resembles this model, with producers obliged to sell to the Pool, then being subject to the authority of the network manager once their prices and costs are known. Up to now there has been no convincing proof of the superiority of this system, as economic optimization is still carried out on a simulated virtual market and this type of market has obviously remained subject to monopolistic behaviour. Given the above, costs are not necessarily reduced more than they would be under a properly organized and regulated third-party access system, where competition between producers might ultimately be more effective.

However, the weighting of these economic arguments in favour of a regulated third-party access, or of a pool, may evolve. The rapid development of
instruments that use information technologies and telecommunications to
manage these networks will undoubtedly put into perspective the extent of
vertical synergies within EdF, on which grounds integration was maintained.
Furthermore, organizational structures emerging overseas seem to combine
third-party access with wholesale markets. These appear to be vital, not only in
providing a basis for the financial markets that are derived from them and
enabling market players to hedge themselves against various risks, but also to
establish an efficient short-term equilibrium, with differenliated prices (*nodal
pricing*). The LMDSPE does not favour the creation and development of such
markets, although they may appear desirable and are no doubt inescapable.

The counterpart to technical integration is non-discriminatory and transparent regulation of network access. To achieve this, regulation must
obviously be distinguished from the authority of the state as EdF shareholder.
Furthermore, it is vital that the inevitable conflicts between operators are
resolved in an effort to establish *jurisprudence*, which implies a high degree of
independence on the part of the regulator, given the major pressure exerted in
the process of any network liberalization. Such regulation is implemented by
delegation, within the regulatory framework defined by the public authorities,
and does not prevent public service plans from being carried out or an effective
energy policy from being installed, the purpose of which is to ensure national
independence. But these plans have to be clearly identified within the regulatory framework, offset at their net cost to the incumbent operator, and
financed on a neutral basis in terms of their impact on competition. After a
great deal of hesitation, the acceptance of a solution involving an independent
electricity regulation body reflects the acknowledgement of these various
constraints.

7.3. REGULATING THE MARKETS

Regulation has essentially two features. On the one hand, it is asymmetrical;
i.e., it subjects the dominant operator to specific provisions which do not apply
to its competitors; this does not mean that the regulation should too actively
favour these competitors. On the other hand, regulation is transitory and
should gradually be phased out as the market develops, or at least the market
should increasingly operate on the basis of incentive rather than directives.

Regulatory efficiency may be assessed using five criteria:

1. the clarity of its objectives and its scope for intervention, specifying the
   sharing of responsibility between the independent regulation authority, the
   general Competition Authority, the relevant ministries and Parliament;
2. the adequacy of resources allocated to various regulatory parties and
   the objectives that are assigned to them, in terms of sufficient budget

allocation as well as appropriate staff allocation, both in numbers and areas of ability;

3. the powers of investigation and sanction granted to the administrative authority, which must be sufficient to make its action effective and establish its credibility;

4. the transparency of procedures, reflected by the rationale for the decisions that are taken, their publication, public consultation procedures, appeal procedures, etc.;

5. the independence of the administrative regulatory authority, as regards market players, state authority and the state's role as both a regulator and a shareholder in the incumbent company, whether it remains public or is partially privatized.

7.3.1 *The legitimacy and powers of regulators*

The European telecommunications markets are still dominated by established national monopolies, so that competition will have little chance of truly taking root without the implementation of a strict regulation. The role of such sector regulation complements that of the general legal framework for competition: while the latter ensures that competition properly operates *ex post*, the role of regulation is to accompany and direct its emergence *ex ante*, specifically by allocating licences to operators, supervising interconnection agreements, and ensuring that public service plans are maintained and funded.

It is clear that the upstream function of regulation, involving the establishment of legal and regulatory frameworks in which competition and regulation can operate, falls within the scope of the government and Parliament; on the other hand, the downstream implementation of regulatory duties is essentially the responsibility of an independent administrative authority in all EU member states. However, in areas such as decision-making and sanctions, executive and legislative powers retain privileges the extent of which varies depending on the member state. French lawmakers have ruled in favour of retaining such privileges, and, while the independent regulator has full powers in terms of interconnection, the telecommunications regulatory authority (ART) only makes a proposal for the net cost of financing the universal service, while the ministry provides the legal *confirmation*, i.e. makes the final decision before this cost is shared between operators; and Parliament is responsible for the proper implementation of the universal service and public service plans overall. The powers of the ART are limited to reviewing applications for the awarding of large-scale licences, where the final decision is made by the minister; this latter choice probably reflects the absence of precepts at the inception of the LRT on the extent to which control over licences is a desirable feature of market regulation.

The first organization responsible for creating a regulatory structure in order to ensure the transition from monopoly to open market was the

Federal Commission for Communications (FCC) in the USA. OFTEL, the telecommunications regulatory body in the United Kingdom, took on board the lessons learned by the FCC in creating its organization and operating methods; OFTEL was then considered an indisputable reference model during the creation of independent telecommunications regulators in the rest of Europe. However, the role and position of this model regulator is to be redefined, as a new law on competition is now being implemented in the UK, granting full powers in terms of enforcing compliance with competition law to sector regulators.

In France the ART has been in place since January 1997, one year before the opening of the market. As already stated, it shares regulatory powers with the ministers in charge of the economy and telecommunications and with Parliament, particularly regarding issues related to public services via the High Commission for Public Post and Telecommunications Services (CSSPPT). While understandable from a conceptual point of view, this fine adjustment of the division of powers sometimes impedes the practical implementation of the regulation and has been a source of recurring tension between the ART and the Minister for Telecommunications, which may weaken the current system in the future. For example, the ART is responsible for intermediate interconnection charges, while the government has the final word on retail prices submitted for approval. Admittedly, in one case it is a matter of ensuring productive efficiency of market entry conditions, and in the other case, of guaranteeing distributive efficiency in the sharing out of profits made by companies and benefits passed on to consumers. However, are the advantages won in terms of the separation between the respective roles of regulators and politicians not actually lost as a result of the separation in the monitoring of intermediate and retail tariffs? In any case, this is the view expressed by the ART in its annual business report.

The sustained growth of the telecommunications sector not only adds momentum to market and regulatory forces, it also tends to shift the existing balance between the various public bodies responsible for supervising this process. In France, the *cursor* was initially set by the law on the regulation of telecommunications (LRT) in 1996 in such a way as to define the powers of the independent authority within a narrower area than in the UK or Germany. The comparison of national experiences seems to indicate that a high level of autonomy for the independent authority on the one hand encourages efficiency, as it guarantees greater procedural consistency, but on the other hand limits operating difficulties and internal disagreements in the overall regulatory structure. It is therefore not unlikely that the French law could be revised in the direction of a greater room for manoeuvre given to the ART, notably in terms of licence granting and price supervision.

As regulation, i.e. the creation of an appropriate environment for the competitive scenario to be played out, is inherently a preliminary and temporary undertaking, efficiency requires that the state commission the project and then give another party *carte blanche* for supervising implementation. Once its job is completed, the sector regulator does not necessarily disappear, but its duties certainly change. The most likely evolution therefore is the one that is currently occurring in the UK, where the authority that was initially responsible for regulation now enforces the common competition law in its specific sector, acting as if it were a specialized sectoral department of the Competition Council. Giving further powers to the ART, therefore, should not be interpreted as engraving the regulation in stone, but rather as the means of accelerating the transitional process in order to reap the full benefits of competition in terms of price cuts, quality improvements, and consumer choice. This analysis applies not only to the telecommunications sector.

French legislation on electricity also separates the role of the government, which is responsible for defining public service duties in the electricity sector, energy policy, and the overall regulatory framework (in accordance with the principles of public service in France, as stated in the Denoix de Saint Marc report), and that of the regulatory authority, the Electricity Regulation Committee (CRE), which is responsible for ensuring the correct implementation of public service plans and for regulating access to public transport and distribution networks, given that the main operator has retained an integrated structure (see Table 7.3).

Following the LMDSPE, the CRE's main role is to define electricity transport and distribution network access charges as well as the total of the expenses arising from public service plans. It will be responsible for making suggestions which the government can either accept or reject, without amendment. The CRE will also be consulted on retail prices set by the government, network concession specifications, and proposed regulations related to the latter (whose rules will be set at a later stage), in addition to network development plans. It will implement tenders for the development of production capacities, consistent with energy policy objectives. It will also ensure that the accounts, in particular those of EdF, meet accounting separation criteria between production and transport. Finally, it will have the power to rule on legal proceedings on network access.

The powers of the ART and the CRE thus appear quite similar. However, there are a number of divergences which reveal the different nature of the two markets. As the vertical structure of the electricity market is well delimited, it appears perfectly normal to define electricity network user charges as a regulated public tariff, while in telecommunications, where reciprocal interconnection is anticipated, the ART monitors the catalogues of powerful operators. However, the term-to-term comparison (Table 7.2) of powers granted to the two authorities leads us to conclude that those of the CRE are more restricted, thereby benefiting the competition authorities in disputes between producers and also the government, whose general regulatory powers are thus reinforced.

Table 7.3. *Regulators' areas of involvement*

Telecommunications (ART)	Electricity (CRE)
• Advice on legislative or regulatory provisions	• Advice on network management specifications and draft regulations related to access
• Review of applications for operating licences for networks open to the public and for providing a public service	• [no: operating licences granted by the Energy Minister]
• Approval of independent networks (review of applications and granting of approval)	
• Proposal for assessment of cost of universal service and allocation of cost between the operators	• Proposal for assessment of cost of public service for electricity production
• Public advice on tariffs for universal service and services not open to competition	• Advice on tariffs for non-eligible clients and emergency charges
• Allocation of available spectrum and numbers	
• Approval of interconnection catalogue for major operators of networks open to the public	• Proposal of rates for use of public transport and distribution networks
• Settlement of disputes related to interconnection, cable networks, and sharing of infrastructure	• Settlement of disputes arising from use of networks
• Mediation in other disputes	
• Administrative and financial sanctions	• Administrative and financial sanctions for failure to comply with specifications regarding access, or for discrepancies in access and market adjustment
• Participation in EU and international negotiations at ministerial request	• Implementation of tenders
• 'Precision' of rules	• Ruling on guidelines applied to transport network

7.3.2 *Public service obligations*

In France the telecommunications law (LRT) of July 1996 specifies public service obligations that are distributed between three categories: (1) public interest duties, such as the development of research and training in the telecommunications sector, together with involvement in defence and national security, duties that are financed partly through public funds and partly by operators on the basis of the obligations they are required to fulfil;

(2) mandatory services, which the incumbent operator is obliged to provide without any external subsidy, such as the integrated services digital network (ISDN), leased lines, or the packet switched service (Transpac); (3) universal service obligations, which are funded on a joint basis by the various operators in the market.

After clearly establishing universal service as part of the public service, the French lawmakers were confronted with the need for a national answer to the four following questions: *who* provides the universal service, *what* are the contents of this service, *how* is it financed, and *how much* does it cost?

1. The answer to the question *who?* is that an operator is required to fulfil universal service obligations over the whole of the national territory in order to be eligible as a universal service provider. This has created a situation whereby the incumbent has a monopoly over the obligations arising from universal service while there is however no monopoly with regard to the provision of services, as the incoming operators are free to compete with the incumbent in market segments related to universal service.

This asymmetrical framework differs from that which has been established, for example, in Germany, where all the operators contribute to the provision of universal service, given that the incumbent is obliged to provide services as a last resort. The French decision to appoint a single universal service operator reflects the wish to entrust the incumbent with public service duties, among which the provision of a universal service features first and foremost, thereby justifying the continuing majority ownership of its capital by the state and the civil servant status of most of its staff.

2. In response to the question *why?* the legislator has ruled that universal telecommunications services in France comprise three elements:

 (i) the universal telephone service, including two structural components: territorial coverage, arising from the obligation to cover unprofitable areas, and a social obligation, arising from the duty to grant preferential terms (discounted subscription charge) to low-income or handicapped subscribers;
 (ii) the universal directory, in both hard copy and electronic format, including the numbers of the subscribers, with all the operators as well as mobile phone numbers, together with the provision of on-line directory assistance;
(iii) public phone booths located in public premises.

This is a rather restrictive definition of the scope of the universal service, and there has been some debate over the potential need for change in this respect. For example, a governmental report, which focused mainly on the partial privatization of France Télécom and was submitted to the Prime Minister in September 1997, recommended an extension of the universal service to the three following areas: urban and rural planning, health, and education. In this respect, the plan to introduce the internet into schools can be viewed as part of the universal service in the broader sense, even though the specific procedures used for implementation are not included in the framework defined in the application decree of the LRT law of 1997 on telecommunications, which is dedicated to the financing of the universal service.

3. Regarding the question of *how?* i.e. the organizational aspects of funding, the latter decree draws a distinction between a transition regime and a permanent regime. The transition regime represents a price rebalancing phase, during which the fall in rates for long distance calls brought about by competitive pressure reduces the contribution from these calls in terms of covering the structural deficit of the local loop (access deficit). This requires both an increase in the subscription charge and the provision of external funds to be divided between the operators, until the subscription charge reaches the target level of FrF 65 excluding VAT, i.e. the amount considered as a cap in terms of the affordability of telephone rates in reference to the British benchmark; this phase was completed by 1 January 2000, and the permanent regime was then settled.

During the transition phase, the tariff rebalancing component and the geographical component of the universal telephone service were funded through an increase in interconnection charges, on a pro rata basis in relation to the traffic conveyed by the various operators. However, the social component of the universal telephone service, together with the amount of compensation provided for the telephone booths and directory services, were covered by a universal service fund under the auspices of the Caisse des Dépôts et Consignations. The operators contributed to this fund on a proportionate basis in relation to the amount of traffic they respectively convey. The operator in charge of the universal service thus receives a net transfer equal to the difference between the cost effectively borne for providing the universal service and its own contribution to the fund.

Once the permanent regime has been established, the tariff rebalancing component and the increase in interconnection charges cease to apply. The geographical component of the universal telephone service is transferred to the fund, which thus becomes the only funding vehicle for the universal service and is completely dissociated from the remuneration provided for interconnection.

4. The last question, *how much*, is obviously the most sensible. The LRT and its decree for universal service stipulate that the ART must submit to the telecommunications minister methods for assessing the cost of the universal service, together with the amount of net contributions from the operators, given that this amount is subsequently confirmed by the minister. The method of calculation used by the ART is similar to that of OFTEL in the United Kingdom and is based on the concept of *avoidable cost*, i.e. the amount that the operator in charge of the universal service would save if it were freed from this constraint and were pursuing purely commercial goals. However, the measurement of avoidable costs is extremely sensitive to the underlying hypotheses

and adopted conventions, particularly in relation to the following:

- the scale of the grid applied to the network in order to calculate the geographical component: an unduly broad grid tends to reduce the number of areas that are basically unprofitable, and therefore to reduce the cost of the universal service, whereas an unduly narrow grid tends on the contrary to incorporate potentially too small technical units to be individually removable from the network, and thus generates an increase in the cost of the universal service;
- identifying relevant costs, together with the method used to assess them, given that the decree recommends a future-oriented valuation, in other words one based on the cost of renewal using modern technology, rather than at the historical cost paid for the equipment by the incumbent operator;
- the return on capital incorporated in costs, which, according to the recommendations made in the decree, should be based on an average of the incumbent's cost of capital and the same cost faced by an investor that is a new entrant into the telecommunications sector;
- the degree of avoidability of costs, which presumably is variable depending on the geographical regions and is lower in profitable areas.

For 1997, in the absence of an approved method, the decree provided for a valuation based on a percentage of fixed telephone service revenues of the universal service provider: 5.5 per cent overall, divided as follows: 2 per cent for rebalancing of tariffs, 3 per cent for the geographical component, and 0.5 per cent for a range of services including phone booths, the directory, and social tariffs. Using these percentages, ART estimated the overall cost for 1997 of approximately FrF 4.8 billion, including FrF 1.8 billion for rebalancing, FrF 2.6 billion for geography, and FrF 0.4 billion for the rest. These figures were subsequently revised in order to better reflect a major gap between France Télécom's forecast revenue (FrF 87.8 billion) and actual revenue (FrF 91.2 billion), implying a universal service cost slightly above FrF 5 billion (cf. Table 7.4). The Directorate General for Competition at the European Commission was sharply critical of this assessment: in an injunction dated 24 July 1998, Commissioner Van Miert stated that France was committing a violation of Directive 90/388, which stipulates that the preservation of the monopoly on voice telephony until 1 January 1998 should have enabled France Télécom to raise the necessary funds in order to meet its obligations; according to the Commission, the universal service has been funded twice in 1997!

For 1998, the provisional forecast of the cost was based on a more sophisticated approach, including a calculation of the avoidable cost based on a grid of the territory representing the geographical component: the avoidable cost is the cost that France Télécom would retrieve by discontinuing the service in unprofitable areas as well as to unprofitable subscribers in profitable areas; however, this cost was calculated on the basis of a fixed percentage (1 per cent of telephone service revenue), in keeping with the provisions of the decree on the

Table 7.4. *Cost of the universal service in France, 1997–2000 (FrF billion)*

	1997 (final)	1998 (final)	1999 (estimate)	2000 (estimate)	2001 (estimate)
Rebalancing	1.824	2.028	2.027	0	0
Geographical	2.736	2.159	1.550	1.446	1.504
Social	0.456	0	1.105	1.211	1.038
Booths		0.187	0.189	0.165	0.185
Directory		0	0	0	0
Total	5.016	4.374	4.871	2.822	2.727

funding of the universal service. This established the cost of the universal service at FrF 4.374 billion, of which FrF 2.028 billion was for rebalancing, FrF 2.159 billion for geographic averaging (approximately FrF 1.3 billion for unprofitable areas and FrF 0.9 billion for unprofitable subscribers in profitable areas), FrF 187 million for phone booths, and FrF 921 million for social tariffs, with no compensation for directory services, which were considered to be financially viable, given the revenue provided by subscriber enquiries. An amount of FrF 921 million had been provisioned for social tariffs but it has not been made effective because of the lack of a mechanism to implement these tariffs.

For 1999, ART's estimates were published in January. In relation to the previous year, the tariff rebalancing component remained more or less stable (FrF 2.027 billion), as an announced increase in France Télécom subscription rates was not implemented at the end of 1998. However, the cost of the geographical component (FrF 1.55 billion) decreased considerably, following the introduction of an economic method for assessing the cost of unprofitable subscribers in geographical areas that are profitable overall: the 1 per cent ratio which was used before the methodological problems were resolved was intended to represent an upper bound. France Télécom, however, questions the method of calculation applied to the geographical component and upholds its own estimate for 1999 of FrF 3.5 billion for the unprofitable areas alone, as for 1998, contrary to the estimates provided by ART. As for the price of the other components, they were slightly increased: FrF 189 million for the booths and FrF 1.105 billion for social tariffs. The estimate for 2000 and 2001 do not show major changes, except for the cancelling of the rebalancing component, which brings the cost of universal service below FrF 3 billion.

Since delivering its injunction in the summer of 1998, the European Commission, no doubt unpleasantly surprised by the high cost of the universal service in France, has criticized the French government and the national legislators for having established a system of financial compensation without checking to see whether providing the universal service would impose an unfair burden on the incumbent operator. Two specific factors regarding the national situation should be examined in view of this criticism, and, while they may not suffice to refute the criticism, they may at least account for the high cost. On the one hand, the telephone subscriber penetration rate is particularly high among French households, at 97 per cent (v. 91 per cent in the United Kingdom); on the other, the geography of the territory is such that population density is low to average over a large area. The latter argument, however, has become somewhat less relevant, given the development of the radio local loop, which is capable of providing less costly connections in low density areas.

What, however, are the real figures behind the financial compensation effectively paid out to France Télécom? In other words, what is the financial impact of the cost of the universal service in terms of the contributions made by operators other than France Télécom? In 1999 the cost of the first two components—rebalancing and geographical adjustment—have given rise to additional compensation of 1.09 centimes per minute, representing an amount of FrF 124 million, given the traffic forecasts for the new operators and the exemption for mobile operators from the contribution to tariff rebalancing, in return for their commitment in terms of geographical coverage. Contributions to the fund representing social tariffs, phone booths, and directory services amount to approximately FrF 91 million and should be added to this figure. The total amount represents a transfer of FrF 215 million versus a total cost of FrF 4.9 billion, of which FrF 4.7 billion were thus contributed by France Télécom.

The amounts involved provide food for thought. On the one hand, the European Commission should be at least partially reassured, as the amount of potential financial compensation looks set to remain relatively modest, although admittedly it is sorely felt by the new entrants and may indeed increase if the competitive pressures become fiercer. On the other hand, it does bolster suspicions that entrusting France Télécom with the supply of the universal service has not placed an unfair burden on France Télécom. Indeed, given that the national regulatory system is able to impose costs of nearly FrF 5 billion versus compensation approaching FrF 200 million, calculated on a proportionate basis in relation to an indicator—i.e. the market share of new entrants—that does not fully reflect the actual impact of the new competitive environment on the former monopoly, the universal service clearly does not represent a pure competitive handicap, and is generating intangible benefits which should be identified and quantified wherever possible.

One admittedly theoretical approach to obtaining an overall assessment of the attendant benefits would be to free France Télécom from its obligation to provide a service and then to ask this operator to specify the amount of compensation it would require in exchange for providing the services representing the universal service on the basis of unchanged retail prices: the value of the intangible benefits would then be equal to the difference between the net monetary cost, as estimated by ART, and the amount of required compensation. If retail prices for the universal service were regulated and no compensation were required, the intangible benefits would be at least equal to the costs. This was the conclusion reached by OFTEL in the United Kingdom, where regulated tariffs for the universal service (annual price increases less than the consumer price index plus 2 per cent) and the lack of a compensation system coexist. Caution should however be exercised when drawing comparisons with the French situation: as the net direct cost of the universal service is far lower in the United Kingdom, given a lower telephone subscription penetration rate and more favourable geographical conditions, a similar amount of benefits might well offset the direct net cost in the UK but not in France.

A more realistic approach, providing greater incentive, would be to establish the value of the universal service, on the basis of *pay or play*: this would involve allowing operators other than France Télécom to provide this service by waiving the mandatory requirement to cover the whole of the territory and to introduce competitive bidding for universal service licences, which is current practice in some areas of the United States. The difficulty in implementing auction procedures should not be underestimated; this particular method would however lead the operators to set a value on the costs and advantages that they ascribe to the universal service. Given the absence of mechanisms that provide both insight and incentive, the regulator is entrusted with estimating the value of the universal service to the incumbent operator and deducting it from the cost of this service; this is the policy currently pursued by ART.

There would appear to be three potential avenues to pursue in order to ensure the continuation and funding of universal service telecommunications under a competitive regime;

1. to make no provision for a compensation system, on the assumption that the universal service will generate for the operator at least as many benefits as costs;
2. to arrange a tender or competitive bidding, in order to award the rights for providing a universal service in a given area, with rights awarded to the operator requiring the lowest subsidy;
3. to calculate the cost of the universal service on the basis of a specific analytical method: this involves apportioning the amount among the various operators on a pro rata basis in relation to the amount of telephone traffic generated, using a universal service fund and/or through increases in interconnection charges.

The main benefit of the first method, currently used in the United Kingdom, is its extreme simplicity; the major drawback, however, is that it does not provide any information either on costs or on the benefits arising from the universal service. The advantage of the second method is that it prompts the agents themselves to reveal the costs through an incentive-based procedure, within which the only element of constraint arises from the technical clauses associated with the specifications for supplying a universal service; however, recent experiments in the United States, using the auction method in the telecommunications sector, have shown that the complex mechanics involved generate substantial organizational costs, liable to offset the favourable theoretical impact of this particular approach.

The third method has been adopted in France. This certainly requires the largest amount of information and is particularly subject to frequent dispute, as it is based on an *ex ante* normative assessment of cost. However, it does represent a crucial benefit, in that it provides some information, however imperfect, on the real costs of the universal service and especially on the relationship between these costs and the various parameters used in the definition thereof, as well as on the extent to which they vary according to the various assumptions used in assessing them.

The United Kingdom and Sweden have chosen the first of the above methods; Germany and Austria are contemplating the second one, and France and Italy have opted for the third route. France is at present the only country in which a quantified assessment of the cost of the universal service has been conducted and approved by the Telecommunications Regulatory Authority (ART). The lack of Community directives specifically covering the universal service accounts in part for the diversity of the methods adopted in the various member countries of the European Union. Admittedly, the 1997 directive on interconnection provides for a minimal amount of content in the universal service, and the 1998 directive on ONP (open network provision) in relation to voice telephony specifies the items eligible for funding. These directives however allow considerable margin for manoeuvre in terms of applying the principle of subsidiarity, in relation to both the exact extension of the universal service and details regarding organization and funding.

The law on electricity reflects a similar approach to that adopted in relation to telecommunications. In this case the concept of *universal* service implies a geographical averaging of the tariffs for non-eligible clients. EdF has the exclusive responsibility for performing these tasks, and the CRE maintains control over the net cost of these obligations and its mutualization. The legislators have however sought to further emphasize the importance of the public service obligations and have stressed that the latter remain a key government prerogative. This has led for example to the establishment of a framework aimed at persons living in poverty or in precarious social conditions. In so far as the market has been only partially liberalized, the regulation of retail prices for non-eligible clients involves even higher stakes than in telecommunications.

First and foremost, the law is a statement of public policy on energy issues. Specifically, this implies the planning of electricity production capacities over several years in order to secure supply and to achieve equilibrium between the various sources of production. In order to implement the latter, the energy minister may use tenders under the auspices of the CRE, whose excess costs are covered by a specific additional fund.

The method for applying this concept of forward planning raises some important questions. If it will be applied only to specific projects, for example technology that produces specific environmental benefits, we can assume that the organizational structure of both the telecommunications and electricity sectors is similar. If on the contrary this particular framework, implying a requirement that EdF should buy the equivalent amount of energy, tends to be used as a way of increasing overall supply, irrespective of contractual agreements with clients under the third-party access framework, the conclusion will be somewhat different: this would represent a shift towards an entry-based industrial policy, or a *per se* competition policy, based on the acceptance of entry despite a major risk that it will prove ineffective. Such an approach has been precluded as concerns telecommunications.

7.3.3 *The state as shareholder*

With regard to telecommunications, there has been a partial privatization of France Télécom, the incumbent operator, in two successive tranches issued in September 1997 and November 1998 respectively. Following the flotation of the second tranche, the state has reduced its stake to 62 per cent. It is still too early to formulate an opinion as to whether the transfer in ownership of part of the capital has contributed to clarifying the role of the state as a shareholder, quite apart from its role of regulator performed via various other bodies, and whether there has been any change in the approach to corporate governance. Further time to adapt and perhaps further privatization will probably be necessary in order for the state to become a 'wise and virtuous' shareholder. It will also take time for the state to distinguish this new role from the more familiar task of exercising its prerogative over the operator's strategic decision-making. It does however seem reasonable to assume that the fierceness of the competition in the telecommunications market and the disappearance of any exclusive right will accelerate the learning curve.

In the electricity sector, we can observe the following developments.

- Partial privatization of EdF is not on the agenda at present, mainly for reasons related to labour relations and because of the continuing belief that only a public-sector operator is able to manage a substantial electric/nuclear power programme.
- The speciality principle of EdF has however been modified in order to enable EdF to diversify and adapt to developments in the relevant markets, particularly overseas (cf. Article 44 of the law that defines EdF's duties).
- The duality arising from the shareholder–regulator status is far more crucial than in the telecommunications sector, given the continued existence of a large exclusive area—i.e. non-eligible clients—which raises the sensitive issue of controlling cross-subsidies between different activities.
- As the market is liberalized, this represents a challenge to existing corporate governance procedures, given the growing number of diversification-related problems of a similar nature to those encountered at the same stage of the process by France Télécom, and of specific problems arising from the

instability in the management structure of the company until recently. Governance-related issues could also further complicate the application of common law to the analysis of anti-competition practices, as the underlying assumption is that the company in question is not allowed to post a loss.

In view of the divergence in terms of the degree of liberalization between the electricity and telecommunications sectors, it is difficult to make a comparative assessment in this regard. It is however tempting to draw parallels, with particular reference to the following points.

1. In the telecommunications sector, where the liberalization process has been rapid, the partial privatization of France Télécom clearly represented a source of revenue for the government, as well as an adjustment factor for the incumbent operator; however, France Télécom at first played only a limited role in the merger process in the sector, given that plans for cooperation with Deustche Telekom aborted and the alliance with Sprint, an American telecommunications carrier, was undermined by the takeover of the latter by Worldcom; in this respect, the situation is now changing rapidly, as is indicated by the merger with Orange in the mobile telephony market and an active involvement in the internet economy.
2. EdF was recently involved in major transactions, for instance the acquisition of London Electricity; however, and in contrast with telecommunications, liberalization in the electricity sector is clearly an arduous task, and indeed, the operator continues to act as a public-sector monopoly.

7.4. CONCLUSION

Despite insufficient attention paid to the scope for new public service obligations, and despite failures observed in some areas, mainly resulting from a lack of cooperation between the ART and the government, the LRT legislation has proved relatively efficient. The ART has however faced recent difficulties in defining its doctrine for new services, such as UMTS (third mobile generation) or ADSL (upgrading of the local loop). On the electricity side, the implementation of the directive has been an uneasy process. The authority of the CRE is somewhat undermined, and there remain uncertainties about the organization of tenders and long-term planning. The fact that the state plays too many roles altogether is potentially detrimental to the transparency of the decision-making process. More generally, there is no strong consensus in France as regards the benefits of energy markets liberalization. Since the breaking up of public operators was banished, which can be defended on economic grounds, the need for a strict non-discriminatory regulation as a necessary counterpart should have been better acknowledged.

Hence the prospect for independent regulators in France remains disputable. Sectoral regulators have to arbitrate complex conflicts between entry, productive efficiency, and short-term and long-term allocative efficiency. Although this requires specific skills, French new regulators do not have enough economists to help them. As a result, they sometimes fluctuate between extreme views: on the one hand, they tend to focus on naïve interpretations of the principle of cost-oriented prices; on the other hand, they sometimes have a priori ideas about the desirable market structure, which could easily lead to capture phenomena.

The choice of placing the regulation of the incumbents' retail prices under the government's responsibility has been made by continuity with previous practices of contractual arrangements between the state and its public firms, and also because there was the fear that an independent regulator would request too much productivity from an incumbent operator. A better cooperation between the state and the regulator clearly appears as an absolute necessity in this matter.

In addition, the regulation of anti-competitive practices, for example predatory practices, by the common competition law requires that all the firms in the market adopt pure entrepreneurial behaviour and do not easily accept losses. The nature of corporate governance of (even partially) state-owned firms is crucial in this regard. In conclusion, there remains a huge conflict of interest in the French organization between the state ownership of the dominant firms and the pricing regulation of monopolistic segments, so that the latter should probably be allocated to an independent regulator.

8

Regulation in the Water and Sanitation Sector in France

PIERRE-ALAIN ROCHE AND BRUNO JOHANNÈS

8.1. INTRODUCTION

In France, the debate on the regulation of public services has often dealt sparingly with the water sector. Indeed, this is one of the few sectors that has not been involved in the postwar nationalization process. If water challenges the analysts, it is first of all because of its decentralized character: responsibility for its quality and price is placed on the communes, which are numerous in France. The multiplicity of contracts accords with the great diversity of local situations. Water is also the subject of health and environment policies, which often resort to economic instruments and consequent intervention on the market.

Today there is a strong social demand for better regulation of the water sector, notably following the political and financial scandals of the 1990s. This chapter is based on a consideration of the French case, and on some reflections about the regulation of drinking water and sanitation services.

8.2. THE ORGANIZATION OF THE FRENCH SYSTEM: A RECORD *A PRIORI* UNFAVOURABLE TO REGULATION

8.2.1. *At the local level: a patchy public service*

Municipalities in France are responsible both for water services, i.e the production and supply of drinking water, and for the collection and treatment of waste water. Whatever the chosen organization of the service, the mayor is accountable for the quality of the services and for the tariffs applied to users. This liability is conferred on him personally, and for a number of years judicial risks have been added to political risks. Indeed, the mayor is liable to personally incur penal condemnation in the case of default in the management of water services.

An ancient regulation, reinforced by the 1992 Water Act, makes it compulsory for the water services to have organizational and financial autonomy

(Accounting Directive M49). Organizing financial transfers between the municipality's general budget and the budget of the water and sanitation services is generally prohibited. (There are dispensations for small communities.) The manager of the service can rely only on the resources brought by consumers' payments and on some subsidies specifically dedicated to water: he is not at liberty, either, to benefit from finance from local taxpayers or to organize cross-funding with other urban services, as the German Stadtwerke do.

Following the principle of free organization of the service by local communities, the municipalities can join together in associations (either rural or urban), local joint authorities, etc. In this case a deliberative assembly, formed by elected representatives of the member municipalities, takes the place of the local council. Finally, the elected representatives can decide to delegate the service to a private firm.

These organizational choices—gathering, delegation—can be made independently for drinking water production, drinking water supply, waste water collection, and waste water treatment. Several (up to four or five) distinct structures, which might have varied statuses and serve different areas, may be involved in the service of each customer.

The public service of water in France, then, is facilitated by a wealth of local services, having various types of organization and various economic sizes. This plasticity undoubtedly permits fine adjustments to local geographic contexts, which are quite diverse in France; it is offset by a certain degree of heterogeneity in the tariffs and in the level of the services, and is frequently denounced by the media and consumer associations.

8.2.2. A POWERFUL OLIGOPOLY

Local communities are faced with an oligopoly, i.e. a small number of very large companies—three in this case (see Box 8.1)—and a large number of very small firms, which these large companies endeavour to take over once they reach a critical size.

The history of these three large groups merges with that of delegated management and hence with that of decentralization. Their birth during the nineteenth century—1853 for La Compagnie Générale des Eaux, 1880 for La Lyonnaise des Eaux—was inspired by a centralist and authoritarian power, which was compelled to resort to the private sector to finance its ambitious town planning operations. Few of the companies that appeared at that time were still in existence at the beginning of the twentieth century; the development of municipal autonomy, and the intervention of local communities in the social and economic life of the country, had got the better of most of them, even if the wave of 'municipal socialism' that was then surging all over Europe eventually influenced France to a lesser degree than England or Germany.

After the Second World War there was a boom in the requirements of the municipal facilities. Municipalities were endowed with relatively important

Box 8.1. *France's water market: The structure of the oligopoly*

Vivendi is the leader in France's water market, supplying 25 million people with drinking water and 19 million with water treatment. Water activities are concentrated in Vivendi Waters. There is a trend towards a simplification of organization in this firm. Water represents 21 per cent of the global turnover of the group (€6.8 billion), coming after the building trade and the real estate business (€11.8 billion) and almost equalling communication activities. Water is also an expanding sector at the international level, with 80 million people being supplied in all. Vivendi has recently bought the American firm US Filter.

Suez-Lyonnaise des Eaux is ranked second on the French market, supplying 14 million people with drinking water and providing 9 million people with sanitation. But this group and Vivendi are evenly matched on the world market, with a total of 77 million people supplied in 1998 and more than 100 million people in mid-2000, not counting the purchase of United Water Resources, which ranks second in the municipal water market in the United States. Water represents 24 per cent of the turnover of the group (€5.12 billion), which is the same as is generated from cleaning activities but a long way behind the energy sector (€11 billion).

Bouygues is first and foremost a building sector company, and water represents only 9 per cent of its turnover. SAUR, its specialized subsidiary, supplies 6 million people in France and 23 million people worldwide. It represents a turnover of €1.35 billion. SAUR is a serious competitor for export, all the more as it forms an association with EdF International which holds 14 per cent of its capital. The company has a presence in China, Canada, Latin America, and Africa, the latter of which is its traditional market.

funds for reconstruction during the growth of the 'Thirty Glorious Years'. Accordingly, they appealed massively to urban service companies. Meanwhile, the philosophy of the system underwent a deep change. The issue was no longer about having the private sector finance facilities and receive payment for the services offered (this vision of delegated management has returned today at an international level and is now influential in relation to European regulations in this area.) Rather, it concerned the relationship between the technical skills of the private sector and the work of the community concerning public services. The established prices became indexed to the cost of living. The 'French way of delegated management' was born, and this led to the issue of regulation. Lyon is a good example of such an evolution. The Compagnie Générale des Eaux (CGE) was created in 1853. Later, under Herriot, a well-known advocate of municipal socialism in France, the service fell once again under the control of local authorities and the CGE was driven back to the suburbs. Since then, however, it has resumed a large part of the water service.

What is the situation today? The French market seems to be close to saturation point: the great majority of the towns now delegate the management of the water service to the private sector. The major French players have undertaken a broad diversification and have extended their activities first to other urban services—waste collection, transport, parking, funerals, school catering, etc.—and then to communication in a broad sense. Each of the three major players owns a television channel.

This redefinition has been paralleled by a spectacular development of international activities, notably in the field of water. Although they have long offered a commercial base for diversification of companies in urban services, the national contracts nowadays appear at best as showcases used by these three main groups for the development of their export activities. These rapid transformations have brought a massive increase of registered capital and structural changes within the groups—mergers, and changes in staff and in shareholding. The three groups of the oligopoly have distinct backgrounds and variously attach importance to water: it plays a minor part for the building and real estate business company Bouygues, but is still important for both Vivendi Waters and Suez-Lyonnaise des Eaux (more than 20 per cent of their turnover), despite their diversification, as attested by the free-for-all on the American market. Suez-Lyonnaise des Eaux stresses that it is first and foremost an engineering group, acting in the sectors of energy, water, and waste and aiming at world leadership in the water sector. Vivendi appears closer to financial circles and is far more diversified, though it does not neglect to generate profits from its core water sector portfolio.

In any case, it appears that the French market today is little more than a matter of image within the global firm strategy. This deeply affects how the companies make policy. Local autonomy is necessary for the contracts. The burden of taking on the responsibility of the service and of negotiating with elected representatives falls to the managers of local services. However, the three main service groups maintain relationships with local representatives. Since the imposition of new laws on the funding of political parties, the contributions of the companies have been published in the *Official Journal*; it should be noted that the water sector finances all the eligible parties, with a careful arithmetic.

8.2.3. *French national policy: environmental regulation and economical intervention by the basin water agencies*

In France, the national authorities seem at first sight to intervene only in terms of regulation, monitoring, and public engineering services, with no economic intervention. In fact it is not like that at all.

To ensure the consistency of the whole at the level of each large watershed, and to make an environmental policy possible, specific institutions were set up following the 1964 Water Act: the six basin water agencies. The water agencies are state bodies, with autonomous budgets, managed under the control of an assembly of water users—elected representatives, industrialists, farmers, associations, etc.—in which the state is in the minority. The water agency levies fees on water consumers and polluters. These fees are adjusted according to technical criteria: the polluting burden, the ecological sensitivity of the area, etc. For domestic use, the water-supplying services collect the fees in the name of the water agency, to cut administrative costs. The amounts collected are redistributed as subsidies to the stakeholders, to support their investment projects and, to a lesser degree, the operation of their facilities. This financial circulation represents about €2.3 billion per year.

Another financial circulation exists alongside that of water agencies: the Ministry of Agriculture manages a fund originally dedicated to water supply in rural areas and recently extended to include other operations concerned with water management. The modest amount involved—€140 million per year—is skimmed half from taxes on the water rates and half from taxes having no connection with the water sector. These subsidies are allocated to communities through the *départements*, which double the contribution from their own budget and sometimes from European subsidies.

The financing of the water sector thus comes from the consumers: 80 per cent of their water rates pay for the service and 20 per cent goes to the water agencies and is reinvested in the sector. Except for a very small contribution made by the *départements*, the water sector is financed totally by the water consumers, not the taxpayers. Through the water agencies, which control 20 per cent of the water turnover, the national authorities play a decisive role in the organization of the water market. Despite this, the French debate on regulation is generally incomplete, and pays no attention to the extent of this economic intervention in the water market.

8.2.4. *The consumers*

The French consumer is only just beginning to have some weight and influence on the economic aspects of the contract between local authorities and the delegated companies. Though it might be difficult to assess except indirectly, it clearly appears that water has become a political issue for voters. As for politicians, they have nothing to gain by water but a lot to lose. Many articles on water, featuring a *fin de millénaire* pessimism, appeared in the media in 1999 and 2000.

As they enter the judicial arena, the importance of the consumer associations has increased. In spite of its age—nearly a hundred years—the French consumer association movement is not nearly as well developed as in northern Europe, either in the field of environmental protection or in the defence of consumers' interests. However, a strengthening of its role has been observed as the associations resort more and more frequently to lawsuits (which, incidentally, have become a source of finance), receive more publicity by the media, and are more closely connected to the Ministry of the Environment and have representatives in the water basin committees. The main consequence of this development is the emergence of real technical skills in the consumer associations on issues related to water quality. As they are more accustomed than technicians to dialogue with lay persons, the associations, if not demagogic, may be able to offer mediation between the specialists of the sector and the general public.

The polls reveal the severe lack of information available to the public generally concerning water issues, whether about environmental concerns, technical realities, or practical organization. The water rate demand, which constitutes the consumers' main source of information, does not invite a critical look at the management of the public services in question. The charge for water depends on the volume consumed and on fixed charges (for the meter rental). The fixed charges are well short of the actual economic costs. They are however a cause of complaint by consumer associations, which would like to have them reduced. The determination of these charges falls exclusively to the managing community. Significant differences have been observed which may be justified in areas with tourist attractions but not in all cases.

Many consumers do not even see their water rate demands: for occupants of most collective buildings, water rates are included in the service charges of the buildings and are divided into two parts: cold water and hot water. In public-sector housing, water represents 18 per cent of the rent. There are increasing pressures for the retrocession of water management in collective buildings to the public water service, as it is the case for electricity.

The water rate demand is issued by the body responsible for the supply of drinking water, which in turn passes on the appropriate amounts to the other institutions sharing in the rate:—the managers of the other services of the water cycle, possibly distinct from each other, either public or private, communal or intercommunal. The rate demand also of course includes taxes and fees, especially those of the water agencies, which are the heaviest.

For some years, the amount of the water rates relating to drinking water has declined, while fees and treatment have increased. Moreover, if the water agencies' fees are reallocated to each type of service they finance, it appears that the cost of waste water collection and treatment now constitutes the major part of the rate demand. The 1992 Water Act took the opportunity to reframe the water rate demand form by making the breakdown of the headings and the mention of their beneficiaries compulsory. The headings must be classified by subject matter, e.g.: supply of drinking water, services to the environment, taxes and fees to public organizations. This improved communication meets an obvious social demand, and most big suppliers have seized the opportunity to redesign their water rate demand forms (copying the electricity rate demand format) as well as to give more information about water consumption via advertisements, etc). Despite these efforts, the French water rate demand is still complicated. Consumers ask for greater transparency and for detailed explanations of the differences in tariffs between the various public services.

Box 8.2. *The diversity of water prices in France*

The Seine–Normandy Water Agency carried out a survey on the price of water in 1999 on the watershed of the Seine and its tributaries and in Normandy (representing about a third of the French population).

Water services are charged €2.7 per m³ on average, which would amount to rates of €325 per year for an average household consuming 120 m³ per year. The great majority of people pay between €2 and €4 per m³, but 5 per cent of people pay less than €2 and 10 per cent more than €4.

Drinking water service represents €1.14 per m³, i.e. 42 per cent of the rate demand, although here too there is great variability. Sewage and waste water treatment represent €0.91 per m³, i.e. 34 per cent of the rate demand.

The fees amount to €0.53 per m³, which is 20 per cent of the rate demand. The fees in question are basically those collected by the water agency, a public body in charge of the coordination and financing of works, which redistributes the levied sums in the form of subsidies to the services of water and treatment.

Finally, the rate demand is subjected to a value added tax that amounts to €0.13 per m³.

The surveys reveal that the delegated water services are about 25 per cent more expensive than those operated directly by municipalities, but also that they correspond to other services, having a higher degree of complexity; with the available data, a comparison of similar services has been possible.

8.3. REGULATION OF CONTRACTS

8.3.1. *Practices and stakes of delegated management*

Today, private companies supply more than 75 per cent of the French people with water. The ratio is lower for sanitation services, which are more recent: probably about 60 per cent. The annual turnover of the delegated services of water and treatment can be assessed at €5.3 billion for the solely domestic market and €3.5 billion for the commercial market. These are only rough estimates: it is still impossible to put forward a global accounting of the sector, despite the recent efforts of the Ifen (the national statistical body specializing in the environment) and the water agencies under the aegis of the Accounting Commission for the Environment (a government commission created in 1998 to stimulate and coordinate these works—see Annual Report, 1999).

The very small municipalities have little concern with delegated management. This might explain how France can simultaneously display a majority of communes with management directly under local authority control and a water market largely dominated by private societies, depending on whether one refers to the number of municipalities or the supplied volume and the number of consumers served.

8.3.2. *A great diversity of contracts*

A certain diversity of contracts is covered under the term 'delegated management'. The existing classifications are inherited from the great French legal tradition and they insist on ideal types such as concession or leasing, depending on how the delegates participate in the financing of the works. In reality, these types are often mixed up, as is testified by expressions commonly used to describe the mixed arrangements, such as 'concessive leasing', 'concessive clauses', 'concessive cores', etc.

This malleability results from the very essence of the delegation contract, which is always drafted *intuitu personae*, that is after a negotiation *in camera* between the delegate and the authority, regardless of the process of competition that has been implemented beforehand. The main work can then be leased, provided the delegate builds any extension that will be in turn conceded. Such provisions can be included in the initial contract or can form the subject of endorsements and settlements during the contract if works prove necessary. The contracts therefore evolve on the occasion of investments and according to the financial capacity of the authorities.

In any case, the contracts are the key to the evolution of the tariffs: the basic price, the updating rules, and the review clauses. Price updating includes a fixed term and several terms corresponding to the main components of the cost, indexed on official indices. Classically, the formula includes a term relating to salaries, which often represents more than 50 per cent and other terms relating to electricity, reagents, etc.

8.3.3. *Why contracts are criticized*

There is no question here of weighing up the pros and cons of delegated management or of propounding elements to assist the local authorities in decision-making on the subject. Our purpose rather lies in drawing up a schedule of conditions for regulation based on the reproaches most frequently levelled at delegated management.

The standard criticism stems from the obvious structural asymmetry that spoils the negotiation and execution of contracts. This asymmetry results from the economic, technical, and human superiority of the delegated company over the local authorities, which are often deprived of the means (or do not resort to them), especially the human ones, to master the economic and technical parameters of the service. It is true that most municipalities are far from taking all the possible steps to attain a balanced relationship with their delegate, especially as the management horizons of the partners are not all the same. When the management of water services was a strictly technical stake rather than a political one, delegation was often deemed to be a way out by elected representatives facing technical requirements that they held to be beyond their reach. The peace of mind of the authorities in charge was well worth this slight loss of sovereignty. The limited predictability of the tariffs offered to consumers for the conceding authorities testifies to this information asymmetry. Indeed, the contracts are settled for relatively long periods, during which the price-updating rule applies. The delegated company undoubtedly holds more elements on the tariff evolution than the local authority. In particular, the big companies justify the charges related to their head offices in return for unquestionable savings by scale effects. But the amount of these effects, transferred to a local level, prove quite difficult to analyse.

The main criticism about the contracts, however, relates to the difficulty in reversing them. There is undeniably a strong inertia in the choice of the delegate; this inertia checks the reversion of the service to public control and its delegation to another company. Otherwise, the Compagnie Générale des Eaux (now Vivendi Waters) points out in its 1998 Annual Report that it has won 100 contracts out of the 111 to which it was a contracting party that had been reopened to competition in 1998. The figures at our disposal confirm this orientation: only a small percentage of the procedures reopened to competition having led to a noticeable change in the management of the service. The few services that nowadays revert to local authority control are probably far more a matter of interest for the media than truly relevant. At the end of a contract, the community has often lost its competent staff as well as its technical heritage. It is difficult to make allowances in this inertia for the trading experience of the firm—accumulated trust, human contacts—and for the asymmetry in information which confers on the delegate, who is already on the inside, a decided economic advantage. As she holds an information stock acquired during the exploitation of the service, the outgoing person is in a better position to assess the risks than her competitor, who has to build up much more information. Moreover, the new firm will often have to buy from the former the remote control system, consumers' data files and/or other technical elements under copyright protection.

The low watchfulness of the local authorities encourages the delegate to be offguard and not to take all possible steps to ensure the reliability of the service—all the more since the possible economic sanctions provided for by the contract are seldom applied. Everything seems to take shape around the issue of staff management. Modern technologies make it possible for the delegate to exploit the facilities with a minimum of employees. That is, it is the reliability of the service that is showing the effect rather than its quality. The 'staff' issue is known to be one of the weightiest, and private firms obviously have a stricter staff management than the municipalities. The reduction of staff can be one of the purposes of a transition to service delegation.

Finally, the issue of the maintenance of the facilities is crucial. As the date of the end of the contract is known, the delegate has no incentive to ensure with the same care as earlier the maintenance of the facilities. Of course, she can—quite rightfully, as we have seen—hope for a renewal of the contract. However, this renewal appears commonly as an opportunity to 'sell' to the authority some upgrading works that would have been prevented or postponed by a proper upkeep. The elected representatives will agree all the more readily, since investments are often more easily subsidized than standard expenses. The wishes of the technicians are then closely in line with those of the financiers.

Postponing necessary maintenance work is also a good way to meet the demand of some elected representatives for a fall in the water price. These representatives will then stand as candidates at the next election on the grounds that they have served their electorate well. The mayor who reduces the water price is doubly popular: as an honest politician (if the price goes down, there can have been no sharp practices), and as courageous champion of the citizens. Nobody thinks to ask if there is another side to these small short-term benefits, such as a reduction in some of the maintenance standards.

There are two ways for the authority to be sure that the delegate sees to the durability of assets and estate: it can supervise the state of the patrimony at regular intervals, or it can monitor the financial flows devoted to its replacement. The second solution is especially enticing: the savings made by the delegate by not using completely the interim payment for maintenance at the end of the contract generally will not benefit the town. The contract might specify that a certain amount of annual expenses must be incurred for the renewal to be assured, but, as it is well known, it is difficult to put an exact figure on the amounts needed. From a more pragmatic viewpoint, some people suggest putting these amounts into a public account and having them distributed *in fine* in a transparent way. However, the first solution is undoubtedly more consonant with the spirit of the service delegation, according to which the contract concerns only the fulfilment of the service and never the means implemented by the delegate. The profit made is offset by the risks related to the exploitation of the service, and this is legitimate so long as the state of the facilities is actually satisfactory. One of the aims of delegated management seems precisely to be the re-introduction of risks into the management of the services. However, difficulties remain in relation to the characterization of the state of the facilities, and particularly of the networks, which are by nature difficult to visit. These difficulties may be overcome through the use of indicators, the monitoring of which should be provided for in the contract. Research is in progress on this matter and should soon lead to experimentation.

8.3.4. *The framing of delegated management by the law*

In 1993, jurists seized on the obligation to update French law in relation to Community law as an opportunity to meet the social demand for regulation. A law known as the Sapin Law (29 July 1993), after the minister who propounded it, was then promulgated to limit the duration of service delegation, to make competition compulsory, and to organize publicity. It is of course difficult to assess a law whose effects are not immediately perceptible. Nevertheless, the first assessments, made by the management research centre of the National

College of Rural Engineering, Water Resources, and Forests (ENGREF) at the request of the water agencies, have produced figures that speak for themselves. The study concerned the year 1998, in which 582 procedures occurred, representing about 4 per cent of the water market; 333 of these have been thoroughly analysed. A palpable decrease in the price of the services can be noticed: on average, a fall of 8 per cent for drinking water and 12 per cent for treatment (13 and 22 per cent, respectively, for the towns of more than 20,000 inhabitants). This decrease was accompanied by an opening up of the market, with the big players slightly losing ground; their part in the concerned cases fell from 98 to 93 per cent of the private market through the procedures they led in 1998. This opening benefited small independent local firms. Neither penetration of foreign groups nor a return to direct local authority control was observed. But most 'Sapin procedures' lie in the future, notably concerning big towns—all the more since the law also has the effect of shortening the average duration of contracts, from seventeen to eleven years according to our study. A peak is forecast in 2003–4, and this might induce a clear change in the face of the French market.

Like all municipal decisions, delegation contracts are subject to legality controls of the prefectural administration and possibly to inquiries led by the regional revenue courts. The prefects receive some documents relating to the contracts for examination and approval. They must reach a decision on the legality of the procedures rather than on economic aspects of the contracts, an aspect that their services, modest and poorly endowed as they are, are not able to study. Suspicious cases are handed over to an administrative tribunal or entrusted to MIEM (an interdepartmental mission of inquiry) for a preliminary inquiry. The controls of the regional revenue courts consist of thorough inquiries into the procedures and economic balances. These courts are not referred to, but they exert their vigilance directly over at least all the largest communities. Sometimes they intervene in situations that have been brought to their attention by the media. As they alternately study parts of large regions, their intervention in a given community is rather rare, but the threat of it is permanent so it might have a deterrent effect.

At the national level, the revenue court is even further from the vagaries of the real world. Its controls are threatened only in big towns, but it exerts an undeniable political authority: its annual report represents an important moment, inevitably followed by political reactions. This is sometimes supplemented by a specific report, as in the case of a report on water in 1996.

The 1992 Water Act gave rise to two instruments that can be connected with a regulatory approach: the Barnier Report, also known as the Report of the Mayor, and the Mazeaud Report, known as the Report of the Delegate. These are annual compulsory publications whose contents are determined by statutory orders. The Mazeaud Report must be handed in by the delegate to the community that is provided with a service. It should include technical and financial information about the course of the contract and should provide the community with a means of control and the ability to stimulate the exercise of this control. The Barnier Report is issued by the mayor for the population with the purpose of supplying information about quality and level of the offered service, its technical constraints and performances, and its financial balance. Both reports are supposed to be endorsed by the town council, and to be made public; they are also supposed to be passed on to the prefect. In fact, the Barnier Report sometimes does not even appear, or is of poor quality; it is seldom released. These reports are often mixed up, and both are written by the delegates. The prefects complain about this irregular delivery, which is of little use to them, and the associations complain about the lack of assiduity shown by the local elected representatives. Part of the fault lies in the fact that the legal text sets out the contents of the report; indeed, it focuses on imparting the vision of a centralized control of the services more than on provoking debates with the population. The problem is exacerbated by a lack of advice in the field.

8.3.5. *Innovations for local regulation*

The time when the system was considered self-regulating, and when the eagerness of the firms to keep their good names would prevent abuse, is over. Today, the social demand is clearly in favour of more visible regulation. The levels of prices and of the investment required probably provide the company with incentives to seek financial room to manoeuvre in the exploitation of the services. Significant sums of money are at stake: the part of the turnover of water services that goes to the delegated firms is probably about €5 billion per year. It is true that the Sapin Law has begun to produce effects on the market, and that it will probably markedly reorganize it during the next ten years. However, there are still pressures for innovations in the field of regulation.

The first temptation would be to rethink the contract itself—its clauses, and its degree of achievement. One of the most promising methods is to play the game of delegated management right to the end: the 'philosophy' of delegation consists precisely in the delegate commiting himself to reach objectives, but by whatever course of action he might judge appropriate. The payment that is received is a reward for both the cost of exploitation and the risk incurred. The idea is to introduce into the contract performance indicators accounting for the quality of the service. The choice of such indicators was not immediate, but a study carried out by the research centre on water management of ENGREF, located on Montpellier and supported by the water agencies, has led to the identification of a list of adequate indicators ratified by a group of European experts. The next step is to reintroduce into the contract a system of financial incentives to promote the quality of the service in relation to the indicators. It is indeed considered that the exploitation of water services today involves fewer risks for the delegated firm than previously, and that this 'peace', acquired over time, distorts the spirit of delegated management. The drafting of such contracts—monitoring the quality, implementing economic incentives—is under consideration and will soon be tested on real contracts. Other researchers think that the nature of the contracts should be more radically changed. Jean Gatty (1998) suggests delegation contracts with an undefined duration—to ensure a good level of replacement of the facilities—but exposing their holders to a possible buy-back by competitors who would commit themselves to provide the service at a better price.

A second way consists in investing in the development of specialized consulting. Thanks to the provisions of the Sapin Law, a consulting market seems to have emerged, albeit somewhat timidly, torn between the interests of the participating corporate bodies—accountants, lawyers, and engineers—whose only point of agreement is the existence of a strong demand. This expanding market for consultants needs to be framed: both technically, via the publication of schedules of conditions and of references, and financially, with financial support comparable to that already granted to the technical studies in the field. Water agencies would probably be in a position to ensure this development, if they were commissioned to do so.

The issue of the role of the state services arises. The local services of the Ministries of Agriculture and of Civil Works are traditionally vested with a mission of project management and technical expertise for rural and town communities that demand it. Those services are paid for and produce an annual turnover of about €180 million. Legal and financial advice represents a part of this activity—assistance in Sapin procedures, assistance in drafting Barnier Reports, control of the delegates. These tasks are justified when they are carried out for small communities, who have neither the services nor the means to pay for private-sector consulting. Because of the evolution of the organization of the state, the long-term future of those structures and their missions might not be assured, and in any case it could hardly face a great rise in demand.

The intervention of consultants in a Sapin procedure is itself an element in favour of regulation. The procedure itself is complex; a precise inventory of fixtures is not always available for the contracting parties, and this lack of knowledge is seldom favourable to the authority. For that reason, some people suggest making the resort to a consultant during the procedures compulsory. Such a provision would make the organizing of the consulting market all the more necessary.

Finally, a third way could be to stimulate the representative's vigilance by performance reviews and comparisons. The idea is regularly to provide the elected representatives with the means to assess the technical and economic performances of their services. An additional motive would be to sustain the political pressure brought by the population and the associations on the elected representatives. This trend is already noticeable, and the question is how to keep it within reasonable boundaries. The associations and the media have begun to publish comparative analyses of the price of water. They have met with immediate success and with a chorus of protests on their rash comparisons. Public authorities are getting themselves organized: first the water agencies, which have implemented monitoring units intended for the general public, then the state, which has mobilized its statistical services. The regular publication of inquiries and econometric studies from a scientific viewpoint will probably induce a decrease in the overwhelming number of studies launched each year in varying degrees of disorder. The actual implementation of statistical competition is not self-evident. The inevitably simplifying discourse of global studies comes up against the great diversity in water service provision in France. That is why some people advocate a grading, using letters, and structured around a set of objective indicators, to reconcile the simplicity of the discourse with the fairness of the judgements. As has already been shown, such indicators do exist. The idea of grading is appealing, but it comes up against the central question concerning the legitimacy of the grading agency. The latter should of course be independent, especially from a financial viewpoint, but it should also be endowed with all the necessary technical skills.

8.4. WATER AS A PUBLIC SERVICE INFRASTRUCTURE: A PROBLEM OF GLOBAL FINANCING

8.4.1. Health and environmental policies and their regulation

There are several arguments for taking health and environmental policies into account in the debate on water regulation. The public policies relating to water and health appear at first sight neutral in relation to questions of market regulation. Their purpose is not to intervene in the distribution of costs and margins among actors. The contract itself is not considered to be important as long as a service that respects the legal standards is ensured. But the impact of such policies on the market is obvious, because of the consequences of the investments they are imposing. In tightening up standards, the authorities compel water services to implement more sophisticated techniques and then to call on new abilities, either internal or external, through delegation. The issue arises of the critical size of water services, that is the size up to which a good level of service can be expected to be ensured in a reliable way. To that purpose, the services could amalgamate; and this does seem actually to be occurring, with a significant effect on the market structure. In speeding up the pace of investment of the municipalities, health and environment policies also provoke more renegotiations of the contracts. Indeed, the implementation of new facilities often appears to be an opportunity to revise the contracts before they come to an end, and to raise the price of water.

Finally, these policies cause noticeable increases in price. Tightening the standards influences the costs, and then the tariffs and possibly the risks, incurred by the delegates and therefore their remuneration. In provoking palpable rises in price, regulations also have a noticeable impact on the acceptance of the price, on the public image of the firms of the sector, on their reputation, and on the social demand for better regulation. The themes of costly water, the lack of transparency of the sector, and the illegitimacy of the disparities in the tariffs have had a great success for some years in the newspapers, because of the political and financial scandals but also because the water rate demands were rapidly increasing as standards were being raised.

The final and more indirect link stems from the very situation of water resources: it argues in favour of a common approach of environmental and economic regulations. The levels of pollution we have reached are close to—and in some places above—the natural capacity for elimination. Locally, the resulting degraded quality of untreated water can confront the 'producers' of drinking water with a problem and impose on them costs they had not anticipated, for instance because of the excess of nitrates. Public policy to control pollution therefore influences the contract, its economic balance, the level of risk accepted by the delegate, its public image, etc. This point is illustrated by the Guingamp trial, in which a delegate who was accused of being responsible for the poor quality of the water supplied brought an action against the state, because of the state's responsibility for controlling diffuse pollution. These relationships explain why the authorities intervene in regulation without acknowledging that they are doing so, and why, conversely, the big water suppliers give priority to the ecological situation over their commercial activity, and take part in European negotiations and in the work of the water agencies.

Finally, authorities are evoking those policies to levy and redistribute about 20 per cent of the water rates, especially through the water agencies. There is a blatant contradiction between the surface neutrality of the authorities and the economic weight of their interventions. As we shall see, the issue of the renewal of the infrastructure is at the heart of the debates on both environmental and economic regulation.

8.4.2. *The question of renewal*

The question of financing the water infrastructures must be analysed in the long term. Indeed, the water sector is by nature capital-intensive; that is to say, it imposes on the owners heavy and rare investments. For a decade, health and environmental policies have induced an increase in the imbalance between the time horizons of local communities' management and the investments they are required to make. Facilities might turn out to be obsolete, for technical reasons or because of their capacity, although their cost may not yet be written off. In the past, the investments in water have been made possible by the intervention of the authorities, and that often happens throughout the world even today. This is not the case in France, however, where the aim is to follow the liberal principle that true prices should apply in the long run ('water pays for water'). However, this seems a realistic approach only because there is an already existing infrastructure that is altered only at the margin. (The annual investments represent about 5 per cent of the replacement value of the existing infrastructure.) The issue is not specific to France: in England, very degraded services have been privatized for want of sufficient provisions; poor quality of the service has justified their sale at a low price. In Germany the problem is circumvented, since the urban services, which have no reason to require investments simultaneously for all sectors, can lean on each other.

The French solution consists of a continuous adjustment of the stock, thanks to a provision method that is compulsory for the owners, through the intermediary of the water agencies: every service regularly has to pay the water agencies' tax, and the water agencies are thereby financially supported whenever they need new investment for renewing or updating. Of course, the agencies also finance stock extensions, but these do not represent more than a third of the amounts granted. If this system did not exist, the owners would postpone compulsory or necessary investments for as long as possible, and that would lead to a general degradation of the stock which would be damaging for the environment. There is no opposition here between a 'mutualistic' logic and an 'environmental' one, as the actual size and financial capacity of the public services is taken into account. Otherwise, it is improbable that the owners would themselves make sufficient provision for long-term time horizons, with the result that they would be led to borrow from the banks to finance their investments, and that would have a greater effect on the price of water. Of course, not all the owners can be assumed to be alike: big towns and big firms can make provisions on their own initiative because of their greater 'management capacity' and the lengthening of their time horizons; furthermore, their investments are proportionally smaller relative to their economic size. Therefore, according to the size and to the management capacity of the actors, it might be necessary on the one hand to regulate the part of the provision that can be given to the owners, and must roughly correspond to upkeep expenses, and, on the other hand, to regulate the part of the provision that must be organized at a higher level, corresponding to rather more expensive investment. Water agencies participate in the latter kind of provision.

8.4.3. *Provisions and regulation*

Both scales of provision are ensured through the good management of services, which is a matter of economic regulation, and through the system of water agencies, which comes within the scope of environmental regulation. Water agencies collect fees which they then reallocate as grants. These fees are determined according to technical criteria and are intended to offer an economic incentive to the actors, who are in a position to reduce the environmental damage they are creating, on the basis of the polluter-pays principle. The money is then redistributed to support projects that are relevant for the environment. The second economic incentive is complementary to the first.

This complementarity enables the same environmental results to be attained with reasonable levels of taxation as would be attained through a higher non-redistributed tax.

A first level of redistribution can therefore be distinguished, which reduces or eliminates the time constraints and makes it possible for anybody to get funds when they are needed, however long they may have paid. The purpose is to serve the general interest, and to enable the national community to take advantage of the pollution reduction without waiting. A second level of redistribution appears as soon as this financial circulation is oriented by health or environmental objectives, determining priorities. Water agencies allocate their funds according to the priorities defined in their five-year programmes. These priorities are the facilities that have been chosen to be focused upon during a period and the geographical areas that are judged vulnerable. Following the same logic, there are grants for the good management of water facilities, depending upon the achievement of good technical results.

To summarize, it could be said that, for good environmental quality, a good level of water service provision is necessary. The provisions can be divided into two parts: the first concerns the shorter term and is the realm of economic regulation; the second concerns the longer term and depends on environmental regulation. These two types of involvement correspond to two modes of intervention by the authorities which are distinct and complementary: on the one hand, the regulation of local delegation contracts of public service; on the other hand, the monitoring of a management system of water resources, instituted at a relevant level, i.e. the watersheds, which is ultimately clearly an environmental one.

8.5. CONCLUSION

The French delegation of local public services seems to have given rise to a model that is spreading all over the world. In fact, this practice cannot be dissociated from the decentralized management of local public services that prevails in France, whereby the numerous local communities have a great autonomy regarding the management of such services as water and purification.

In this context, the issue of water regulation can be stated in a specific way: how can the state intervene in contracts that are basically local, when it is not the principle upon which the system is based? Similarly, is it possible to do without a national regulator, given the huge asymmetry characterizing these contracts? What kind of role could the national regulator play?

It is our belief that there are three such roles: that of producing norms, a role of the state that no one would dispute because of the environmental and health stakes attached to these services; that of organizing the system of economic incentives and redistribution that is necessary to water policy; and, finally, that of producing and circulating the information needed to enable players in the market (references, methods, etc.) to be in a good position to act, without endeavouring to intervene in each local contract. This latter function has yet to be organized in France.

REFERENCES

Agence de l'Eau Seine-Normandie, *Rapport de l'Observatoire des prix et des services de l'eau et de l'assainissement*, Nanterre, 1998.

Barraque, B., *Les Politiques de l'eau en Europe*, Paris, 1995.

Bourdin, J., *Les Finances des services publics de l'eau et de l'assainissement*, Paris, 1998.

Cabal, F., Duroy, S., Grand D'Esnon, A., and Tricot, H., *La Commune et l'eau potable*, Paris, 1999.

Commission des Comptes et de l'Economie de l'Environnement, *Rapport 1999: Données économiques de l'environnement*, Paris, 1999.

Cour des Comptes, *La Gestion des services publics d'eau et d'assainissement*, Paris, 1997.

Drouet, D., *L'Industrie de l'environnement: dynamique et enjeux de la constitution d'un nouveau secteur d'activités*, Paris, 1997.

—— *La Régulation économique des entreprises de services eau et assainissement: observations sur les politiques et les outils en vigueur aux Etats-Unis*, study undertaken for l'Agence de l'eau Seine-Normandie, Paris, 1998.

—— *La Mondialisation des exploitants privés de services dans le domaine de l'eau : tendances et enjeux*, study undertaken for l'Agence de l'eau Seine-Normandie, Paris, 1999.

Ecole Nationale du Génie Rural et des Eaux et des Forêts, Laboratoire de Gestion de l'Eau et de l'Assainissement, *Analyse des délégations de services d'eau et d'assainissement menées en 1998*, Montpellier, 1999.

Gatty, J., *Quelle concurrence pour les services d'eau et d'assainissement?* Nanterre, 1998.

Haut Conseil du Secteur Public, *Quelle régulation pour l'eau et les services urbains?* Paris, 1999.

Henry, C., *Concurrence et services publics dans l'Union Européenne*, Paris, 1997.

Lorrain, D., *Gestions urbaines de l'eau*, Paris, 1995.

Martinand, C., *L'Expérience française de financement privé des équipements publics*, Paris, 1993.

Nowak, F., *Le Prix de l'eau*, Paris, 1998.

Nicolazo, J.-L., *Les agences de l'eau*, Paris, 1997.

OECD, *The price of water: trends in OECD countries*, Paris, 1999.

Pezon, C., *La Gestion du service de l'eau en France: analyse historique et par la théorie des contrats (1850–1995)*, thesis deposited with Conservatoire National des Arts et Métiers, Paris, 1997.

Roche, P.-A., *Toward a basin integrated water resource management*, International Water Association, 2000.

9

Independent Regulators in Italy

FRANCESCO BAVAGNOLI

9.1. INTRODUCTION

As a result of the implementation of EU directives on liberalization,[1] the evolution of the Italian energy and telecommunication industries could become a paradigm for the reform of all public utilities, in Italy, from the postal service to the railway network.

This paradigm requires three changes in the government's role and in the industry structure. First, the government will lose its exclusive right to operate in the field, a right thus far reserved to a public operator or to a government-controlled, yet formally private, operator. Second, it will no longer fulfil the convenient role of being both producer and regulator; the property of the ex-monopolist, through a huge privatization process, will come under the control of the financial market control. Third, new bodies, independent of political, economic, and bureaucratic power, will regulate the industries, guaranteeing equal access to them and imposing fair play rules in the competitive arena.

This paper examines this paradigm, focusing on the new bodies as the centre of the new regulatory scheme. It falls into six parts. Section 9.2 describes the historical and theoretical background of the state as both producer and regulator. Section 9.3 traces the failure of the traditional form of state intervention, while Section 9.4 examines the independent powers' *raison d'être*, giving a brief history and an analogy with North American, British, and French independent bodies. The common and qualifying features of the new bodies are described in Section 9.5, their all but easy compliance with principles at the core of the Italian public administration model as outlined in the Constitution in Section 9.6, and, in conclusion, the factors that are likely to determine their impact on public utility industry in Section 9.7.

---

[1] On telecommunications, directive 301/88, and directive 388/90, revised by later directives 94/96, 95/51, 96/2, 96/19; on energy, directive 96/92 (electricity) and 98/30 (gas).

9.2. THE *ANCIEN RÉGIME* OF PUBLIC UTILITY REGULATION IN ITALY: HISTORICAL AND THEORETICAL BACKGROUND

Before the 1990s and the shift towards liberalized markets in public utilities, the Italian government had long held the sole role of being both regulator and player. The conviction that only the government could provide energy and telecommunications services in the public interest can be explained in terms of the theory of market failures—notably the natural monopoly argument— which backed a monopolistic configuration of the industries and was framed in terms of certain historical circumstances and cultural reasons that supported a public rather than private monopoly.

A competitive configuration of the market was excluded by the relevant market failures that affected the industries. It seemed that only a monopolist could attain the critical mass necessary to reap the requisite scale economies for providing basic telecommunications and energy services to the entire popula-tion — including the 'unprofitable customers' in rural areas—at a reasonably low price.

This scheme also required a cross-subsidization of unprofitable business areas by profitable ones, which was possible only by forbidding access to the industries and raising the prices of the price-inelastic services, such as long-distance calls made by business operators. Otherwise the cream-skimmers, which would choose to operate only in the most lucrative parts of the market, forsaking the unprofitable ones, would drive out companies covering the market as a whole.

Three basic issues influenced the choice between a public monopoly and a privately regulated one.

1. The huge and high risk investments needed for building and maintaining the fast growing public utility networks made it questionable whether the 'invisible hand' of the market could provide sufficient financial resources.
2. A private monopoly was considered too difficult to control, on account of the weakness of the Italian public administration bureaucracy.
3. A public monopoly was consistent with the dominant postwar *dirigisme*, which favoured an active role of the government in the economy.

In line with this third point of view, two apparently clashing factors con-tributed to establish a public monopoly in the utilities. First was the *étatiste* policy, which imposed an active role on the government and gave priority to the public interest in the economy. And second, the government's weakness paradoxically ruled out a private monopoly controlled by an independent agency, and supported the government's presence as both producer and reg-ulator. The implicit (wrong) assumption was that, once they acquired the property of the monopolistic operator, there would no longer be the need for any controller.

9.3. PUBLIC FAILURES AND 'DEREGULATIVE' POLICIES

Such a system brought benefits and losses. It had the merit of allowing the development of basic public services and of providing them even to the unprofitable customers. On the other hand, the public monopoly has caused a welfare loss — in terms of poor quality and scarce innovation—similar to that typical of private monopolies. Ruling politicians have contaminated companies' strategy with not-profit-oriented hidden goals such as fund raising for their parties and full employment, inevitably weakening the efficiency of the enterprises. The proximity of the monopolists to the government and the lack of strict control over them prevented a regulation policy from limiting the expansion of public enterprises and fostering larger competition.

Given this conservative trend, some momentous changes in technology and policy have brought a far-reaching shift in government's approach towards the regulation of public utilities. The turbulent technological evolution has reshaped the borders of natural monopolies in the industries,[2] allowing a competitive configuration of the market, and has made monopolists incapable of meeting the ever growing volume and complexity demands by sophisticated customers. Even the very notion of a natural monopoly linked with exclusive rights is now questionable. When the incumbent is efficient there is a natural barrier to entry, arising from economies of scale and scope, which makes exclusive licensing unnecessary. Benefits that potential (actual) competition may bring often outweigh the occasional waste and duplication created by new entrants.

These factors—(1) the distrust in the traditional forms of public intervention, backed on the doctrinaire side by the theory of market failures, which holds that we might expect larger inefficiencies in public rather than private enterprises, and (2) the awareness of the distortive effects of heavy regulations— explain the radical shift towards policies often labelled as 'deregulative'. These policies involve three major changes in the industry structure.

1. The government has to dismiss the shares that granted control over ex-monopolists, thereby separating production and regulation, which had been gathered — in the *ancien régime* — into its hands.
2. Exclusive rights of operating in the fields have to be abolished.
3. Ex-monopolists, new entrants, and the whole industry, have to be subject to the authority of new bodies, independent of economic, political, and bureaucratic power.

Although these policies have been labelled as 'deregulative' — correctly, to the extent that they imply a shift towards a market-driven economy and a less intrusive government — *re-regulation*, rather than outright *deregulation*, better

---

[2] Nowadays the telecommunications industry and the energy generation sector of the energy industry are no longer natural monopolies, as it was argued in the past.

describes the whole process, inasmuch as an overhauled regulatory scheme is essential to effect a smooth transition to a competitive configuration of the industries, and to guarantee equal access conditions and fair play rules among the competitors.

9.4. A NEW ADMINISTRATIVE MODEL: *AUTORITÀ AMMINISTRATIVE INDIPENDENTI*

In the public utility industries the option for regulators independent of political, economic, and bureaucratic power can be explained in terms of: distrust in politicians' moral integrity; the need for impartiality in the presence of the state-run company during the transition from public monopoly to a multi-player competitive arena; hostility to postwar *dirigisme* and a preference for new tools to regulate the more sensible and more market-oriented economy. Sceptics view the change in approach as a deceptive strategy of the government to side-step difficult issues by giving responsibility to regulatory bodies with apparently technical but actually political power.

In a broader perspective, the creation of independent powers has recently been a dominant issue in the reform of the Italian public administration. The public utilities regulatory agencies are part of a larger category of administrative bodies — the *autorità amministrative indipendenti* (AAI) — which engage in a wide range of activities and sectors. Although there are some similarities, in terms of independence of political influence, between the AAI and the long-established Banca d'Italia, Consiglio di Stato, and Corte dei Conti, the independent powers in Italy are quite an innovative and fairly recent model, having started only in the mid-1980s, when a parliamentary think-tank first mentioned the new category, referring to Consob,[3] Isvap,[4] and Garante per l'Editoria.[5]

The new model, apparently viewed as a panacea for all the shortcomings of Italian public administration, has been adopted extensively, in matters ranging from competition[6] and privacy law[7] to public utilities regulation.[8]

---

[3] *Commissione Nazionale per le Società e per la Borsa*, created in 1974 (L. 7 June 1974, n. 216), and transformed in an independent body in 1985 (L. 4 June 1985, n. 281), has regulatory powers in the financial markets.

[4] *Istituto per la Vigilanza Sulle Assicurazioni Private e di Interesse Collettivo*, established in 1982 (L. 12 August 1982, n. 576), regulates insurances.

[5] Established in 1981 (L. 5 August 1981, n. 416) this has progressively gained authority over the whole multi-media industry, including press, television, and telecommunications; it was absorbed in 1997 by the telecommunications regulatory agency.

[6] *Autorità Garante della Concorrenza e del Mercato* (L. 10 October 1990, n. 287).

[7] *Garante per la Tutela delle Persone e di Altri Soggetti Rispetto al Trattamento dei Dati Personali* (L. 31 December 1996, n. 675).

[8] In the energy industry, *Autorità per l'Energia Elettrica e il Gas* (L. 14 November 1995, n. 481); in the multi-media industry, *Autorità per le Garanzie nelle Comunicazioni* (L. 31 July 1997, n. 249).

Such a proliferation of independent bodies typical of common law systems[9] in the Italian civil law system also exemplifies the convergence towards more similar administrative structures, confirmed by the French experience of the *autorités administratives indépendantes*, where the common law influences meet the French administrative tradition, which is very close to the Italian tradition.

9.5. FEATURES OF THE INDEPENDENT AUTHORITIES

The common and qualifying feature of the *autorità indipendenti* is the independence they enjoy from political, bureaucratic, and economic power. This independence resides in the power granted to the new bodies to determine their own organizational structure without interference from government regulation, and in the autonomy of acting regardless of any political guidance. The independence of the authorities' officers is guaranteed by strict professional and legal prerequisites, by bipartisan appointing procedures, by the considerable length of the term served by the officers (usually five years or more), and by severe incompatibility rules (i.e. the prohibition forbidding officers to engage in other businesses or employment or to have any interest in the sector subject to authority regulation while serving their term and for a short time after).

The great scope and variety of AAI activities — which range from issuing regulations that have the force of law, rate-making, and *moral-suasion* (direct to Parliament and to the executive) to adjudicative hearings which lead to the imposition of sanctions such as monetary penalties or licence revocation — and the authorities' independence from political influence makes it unclear whether the new institution belongs to one of the three branches of government (and if so to which one), or if it belongs to a different kind of public body, i.e. a new fourth branch of government, as the doctrine has often held.

On the other hand, the authorities seem to engage in a quasi-legislative, quasi-administrative, quasi-judicial action, constrained only by the law that establishes them and by judicial review. The AAI may therefore be considered wholly responsible — within the economic sector and the range of issues subject to their authority — for the achievements of certain public goals.

9.6. CONSTITUTIONAL PROBLEMS

The introduction of independent authorities raises the question of their positioning in the existing constitutional framework, with which they appear to be in opposition to a certain extent.

---

[9] The archetype of the 'common law' category is probably the North American *independent regulatory commissions*; similarly devised are the British *'quasi-autonomous non-governmental organizations' (quangos)*.

A dichotomy can be perceived with respect to the principles at the core of the public administration model devised in the Constitution: that is, between the principle of *legality* (art. 97 Cost.), which requires that the law determine the attributions and the responsibilities of public administration officers, and the principle of *responsabilità ministeriale* (art. 95 Cost.), which implies that the entire executive branch be subject to the political guidance of the Presidente del Consiglio dei Ministri and of the competent *ministro*.

These principles seem to contradict the autonomy the *autorità indipendenti* enjoy when they outline their organizational structure, and the political influence they are likely to yield, being independent of political directives, and owing to the extensive powers and attributions given to their officers. Nevertheless, the establishment of public bodies independent of political, economic, and bureaucratic power does not appear to be completely alien to the constitutional profile of public administration. One could regard it either as an implementation of the principle of administrative impartiality (art. 95 Cost.) or as an abiding by the 'autonomy and devolution requirement' (art. 5 Cost.).

A solid constitutional legitimization of the authorities could otherwise be found in the superior force of the European Union law compared with the national one (art. 11 Cost.), inasmuch as the new bodies are often called to investigate compliance with, or to actually implement, EU law. This argument seems particularly suitable to Consob (Commissione Nazionale per le Società e la Borsa) and Community rules on financial markets, to the Autorità Garante della Concorrenza e del Mercato and the competition law, to the public utilities' regulation authorities, and to the European directives for the market liberalization.

There is a strong case, however, for a specific provision in the Italian constitution for independent authorities. In such a way, two goals could be reached: first, an undisputed constitutional legitimization would be given to the *autorità indipendenti*; second, the essential and qualifying features of the new model would be established, setting some limits to a decidedly extensive but not always appropriate use.

9.7. CONCLUSION: THE IMPACT OF INDEPENDENT REGULATORS ON THE PUBLIC UTILITY INDUSTRY

While the authorities' advocates consider the *autorità indipendenti* a guarantee of impartiality, their critics fear that they could be easily captured by better organized lobbyists. Moreover, there are doubts regarding the effectiveness of the control over the new bodies, which are often viewed as an unchecked fourth branch of government.

Although it is too early to evaluate the impact of the new regulatory scheme on the utilities industry, the time is opportune to raise some decisive issues in determining that impact. Four questions need to be answered: (1) How intrusive will the government's attitude towards meddling in the sector be? (2) Who will supervise the regulator's actions? (3) What will the long-term functions of the regulator be? and (4) What will the regulator's relationship with the anti-trust authority be?

1. With regard to government's attitude towards meddling in the industry, the less intrusive it is, the more effective will the regulator be. An intrusive executive would bring a duplication of powers and conflicting views on the future development of the industry, given the strong bonds between the ministerial structure and former monopolists.
2. An effective check on the regulator's actions would be assured by deferential — but not indulgent — judicial control, by the openness of the regulator to public opinion, and by procedures in the rule-making and adjudication activity of the regulator. That would give all the involved and interested parties a chance to take part in those processes and would surely represent a preferable alternative to hiding the political content of such issues as rate-making and access to the industry (above all in the multi-media sector).
3. Conclusively, the functions of the regulator should be dynamically revised in accordance with a rapidly changing environment. The Italian attitude towards regulation is not as hostile as the North American, where regulation is viewed as a necessary evil which should be avoided whenever possible in favour of the most competitive configuration of the relevant industry. However, in the long term the functions of the regulator should not be prevented from changing, whenever further technological or economical developments require it.
4. The division of labour between the regulator and the antitrust authority is crucial. It might turn out in the mature development of the industry that some of the activities of the regulator should be absorbed by the antitrust authority. During the transition from monopoly to competitive market the relation between the regulator and the antitrust authority seems to be synergic. The first fosters competition by enforcing specific rules, and the latter enforces — and investigates compliance with — the competition law, defined only in terms of broad principles and not in terms of detailed rules.

REFERENCES

Alpa, G., *et al., Attività regolatoria e autorità indipendenti: l'Autorità per l'energia elettrica e il gas* (Milan: Giuffrè, 1996).

Amato, G., *et al., Regolazione e garanzia del pluralismo: le autorità amministrative indipendenti* (Milan: Giuffrè, 1997).

Bassi, F. and Merusi, F., *Mercati e amministrazioni indipendenti* (Milan: Giuffrè, 1993).

Baumol, W., Panzar, J. and Willig, R., *Contestable Markets and the Theory of Industry Structure* (New York: Harcourt, Brace, Jovanovich, 1982).

Caianiello, V., 'Le autorità indipendenti tra potere politico e società civile', *Il foro amministrativo*, 1 (1997), 341–75.

Cassese, S., 'Poteri indipendenti, Stati, relazioni ultrastatali', *Il foro italiano*, 1 (1996), 7–13.

Cavazzuti, F. and Moglia, G., 'Regolazione controllo e privatizzazione nei servizi di pubblica utilità', *Economia italiana*, 1 (1994), 9–30.

D'Alberti, M., *Diritto amministrativo comparato. Trasformazioni dei sistemi amministrativi in Francia, Gran Bretagna, Stati Uniti, Italia* (Bologna: Il Mulino, 1992).

Franchini, C., 'Le autorità amministrative indipendenti', *Rivista trimestrale diritto pubblico*, 3 (1988) 549–84.

Gardner, A., 'The velvet revolution: article 90 and the triumph of the free market in Europe's regulated sectors', *European Competition Law Review*, 2 (1995), 78–86.

ID., ' "Amministrazioni indipendenti" e posizione istituzionale dell'amministrazione pubblica', *Diritto della Banca e del Mercato Finanziario*, 1 (1993), 33–55.

Kahn, A.E., 'Regolamentazione e concorrenza nelle imprese di pubblica utilità: un "inquadramento teorico" ', *L'industria*, 2 (1992), 147–66.

Longobardi, N., 'Le autorità amministrative indipendenti, laboratori di un nuovo diritto amministrativo', *Jus*, 3 (1998), 685–720.

Majone, G. and La Spina, A., 'Lo stato regolatore', *Rivista trimestrale di scienza dell'amministrazione*, 3 (1991), 3–62.

Stiglitz, J.E., *et al.*, *The Economic Role of the State* (Oxford: Basil Blackwell, 1989).

Vesperini, G., 'Le funzioni delle autorità amministrative indipendenti', *Diritto della banca e del mercato finanziario*, 1 (1990), 415–50.

10

Regulating Energy in Italy

PIPPO RANCI

10.1. INTRODUCTION

What I am presenting in this chapter is not an essay on regulation: rather, it is an observation on the main issues I have found myself dealing with in three years as president of the Autorità per l'Energia Elettrica e il Gas in Italy. I hope that a brief description of Italy's national experience may offer some food for thought on regulation in general.

10.2. A COMPLEX INITIAL SETTING

Regulation is highly sector- and country-specific. Present challenges, difficulties, and opportunities arise from previous choices. History matters.

The Autorità per l'Energia Elettrica e il Gas was created in November 1996 on the basis of Law no. 481 of 14 November 1995 (henceforth referred to as the Energy Authority or simply 'the Authority'). It consists of a three-member board, with a staff that cannot exceed 120 people. Its tasks include the setting of tariffs, which was previously entrusted to the Minister of Industry; the introduction of compulsory quality standards; the definition of network access conditions; and the issuing of rules for accounting separation. It can make recommendations to the government and to Parliament on the services in general, can propose to the Minister of Industry changes in the terms of licences, and can even recommend that licences be revoked. In general, it has a mandate for promoting competition. The Authority is responsible for promoting the interests of consumers, assessing complaints and appeals from consumers, ensuring the publication and transparency of the conditions under which services are supplied, and settling disputes.

Before the introduction of an independent regulator, the Italian electricity and gas sectors presented a mixture of non-competitive market forms. A legal, regulated monopoly prevailed in electricity after nationalization in 1962, although small-scale private generators and municipal (and some very small private) distributors existed alongside the dominant state-owned Enel. A *de facto* unregulated and loosely supervised monopoly characterized the gas service, where state-owned Eni, through its subsidiary Snam, supplied almost all the gas consumed in the country, selling either directly to large consumers or to the country's numerous, mainly small, municipal and private local distributors. Regulation was weakly managed by ministerial offices, with the help of the same state-owned monopolistic enterprises that were subject to regulation.

The legal framework was unclear in many cases. For example, it was never specified whether the municipal electricity utilities were subject to public service obligations on an equal footing with Enel, which served over 90 per cent of the customers and provided the same municipal utilities with all the electricity they needed in addition to what they could produce in their generating plants.

Another case of unclear regulation can be seen in gas prices applied by *de facto* monopolist Snam to distributors and large industrial consumers: such prices were 'freely' contracted and formally subject to a government 'surveillance', which was never explicitly carried out. Yet final supply by local distributors to medium and small consumers was subject to an administered tariff. A local distributor was therefore selling at an exogenous tariff set by a government office and buying at an equally exogenous price set by a monopolist, without any guarantee that the two would be mutually consistent. In actual fact, however, the two always varied simultaneously, and in such a way as to leave the margin reasonably stable, as a result of an informal, opaque understanding between government offices and the monopolist.

In many cases legal disputes arose. One clear example is the way the dismantling of all nuclear generators was handled after a political decision to abandon nuclear generation, taken in the wake of a referendum in 1987. In principle, the costs of decommissioning were charged to electricity consumers, via surcharges on the tariff; but endless legal disputes arose regarding the definition of the amount involved, with respect both to existing power stations and to those under construction.

It is part of the Authority's task to manage such unclear regimes, to try to replace them with new and more rational frameworks (sometimes dealing with inconsistent legal provisions which the Authority itself cannot overrule), and to handle old disputes and apply the courts' decisions—all in all, a number of difficult and time-consuming operations that fall mainly outside the bounds of the regulator's usual remit, or at least the handbook version of it.

Independent regulation was introduced rather late with respect to pioneering countries: at the very time the process of liberalization was being started, and when the European directives for the internal market for electricity and natural gas were being finalized. The mandate of the regulator is therefore two-fold: the first task is to set limits to existing monopoly power, as in the classic case of regulating monopoly; the second task is to introduce competition so that monopoly can be eliminated, and with it the regulator's initial task.

The great issue, therefore, is whether the survival of at least some degree of monopoly in operating the network implies a permanent role for regulation. An extreme view of liberalization implies the elimination of all sectoral regulators and exclusive reliance on the Antitrust Authority. Political interference was occasionally apparent, e.g. at times of high inflation, when tariffs were temporarily frozen, and when cross-subsidies were introduced due to social or industrial policy goals or constraints.

All this is part of the current debate on regulation in network services. Yet in a country where tradition in regulation is weak, and where the main remedy to monopoly has long been regarded as nationalization, the sudden introduction of an independent regulation of monopoly and liberalization can be somewhat confusing. Legal (formal) liberalization can be taken by monopolists as indicating that they are now free competitors, long before their market shares have been reduced to levels consistent with competition; this induces them to fight the new rules the regulator is trying to introduce as though they were merely an exaggerated form of bureaucratic interference. Adversaries of regulation, including supporters of monopoly for nationalistic reasons, might appeal to the principles of extreme liberalism to demand the elimination of a newly established regulator. This is why we at the Authority are keen to explain our actions to the public, and to ensure that the channels of communication with public opinion are kept open. To this end, it has been helpful that widespread dissatisfaction with the working of the old system of regulation as run by government has emerged: the Authority has thus benefited from favourable attitudes right from the outset. These have on occasion given way to disillusion when it has appeared that regulation cannot satisfy all parties, or be simple and clear when issues are complex and interests manifold. Nevertheless, there is widespread respect for the integrity and competence of the Authority.

Liberalization is often confused with privatization, which in the Italian context was introduced in the early 1990s as a part of an emergency programme for reducing public debt. It then became apparent that privatization without liberalization would create dangerously powerful private monopolies. Yet, while the privatization process was still in the making, the floating of shares of the old state-owned monopolies would have been much easier, and revenue for the Treasury much higher, if liberalization had been defined in such a way as to let the company maintain some elements of monopoly power, and if tariff-setting and other rulings had stayed in the hands of government rather than pass to the hands of an independent regulator.

In actual fact, the Italian government sold one-third of Enel and reduced its stake in Eni to below 50 per cent during 1998–9, just when the legislation for liberalization and tariff reform was being introduced. Despite gradualism and certain weak aspects in the liberalization process, and some degree of tension, the process has been carried through in a way that can be considered as acceptable, and the independence of the regulator has been respected.

Liberalization is often opposed on the grounds that it could damage public service and weaken national industry. We have taken quality of service as one of the main targets of regulatory action, the aim being to demonstrate that liberalization plus regulation will produce *better* quality than did the previous regime.

10.3. TRADITIONAL TASKS, NEW CHALLENGES

A legal and economic transition requires cultural change. The following are some of the main differences between traditional culture and modern regulation, and illustrate some of the difficulties we have been encountering as a result.

1. *Incentive regulation*   The regulator inherited the setting of administered prices, with the mandate of moving from a cost-plus criterion to a price-cap, incentive-compatible type of regulation. The new approach to tariffs could be considered as unfair, since it clashes with the old idea that costs actually incurred should always be recognized. The old idea has a strong appearance of equity which is appealing to the legal culture of the courts, to which most regulatory decisions are submitted by one of the parties involved. It has turned out to be very useful that each decision is accompanied by a 'technical report' explaining its rationale.

2. *Cross-subsidies*   The old tariff system was heavily distorted by cross subsidies.

Household electricity tariffs were (and in part still are, as a result of the gradual transition process) set below costs for low levels of consumption; this was compensated by extra high tariffs for higher levels of consumption and for second homes. Household gas tariffs were (are) differentiated in favour of cooking and hot water usage, with tariffs for domestic heating making up the distributors' revenue.

Outside the household sector, electricity tariffs were heavily weighted in favour of agriculture and energy-intensive sectors, and against small industrial and commercial customers, which can bear heavy unit costs of the kilowatt-hour since energy accounts for a very small share of their total production costs.

Cross-subsidies are gradually being eliminated and tariff levels are being aligned to costs. This is widely considered to be fair in principle, yet it raises protests by those categories facing increases.

Energy-intensive industries point to the lower costs of energy borne by their competitors in Europe, and claim that it is a duty for industrial policy-makers to provide them with an even playing field. The issue is a thorny one, since substantial differences in the cost of electricity do exist; these are due in part to the higher average price of energy in Italy, and in part to existing, mostly non-transparent, cross-subsidies in other countries.

Political criticism has been directed at the general adoption of *cost-reflective tariffs*, since this implies abandoning the use of tariff policy as an instrument for pursuing social, environmental, and industrial goals: it is seen as an abdication of political responsibility. Such an attitude generates either a pressure on the regulator to depart from rigid cost reflectivity, or a radical proposal to withdraw tariff-setting responsibility from the independent regulator and restore it to a 'politically responsible' body.

3. *Planning* Privatization plans in electricity, and actual privatization in gas, are changing the national framework: public enterprises, previously in charge of defending the public interest, cannot maintain their powers of planning and coordination for the whole sector once they have been turned into profit-maximizing corporations. The question is then raised on many sides: who is now in charge of planning investment and long-term import contracts in order to guarantee the availability of energy for the country? It is clear that market forces will play a larger role in providing security of supply; what is not clear is how large this role will be, and in any case it is not easy for political and public opinion to rely on an invisible hand when they have been educated to believe in a visible hand, and to seeing it operate for decades.

4. *Complication v. simplification* Comprehensive tariffs for energy supply to final consumers are being replaced by a tariff system where the final price is a sum of the prices of generation, transportation, distribution, and supply. Some of these prices are set through free negotiation on more or less competitive markets, and some are still set by the regulator. The picture is much more complicated than it was before, and this complication is sometimes decried as the product of a bureaucratic approach. In particular, tariffs are becoming much more complicated in their gradual transition to market prices, since the old tariff has co-existed with the new one for some time; this gradual approach is necessary in order to avoid big leaps in low, subsidized tariff levels.

In an effort to introduce flexibility and customer care to the captive market, the Authority has replaced administered tariffs with a system of revenue ceilings, and is allowing suppliers some freedom to offer a variety of tariff options below these ceilings. This allows for some yardstick competition in price-setting. Monitoring of the ceilings is a challenge to the very small suppliers, who are unfamiliar with sophisticated accounting procedures. However, the new flexible system has been interpreted by Enel as allowing for a wider flexibility than was actually intended by the regulator and set out in its decisions: this led recently to a minor conflict.

5. *Liberalization and regional disparities* A political decision has been taken that electricity tariffs should be uniform throughout the country, to avoid regional disparities. This is not easy to combine with a flexible, incentive-compatible tariff system. The Authority is complying with this requirement by setting national uniform ceilings, and by introducing compensation for regional differences in those distribution costs that are due to objective,

geographical factors. The new system has been generally praised for its rationality, yet it is much more complicated than the old one, a fact that is not generally well received. Regional compensation parameters are presently under study, and it is likely that they will supply the utilities with an opportunity for conflict with the regulator.

In order to maintain easy access to gas in all regions, in the Gas Liberalization Act Parliament has introduced criteria for the gas transportation tariff, thus limiting the general power of the regulator to set tariffs. While the political intention was to impose regional equalization, the criteria written into the law are in fact far too technical to be fully appreciated by members of Parliament.

6. *Environmental provisions* Support for electricity generation from renewable sources has been maintained. This is financed through surcharges on tariffs, which are strongly resented by consumers, particularly energy-intensive industrial consumers. The transition is under way from traditional instruments such as guaranteed electricity prices to new, market-oriented instruments such as green certificates.

One cultural difficulty in this transition phase is the widely held belief that generation from renewables, being socially beneficial, should be exempted from economic risk or uncertainty, in which case guaranteed prices and quantities would appear to be the most appropriate solution. The Electricity Liberalization Act is innovative in this respect. In coming years each generator using fossil fuels will be obliged to provide additional electricity produced from renewable sources, either by generating it directly or by buying it, in a fixed proportion of 2 per cent of total production. As a consequence, a market for 'green' certificates will develop, endogenously generating the amount of the subsidy. The difficulty with such a scheme is that, while neatly defined at the national level, it is not easy to manage with respect to electricity imports and exports.

10.4. IS LIBERALIZATION CONDUCIVE TO ACTUAL COMPETITION?

Transition from a monopolistic to a competitive framework is understood as a consequence of enacting the European directives for the internal market of electricity and natural gas. Yet the emerging organizational structure of the two markets looks far removed from the framework that real competition requires.

The transposition of the two European directives into the Italian legal system has been operated by two government decrees upon mandate by Parliament: in February 1999 for electricity and in May 2000 for gas. It is opening the way to a profound restructuring of the two sectors, which was in any case necessary. The Energy Authority has been involved in the legislative process through hearings before parliamentary committees and consultation with government. Although this is part of its statutory remit, and the promotion of competition is clearly laid down in the law as one of its tasks, every time the Authority has publicly argued in favour of competition during a parliamentary debate on liberalization, its intervention has been taken by some opinion makers as evidence of a technical body unduly taking a political position and acting outside the boundaries of its statutory powers.

Raising the doubt that what is emerging from the present trend in energy liberalization is anything other than a competitive framework can be taken as an act of destructive criticism. Yet the question is a real one.

Competition is now beginning to operate, while largely dominant positions persist. Abuse of dominant positions is easy, and public officials have a duty to consider it as a real possibility. In principle, the abolition of legal monopolies should be followed by the abolition of price controls on the wholesale markets for electricity and gas: as a consequence, the competition authority, rather than the energy authority, should then take care of the price-setting mechanism. In the presence of persistent, largely dominant positions held by former monopolists, it is reasonable that some control be maintained and be eliminated only gradually. The possible instruments for such control are currently under scrutiny at the Energy Authority. Cooperation between the two authorities is very satisfactory, while their joint efforts in introducing a culture of competition are both desirable and necessary.

10.5. INDEPENDENT AUTHORITIES AND THE WORKING OF THE PUBLIC ADMINISTRATION

A number of new bodies, confusingly grouped under the same heading of *autorità indipendenti* or 'authorities' (the English word is often used), are being created in Italy, in an attempt to modernize the public administration and limit political interference in administrative processes. Among them are the regulating authorities for services 'of public utility', such as the Authority for Electricity and Gas and the Authority for Communications, including telecommunications and television. An intense debate is taking place around these new institutions.

The creation of the new authorities coincides with a crisis in the traditional state administration, owing to its low level of efficiency and to the present massive decentralization towards regional government on the one hand, and the transfer of powers to European institutions on the other. The authorities can be seen either as an attempt to experiment with new forms of public administration that can help in modernizing and reshaping the whole body public, or alternatively as further evidence of the distrust in which the traditional public administration is held, something that would increase the malaise experienced by public officials and exacerbate the decline of the existing institutions.

Working methods in the new authorities are generally better than those practised in traditional public offices: they include transparency, consultation papers, public hearings, flexible labour contracts, and strict independence criteria. We have been particularly keen on transparency and consultation, and this has been widely appreciated by operators and consumers alike. A careful approach to the demands of consumers is both required and appreciated in providing accurate information, responding to enquiries, and settling disputes. The difference with respect to ministerial offices is evident.

A reaction against the new authorities has been fed by a widespread fear that they may become privileged, politically unaccountable centres of power. Scores of conferences have been held on the subject and scores of articles written, mainly by legal experts and politicians, over the last three years. The central issue is well represented by the dilemma of Ulysses before the sirens: is it advisable for political representatives to tie their own hands and lend their powers to an independent body in order to set regulation free from their interference? Many believe that it is, but the actors in the drama do not seem to be fully aware of the powers they will be giving up when they make the decision, and will discover this, with dismay, only when the new independent body begins to make its own decisions.

10.6. EUROPEAN INTERDEPENDENCE AND COOPERATION

For liberalization to be possible in each country separately, the existing monopolistic enterprises would have to be broken down into many small competitors, something that might be economically unsound and is certainly politically unacceptable. At the same time, an effective unification of the national markets into one European market comes up against physical constraints in the capacity of existing networks for electricity and gas, the political and environmental difficulties of extending the networks, and the numerous legal obstacles to trade that have been created during decades of separation and are still maintained by persisting monopolistic positions in some countries, including non-EU countries like Switzerland.

Liberalization in each country is largely dependent on what neighbouring countries are doing. National interest may contest, and national pride will certainly oppose, any unilateral liberalization. When a national company can show that its expansion abroad is hindered by lack of access or entry possibilities, then granting foreign companies access to the domestic market becomes almost impossible on political and psychological grounds. Even if liberalization can be shown to be beneficial to consumers, it is seen as damaging to the country's interests, since it is opposed by producers: concentrated interests are always more vocal than diffused interests. Reciprocity clauses, which have been included in the European directives, are helpful, but only in part: they can be circumvented by aggressive firms operating through subsidiaries located in third countries.

Coordination is therefore necessary if liberalization is to proceed. It is wise not to leave this entirely to governments, particularly in countries where state-owned firms are influential in ministries, or traditional protectionist industrial policies are popular with ministerial bureaucracies. It may be that regulators, being new institutions created during periods of liberalization, are more immune to complicity with old incumbent firms. The recently created Council of European Energy Regulators reflects the regulators' will to organize European action in favour of coordinated liberalization.

An obstacle to coordination is the variety of legal frameworks in the various European countries. Regulators have different degrees of autonomy with respect to governments. In some countries, such as Germany, no regulator has been created. In such a context, it is difficult to establish common rules even where they are necessary, as in the case of cross-border exchanges.

Regulators see a common tariff for cross-border transmission of electricity as a necessary guarantee against any discrimination or barrier to trade: since a transmission tariff is usually, for technical reasons, largely independent of distance, the lack of common regulation would make an electricity supply contract from country A to country B across country C at least twice as expensive as a similar contract involving transmission within one country. The regulators' approach is to set up common tariff criteria: for example, one very simple criterion could be that only the purchaser of electricity should pay the transmission fee to the transmission system operator (TSO) providing the service, and the TSO should then share the revenue with all other TSOs involved, irrespective of their number.

An alternative approach is to leave such decisions to the TSOs, albeit within limits set by some framework agreement, as has been decided in Germany. Each TSO, or any group of TSOs, would set transmission tariffs, publish them, and be subject to inquiry by antitrust authorities only against possible discrimination. This would make regulators redundant and would lay most of the responsibility at the door of each country's antitrust body (such as the Bundeskartellamt) and of the competition directorate of the European Commission. My own feeling is that the regulators' approach is more equitable and practical; that it allows for timely prevention of monopolistic abuses, rather than relying on *ex post* repression; and that it does not involve a greater degree of bureaucratic interference with business than is strictly necessary.

An interesting case illustrating the need for coordination is the treatment of electricity imports into Italy. Imports account for 15 per cent of Italy's electricity consumption, and its interconnection capacity was utilized by Enel before liberalization. The Authority has been charged by law with the task of allocating the limited import capacity. Since about half the capacity is used for Enel's long-term contracts, the other half was available for the year 2000. The Authority has distributed this capacity among forty-four different contracts involving twenty-four operators, by limiting the amount allowed for each operator. For 2001 competitive bidding is to be introduced. There were no alternatives in 2000 to this one-sided allocation process, which should be replaced in future by a set of bilateral agreements with the neighbouring TSOs and regulatory institutions, thus opening up trade to all competitors, even when a vertically integrated company is in charge of the network. Agreements should also allow for free electricity trade between Italy and, say, Germany or other non-bordering countries.

All this requires the breaking of new ground, in an area where old habits of bilateral informal agreements between integrated monopolies have long prevailed; the enactment of the European directive provides a decisive help only in the cases of France and Austria, while it does not apply to Switzerland (where interconnections are most developed) and Slovenia.

10.7. A FINAL REMARK

A regulator in a previously monopolistic context is charged with very challenging tasks: to introduce competition and foster efficiency; to preserve public service obligations and protect consumers against a new profit-oriented attitude on the part of service providers; to help separate public from private interests where a tradition of state-owned enterprises and protectionist industrial policies has established strong and deeply-rooted ties between the two; to provide an example of a modern, skilfully operated, and reliable public office; to help set up common rules for European energy markets.

These tasks are highly technical in content, yet they are rich in ideals and significance. So they can be performed only if appropriate personnel selection procedures are followed, if employees are well led and the organization is well managed, if the workings of the board run smoothly, if the whole staff is pervaded with a common sense of purpose. These factors should not be taken for granted when setting up a regulator's office: they form an important part of the regulator's challenge.

11

The Electricity and Telecommunications Sectors in Spain: Rapid Change, Regulators at the Crossroads

NICOLAS CURIEN AND MICHEL MATHEU

11.1. INTRODUCTION

There is certainly no 'Latin' model of industrial organization and regulation of public services and networks. Spain provides proof of this, if proof were needed. It is a country where the postal monopoly is circumvented—in fact, there is no flat postal rate—where the electricity sector has long been very fragmented, where private operators already have a major presence in several sectors, and where, for some years, the government has been very quick to take measures to open up to competition—measures that go well beyond European requirements.

In view of these specific features, and some more, can we conclude that Spanish markets are rapidly moving towards a more northern European model, with very strong competition and fairly numerous private operators? A study of the electricity and telecommunications sectors—chosen in view of the scale of the changes they are undergoing—leads us to qualify this argument.

As we will see, there is definitely a real political will for reform in the various sectors. But the actual organization and the concrete form of regulation, which are the main issues discussed in this study, highlight limits. Clearly, the regulators are truly independent, in the sense that they have many guarantees over appointments and funding, but they are only consulted on major decisions. Many matters relating to public services and networks can be referred to the competition authority, namely the Competition Court, but the Court does not appear to have adequate resources to make effective rulings: it has very limited access to outside expertise and is highly dependent on the Ministry of Finance in terms of investigating individual cases. The monopoly has virtually ceased to exist, and the operators are private, but in both sectors studied a duopoly or a single dominant operator had succeeded in achieving an important position before competition was really introduced, which has considerably complicated the task of the regulators, who would like to see the market shares of these dominant players reduced.

11.2. REGULATION OF ELECTRICITY: A VERY LIBERAL LAW, BUT A STRONG DUOPOLY AND A RATHER TOOTHLESS REGULATOR

There are still strong barriers in the electricity sector. In recent decades the Spanish electricity system, which was very fragmented during the Franco era, has consolidated, without however establishing any strong connection to the continental electric grid. The 1997 Act opened up the market considerably, and the implementing decrees provide for a more rapid rate than that required in terms of the minimum legal thresholds. However, competitive practices do not appear to be increasing as rapidly as might be expected in view of the objectives announced by a government with liberal leanings. Nor is the fall in prices to consumers, including industrial consumers, great enough to put the country among the European leaders. The power of a private duopoly which is difficult to challenge and the relative weakness of the regulatory authorities—in that order—appear to be the two major reasons for this.

11.2.1. *The structure of the Spanish electricity market*

As far as the continental part of the country is concerned, the Spanish electricity system is constrained basically by the fact that the country is a peninsula. Interconnection with the European network is extremely limited: it is restricted to a link with France, which is now saturated, and the creation of a new link has come up against strong opposition from local inhabitants and ecological groups. In such conditions Spain cannot import competition from the neighbouring countries, as is possible for highly interconnected European countries located in the central part of Europe, i.e. most of the Continent except for Scandinavia, Eastern Europe, and the peninsulas.[1]

Total demand for electrical energy in Spain, including the island regions, was 182 TWh in 1998, which represents a comparatively low level of per capita consumption—roughly one and a half times lower than in comparable

---

[1] There is also a link with Portugal and Morocco, but this does not solve the problem of 'importing' competition: the Iberian peninsula as a whole has limited connections to the continental European grid which otherwise could be the source of significant flows.

European countries. In terms of *generation*, no single energy source has any significant edge on the others. In terms of *consumption*, the coal and nuclear segments—which supply basic energy—clearly prevail, with 35 per cent and 34 per cent respectively of the total in 1998. In terms of *installed capacity*, hydroelectric power predominates, but this source was used only at just over half of its maximum potential. It is worth noting that the national coal industry benefited, and still benefits, from significant public aid (Pta 50 billion in 1998, or the equivalent of about €300 million). Autoproducers supplied some 11 per cent of total electricity consumption in 1998. This represents a rapid increase, since their contribution was virtually nil up until 1989. Co-generation has also been growing rapidly, reaching 8 per cent in 1998. Spanish electricity has long been expensive: assuming a constant currency, the price hardly fell between 1982 and 1991. Between 1991 and 1999 there was a drop of just over 30 per cent, which was most marked since 1993. Between 1996 and 1998 Spain improved its European ranking for most categories of consumers. If we consider the standard basket of consumption by private and industrial users set by the International Energy Agency (IEA), the Spanish price to consumers was still the second highest in Europe in 1998. For industrial consumers, Spain was in the middle of the range, but only in the ante-penultimate position after adjustments for purchasing power parity.

In recent years, the Spanish electricity market has moved towards rapid concentration, resulting in the creation of a real duopoly. Initially, there were a very large number of generation and distribution companies, each with an operating area the size of an autonomous region, or smaller. With the backing of the government, which considered that this fragmentation was detrimental to the efficiency of the national electricity system, many new groups were created, centred on the two major companies, Endesa and Iberdrola. In late 1998,[2] the combined market share of the two main operators and their subsidiaries was 81 per cent, both in production—where Endesa had a clear edge—and distribution, where their shares were balanced.[3] A merge of the two operators of the duopoly was even being contemplated at the end of 2000. This vertically integrated organization based on a duopoly exacerbates the relative isolation of the Spanish electricity system, making it very difficult to bring about effective competition. The transmission system operator REE is far and away the major carrier on the Iberian peninsula: it owns 98 per cent of the extra-high-voltage 400 kV network, but only 27 per cent of the network for voltage below 220 kV.

[2] Most of the figures are taken from Comision Nacional del Sistema Eléctrico, *Información básica del sector eléctrico 1998*, CNSE Publication, 1999.
[3] Excluding the islands and Morocco, which account for about 5% of the country's total consumption. In the islands, integrated companies account for all generation, transmission, and distribution services.

11.2.2. The liberalization of the Spanish market

It was the Electricity Act of 28 November 1997 that paved the way for the liberalization of the Spanish electricity sector. This was supplemented by various decrees, most of them dating from 1998, which govern tariffs and regulation. The Hydrocarbons Act of 8 October 1998 indirectly involved electricity in so far as it led to the establishment of a single regulatory body for electricity, gas, and liquid hydrocarbons.

Prior to the 1997 Act, the Spanish electricity system was fragmented, but the companies involved were for the most part vertically integrated. From 1985, the operator REE (Réd Eléctrica de España—Electricity Network of Spain) was recognized as being responsible for managing the transport network, even though it did not own the whole network. An initial Act for liberalizing the sector was passed in 1994, but was not implemented. The government undertook negotiations with the electricity industry, and in 1996 it reached a draft agreement which formed the basis of the 1997 Act.

This Act created a new organizational model for the sector. It created a wholesale market, managed technically by a transmission system operator and financially by a market operator. It authorized a forward market. As well as the spot market, there are bilateral agreements. The competitive framework adopted for access to the network is that of regulated third-party access. Competitive areas are regulated by a licensing system. The implementation of the system was wound up in late 1998. In the last quarter of 1998, transactions carried out with eligible customers, who were still rather scarce, and dealers accounted for 6 per cent of the market.

The eligibility thresholds set by the Act are as follows: 15 GWh (or half of the ceiling set by the directive for 1999) from 1 January 1999, 9 GWh from 1 January 2000 (or the ceiling provided for by the directive for 2003), 5 GWh from 1 January 2002, and 1 GWh from 1 January 2004. Unless another Act is passed, all consumers must be eligible by 1 January 2007. In practice, the government is going ahead more rapidly, with a series of decrees. The threshold of 1 GWh was reached on 1 October 1999; this corresponds to 42 per cent of the market. Immediately after he was re-elected, the current prime minister announced that he intended to achieve universal eligibility by the end of his present term of office. The pace of liberalization is thus much faster than the minimum set by European legislation. In addition, production and distribution activities had to be separated by the end of 2000. Separate accounts were already required for regulated and unregulated activities.

Planning applies only to the field of transmission. A system of sunk costs is to be implemented for a maximum period of ten years. Finally, a system of special benefits applies for renewable energy and co-generation. The intention is to cut aid to the national coal industry, but without abolishing it entirely. Between now and 2004, aid should apply to no more than 15 per cent of total consumption, and it must be granted 'in keeping with the principle of fair competition', which could raise practical problems on which the Act does not elaborate.

11.2.3. *The regulatory system: institutional aspects*

Regulation is shared by the ministry responsible for energy, an independent body—currently the Comisión Nacional de Energía (CNE)[4] (National Energy Commission)—the autonomous regions,[5] and the body responsible for competition, the Tribunal de Defensa de la Competencia (Competition Court). As we will see, although the CNE is independent, the system provides for a large role to be played by the government.

The Commission includes nine full members, including the chairman, and a secretary who has a consultative role. The chairman and commissioners are appointed for a term of six years, and the terms of office of half of them are renewed every three years by Royal Decree, further to recommendation by the Ministry of Industry and after an opinion from the relevant parliamentary committee. They cannot be dismissed except in the event of misdemeanour, serious neglect of their duties, or the simultaneous pursuit of business interests which is forbidden. The minister or a high-level representative may request to take part in meetings when this is deemed necessary.

A very keen political debate surrounded the 1998 reforms. The members of the previous Commission, responsible solely for electricity, were appointed on a political basis. The seats were allocated to individuals with close links to the major parties in proportion to the importance of those parties. Seats on the CNE were officially allocated purely on the basis of know-how. The opposition parties lodged an unsuccessful complaint to the effect that the new arrangements were heavily biased in favour of the governing People's Party. It is worth noting that reports are often adopted on a simple majority basis. In 2000, it even happened that a proposition was rejected after the Chairman had voted with the minority.

Before the creation of the CNE, its predecessor responsible for electricity, the CNSE, had seventy-three salaried staff. Its funding was based on sales in the electricity sector (0.094 per cent of the total), which meant that in 1997 it had a budget of just under Pta 2 billion (€12.2 million).

The CNSE produced many valuable reports, using its own staff, since it was not able to outsource much work with the resources at its disposal. The dark part of the picture is that, according to the directors of the Commission, salaries in the electricity sector are significantly higher than those that the regulators

---

[4] Until the implementation of the 1998 Act, the scope of authority of the Commission, then called the Comisión Nacional del Sistema Eléctrico, was restricted to electricity.

[5] Which are charged with regulating electricity companies whose activities only cover their territory.

can offer, even though these themselves are considerably above the level of salaries in the state sector. As a result, turnover is very high: according to the directors of the Commission, it rose to 60 per cent in 1998.

The Commission's remit was extended to liquid and solid hydrocarbons as soon as it became necessary to have a law regulating competition in the gas sector. There does not appear to have been much debate on whether this extension was appropriate. For Spanish experts in the sector, the idea that it is necessary to regulate gas and electricity jointly, taking account of the overlap of their markets and production processes, is considered to be self-evident.

The CNE requires on a mandatory basis a considerable amount of accounting information, including information on transport and distribution costs, costs arising from obligations in respect of security of supplies, sunk costs, and supplementary costs for the island markets. It has access to information on costs borne by network and market managers. Most information is provided on a monthly basis.

In addition to the CNE, there are two consultative councils, in which major interests, including those of consumers, are represented. These councils are systematically consulted on many of the Commission's acts.

Decisions by the CNE are open to appeal before the Ministry of Industry, except for those concerning the settlement of disputes and documents (*circulares*), which require that the operators provide it with information necessary for the due exercise of its functions. In such cases, appeals are submitted to administrative tribunals.

11.2.4. *Regulating competition*

The government grants licences to the operators. The CNE is not able to issue opinions in this respect. The CNE is empowered to make suggestions or issue opinions in matters of implementing regulations pursuant to the Electricity Act and the planning of transmission infrastructures. Its only real powers involve the settlement of disputes relating to network access and the issuing of rules within the framework of decrees governing regulation. In addition, the Commission authorizes companies that exercise a regulated activity to take stakes in trading companies, subject—and we will come back to this later—to these being duly notified. It does not have real powers to impose penalties.

In theory, the Commission is responsible for ensuring a competitive framework for activities in the electricity sector. In practice, if it becomes aware of a breach of the competition rules, it must duly inform the department in control of competition at the Ministry of Finance, which is responsible for bringing action before the Competition Court. The Court is the real body in charge of competition. In practice, it is possible for one and the same matter to be considered by the two bodies.

The Commission was also consulted on the calculation of sunk costs. It issued an opinion, which was not taken up, against the calculation proposed by the government, which grants about Pta 2 billion (€12.2 million) a year in all—this amount will be reduced if the generation price of electricity does not fall below a specified threshold.

The decreases expected in terms of price correspond to the productivity gains that can be made by operators. The figures are comparatively modest, considering the rather high price of Spanish electricity: the basis for calculation is −1 per cent for the period 1999–2001, and this figure may be revised downwards if interest rates are low, if demand increases more rapidly than expected, or if repayments in respect of sunk costs do not fall.

Quality is controlled in accordance with regulations whose principles are set by the government, with the autonomous regions being responsible for applying the regulations. The quality criteria vary according to whether the area concerned is urban, suburban, or rural. The new law provides for consumers to be compensated in the event of failure to comply with quality standards. The parameters measured are the differences in theoretical voltages and an indicator of breakdowns in service.

11.2.5. *A system whereby competition is being introduced only gradually*

All in all, observers—including local observers—consider the Spanish system rather uncompetitive, and there are doubts about the possibility of making it more competitive in the short term. The regulator's powers seem to be rather limited, although it does seem to be truly independent. Essentially, it formulates proposals, but it does not set tariffs and its recommendations are by no means systematically implemented. In several cases it issued opinions that were not followed up and which were all more favourable to competition than the government's position. For instance, the CNSE was against the merger between Endesa and Sevillana, which gave the duopoly's competitors an excessive share. In practice, the regulator does not seem to have influence over mergers. According to the regulatory body's directors, the competing bodies often are not notified of proposed mergers, as they should be, and therefore the Commission is not consulted. When the regulator proposed an amount of sunk costs significantly lower than that adopted by the government, this aroused sharp criticism from other European electricity companies. For 1999, the regulator suggested a price-cap much lower than that adopted by the Ministry of Industry, an average fall of 5.8 per cent instead of 2.1 per cent. Its point of view did not hold sway, even though in its method of calculation it referred to the draft agreement signed with the industrial operators in the sector in 1996.

The other independent body, the Competition Court, also appears to be rather powerless. In particular, the Court is dependent on the Ministry of Finance, whose competition unit refers cases. According to specialist regulators and some experts, the Court is not sufficiently independent to fulfil this mission adequately. Its resources—in terms of both staff (fifteen people) and budget resources (about €1.5 million)—mean that in practice it hardly has the resources required to exercise its powers effectively. Only one person in the department knows about energy problems, and that person has other areas of responsibility. This results in considerable delays (sometimes up to a year) in bringing cases. There are additional delays in the appeal procedures with the Administrative Disputes Tribunal and the Supreme Court in the event of a further appeal. In addition, the government often shows excessive meddling, by bypassing the decisions of the Competition Court, particularly with a view to promoting sector consolidation. A new Competition Act should help to improve the situation, but, according to those involved, its major thrust will be to reduce delays in handling disputes, without supplying the human and material resources concomitant with its objectives.

In addition, the opinions of the Court may differ from those of the Electricity Commission, or even the ordinary courts. Admittedly, this does not worry those in charge. The chairman of the Court is certain that the unification of the criteria for fair competition will come from the authorities in Brussels and Luxembourg.

All in all, the liberalization of the Spanish electricity sector seems paradoxical. In some respects, it seems to have been far-reaching and rapid. As we have seen, the eligibility thresholds are advancing much more rapidly than required by Community legislation, and the objective is universal eligibility within less than six years, possibly less. Sophisticated markets are already up and running, and the system of a spot market linked to bilateral transactions opens up the range of possibilities. The regulatory Commission estimated that as soon as the end of 1999 total transactions effected on the wholesale market accounted for almost half the total opened up to competition.

But at the same time, the conditions for a rapid increase in competition do not appear to be in place. Few large customers have switched suppliers. At the time the Act came into effect, the Spanish electricity system was run almost entirely by a duopoly. Under these conditions, the effectiveness of opening up sales to important customers is questionable.

In practice, competition has to be mainly imported. The interconnection with France is not sufficient for this. It would have been possible for a company to take advantage of the gradual increase in electricity consumption in Spain to facilitate the entry of new operators; for instance, it might have been feasible for a large foreign operator to buy up one of the remaining small Spanish operators and gradually develop it. In the first quarter of 2000, however, the government opposed an attempt of this kind involving Hidrocantabrico, whose situation was not completely settled at the beginning of 2001.

In addition, in common with a large part of Europe, Spain has surplus installed capacity, so that the development of a third producer will not in any event be easy. The gas market is also very concentrated and relatively isolated from the rest of Europe, so that the path to competition using gas production is not very feasible either. In practice, the dominant operator—Gas Natural, linked to the Repsol oil company—cooperates with the two companies in the electricity duopoly, mainly at international level with one of them and mainly in Spain in the generation of electricity from gas with the other.

In short, it is not easy to bring about competition in a sector that has already been privatized and has powerful players. The method involving restructuring a sector while it is publicly owned and then partially privatizing it is certainly less onerous, but this did not apply in Spain. In view of the above, the directors of the regulatory Commission think it would have been better to follow the UK example: to oblige operators in the duopoly to sell off some of their assets to achieve a significant number of competing producers. The Spanish government decided otherwise.

Finally, things are proceeding as if some sort of compromise had been negotiated, which leaves room for competition, but slows its effects; there are low eligibility thresholds, improved tariffs but no excessive pressure on the existing producers, and high sunk costs which protect the Spanish operators. In the current situation, it will no doubt be difficult to obtain meaningful results in the short term. The private duopoly is powerful. On the other hand, the bodies responsible for competition and regulation both have limited resources and powers. The main question is: after a transition period making it possible, *inter alia*, to solve the problem of coal production, will the Spanish government come round to the view that the disadvantages of the duopoly outweigh its advantages?

11.3. REGULATION OF TELECOMMUNICATIONS: A POWERFUL PRIVATE OPERATOR AND REGULATION REQUIRING FURTHER ADJUSTMENT

Spain was initially one of the few countries for which the European Commission pushed back the deadline for opening up the telecommunications sector by five years, to 1 January 2003. With the change of government in 1996, this position was reviewed and the final date was brought forward to 1 December 1998, less than a year later than the 1 January 1998 deadline applicable to most member states. The new General Telecommunications Act (GTA) came into force in Spain on 24 April 1998, and the specific regulations for interconnection, dialling, universal service, and granting licences were implemented in the third quarter of 1998. Without waiting for the statutory deadlines, 'limited liberalization' was introduced between 1996 and 1998: two new fixed telephony operators, Retevision and Uni2 (Lince), and two new mobile operators, Airtel and Armena (Retevision), obtained licences during this preliminary period. In addition, in most regions cable network operators were authorized to offer combined telephony and cable television services.

Concomitant with this reform of the telecommunications sector, a new legislative framework was also set up for the audio-visual sector, including cable/satellite and land-based digital networks. This constitutes a regulatory field separate from that for telecommunications. However, there is an exception, concerning the provision of telephony service over cable networks on the one hand and the allocation of frequencies on the other, both of which are subject to the telecommunications legislation.

11.3.1. *The institutional framework of regulation*

In accordance with Article 67 of the GTA, the Minister of Public Works (*Ministerio de Fomento*) is responsible for submitting proposals on the policy for developing the public telecommunications service to the government. Within the Ministry, the General Secretariat for Communications drafts and proposes the regulatory standards governing the sector, including allocation of scarce resources—especially frequencies—and assessment of service quality. In the last governmental change, the General Secretariat was extended as a new Secretariat in charge of both telecommunications and information technologies and was transferred from the Ministry of Public Works to the Ministry of Science and Technology (*Ministerio di Ciencia y Technología*). In parallel, a Telecommunications Consultative Council, chaired by the Minister of Public Works, has been set up: this examines all draft laws and decrees issued by the Ministry and can also issue advices spontaneously, following an internal referral procedure. The members of the Council are appointed by the government and include representatives of users, service providers, equipment producers and suppliers, unions, and the government.

Exactly one year after the promulgation of the GTA, on 24 April 1997, an initial Act on the liberalization of telecommunications led to the setting up of an independent regulatory body, the Telecommunications Market Commission (*Comisión del Mercado de las Telecomunicaciones*, CMT). The powers of the CMT are set out in a ministerial decree dated 9 April 1997; they apply both to the telecommunications and audio-visual sectors, apart from the regulation of information contents. The stated objectives are to provide and maintain the conditions for effective competition in the telecommunications markets, to control 'fair' price-setting, and to mediate disputes between network or service operators. To achieve its objectives, the powers of the regulatory Commission comprise:

- granting licences and authorizations, with the notable exception of the most important licences and those involving frequencies (mobile networks and local radio loops) that are subject to public tender and government decision;
- assigning numbers and managing the numbering system;
- monitoring the public service obligations and their funding;

- determining the technical and tariff conditions and settling disputes between operators over interconnection of networks;
- promoting and maintaining competition by means of resolutive decisions, with the proviso that regulation of the retail prices of Telefónica, the incumbent operator, remains the prerogative of the government, as does authorizing new services for which the legislative and regulatory framework is not yet in place.

The CMT has to submit a report to the government every year, and this report is also presented to Parliament. It employs about sixty people and is managed by a board, comprising a chairman and vice chairman appointed by the government and six other members appointed by the Minister of Science and Technology. Appointments are submitted to Parliament for ratification, and the six-year mandate can only be renewed once. In theory, the decisions of the CMT can be revised only by the government and appeals are brought before the Administrative Disputes Tribunal (*Tribunal di Contenzio Admistrativo*).

Although at first sight the CMT's institutional characteristics appear to guarantee its independence from industry and the government, there is still some concern as to the possibility of 'capture', considering that on the one hand the present chairman of the Commission comes from the dominant company, Telefónica, and on the other hand that a former director general from the Ministry is a member of the board. In addition, the role of the CMT is often considerably reduced in practice by the fact that the government retains substantial regulatory powers—particularly regarding licences and frequency allocation—that the ministerial departments themselves are submitting many cases, and that they even gather and directly process some complainants' claims. Seen *ex post*, these practices may originate from the fact that the creation of an independent sector regulatory body in Spain was not considered *ex ante* to be self-evident, since the state, which held only a minority stake in the incumbent company Telefónica, sold off that stake before the market was opened up.

In the absence of political debate and a ruling on the issue of clearly defining the respective fields of regulation and implementation of competition law, the tasks of market control are shared *de facto* by the CMT and the antitrust body, the *Tribunal de Defensa de la Competencia*. This court, which comes under the auspices of the Minister of Finance and Economic Affairs, submits an annual report to the government on the state of competition in various economic sectors, and issues judgments to settle competition disputes from private industry. As concerns telecommunications services, the market players can refer directly to the Competition Court, except in the event of disputes over interconnection. These fall under the sole jurisdiction of the CMT, which must give a ruling within three months. As has been observed before, the Competition Court is not as independent and influent as many of its European counterparts.

The final body for institutional regulatory mechanisms, an interministerial Committee for Price Control (which arose from the inter-ministerial Commission of Economic Affairs), is responsible for submitting proposals on all regulated prices, including those relating to the tariffs of the dominant operator in the telecommunications sector.

11.3.2. *State of the market*

The Spanish telecommunications market is an exception in Europe, in so far as services have always been provided by a mainly privately owned company—Telefónica—and not by the public sector. This feature has probably boosted the process of adapting the sector to European requirements in respect of liberalization. However, prior to liberalization, the state was a minority shareholder, with a right of veto ('golden share') on strategic decisions by the company, and Telefónica still operated under a framework agreement drafted in 1991. Only recently has Telefónica been fully privatized, in order to adapt to the new open environment.

The incumbent operator has an ambitious strategy of acquisitions and alliances and has taken significant stakes in the telecommunications sector in Venezuela, Chile, Argentina, Peru, Brazil, and Puerto Rico. In 1998 the company posted sales growth of 20 per cent and earnings growth of 14.5 per cent; its shares rose by 52 per cent. Most of this growth was due to the company's expansion in Latin America and on the mobile telephony market.

As for Retevision, it was created in 1989 to transmit the television signals of the two public channels and three national private channels. It is a private company, with a minority public shareholder base. In the pre-liberalization phase the government chose Retevision to become the second national telecommunications operator. This decision was enacted pursuant to the decree law on the liberalization of telecommunications of 6 June 1996, whereby this company obtained a licence enabling it to provide telecommunications services, including voice telephony. Finally, the Lince consortium, in which France Telecom is the major shareholder, obtained (under the name Uni2) the third fixed operator licence in 1998. It was the only bidder on this occasion. The fixed telephony market is still very asymmetrical today, with Telefónica's market share standing at around 90 per cent.

In the mobile telephony market, Telefónica has been using analogue cellular networks since 1988. Since 1992 the company has offered the Movistar mobile phone service and this makes it the leading mobile operator operating under public contract. Having won a tender, the Airtel consortium, comprising Banco de Santander, Airtouch International, and BT (British Telecom), became the second mobile operator on 29 December 1994. Finally, the third mobile licence, using DCS-1800 technology, was allocated to Retevision in 1998 under the brandname Armena. Like the fixed telephony market, the mobile telephony market is asymmetrical. In 1999, Movistar had a market share of 63 per cent, compared with Airtel's 34 per cent and Armena's 3 per cent.

The liberalization of the cable television segment started in January 1996. The process of choosing the successful applicants for the regional tenders is virtually complete. The result is a concentration centred on two large companies, Retevision and Cableuropa. Prior to the deadline of 1 December 1998, cable operators were authorized to offer fixed telephony services; this authorization was counterbalanced by obligations in terms of levels of investment. Telecommunications companies that have entered the market after this deadline are not subject to the same obligations, but nor do they have the commercial advantage resulting from a bundled offer of 'cable and phone'.

Finally, as concerns data transmission, BT Telecommunicaciones, the first of sixteen operators that have obtained an operating licence since liberalization in 1993, remains the only real alternative on the market. Since 1996, this company has also offered a telephony service to closed user groups (CUGs), a segment in which liberalization started in 1995.

11.3.3. *The state of regulation*

Although the independent regulator has been in place since 1997, some major aspects of regulation are still in government hands (the Ministry of Science and Technology), in particular with regard to granting major licences and allocating frequencies. This has the effect of creating a certain amount of confusion, exacerbated by a lack of transparency. In addition, although several recent decisions by the CMT have revealed a clear wish to introduce effective competition in Spanish telecommunications, there are still major efforts to be made, and it will be necessary to take a more proactive stance in order to offset the dominant position of the incumbent operator.

Telefónica's offer of interconnection (RIO) was published in October 1998 and is now accessible to all licence-holders. Tariffs comply with the recommendations of the European Commission and the pre-selection of the long-distance operator is already available, but the range of services has not yet been fully defined. In respect of transferability of numbers, Spain is rather advanced compared with the European average, since the CMT has made the service available as from 2000: after consultations with operators in the first quarter of 1999, the Commission submitted a draft to the parties concerned and the operators reached a consensus in respect of technical specifications as well as a compromise between divergent views on the procedures to be adopted, and on the extent to which the Commission should be involved in managing and funding the entity that will administer the reference database. Finally, although the law explicitly provides for the requirement of transparency and separate accounts for the incumbent operator, Telefónica, and although the CMT has shown an unequivocal wish to impose this, methodological problems remain and there is still a considerable gap between theory and practice.

Universal service includes basic telephony and slow-speed (less than 32 Kbit/s) data transmission services. For the year 1999 the net cost of this service has been assessed at some Pta 30 billion (nearly €200 million), or almost 3 per cent of Telefónica's turnover, but no funding system has yet been set up. The monthly subscription is an 'affordable' Pta 1,200 (about €8). This has not given rise, as was the case in France, to increased subscription charges to offset lower call costs. The subscription fee is reduced to Pta 700 for senior citizens.

Regarding *the allocation of licences*, the General Act's promulgating decree provides for three standard categories of licence: licence A for service providers not operating their own network, licence B for service providers operating their own infrastructure, and licence C for network operators not providing services themselves. At the end of 1999, 60 type A, 20 type B, and 500 type C licences had been allocated. Although the law allows market newcomers to set up their own infrastructures without restrictions, two major problems have emerged in practice. On the one hand, permits for civil engineering works are granted by the municipal authorities only after a long, arduous procedure. On the other hand, no clear, transparent rule was stipulated at the outset that operators should share the infrastructure. However, there have been developments in this respect, since a Royal Decree of 22 February 1999, supplementing a decree-law of 27 February 1998, stipulates the technical standards which the joint telecommunications infrastructures inside buildings have to meet in order to open these up in a competitive way to telephone and cable television operators.

As in all European countries, the unbundling of *the local loop*, the monopoly's last line of defence, is an extremely sensitive issue. A ministerial order of 26 March 1999 regulates the deployment of the high-speed ADSL (Asymmetric Digital Subscriber Line) technology in Telefónica's local loops. This technology is limited to internet access, excluding voice telephony, and three modes have to be made available throughout the country, with the highest speed offered being 2Mb/s. Data flows coming from the ADSL loops are channelled through a network using ATM (Asynchronous Transfer Mode) technology to a hundred or so points of transfer to which the access providers (NSPs) and service providers (ISPs) can be interconnected. NSPs and ISPs are billed at flat-rate charges—that is, charges which do not depend on the volume of traffic. Modems have to be supplied by the NSPs and ISPs in accordance with specifications which have to be made public, and the extension of the public network to all local automatic switching machines has to be achieved by the end of 2001.

These measures have brought mixed reactions. On the one hand, cable operators denounce them as not complying with the moratorium imposed on Telefónica in respect of cable television and are demanding that this moratorium be extended for five years. On the other hand, global or long-distance operators think that the measure poses—in relation to competition law—a dual problem of bundled offers: on the one hand, an access network (ADSL) with a transport network (ATM), and on the other hand, a voice service linked with a data transmission service. In addition, these operators consider that the projected service quality for the ATM network is not adequate and thus is likely to put up barriers to entry to the markets in those services that are most demanding in terms of speed, such as voice under IP internet protocol, or video on demand.

To conclude, the two sectors reviewed above are obviously different, from both a technical and an economic point of view. Both systems of regulation, however, may be considered relatively weak, and the introduction of competition in both cases seems to be hampered by the strength of former public companies or by mergers supported by the government itself.

Is the current period one of transition towards a more competitive industrial organization and more powerful regulation, in terms of human and financial resources, and in terms of decision-making powers? It would be rather premature to suggest an answer to that question during this period of very rapid development in Spain.

12

The Spanish Experience of
Regulation within the
Telecommunications Sector

JOSÉ MARIA VAZQUEZ QUINTANA

12.1. INTRODUCTION

The change of government that occurred in Spain in 1996 was the occasion
for a revision of Spanish telecommunications liberalization plans. At that
time there was a clear awareness of the imbalances affecting the telecommunications market, which was then a monopoly, and of the time and effort that
would be needed to correct them and transform the market into a competitive
structure.

The difficulties encountered in liberalizing the market were of two orders,
one legal and one economic. From a legal perspective, designing a new regulatory framework that relied on free market enterprise rather than public service had far-reaching implications. The telecommunications system in
Spain had up to then been enmeshed in the Spanish legal system, with references and links to a large number of legal instruments. Reform entailed
calling into question constitutional principles and statutory rights with regard
to local government. Therefore a number of legal changes were going to be
necessary and these would involve complex issues in terms of legal techniques
and the way local authorities were to be empowered to make use of the new
regulatory tools.

From the economic point of view, the most onerous imbalances concerned
the lack of harmonization between prices and costs. In the monopolistic telecommunications market, integrated both vertically and horizontally, it was
sufficient for prices to cover total costs incurred by the monopolist. In a
competitive setup this market structure could not be maintained, because it
would force each new entrant to produce an equally integrated offer from its
own resources. But competitors are operating in different segments of the
market; this forces the incumbent to segment its value chain, as it is required to
provide the missing links in the value chain which entrants are not (yet) prepared to uphold with their own resources. It therefore follows that the existing

harmony between prices and costs of service provision would need to be replicated at the level of each link in the value chain.

A number of these links are defined before competitors identify them; this applies to links identified in the Reference Interconnection Offers of the incumbents. For instance, local, single, or double transit interconnection are identified in all EU countries as partial services which any new entrant may claim from the incumbent, at prices that are oriented to the production costs of the segment of the complete service. Identification of the value chain segments to be made available to new operators, and preparation of the technical installations necessary for effective operations, take some time. Moreover, it is usually difficult to obtain data from the old accounting system of the incumbent that adequately reflect the costs of the new segments.

Once technical difficulties have been resolved and prices for each segment have been decided on, in cases where only transference prices between operators (the interconnection prices) are affected, application is immediate. However, some of these segments may correspond to services that, in addition to be being provided among operators, also appear in the end market between an operator and one of its clients.

This is the case regarding access to the local loop, where the distribution of the overall balance that insures equilibrium in each of the segments of the value chain has a direct effect on end-user prices, for instance through the monthly subscription rate for voice telephony. Inertia immediately appears rooted in the population's reluctance to acknowledge the need for price increases of some services or the introduction of new tariff concepts, precisely when considerable reductions in prices were the promised and expected benefits of liberalization. This social inertia entails dedicating time to the process of tariff rebalancing in the local loop, which, until achieved, disturbs the balance of other segments.

In accordance with EU legislation, Spain is one of a number of countries that were granted a five-year derogation period, until 2003, to implement the necessary modifications before fully liberalizing its telecommunications market. In 1996 however the situation in Spain was re-examined and it was decided that liberalization would take place as soon as possible.

Once the possibilities of reformulating and developing the legal framework had been analysed, it was decided that the date for opening the market to competition should be 1 December 1998, which meant speeding up the process by more than four years. It was decided that, while the new legal framework was being designed, it would be a good idea to introduce a limited amount of competition, by opening some gaps in the pre-existing legal structure. In the interim, therefore, two new fixed voice telephony operators were allowed to enter the market and compete with Telefónica. In addition, licences were granted to cable operators through different bidding procedures at the regional level, across most of the country. These licences were for voice telephony, television, and other services that could be provided over the broad-band networks that all licensees were committed to deploy.

The aim of this policy was to anticipate full competition and familiarize users with its benefits. The intention was also to use this time lapse to encourage the deployment of alternative infrastructure to provide information society services. As part of this initial set of measures, the Comision del Mercado de las Telecomunicaciones (CMT) was established as the independent regulator to safeguard effective competition within the communications market. Until then, the powers allocated to the CMT had been governmental powers.

The exercise of CMT powers is subject to the same jurisdictional revision as affects government resolutions. In enforcing regulation, CMT is subject to similar judicial review (or appeal procedures) as is government. Appeal against CMT decisions is made to the Contentious Administrative Judges, as for government resolutions; hence the CMT criteria for reaching decisions will be very much structured by that body and will not necessarily be in line with criteria that would have the government's preference (or orientation).

12.2. INSTITUTIONAL POSITION OF THE TELECOMMUNICATIONS REGULATORY AUTHORITY

Against the general background given above, it is now possible to explain the institutional position of the Spanish regulator.

European directives have provided the National Regulators Authorities (NRAs) with straightforward independence. However, this independence applies mainly to the bodies that developed the telephone monopoly, particularly in those European countries where such bodies were a part of the civil service and thus depended directly on the government.

In some countries the condition of independence is understood to be automatically satisfied through privatization because the responsibility for telecommunications operations has been separated from the government, even if regulation activities have not. It is not infrequent to see such NRAs depending directly on the government without this being regarded as compromising their independence. In Spain, however, Telefónica, the monopolist, was a private company in which the state had a minority share, which it gave up before liberalization. It could have been acceptable for the CMT to belong to the institutional structure of a ministry, in the same way as the Tribunal de Defensa de la Competencia (the Spanish Competitive Authority) does. However, it was decided to reinforce the independent character of the CMT by creating a body with its own budget, and directed by a board appointed by the government, members of which cannot be removed for six years. This board is composed of nine independent individuals of recognized prestige in the sector. For the sake of transparency, the government is required to present names to Parliament during the selection process for members of the board.

The CMT makes its own decisions, which the government may not revise under any circumstance. The appeals are to be presented directly before the courts. The CMT enjoys economic independence, which reinforces its immunity from government interference. The board has a mandate to ensure independence of criteria. This is not only welcomed by the board members, but also demanded by the courts, which back very strongly the exercise of that freedom. Other sector-specific regulators do not share the characteristics of the CMT since such independence was not required to regulate markets that had already been organized. Thus, for instance, the enforcement of horizontal competition laws need not necessarily be achieved without government criteria; indeed, government criteria are sometimes applied explicitly, as for the regulation of mergers and acquisitions.

Conflicts might arise between these two distinct institutional models, since the horizontal regulation of competition is bound to be more and more applicable to the emerging telecommunications markets. Gradually, the monopolistic structure could evolve towards a market driven by competition.

The European Union aims at a halfway house between both types of regulation, and this could lead to cases where different regulatory bodies intervene, bodies maintaining different types of institutional independence from their governments. In theory, one would witness the weakening of NRAs, which by nature operate according to independent criteria, in favour of regulatory authorities that are institutionally more dependent on government criteria.

The Spanish Competition Authority, although answerable to the government, has so far made decisions according to independent criteria, but this has been due to a strong commitment on the part of the Spanish government rather than to the invulnerability of the institutional model.

12.3. REGULATORY PROCEDURES

The regulatory process in Spain, as in other countries, is two-fold, consisting of:

1. the establishment of rules governing the behaviour of the competitors in the market; in Spanish terminology this function is called '*reglamentación*';
2. the enforcement of these rules, or '*regulación*' in Spanish.

Before the establishment of the CMT, both processes were the government's responsibility and no special efforts for clarification between them was deemed necessary. Since the establishment of the CMT, there has been a relatively clear distinction between its own competences, mainly as regards the application of the rules (*regulación*), and those pertaining to the government. However, there are several exceptions, which can be classified in three categories.

1. *Regulatory functions* (in the sense of *regulación*): these are reserved for the government when market entry is limited by scarce resources and full effective competition cannot be expected.
2. *Regulatory activities* (in the sense of *regulación*): these are maintained within the sphere of government responsibilities for the period of transition from monopoly to competition. These regulatory activities are carried out under national political criteria related to special sensitive aspects, and they

include the transitory regulation of retail prices applied by Telefónica or the provisional authorizations for the development of new services for which the government has not yet established the appropriate rule.
3. *Regulatory functions* (in the sense of *reglamentación*): these functions, reserved for the CMT, allow it to instruct the market on its criteria when applying general rules in repetitive situations.

The stable division of work between the legislator and the regulator does not create excessive administrative difficulties in most European countries; however, the diversity of practice across these countries should be acknowledged, as it may disconcert entrants.

In Spain, all the authorizations or licences providing telecommunications services are granted by the CMT, with the exception of those corresponding to services that make use of scarce resources—such as the radio frequency spectrum—which are granted by the government. Specifically, this refers to mobile licences.

As regards exceptions of a transitory nature, the regulation of Telefónica prices is bound to disappear, but the exception concerning authorizations for new services, so far non-regulated, may remain for a time.

In an attempt to present the regulatory setting for the Spanish market in broad terms, the final goal to be envisaged would be the establishment of a clear division between the rule-making competence of the government and its responsibilities in the implementation of those rules with the CMT. The implementation of rules includes the licensing of telecommunications services.

The administration of the spectrum of radio frequencies remains a government responsibility. This includes the concession of portions of this spectrum to would-be operators. The allocation of radio frequencies, which includes the licence to provide a service and the conditions imposed on its position when such a service requires the allocation of spectrum, remain the responsibility of the government. This includes mobile telecommunications services of home access to information services using a wireless local loop. The provisional authorization necessary to provide such services for which the government has not yet established the necessary rules remains the responsibility of the government, which will also assume the development of all relevant legislation applicable to the new situation. On the other hand, the CMT grants all other types of licence and authorization, and administrates all resources that are not naturally limited (including the administration of the National Numbering Plan). Moreover, the CMT may anticipate general rules of behaviour in the competitive market to avoid having to position itself repetitively on a case-by-case basis in identical situations.

At present, in Spain the government retains a number of transitory functions aimed at controlling and weakening possible anti-competitive behaviour in an insufficiently established competitive market. These transitory aspects, which mostly affect price regulation, were recently allocated to a ministry different from the one whose responsibility is to develop sector-specific rules. This has clarified the distribution of responsibilities among the different regulatory units. The legislative development remains the responsibility of the Ministry of Science and Technology, the responsibility of direct intervention in the market, that of the Finance Ministry. Finally, there is some degree of convergence between authorities applying general competition laws and the sector-specific regulators, although each has set its own independent character.

12.4. RESULTS AFTER A FIRST STAGE OF LIBERALIZATION

The first competitors to break into the Spanish telecommunications market before the new legal framework was established were favoured with special conditions which also entailed some obligations, including certain investment commitments.

New entrants encounter a very favourable situation, because the new regime only requires them to ensure the inter-operability of services or contribute to the obligations of Universal Service, allowing them complete freedom to decide on the necessary investments, the time frames, and their activities. Moreover, the Reference Interconnection Offer requires Telefónica to provide for any need new entrants may have in order for them to put together an attractive offer for their clients.

Some aspects of regulation that were considered minor in other countries, such as carrier pre-selection or number portability, have become extremely important in Spain for new entrants. This indicates that some major difficulties that have arisen during the process of liberalization in more advanced countries have hardly appeared in Spain, while relatively secondary aspects represent some of the major requests from new entrants. Severe difficulties were encountered, including the creation, financing, and maintenance of the administrative structure and technical systems to implement number portability and carrier pre-selection facilities. Spain intends to adopt long-lasting solutions, which have ruled out some relatively temporary technical solutions (in terms of liberalization) adopted in more advanced countries.

Up to now, we have identified interconnection, number portability, and carrier pre-selection as the main concerns and requests of new operators, to be addressed with sector-specific regulation. Another concern is granting rights of way through the public estate. The public estate is governed by law and regulations whose primary objective is not to foster new competitive entry into telecommunications. Therefore, this law and its regulations apply equally to operators in the telecoms sector and to any other agent that is entitled to a right of way.

Most new entrants have placed themselves in niches where they have identified potentially larger and faster-growing revenues and lower fixed and variable costs. To that end, they have identified segments of the integrated value chain with the larger price–cost balances. As a result, tensions appear in the process of establishing the price–cost balance in each segment, in order to break vertical integration.

Some new entrants have instead chosen market niches characterized by the category of clients, generally large business consumers who recognize the value of high-quality communication. These operators are normally involved in all stages of production of the telecommunications service they provide, and ensure a higher quality of the product.

Finally, operators that were granted licences under conditions of investment commitments, and other obligations are still in the market. This includes mobile operators and cable network operators, who received a licence to operate within a specific region under a duopoly regime in competition with Telefónica. These bodies are developing their activities in compliance with their investment commitments, and they are concerned about the risk posed by other operators entering the market under the new liberalized regime, which no longer imposes the previous heavy obligations. It was somewhat understandable that the government, promoter at the time of a licensing system based on balanced rights and obligations, should feel inclined to protect the incumbents from the effects of competition until all operators were on an equal footing. Hence those cable network operators were granted the opportunity to provide a bundle of telecommunications services and television transmission services which, as broadcasting services, still retain their public service characteristics and are not yet liberalized.

Since this is the case, those operators who wanted to compete with the cable telecommunications operators could deploy networks as they saw fit, instead of meeting the obligations fulfilled by the latter. However, the advantage is offset by the difficulty of offering the same package of services on the market.

As for the mobile communications operators, their vulnerability would derive from the right of access of potential competitors to their infrastructure, according to the same rules as those governing the interconnection to local networks of dominant fixed voice telephony operators. This existing protection of business widened with investment commitments is not specific to Spain, but applies in principle across all EU countries, with rare exceptions. The Spanish case may stand out because this principle is applied to cable network operators providing telecommunications services, a rare occurrence in the EU.

As a consequence of all the above, general public fixed voice telephony offers proliferate, owing more to the decrease in prices of long distance communications than to the provision of new or higher-quality services. When facilities such as carrier pre-selection or number portability appear, customers have to select one operator. This results in a diversity of offers which creates an initial confusion, not uncommon in the aftermath of such a significant change in the market model.

So far, the Spanish market has not encountered in an acute manner any of the greatest inconveniences that were experienced in other countries for example, citizens have not been tricked into making undesired consumption commitments, though one should keep in mind that, as competitive pressure increases, some incidents of this kind may occur.

An overview of the Spanish market with regard to the number of operators, market shares, and the development of the market as a whole is presented in Tables 12.1–12.6.

Table 12.1. *Status of Implementation of Carrier Pre-selection in Spain*

	No. of telephone lines requesting carrier pre-selection		
	Requested	Granted	Rejected
11 March 2000	45,065	25,555	16,319
9 April 2000	99,986	68,020	26,000
22 April 2000	138,419	81,732	35,248

Table 12.2. *The Spanish Telecommunications Sector: Revenues, 1999*

	Revenues for retail services and retail income	
	pta m	€m
Sector revenues	3,019,188	18,146
Fixed telephony	1,362,560	8,189
Mobile telephony	717,359	4,311
Audio-visual services	553,417	3,326
Others (including leased lines, corporate communications, internet access, satellite, data transmission, and TV broadcasting networks)	385,852	2,319
Revenues per capital	76,594	460
Revenues over GIP	3%	—
Income (net values)	(49,105)	(295)
Mobile telephony	79,247.951	476
Fixed telephony and other	(128,353.908)	(771)
Total revenues for the sector (including retail market and intermediate market)	3,500,000	21,035

Table 12.2. *(Continued)*

	Revenues for retail services and retail income	
	pta m	€m
Investment	1,027,992	6,178
Fixed voice telephony, data transmission, and corporate communications	534,556	3,213
Mobile telephony	339,237	2,039
Cable TV network operators (contents not included)	123,359	741
Investment per capita	26,079	157
Employment (workers)	88,033	—

Table 12.3. *Variation in the Spanish Telecommunications Sector, 1998–1999*

	1999	Variation, 1998–9 (%)
No. of fixed lines installed (m)	17.6	—
No. of users with direct access (m)	16.7	2.6
No. of users using carrier selection codes (m)	3.6	—
Penetration rate for fixed telephony (direct access) (%)	42.98	2.45
No. of net mobile connections (m)	15	133
Penetration rates mobile telephony (%)	37.65	21.3 per person

Table 12.4. *Market Share of Fixed Voice Telephony Operators in Spain, 1999*

Operator	Share of total operations revenues (%)	Share of long distance revenues (%)
Telefónica de España	94.34	90
Retevisión	3.06	5.73
Lince	1.09	1.82
Euskaltel	0.51	1.01
Jazz Telecom	0.28	0.48
Comunitel	0.17	0.13
RSL Com	0.15	0.28
Rest	0.4	0.55

Table 12.5. *Market Share of Mobile Voice Telephony Operators in Spain, 1999*

Operator	Share of total operations revenues (%)
Telefónica Servicios Móviles	63.11
Airtel	33.88
Amena	3.01

Table 12.6. *Telecommunications Licences Granted in Spain, 1999*

	Existing at 31/12/98	Granted during 1999	Converted or revoked	Existing at 31/12/99	Existing at 31/3/2000	Existing at 30/4/2000
Individual licences						
Type A	3	20	1	22	24	26
Type B1	6	26	—	32	34	35
Type B2	2	—	—	2	2	2
Type C1	1	7	—	8	10	10
Type C2	—	3	—	3	3	3
General authorizations						
Type A	24	35	1	58	59	59
Type B	—	18	—	18	18	18
Type C	127	291	2	416	452	482
Cable TV network licences						
Provisional	432	—	64	368	368	368
Ex Lege	210	—	27	183	183	183
Special	5	4	—	9	9	9
Authorizations for satellite TV services						
TV conditional access services	2	0	—	2	2	2
Broadcasting services without network	3	2	—	5	5	5

13

Contrasts in Germany: Decentralization, Self-regulation, and Sector-specific Regulators

KATHARINA GASSNER

13.1. INTRODUCTION

This chapter offers an overview of the recent liberalization of three German network utilities and the regulatory framework established in these industries. Legal, structural, and institutional changes that have been implemented in the past few years in telecommunications, electricity, and railway services are surveyed, and the success of introducing competition into these industries is evaluated.

The introduction of competition into Germany's network utilities is part of the overall European effort to open up these industries with a view to creating a single European market. However, apart from its obvious size, Germany displays a number of characteristics that make it stand out among the European countries. This paper discusses in some detail the unusual decentralized approach that has been adopted in the reform of both the electricity and the rail industry. Unlike the integrated, monopolistic markets that are observed in many European network industries, these two German industries display a fragmented structure with a relatively large number of companies. Because of this particular initial setting, the regulatory regimes that have been established differ in their design from regimes in place in other countries.

The German case illustrates that the common economic principles underlying the introduction of competition into utility networks, such as non-discriminatory access to the monopoly network, or price regulation, coexist with and are adapted to idiosyncratic national environments. In particular, in the German electricity sector the presence of numerous companies has led to a regulatory framework relying more on self-regulation than on structural

Initial work on this chapter took place at the London School of Economics and the Université de Lausanne. Major revisions and updates were necessary at a later stage when I was employed by Oxford Economic Research Associates (OXERA). I gratefully acknowledge the company's support of this project; however, the views expressed are my own and are not attributable to OXERA.

reform. In the railways sector, the regulatory institutions in place reflect the strong regional and local element present in German public transports. So far, an independent, sector-specific regulator, modelled after the British example, has been set up only for Germany's telecommunications and postal markets.

The idea of this contribution is to survey the multiple changes that have occurred in Germany's utility industries in the recent past, to highlight national characteristics, and to draw attention to remaining structural problems. Its goal is not to explore in great depth any particular issue, but rather to give an impression of the variables that shape the way in which German network utilities have been liberalized.

In spite of this objective, an important aspect of recent German developments has largely been omitted from discussion. Complexity has been added to regulatory reform by the impact of reunification. The costs of this act, and the associated task of rebuilding the utility networks in the former German Democratic Republic (GDR), were considered by some a reason to request an exceptional status for Germany in the European liberalization efforts. Germany's policy-makers mostly resisted these calls and went ahead with their liberalization agenda, while allocating additional public funds to infrastructure investments and granting transitory exceptions, for instance in the case of mandatory third-party access to the electricity grid of the new *Länder*. None the less, the debate surrounding the appropriate treatment of undertakings with substantial investments in the new *Länder* illustrates conflicting regulatory priorities. The introduction of competition needed to be balanced against the protection of investment incentives, as well as against social and political objectives often linked to employment issues. The issues raised go beyond the remit of this paper and are not treated here.

The remainder of this chapter is structured as follows. In the next section, the main market characteristics as well as recent liberalization measures are surveyed for each of the three utilities, electricity, rail, and telecommunications. The subject of Section 13.3 is the regulatory framework that has been set up in the three sectors. Section 13.4 provides an account of how the three markets have developed since the introduction of competition, and Section 13.5 evaluates the success and potential pitfalls of the reforms. Section 13.6 concludes.

13.2. MARKET STRUCTURE AND LIBERALIZATION

13.2.1. *Electricity*

Industry Structure

Germany's electricity supply industry (ESI) possesses, for historic reasons, a decentralized structure which results in a large number of companies on the market.[1] Among the nearly 1,000 German electricity utilities, three different

---

[1] A summary account of the history of the German electricity industry is found in Müller and Stahl (1996). For more detailed discussions regarding the industry structure, see also Sturm and Wilks (1997) and IEA (1997).

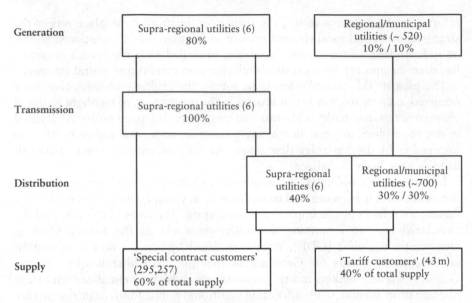

Figure 13.1. *Structure of the German electricity supply industry*
Source: Schulz (1996), updated by the author: VDEW(1998) and IEA(1997).
Note: Percentages represent market shares.

groups can be identified. These are distinguished by size and by different core-activities; however, all are vertically integrated. Figure 13.1 gives a schematic overview of the industry structure.

Until two recent mergers, there were eight *supra-regional* utilities, which generated between them 80 per cent of total electricity production. In June 2000, the mergers between the second and third largest of the eight utilities, VEBA and VIAG, and the largest and fourth largest, RWE and VEW, were approved by the European Commission (EC) and the Federal Cartel Office (FCO), the German competition authorities.

The supra-regional utilities are also solely responsible for the operation of the high-voltage transmission grid. They sell electricity both to large industrial end-users and to regional and municipal distribution companies. At *regional* level, there are around eighty regional utilities, which purchase electricity from the supra-regional producers, but also generate their own power (around 10 per cent of total production). The regional utilities are active mainly in distribution and electricity supply, with supply activities taking place predominantly in the rural and less densely populated areas. Finally, there are around 850 *municipal* electricity companies (*Stadtwerke*), which deal mainly with distribution and supply to residential consumers; however, they also generate a small part of total electricity production (10 per cent). The municipal electricity companies often operate as part of municipal multi-utilities.

Sales to end-users are split evenly between the three categories of suppliers. German end-users of electricity are divided into 'tariff customers' (*Tarifkunden*), mostly households and small commercial users, and 'special contract customers' (*Sondervertragskunden*), mostly large and medium industrial users. In 1997, supra-regional utilities had a 33 per cent share of total electricity sales to end-users, regional utilities a 36 per cent share, and municipal companies a 31 per cent share (VDEW 1998: 17).

The ownership structure of the industry is mixed, with public owners being overwhelmingly the *Länder* and municipalities rather than the federal government. It is also worth noting that the public influence in the industry is often greater than the ownership of capital would indicate, as the public owners have frequently secured majority voting rights, even if their capital stake is minor.[2]

Another characteristic feature of the German ESI is its high degree of vertical and horizontal integration. Cross-shareholdings between the different companies are common, and long-term contracts have long been an important part of the functioning of the industry. A large number of regional and municipal companies are directly or indirectly at least partly owned by the supra-regional utilities, which also act as their main suppliers. Because of cross-shareholdings, only four of the pre-merger eight supra-regional utilities were independent from each other. An important condition for the approval of the mergers between VEBA and VIAG, and between RWE and VEW, by the European and German competition authorities was a commitment by the four companies to divest mutual cross-shareholdings. Significantly, the East German supra-regional utility VEAG was jointly owned by the West German companies. Following the concessions made by the merging companies, VEAG is now independent from its former owners; it is by size the third-largest German utility, and its independence is hoped to improve the competitive situation in the industry.

Beyond the integration within electricity supply, the industry is deeply embedded in other sectors of the German economy. There exist vertical links and cross-shareholdings to related industries, notably coal and lignite, and some of the large electricity utilities are part of industrial conglomerates with interests ranging from the chemical to the telecommunications industries.

Industry reform

Despite the large number of players, the German ESI was far from competitive before liberalization. The legal framework within which it functioned created an environment of regional and local monopolies, organized in a cartel-like fashion. A set of private industry contracts taking the form of vertical and

---

[2] An illustration of this is provided by the pre-merger RWE Energie. Its shares were owned 30% by a group of 70 municipalities and 70% by private investors, but municipalities held 60% of the voting rights (IEA 1997: 96).

horizontal demarcation contracts defined the geographical areas and activities in which each company could be active. These anti-competitive agreements had developed historically and were granted an exception from the general competition laws.[3] In addition to the demarcation agreements, exclusive concession contracts existed at the municipal level. These were grounded in municipal rights of way and created monopolies for the supply of end-users. In exchange for rights of way, concession holders had to pay municipalities a share of their revenues.

The liberalization policies emanating from Brussels played an important role as catalyst in breaking the long-standing mould of the German ESI. Various previous attempts at reform undertaken by the German federal government were dwarfed by the many vested interests. Above all, the public–private ownership structure, as well as the municipal rights of way, raised property issues anchored in the Constitution which forestalled all attempts at reform.

Following the implementation of the European electricity liberalization directive in 1997, the new German law for energy markets (*Energiewirtschaftsgesetz*) came into force on 28 April 1998, thereby transcribing the European directive into national law. With the new law, the totality of the German electricity market, including the residential market, was opened to supply competition in a single step.

The new electricity law abolished all demarcation agreements with immediate effect, and, while concession contracts continue to exist at municipal level, they are no longer exclusive, giving end-users the possibility to bypass the local distribution network. Simultaneously with the abolition of the demarcation contracts, the German Competition Act was amended and the protected status of the industry ended. An essential facilities clause was introduced declaring as unlawful the unjustified denial of access to an essential infrastructure. The amendment of the competition law was strongly supported by the Federal Cartel Office, which became the main regulatory institution for the industry (see also Section 13.3.1).

13.2.2. *Rail services*

Industry structure
Similar to electricity, an element of decentralization is present in German rail services, with non-federal rail undertakings playing an important role both regionally and locally. Their owners are mostly federal states or municipalities, with a small number of private operators also being present.[4] However, a distinct asymmetry between the federal and regional players exists. The federal rail operator Deutsche Bahn AG (DB AG) is not only by far the largest rail

[3] Sturm and Wilks (1997) offer a comprehensive overview of the legal conditions of the pre-liberalization industry.
[4] Hass-Klau (1998) provides an extensive account of the history and present structure of the German rail system.

service operator, it also owns the quasi-totality of the public rail infrastructure. One of the most interesting aspects of the reform of the German rail sector undertaken between 1994 and 1996 is arguably that it has strengthened the regional element at the expense of the federal operator in a devolution of responsibilities.

Industry reform
The federal rail industry was the first German network utility to undergo far-reaching reform in the 1990s. High subsidy payments and accumulated debt were the main drivers for change. In 1989 a multi-disciplinary government commission was charged with the task of finding a new structural concept for rail transport. Reunification and the investment demands generated by the modernization of the public transport network in the new federal states accelerated change, as did policy emanating from Brussels. The reform of the German railways sector was implemented in 1994 with a new Railways Act (*Eisenbahnneuordnungsgesetz*), after a change in the German Constitution abolishing the federal monopoly of Deutsche Bundesbahn in 1992.

The reform was based on three main elements: separation of commercial activities and public domain obligations; separation of network operation and service provision; and regionalization of short-distance passenger services.

The separation of commercial activities from other obligations falling into the public domain was achieved through the complete reorganization of the public federal rail operator Deutsche Bundesbahn. On 1 January 1994, all commercial activities were transferred to the new corporation Deutsche Bahn AG (DB AG), a private company. The capital of DB AG is for the moment entirely held by the federal government, but privatization is planned.

The non-commercial obligations of the federal railways were honoured through the creation of two new public administrations. The first was the Fund of Federal Railways (*Bundeseisenbahnvermögen*), which took over all debt and other public obligations from the old federal operator, which at this stage comprised the merged East and West German operations. The obligations concerned for instance the management of the pension fund of former civil service staff. The new commercial undertaking DB AG could thus start business without being burdened by old liabilities. The second public body created in the course of the 1994 rail reform was the new Federal Office for Rail Services (*Eisenbahn-Bundesamt*, EBA). It became functional on 1 January 1994 and is in charge of key regulatory tasks such as licensing (see also Section 13.3.2).

While the first element of the reform dealt with reforming the financial basis of the rail sector, the objective of the second element was the creation of an environment favourable to the introduction of competitive forces into the sector. The separation of network operation and service provision was implemented through the establishment of separate legal units within the new operator DB AG. In 1994, Germany's policy-makers decided against structural separation and different owners for network and competitive activities.

However, the privatization of the separate business units of DB AG was always planned for the moment their financial health had stabilized; only the infrastructure unit, DB Netz, was to remain permanently under public ownership. Continued public ownership is therefore the strongest regulatory instrument used to constrain the monopoly position of the infrastructure operator.

The third element of the German rail reform reinforces the regional element of the rail service. With the objective of improving the overall efficiency, quality, and coordination of regional services, the *Länder* have been granted responsibility for regional passenger rail transport in terms of finance and planning.

Traditionally, urban and suburban public passenger transport (tram, bus, underground, and light rail) is controlled by a number of local or regional authorities, the most important of which are passenger transport authorities known as *Verkehrs–Verbünde*. These are legal bodies coordinating, but not owning, the public transport operations of their members. A typical Verkehrs–Verbund comprises the local public transport operator or operators, DB AG (which runs and operates 95 per cent of all suburban and regional rail passenger services), and possibly a small number of private bus companies.[5] By 1997 Germany had twenty-eight Verkehrs–Verbünde covering about 47 million people, and new authorities were still being created in the new *Länder*.

On 1 January 1996, DB AG transferred all activities related to regional passenger rail service to the *Länder*.[6] Some differences exist in terms of how the *Länder* have then chosen to pass on this newly acquired authority. In some cases, the *Land* has kept all control over regional transport, or else responsibility is to be transferred to local authorities only at a later stage; still other *Länder* have devolved power to the local authorities of the major cities only. However, in most cases the Verkehrs–Verbünde have seen their power increase. The reform has notably increased the bargaining position of local and regional authorities *vis-à-vis* DB AG. Prior to reform, all regional railway costs were reimbursed by the federal government via DB AG. The federal operator was a powerful partner who could veto or amend new investment or planning decisions. Today, regional rail is integrated into the existing regional transport programmes, the funding of which is assured by federal, regional, and local finances. A substantial share of the tax revenue generated by the energy tax is transferred to the *Länder* to fund regional transport services.

In order to achieve quality and efficiency improvements of regional public transports, decentralized bodies dispose of considerable flexibility and autonomy. (See Section 13.4.2 for an example of regional transport initiatives.) Funds can be transferred between modes of transport, leaving the

---

[5] There exist however great differences between different Verkehrs–Verbünden. The Verkehrs-Verbund Rhein–Ruhr, for instance, comprises 15 cities covering over 100,000 inhabitants and their respective public service operators.

[6] Regional passenger services are defined as journeys taking less than an hour or covering a distance of under 50 km.

local authorities to decide which means of transport services a given route most cost-efficiently.

13.2.3. *Telecommunications*

Industry structure and reform

While decentralized market structures prevail for German electricity supply and rail, the pre-liberalization German telecommunications services were organized in a monopolistic market. Both telecommunications and postal services were provided by a single operator, Deutsche Bundespost, part of the Federal Ministry of Post and Telecommunications. As a general rule, the liberalization of the German telecommunications sector has closely followed European legislation in the domain.

The government proceeded to restructure the Federal Ministry in 1990. Three public companies, responsible for telecommunications, postal services, and the financial services of the post, were split from the ministry. In 1994 an amendment to the Constitution, necessary to implement the changes requested by Brussels in view of the liberalization of the sector, was voted. The three public companies created in 1990 were transformed into private corporations and their statutory monopoly rights to service exclusively the telecommunications and postal markets were abolished. The private company that took over the telecommunications business from the public operator is called Deutsche Telekom AG (DT AG).

In August 1996 the new German Telecommunications Act came into force. All telecommunications services with the temporary exception of voice telephony were opened to supply competition.[7] The law also abolished the infrastructure monopoly of DT AG with immediate effect, and a number of alternative network operators appeared at this stage, often basing their networks on existing facilities such as rail or electricity infrastructures. Competition developed first for services such as data transfer and corporate networks. In 1996 the government sold the first slice (26 per cent) of DT AG to the public.

The last step in the liberalization of the telecommunications market was taken on 1 January 1998. In accordance with European prescriptions, the monopoly for fixed voice telephony was ended. At the same date, the first and so far only sector-specific regulatory agency in Germany, the Authority for Telecommunications and Post (*Regulierungsbehörde für Telekommunikation und Post*, RegTP), started its activity.

13.3. REGULATORY FRAMEWORK

For each of the three industries discussed, the regulatory institutions monitoring the introduction of competition differ. In electricity the historically

---

[7] Only fixed telephony services are considered here. Mobile voice telephony has been provided in a duopoly market since 1990.

fragmented, mixed-ownership organization has led to the unique establishment of a system based largely on self-regulation, with the Federal Cartel Office acting as watchdog over competition. In the rail industry, an important regulatory role is still held by the federal government through its continued ownership of the network operator. A federal rail authority has been set up; however, its brief concentrates on technical regulation. Perhaps most importantly, reform has strengthened the role of regional transport authorities which foster competition on regional level. Only in telecommunications has a sector-specific regulatory authority been put in charge of regulating DT AG and promoting competition as one of its primary duties.

13.3.1. *Electricity*

The decentralized structure of the German ESI is reflected in the existing regulatory institutions. At the federal level sector policy is devised, and legislation elaborated. The larger part of energy policy is the responsibility of the Federal Ministry of Economics and Technology, although the important area of nuclear energy policy falls under the competence of the Ministry of Environment. Federal and regional legislation is implemented at *Länder* level through regional government offices. The *Länder* authorize new plants, and approve the retail tariff that customers are charged. Municipalities, for their part, have retained the right to levy concession charges in exchange of rights of way. This basic regulatory setup has not changed with the opening up of the industry to competition.

Network access

The new German electricity law emulates the key ideas of the EU electricity liberalization directive. It is based on the vertical separation of the different functions of the ESI, that is upstream generation, transmission, and downstream distribution and supply. However, neither the directive nor the new German electricity law imposes structural or ownership separation of potentially competitive and naturally monopolistic activities. Only the management separation of businesses and the functional unbundling of accounts is required, and liberalization has done nothing to change the integrated nature of the German ESI.[8]

In a decision unique in Europe, the German government decided to grant the industry the right to self-regulate in the crucial area of network access. Simultaneously with the elaboration of the new electricity law, the main parties involved in the industry have concluded an access agreement (known as Verbände–Vereinbarung, or V–V[9]), which forms the basis for negotiated

---

[8] Sturm and Wilks (1997: 22) argue that such a structural reform would have been virtually impossible given the ownership conditions in the industry.

[9] The agreement was negotiated between the Association of Electricity Producers (Vereinigung Deutscher Elektrizitätswerke, VDEW), the Association of German Industry (Bundesverband der Deutschen Industrie, BDI), and the Association of the Industrial Energy Sector (Verband der Industriellen Energie- und Kraftwirtschaft, VIK).

third-party access to the grid. Only if the self-regulation of the industry fails and the development of competition is judged insufficient has the Federal Ministry of Economics reserved the option to legislate for access, and move *de facto* to a system of regulated third-party access.

The V–V sets out the rules for negotiated third-party access.[10] It lists the cost elements to be included in transmission charges, but does not set any price levels. These are the subject of negotiation between the network operator and the third party requesting access. Indicative transmission prices are to be published by all network owners six months after the implementation of the agreement.

The V–V has already been re-negotiated once since 1998, with the new version, V–V2, in place since the beginning of 2000. The V–V2 responded to criticisms of the first agreement, simplifying significantly the structure of the transmission charges. However, the highly contentious distance element in the charges did not entirely disappear with the new agreement, which divided Germany into two trading zones, North and South, with a surcharge being levied on all net traffic between the two. The same surcharge applied to transmissions over the national border, a fact that has angered foreign suppliers. Only the negotiations regarding the approval of the two big mergers discussed in the previous section have led to the disappearance of the distance charge for transmissions within Germany.

In parallel with the concessions gained by the competition authorities, negotiations aiming at a harmonized cross-border tariff system for all European countries by the so-called Florence Forum took place. Once the Europe-wide cross-border tariff agreement overseen by the European Commission comes into force, the German access agreement will lose its relevance for cross-border transactions.

Consumer price regulation

A federal law on electricity tariffs (*Bundestarifverordnung für Elektrizität*) sets out the principles of retail price regulation for tariff customers, but there exist differences in the interpretation of the law between different *Länder*. Moreover, the regulatory process is far from transparent. Utilities submit their tariff proposals and the cost information requested to the relevant regional authorities, but only the approved tariffs are published. Attempts to introduce elements of yardstick regulation into the system have proved only moderately successful so far.

With the liberalization of the ESI, the official stance taken by the government with respect to retail price regulation has consistently been that it would abolish the remaining regulation once competition has taken root. With the rapid (and larger-than-expected) advent of price cuts for residential customers (see Section 13.4.1), a representative of the industry association VDEW has

---

[10] For a very complete analysis of the first V–V, see Brunekreeft (1999).

confirmed that the regulated prices are maximum prices which have now lost their significance, and their disappearance is seen as a formality.

Environmental and social obligations

An important role in the regulation of the German ESI is played by environmental regulations. Apart from the subsidy programme for domestic coal,[11] it is the increasing support given to renewable energy sources, as well as severe emission controls, that have most influenced the industry in the last decade.

In 1990, the electricity feed-in law (*Stromeinspeisegesetz*) was adopted to promote the use of renewable energy sources. It guaranteed access to the public grid for hydro, wind, and solar generators. These received a standard payment of 90 per cent of the tariff customer retail price. The law has had a particularly important impact on wind-based power generation, making Germany the most important producer of wind-based electricity worldwide. On 1 April 2000, a new Renewables Law (*Erneuerbare–Energien–Gesetz*) became effective, replacing the electricity feed-in law. This expands the range of input fuels eligible for support. Importantly, the new law also ruptures the link between the price that utilities have to pay for 'green' electricity fed into their grid, and the retail price. Under the new Renewables Law, electricity suppliers are held to purchase renewables-generated electricity at fixed prices varying as a function of the input fuel between Pf 13 and Pf 19 per kWh. In comparison, according to the industry association VDEW, the price for wholesale traded electricity in Germany was below Pf 10 per kWh in April 2000.

In addition to the promotion of renewable energy sources, the imposition of some of the most severe emission controls worldwide have played an important role in Germany's notoriously high electricity prices during the 1990s. The success of the environmental policies is however also apparent. Between 1987 and 1997, carbon dioxide (CO_2) emissions of public electricity suppliers fell by 23 per cent, from 339 mt (million tonnes) to 261 mt (VDEW 1998: 53).

In contrast to the extensive environmental regulation, no social obligations are imposed on the German ESI. The protection of vulnerable consumers is part of the general social security policy. Geographical averaging of electricity prices has never been pursued in Germany and a multitude of residential electricity tariffs exist. It can be argued that this lack of social obligations directly linked to the industry has reduced political resistance to the speedy liberalization of the industry.

13.3.2. *Rail*

A decentralized regulatory structure is also in place in the German rail industry. The federal government continues to play an important role, and a federal rail agency was established in 1994. At the same time, however, regional

---

[11] This complex issue goes beyond the scope of this chapter; see IEA (1998) for an overview of the coal subsidy programme.

transport authorities have seen their responsibilities increase since 1996. Similar to the electricity sector, the Federal Cartel Office acts as ultimate guardian of competition.

The Federal Rail Office

The Federal Rail Office (EBA) is an independent authority under the supervision of the Federal Ministry of Transport. It acts as representative of the government in its function of supervising DB AG investment projects. The regulatory brief of the EBA comprises first and foremost technical matters. It issues federal rail licences, which are either service licences needed for operators desiring access to the federal rail network, or network licences for the operation of a rail transport network. Related to the issuing of licences, the EBA also monitors technical and safety standards and is in charge of accident investigations.

Moreover, the federal rail agency decides upon the closure of rail lines. It is however important to note that political factors play an important role here, and local and regional pressure groups often prevent the closure of a given route. With the regionalization, a certain number of financially unviable lines have been purchased from DB AG by regional transport operators (see also Section 13.4.2).

The EBA is also responsible for supervising non-discriminatory access to the federal rail infrastructure, although its role is essentially advisory. It acts as mediator between different rail operators and provides clarifications. The EBA intervenes only on request, and only in the negotiation phase. Non-discriminatory access for third parties is monitored by the agency only with respect to third parties. Preferential treatment within different business units of DB AG is considered a problem by many observers, but goes beyond the remit of the EBA. Inquiries into anti-competitive practices are undertaken by the Federal Cartel Office. No price control has been set up for network access charges, which are discussed below.

Network access

Under the new legislation, the infrastructure unit of Deutsche Bahn, DB Netz, is obliged to provide non-discriminatory access to the federal rail network on the basis of an indicative access price list. DB AG is held to act as a commercial undertaking and as such is free to set access prices at a level that allows it to cover maintenance costs of the network. New investment in infrastructure is funded by the federal government.

The first track prices were published in June 1994. Basic charges are cost-based and as such depend upon the type of train being operated, its weight, maximum speed, and planning quality. (The planning quality allows time-tabling by attributing different priorities to trains.[12]) Important discounts are

---

[12] For illustrative examples of the pricing system, see Hass-Klau (1998: 57–8).

offered by DB Netz on the number of kilometres run, a practice that has been criticized by competing companies because of the clear price advantage it confers to DB AG. The discounts have subsequently been investigated by the competition authorities.

Track charges are not inclusive, as further payments are levied for using tracks to collect carriages and locomotives together to form a train, for leaving a train overnight, or for reimbursing electricity charges. The overall ratio between track access and other charges is about 65 : 35 (Hass-Klau, 1998: 60).

The continued influence of political factors in the rail sector can be seen in the fact that end prices for infrastructure services, and also for other services provided by DB AB over the network, may be reduced following negotiations between DB AG and the *Länder*. As outlined in Section 13.2.2, regional rail services since 1996 have been reimbursed by the *Länder*, either directly or via local authorities. All these bodies agree an overall price with DB AG for the services it provides for them regionally.[13] A *Land* or Verkehrs–Verband may share the cost of new trains or station improvements, and the price per kilometre for services provided by DB AG varies as a function of a *Land*'s own rail investment. Some bodies conclude annual contracts with DB AG to increase their bargaining power; others renew their contracts every two or three years.

At regional level, the network access principle is combined with competitive tendering organized by the regional authorities for exclusive service licences. The tenders are open to DB AG as well as to all other licensed operators. DB AG has already lost several regional service licences to smaller companies which were better able to cater for specific needs at the local or regional level. Regional operators winning a licence will pay access charges for the use of the tracks, which can be owned either by DB AG or by local bodies. Since 1996, a number of railway lines have been transferred from DB AG to other operators, often at a nominal price.[14]

Price regulation of regional passenger services (no other prices are regulated) are the responsibility of regional authorities, and take the form of price caps.

13.3.3. *Telecommunications*

The Regulatory Authority for Telecommunications and Post
The Regulatory Authority for Telecommunications and Post (RegTP) is so far the only sector-specific regulatory institution in Germany in charge of all aspects of telecommunication (and postal) regulation. Regulatory action in the

---

[13] The passenger transport unit of DB AG still runs 95% of all regional rail passenger services, either on its own or on non-federal tracks. It also operates urban and suburban bus services.

[14] These routes were often unprofitable for DB AG, and local bodies have purchased them to avoid closure, often finding innovative solutions to future service provision.

sector is as a general rule limited to dominant undertakings, which makes DT AG the only operator subject to price and quality regulations, both in network and end-user services.

The RegTP has taken over the regulatory tasks of the former Ministry for Post and Telecommunications and the supervisory role for technical harmonization, formerly the responsibility of the Federal Office for Post and Telecommunications. The new authority has a staff of nearly 3,000, most of whom are civil servants taken over from the now defunct federal administrations.

The regulator is organized in five independent 'decision chambers', each of which is in charge of a different regulatory domain, such as price regulation, dispute settlement, or network access. This organizational form allows internal independence, increases transparency, and limits regulatory discretion.[15] The role of the *Länder* was a contentious issue during the elaboration of the new regulatory framework, and a compromise was reached through the creation of an advisory council, which works alongside the regulatory chambers. One-half of the council's eighteen members are appointed by the *Länder*, the other half by the Bundestag, Germany's federal parliament.

Network access and price regulation

The new Telecommunications Act obliges dominant network operators to grant network access and to allow its competitors to interconnect to its network on non-discriminatory terms. The equal network access regulation implied that direct resellers entering the market (offering mostly call-by-call services) would be able to offer services without substantial investments. Similarly, the interconnection obligation meant that alternative network providers would be able to attain universal coverage regardless of the initial size of their networks. The regulatory decision that number portability had to be free of charge helped keep switching costs low for consumers.

The interconnection tariffs DT AG is allowed to charge are determined by the RegTP. They are cost-based and the initial price levels have been determined by international benchmarking in 1997. Since then, two analytical cost models for national and local network access have been set up and were the object of an extensive public consultation process (WIK 1998).

In addition to network-related service prices, the retail prices of DT AG are regulated by a price cap. DT AG was held to reduce the average price level for each of two separate service baskets by 4.3 per cent in the two-year span 1998–9. (The first basket contains local and long-distance services for private customers, the second, similar services for business customers.) However, strong competition has made prices fall considerably faster than the regulatory rule implied, and the retail price-cap has proved to be non-binding for DT AG.

---

[15] The organization in 'decision chambers' can also be found in the Federal Cartel Office (FCO).

Public service obligation

The new German legislation provides for a universal service fund for telecommunications, following the approach advocated in the European directives. The level of service that has to be made available by service providers to all persons requesting it is defined in the Telecommunications Act. Intervention in the market in order to guarantee this level of service is however kept to a minimum. The regulator intervenes only when the provision of services resulting from commercial decisions is insufficient. In such a case, the dominant operator is given the option to provide the missing service without financial compensation. If it refuses to do so because it judges the cost of the service too high, the right to provide the service in question is allocated via competitive tender, and the service is funded through the universal service fund. All telecoms operators above a certain market share contribute to the fund. So far, however, the reimbursement scheme has not been used in practice. DT AG remains the only universal service provider and thus far has requested no financial compensation.

13.4. MARKET DEVELOPMENT SINCE LIBERALIZATION

13.4.1. *Electricity*

Since the German ESI has been opened up to competition in April 1998, prices have fallen sharply and the industry has been consolidating. In a stagnant market, price competition is expected in defence of market shares, so it is not the fact that prices were falling, but rather the speed at which it was happening, that has surprised observers.

Germany has for a long time been known for its high electricity prices. This is explained partly by the cartel-like organization of the industry, and partly by the high costs of coal subsidies and environmental policies borne by German electricity consumers. The abolishment of the protective industry agreements through liberalization, the disappearance of the coal levy in 1996, and the coming to an end of most of the environmental investment programmes all have coincided to allow price cuts. Moreover, according to a recent report by McKinsey (2000), the German electricity industry displays large over-capacities: of a total of 118.0 GW installed capacity, only 66 per cent is necessary to satisfy peak demand. This implies that the marginal cost of generation is close to zero, and that companies can sell at very low prices indeed at least for a limited period.

According to a monthly price survey undertaken by the Federal Association of Energy consumers (VEA), German electricity prices for industrial customers have on average, in the twelve months between July 1998 and July 1999, fallen by 13 per cent, with some price cuts exceeding 25 per cent.[16] The renegotiation

---

[16] Average price for different industrial usage profiles; net prices excluding all taxes. Bundesverband der Energie-Abnehmer (1999) *VEA-Strompreisvergleich, Stand* 1.7.99.

Table 13.1. *Tariff offers for German residential users, 1999*

Electricity brand	Unit price[a] (Pf/kWh)	Difference from average price (%)
EnBW 'Yellow'	25.4	−20
PreussenElektra 'Direkt'	26.77	−16
RWE 'Avanza'	28.15	−11.5
Bayernwerk 'Power'	29.09	−8.5
Federal average[b]	31.8	—

[a] Domestic user with 4,000 kWh annual consumption.

[b] Includes eastern German prices.

Source: Power in Europe, 3 February 2000.

of contracts is the main instrument through which price reductions are realized for large end-users. One of the most successful instruments for renegotiating contracts has been the emergence of customer pools, the largest of which is the Hanover-based Association of Energy Consumers VEA with 2,500 participants; in 1999 it succeeded in renegotiating the power supply of its members with the regional supplier PreussenElektra at a price 30 per cent below pre-liberalization levels for some of its members.

Price competition has also surprisingly quickly reached the residential market, and competition for small tariff customers is fierce, with a wide range of individually tailored tariffs emerging, including 'green' tariffs, promising variable contents of renewables-generated electricity. Table 13.1 gives an indication of the tariff offers available to tariff customers in 1999.

Despite the important price cuts offered by electricity suppliers, switching numbers for residential customers are so far low; in a recent speech, a VEW board member put the number of residential customer switching at 3 per cent. In part, this low number can be explained by initial uncertainty about the terms and prices at which alternative suppliers could gain access to residential customers. This uncertainty has since been substantially reduced by the pro-competitive stance the Federal Cartel Office (FCO) has taken, having refused so far to accept the denial of access by incumbents and decided systematically in favour of competitive entrants.[17] Low residential switching can also be linked to customer loyalty to municipal suppliers. Many end-users are aware of the role that revenues of the municipal supply company play in municipal budgets and are willing to accept marginally higher prices on the basis that they cross-subsidize other loss-making local public services, such as public transport. According to a January 2000 report on VEBA/VIAG by Deutsche Bank, price

---

[17] According to the information published on the FCO web page, of six access cases brought in front of the authority in 1998 and 1999, none were decided in favour of the incumbent refusing to grant access.

falls for all domestic customers, not only those willing to switch, will be 10 per cent in 2000, 3.6 per cent in 2001, and 1.2 per cent in 2002.[18]

As a reaction to the price falls, German electricity utilities are consolidating to reduce costs. The two biggest mergers were announced at the end of 1999, involving, respectively, RWE and VEW, and VIAG and VEBA. Both German and European competition authorities expressed their concern that the two mergers would reduce the number of independent supra-national electricity utilities to three (RWE/VEW, VEBA/VIAG, and EnWB), with the two newly merged companies effectively gaining a duopoly position in the market, controlling between them 80 per cent of power supplied over the high-voltage grid. As a consequence, the competition authorities have made the divestiture of cross-shareholdings a precondition for the approval of the mergers. Parallel to the concentration taking place between supra-regional players, many regional and municipal utilities are either being further integrated with their main upstream suppliers, or forming consortia to cut fixed costs, such as marketing costs. A number of foreign investors have also seized the opportunity offered by the profound changes in the industry and have entered the market through acquisitions of large municipal companies in Berlin and Hamburg, for instance.

13.4.2. Rail

In 1998, there existed around 200 licensed rail operators in Germany.[19] About thirty of these are independent passenger rail operators, but many more are involved in freight. Many are operational units of DB AG, others are non-federal and private undertakings. A number of new entrants have been recorded, one of the most important being KAP Lock, a logistics company jointly owned by the federal postal operator Deutsche Post AG and UPS. Access to the federal network by national and international rail services (often high-speed services) is increasing. The success of the existing high-speed passenger services has led DB AG to invest heavily in the expansion of its high-speed tracks.

On local level, all of the larger German cities have undertaken substantial investments in urban and suburban public transport networks. One of the most substantial investments planned is the major refurbishment of twenty-five railway stations (e.g in Stuttgart, Munich, and Frankfurt), with surface tracks being brought underground to free attractive city centre building sites.

The devolution of responsibility has enabled local service providers to display greater initiative in terms of service innovation. An example of regional projects is provided by the local railways in Düren, cited in Hass-Klau (1998). The Dürer Kreisbahn is 45 km long and runs between Cologne and Aachen. In 1993 DB AG wanted to close the line, but a local campaign prevented this, and

---

[18] Report cited in *Power in Europe*, 3 February 2000.
[19] Internal EBA document, 1998.

instead the line was taken over by the local transport operator in Düren, which had previously been running the public bus services in this town of 91,000 inhabitants. The tracks were bought for 1 DM from DB AG. New lighter and cheaper trains were specially developed and built for the route. Moreover, the timetable was changed to an hourly service with interchange facilities to other public transport services along the route. Flexible timetabling was made available for special events. By 1996, a 360 per cent increase in passenger numbers with respect to 1989 had been realized. Funding for the operation was 60 per cent provided by the *Land* government of North Rhine–Westphalia.

A big problem remaining for entrants into the German rail sector is the provision of rolling stock. Rolling stock is a large investment for new companies and, once again, DB AG is at an advantage with its large existing and flexible stock and often preferential relationship with the big rolling stock companies. None the less, two ways of addressing this problem have emerged. Subsidies of 50 per cent and more are available from the *Länder* for the purchase of new rolling stock. Moreover, franchise periods for private firms are generally longer (with seven- to ten-year leases) than those offered to DB AG (two- to four-year leases), to take into account the greater need to recover fixed setup cost.

13.4.3. *Telecommunications*

Every two years the RegTP is held to present a report on its activity to the two chambers of the German parliament, Bundestag and Bundesrat. The first of the regulatory reports was submitted in December 1999 (RegTP 1999), and it highlights the success of the introduction of competition in the first two years of the liberalized market.

At the end of June 2000, 150 providers of voice telephony offered their services (RegTP 2000*b*). Among them, over ninety possess own network facilities, and over fifty specialize in resale.[20] Overall, over 1,800 companies were offering telecommunications services by mid-2000. This number includes the growing group of internet service providers (ISPs). Three new fixed network operators with national scope—o.tel.o, Viag Intercom, and Arcor—have entered the market since 1996. Their networks are based on existing backbone infrastructure (electricity transmission in the case of o.tel.o and Viag Intercom and railway infrastructure in the case of Arcor). Other network operators have restricted their infrastructure to a region or city. So-called 'city carriers' include NetCologne and ISIS, but many of these carriers are at present expanding their scope by connecting their local networks. Competing network operators have invested mainly in optic fibre technology, and by the end of 1999 the combined

---

[20] Considerably more companies have been granted voice telephony network or service licences by the regulator. However, a great number of licence holders have yet to offer services to end consumers. See RegTP's web page for the full listing of the 305 (30 June 2000) licence holders.

length of the optic fibre network operated by companies other than DT AG reached over 40 per cent of DT AG's optic fibre network (RegTP 2000*a*).

The sector regulator also draws attention to the emergence of inter-carrier business as a new growing market segment. Revenues from interconnection deals between fixed, and between fixed and mobile, networks have more than doubled between 1998 and 1999 (RegTP 2000*b*). Carrier exchanges allow network operators and service providers to optimize their investments in call and transmission capacities. Brunekreeft and Gross (1999) argue that substantial excess transmission capacity exists in the short run as infrastructure entrants have chosen the size of their network in anticipation of strongly increasing demand. This explains in part the aggressive price competition taking place at present (see below).

In 1998 the new entrants in the voice telephony market held a market share of 4.9 per cent in terms of call volume.[21] By mid-1999, their share had grown to 14.4 per cent, and a year later, to 20 per cent. The market share of new entrants is highest for the group of long-distance, international, and fixed-to-mobile services: over 40 per cent of call minutes were attributed to competitors of DT AG in July 2000. Traffic growth was 10 per cent in 1997/8 and 17 per cent in 1998/9, owing to the strong increase in internet-related traffic and fixed-to-mobile calls. The presence of companies other than DT AG in local call services and as providers of access services is considerably weaker, but competition is also increasing for those services. While in 1998 only 0.5 per cent of the former and 0.3 per cent of the latter were attributed to new entrants, these numbers had changed to 4.8 and 1 per cent by mid-1999.

Competitive end-user access is so far based largely on lines rented from DT AG, either by city carriers, or by network owners in the process of building up universal networks. Germany's regulator had implemented local loop unbundling obligations for DT AG by 1998, and by mid-2000 eighty-two local loop contracts had been concluded between the incumbent and its competitors. Entrants are also increasingly exploiting two further means of bridging the final link to the end-users, the first being the wireless local loop (WLL) and the other, broad-band cable connections. In 1999 and 2000, over 160 WLL frequencies were allocated by the regulator.

Moreover, Germany has one of the world's most developed cable TV networks. In January 1998, 48.2 per cent of all households with TV were already connected to broad-band cable (WIK 1999).[22] The percentage of *connectable* households is even higher, at 85.0 per cent. While DT AG dominates the trunk cable network, many small local providers (between 4,000 and 6,000) are active in the local loop segment. Only a third of households are directly serviced by DT AG. On the basis of unbundled local loop contracts and alternative

---

[21] Figures in this paragraph are drawn from WIK (1999), as well as RegTP (2000*b*).

[22] In comparision, 65% of US households have cable TV, but the number is only 14% in Spain, 13% in Japan, and 11% in France and the UK.

infrastructures, approximately fifty-five licensed operators were offering access services to end users by mid-2000.

In July 1999 the telecommunications consumer price index computed by the Federal Statistical Office was 12.3 per cent lower than eighteen months earlier at the moment of market opening (RegTP 2000*a*). The price index fell most impressively for national long-distance calls: consumers faced prices that were on average 42.5 per cent lower than in January 1998, and maximum savings of 85 per cent could be realized. Similar maximum savings were realized for the most frequent international call destinations. The cost of local calls and telephone connections, by contrast, has not changed since liberalization, because of rebalancing and slower take-off of competition for these services.

Industry turnover figures show the shift occurring between telecommunications activities very clearly (RegTP 2000*b*). In 1999 overall turnover increased by 10 per cent compared with the previous year. Three new activities drive growth and compensate for the 10 per cent fall in turnover generated by fixed telephony services: first, mobile services have grown by 34 per cent; second, inter-carrier business has doubled; and third, other activities, including notably internet service providers, have seen their turnover increase by 25 per cent.

13.5. ASSESSMENT

The introduction of competition in the German utility markets surveyed in this chapter should be considered a success. Prices have fallen by double-digit figures since the liberalization of the telecommunications and electricity industries and new services and tariff options proliferate in all industries surveyed. However, in view of the long-term sustainability of this competition, a number of structural concerns arise, notably in the electricity industry.

The over-capacity in generation assets and the resulting price war makes entry into the German electricity market at present unprofitable and confers a strong position to the consolidating incumbents. While consolidation is driven by the need to reduce costs, and is arguably desirable in an industry with nearly 1,000 players, the question remains whether the survivors of the price war will be able to dominate the energy market once more and revert to collusive behaviour and/or the erection of entry barriers.

I argue that three market developments can help the competition authorities in their task to constrain possible future abuse of market power. First, dominant positions in the domestic market can be mitigated by competition from abroad. The high degree of interconnection of the German grid and the finalization of a European agreement on trans-border transmission charges by the Florence regulatory forum and the European Commission create favourable conditions for cross-border trade. Germany is surrounded by highly competitive markets, which will make it harder for incumbents to raise prices above the competitive level. Second, German consumers have very rapidly adopted their power purchasing behaviour to competitive markets, and successful strategies such as the formation of consumer pools are unlikely to be forgotten. Third, the introduction of competition in European electricity markets has led to the emergence of standardized power exchanges. These facilitate upstream or downstream entry by national or international companies and thus have a beneficial effect on the development of competition. In Germany power exchanges have taken up operation in Leipzig and Frankfurt. Moreover, the Amsterdam Power Exchange (APX) has opened a regional hub in Germany.

Despite these positive market developments, serious concerns remain regarding the German ESI because of the lack of structural separation between the transmission system operators and upstream and downstream undertakings. The utilities have unbundled their accounts following the prescriptions of the European directive, but no physical separation has been imposed, and the owners of the monopolistic grid and competitive generation and supply operations are identical. Such a setting leaves room for doubt about the fairness and non-discrimination of grid access with respect to third parties, in particular given the important element of self-regulation. The FCO has shown its determination to protect competition in electricity supply; however, no systematic information collection for the purpose of benchmarking or cost modelling occurs in the absence of a specialized regulator. Without instruments to overcome the information asymmetry between the industry and the competition authorities, it might be difficult to assess the anti-competitive potential of price and entry strategies in the future market.

The regulation of the monopoly network is also one of the least transparent elements of the reformed German rail industry. The principal safeguard against DB AB abusing its monopoly position is the continued public ownership of the infrastructure unit. Access charges are supposed to be cost-based and to cover all maintenance costs of the rail infrastructure. However, there exists no formal price control, and incentives for cost reduction are not explicit. Nor have anti-competitive practices such as volume discounts, which favour operational units of DB AG, been addressed in a systematic manner.

The incumbent rail operator is constrained in its actions by political involvement, which remains strong, in particular after the devolution of authority for all regional passenger transport services to the *Länder*. The prices published by DB AG are often not those eventually paid by regional authorities. Overall service contracts are subject to negotiations between regional authorities and DB AG, and public service considerations play an important part. It has to be noted, however, that the very flexible approach shows its advantages in the emergence of innovative and efficient public transport services at regional level.

It is in the telecommunications market that competition is arguably most firmly established. The incumbent DT AG has lost up to 40 per cent of market share in the first two years of competition and prices are falling rapidly. The entry of numerous operators with own transmission capacity means that the industry is at present displaying over-capacity and price competition is fierce, a development very similar to the electricity market. The significant difference between the two industries is that over-capacity in telecommunications is due to competitive entry in the infrastructure domain, thus eroding the network monopoly argument.[23] Moreover, the telecommunications market is still expanding rapidly, leaving room for new entrants and services. In electricity, duplication of the grid infrastructure is still considered uneconomic, and over-capacity in generation will disappear only in the medium term to leave room for more efficient generating plant to replace current capacity.

13.6. CONCLUDING REMARKS

While not one of the pioneering countries of liberalization in Europe, Germany has in the past few years gone far in introducing competition into the three network utilities discussed in this chapter. German reforms embrace the principles of European legislation for the industries in question; they have however gone beyond the minimal prescriptions of the European directives where electricity and rail are concerned. An important conclusion from the survey provided above is that idiosyncratic national features, in particular the decentralized nature of electricity supply and of rail transport services, have shaped the regulatory framework that has been set up parallel to the introduction of competition. Only in the telecommunications industry has a sector-specific comprehensive regulatory body been established, emulating what has become the UK model. For both the electricity and the rail industries, it is the Federal Cartel Office that acts as guardian of competition. Long-term structural problems remain in electricity and rail, but in the short term the overall success of the liberalization measures in introducing competition cannot be questioned.

REFERENCES

Brunekreeft, G. (1999). 'Germany: negotiating access', in, *A European Market for Electricity? Monitoring European Deregulation 2*, London: Centre for Economic Policy Research.
—— and Gross, W. (1999). *Price Structures in the Market for Long-Distance Voice Telephony in Germany*, Discussion Paper 61, Institut für Verkehrswissenschaft und Regionalpolitik, Universität Freiburg, June.
Bundesverband der Energie-Abnehmer (BEA) (1999). *VEA-Strompreisvergleich*, Stand 1.7.99.
Hass-Klau, C. (1998). *Rail Privatisation: Britain and Germany Compared*, London: Anglo-German Foundation.

---

[23] Consolidation because of over-capacities is also occurring in the telecommunications industry. Arcor bought o.tel.o in April 1999, so that only two of the initial three alternative national network operators remain. However, new entrants keep concentration ratios low even in the network activities.

IEA (1997). *Energy Policies of IEA Countries: Germany 1998 Review*, Paris: OECD/ IEA.

McKinsey (2000). 'A Shopper's Guide to Electricity Assets in Europe', *McKinsey Quarterly*, No. 2, Europe: 60–7.

Müller, J. and Stahl, K. (1996). 'Regulation of the Market for Electricity in the Federal Republic of Germany', in R. J. Gilbert and E. P. Kahn (eds.), *International Comparisons of Electricity Regulation*, Cambridge: Cambridge University Press.

RegTP (1999). *Tätigkeitsbericht 1998/99 der Regulierungsbehörde für Telekommunikation und Post gem. § 81 Abs. 1 TKG und gem. § 47 Abs. 1 PostG*, Bonn, December.

—— (2000a). *Telekommunikations- und Postmarkt im Jahre 1999*, Bonn, June.

—— (2000b). *Halbjahresbericht 2000: Marketbeobachtungsdaten der Regulierungsbehörde für Telekommunication und Post*, Bonn, July.

Schulz, W. (1996). 'Alternatives for Introducing Competition in the German Electricity Industry', in R. Sturm and S. Wilks (eds), *Wettbewerbspolitik und die Ordnung der Elekrizitätswirtschaft in Deutschland und Grossbritannien*, Baden-Baden: Nomos.

Sturm R. and Wilks, S. (1997). *Competition Policy and the Regulation of the Electricity Supply Industry in Britain and Germany*, London: Anglo-German Foundation.

VDEW (1998). *Strommarkt Deutschland 1997*, Frankfurt am Main: VDEW.

—— (1999a). *Jahresbericht 1998*, Frankfrut am Main: VDEW.

—— (1999b). *Electricity 1998*, Frankfurt am Main: VDEW.

VEA (2000). *Strompreisvergleich Deutschland*, Hannover: Bundesverband der Energie-Abnehmer VEA.

WIK (1998). *Ein analytisches Kostenmodell für das Ortsnetz*, Wissenschaftliches Institut für Kommunikationsdienste.

—— (1999). *Entwicklung der Märkte für Telekommunikationsdienstleistungen*, Wissenschaftliches Institut für Kommunikationsdienste, November.

14

Liberalization of Energy Markets: The German Way

ULF BÖGE

14.1. THE EUROPEAN CONTEXT

The European Commission set the course for competition in the European energy sector with the Single Market directive on electricity[1] and gas.[2] The aim was to liberalize the monopolized gas and electricity markets in all EU member states by introducing rules on open network access.

Although the electricity directive places an obligation on the member states to open up their markets, it does give them a certain amount of leeway regarding how they go about doing this. Germany decided to liberalize its electricity market immediately and completely, so that small enterprises should also have the opportunity —not least for competition reasons—to choose their electricity suppliers freely. Therefore, in contrast to other member states, Germany has gone beyond the provisions of the directive, which merely provides for a gradual liberalization of the markets.

It would be desirable, however, if market liberalization could proceed more quickly in the neighbouring countries too, especially in France, to avoid difficulties arising in cases of cross-border mergers, for example. The International Energy Agency also recently criticized the French law liberalizing the electricity market for having made hardly any contribution to the development of competition.

14.2. THE MARKET SITUATION IN GERMANY

Competition in the electricity sector in Germany has taken hold more quickly than many people expected. Electricity prices to large customers in Germany have fallen by up to 60 per cent, and are thus among the lowest in the EU. Consumers too have profited from this development, indirectly, since the prices for energy-intensive products are tending to fall. Consumers are also benefiting

---

[1] OJ EC no. L 27/20, 30 January 1997.   [2] OJ EC no. L 204/1, 21 July 1998.

from liberalization directly, since the electricity tariffs for private households have fallen by around 20 per cent since liberalization was introduced.

Similar results have not been achieved so far in the gas sector, although it must be remembered that liberalization of this sector began two years after the electricity markets were opened to competition.

14.3. THE GENERAL CONDITIONS UNDERLYING ENERGY LIBERALIZATION IN GERMANY

The general conditions applying to the transmission of gas and electricity via rival companies' networks are of central importance to competition. The Single Market Directive stipulates that network access can be achieved by negotiations between the parties concerned or by means of state regulation.

Germany has consistently followed the path via the market and has thereby also broken new ground. It preferred not to have a state regulation or to issue a network access regulation, but decided instead on a flexible solution of negotiations between energy producers and their buyers. So-called negotiated network access takes into account the experience and knowledge of the market participants and, unlike the often inflexible state requirements, is open to change.

The first Associations' Agreement on electricity was concluded in 1998 between the relevant associations of electricity producers and representatives of the electricity customers. This set down for the first time the criteria for determining the fees charged for third-party access and network use. It was replaced by an improved version just eighteen months later. This second Associations' Agreement ended the controversy surrounding the network use charge by no longer making it dependent on the distance between electricity suppliers and electricity customers. Instead, two trading zones were formed, one in the north and one in the south. No distance-related charge was made for transmissions within a zone. A fee was charged, however, for electricity transmissions from one zone to the other. This fee poses a considerable barrier to new firms wishing to enter the market.

The two-zone model itself has in the meantime been superseded. The Bundeskartellamt's examination of the proposed merger of the two power utility companies RWE and VEW, and the European Commission's examination of the proposed concentration of VEBA and VIAG, were decisive in bringing about this change. In the course of these merger investigations, the companies concerned stated that they were prepared to refrain from charging a transmission fee. The competition authorities made the abandonment of the two-zone model one of the prerequisites for clearing the mergers.[3] Meanwhile,

---

[3] RWE/VEW: BKartA 03.07.2000 = WuW/E DE-V 301; also www.bundeskartellamt.de/fusion.htm, B8-309/99; VEBA/VIAG: European Commission 13.06.2000 = WuW/E EU-V 509.

all the German power utilities have decided to stop charging a transmission fee for supplies between these zones. This is an extremely positive development in competition terms.

The development in the gas sector is less promising from a competition point of view. So far there have been hardly any transmissions by third parties that would have had the effect of introducing competition into the market. The Associations' Agreement on gas, which, like the Associations' Agreement on electricity, was worked out by the associations operating in the sectors of the economy concerned, has not improved this situation to any significant degree. A follow-up agreement is already being discussed, however. It is important that the shortcomings of the first agreement, i.e. a lack of transparency and practicability, are not repeated.

14.4. THE MARKET FOR BALANCING ENERGY

The Bundeskartellamt is also endeavouring to improve the framework conditions for competition that go beyond the scope of the Associations' Agreements. During its examination of the RWE–VEW merger, for example, it opened up the previously closed market for balancing power.

Every electricity supplier depends on the respective transmission network operators providing so-called balancing energy. The reason for this is that, although electricity supply is determined by the electricity consumption expected by the supplier, this may not fully coincide with a customer's actual electricity consumption. The resulting discrepancy between expected and actual consumption is compensated for by the balancing energy provided by the network operators. It is easier for very large suppliers such as utility companies than for new entrants supplying small amounts to forecast and compensate for fluctuations in supply. The new entrants' costs for balancing energy are difficult to forecast and therefore are comparatively high.

The Bundeskartellamt stipulates that this energy need no longer be obtained from the network operator in the network territory of RWE and VEW. It can be obtained from other suppliers as part of a competitive tendering procedure. The tendering procedure is now under way and the market for balancing energy in the territories of REW and VEW is expected to be open to competition by the beginning of February 2001.

In the course of another merger investigation, the Bundeskartellamt also placed the utility E.on (formed as a result of the VEBA–VIAG merger) under obligation to invite tenders for the procurement of balancing energy in its network area.[4] It is expected that the progress made here with regard to competition will soon also assert itself in the other network areas of Germany.

[4] E.on/Hein Gas, available from www.bundeskartellamt.de/fusion.htm, B8-132/00.

14.5. APPLICATION OF THE ACT AGAINST RESTRAINTS OF COMPETITION (ARC)

The Bundeskartellamt has in certain cases applied the essential facilities criterion of Section 19(4), no. 4, of the ARC to push through the competitive liberalization of the market. This provision binds an energy provider in principle to allow third parties to transmit electricity via its network.

In the electricity sector the parties concerned have agreed on modalities of transmission in several proceedings after being placed under pressure by the Bundeskartellamt. The first case in this sector involved the electricity of an American energy company being transmitted to a German municipal utility via the network of a regional electricity supply company.[5] In other cases a formal decision was issued. This occurred for example in September 1999, when the Bundeskartellamt bound the Berlin electricity company BEWAG to transmit electricity to interested commercial buyers, public services, and final customers.[6] The company had refused to grant third-party access by arguing that the capacity of the line used for the transmission was not sufficient. In its decision, the Bundeskartellamt concluded that a network operator must remain neutral and treat the interests of third parties wishing to use the network on equal terms; the owner of the network cannot claim general priority for its own electricity supplies.

After putting a new high-voltage cable system into operation, BEWAG gave up its resistance to the transmission.[7] Full third-party access is being granted now that Berlin has better connections to the German interconnected electricity network. During the proceedings, which lasted a good twelve months, the Bundeskartellamt's decision ensured that BEWAG's competitors were able to supply their own electricity to their customers within the limited capacity.

Hardly any third party access has been granted in the gas sector. The Bundeskartellamt is, however, implementing non-discriminatory network access in individual cases here too. In the summer of 2000 a foreign gas company wishing to operate in the German market approached the Bundeskartellamt. The incumbent network operators were refusing to transmit the gas via their networks, particularly because of the discrepancies over what the transmission charge was to be. The Bundeskartellamt achieved immediate third-party access in return for the payment of a provisional fee. The proper fee is being calculated by the Bundeskartellamt in the course of the proceedings that are now pending and will then be charged with retroactive effect in place of the provisional solution.[8]

---

[5] 1997/8 *Activity Report* of the Bundeskartellamt, p. 29.

[6] BKartA 30.08.1999—Berliner Stromdurchleitung = WuW/E DE-V 149; also www.bundeskartellamt.de/kartell.htm, B8-99/99.

[7] Bundeskartellamt press release of 15 November 2000, www.bundeskartellamt.de/news.html.

[8] Bundeskartellamt press release of 24 August 2000, www.bundeskartellamt.de/nachrichten.html.

14.6. FURTHER LIBERALIZATION FOR THE BENEFIT OF PRIVATE CUSTOMERS

Although electricity prices for private households have fallen by up to 20 per cent in Germany, competition on the market for private customers is still not satisfactory. It is precisely in this market that incumbent network operators are impeding new electricity suppliers from supplying their newly acquired customers.

The Bundeskartellamt and the competition authorities of the German *Länder* have received numerous complaints of incumbent electricity companies charging excessive fees for the use of their networks and making other unjustified demands such as charging a fee when customers switch to another supplier.

The main task of German competition authorities in creating extensive and effective competition in the energy supply via networks will be to prevent this widespread form of hindrance of new market participants by applying the instruments of competition law.

14.7. NO REGULATORY AUTHORITY FOR GAS AND ELECTRICITY

There are good reasons why Germany has no regulatory authority for gas and electricity. A regulatory authority would undermine the aim of the lawmaker and also the wish of the business community to enable competitors to acquire network access by means of negotiation, i.e. via the Associations' Agreement.

There are fundamental reasons for not having a regulatory authority. A fragmented competition law preserves competitively unjustifiable features of the sectors concerned. It was not for nothing that the lawmaker endeavoured to remove sector-specific rules as part of the amendment to German competition law in 1998.[9]

Politicians and electricity traders are now calling for a regulatory authority, citing the example of competition in the telecommunications sector. The two sectors are not comparable, however. The market structure in the telecoms sector is clearly different from that of energy supply via networks. In the telecoms markets Deutsche Telekom had a state-controlled monopoly. In the electricity sector there were a multitude of private enterprises and municipal utilities with regional monopolies. It is therefore logical that the lawmaker has provided for sector-specific regulation to end in the telecoms sector as soon as the former state-controlled monopolist has lost its dominant position.

---

[9] Explanatory memorandum on government draft, BT-Drucksache 13/9720 of 29 January 1998, published in WuW, special edition on the ARC, p. 64.

Market results (e.g. a 60 and 20 per cent drop in electricity prices for large customers and private households, respectively) are another reason why setting up a price-regulating authority is not advisable. By using the instruments of competition law, the Bundeskartellamt will achieve further improvements also in areas where competitive deficits still exist, especially for tariff-rate customers in the electricity sector, and in the entire gas sector.

PART III

NEW REGULATORY ISSUES IN EUROPE AND BEYOND

15

Network Utilities: The EU Institutions and the Member States

P.A. BUIGUES, O. GUERSENT AND J.F. PONS

15.1. INTRODUCTION

This chapter draws general lessons from the European perspective. It clarifies the fundamental roles of Community regulatory policy and competition law, in particular in coordinating national regulatory approaches and promoting liberalization in the context of the integration of European network industries.

In network industries, regulatory reforms and liberalization are expected to improve the static and dynamic efficiency of an enterprise by ensuring a better allocation of resources and fostering the availability of new products and services by encouraging technological innovation. The whole process should, therefore, lead to a reduction in costs and prices as well as an increase in demand and supply.

However, changes brought about by liberalization also imply adjustment costs. The main challenges are to encourage efficiency, competition, and general public acceptance with the liberalization process. To ensure that the benefits of liberalization will be shared, political decisions need to be made. At the European level, these include:

1. the question of the appropriate level of public intervention (European, national, local), taking into account the principle of subsidiarity; and
2. the question of the respective roles of competition authorities and sector-specific regulatory authorities.

The following section summarizes the present EU governance model adopted for network industries, and the choice made of the different possible approaches (liberalization *v.* harmonization) and different policy instruments (directive, regulation, recommendation). Network industries have in common the fact that network infrastructure entails both a heavy fixed cost and potential substantial economies of scale. However, at the same time network industries differ widely in terms of their importance from a public service

We express our gratitude to Karen Frazer for her contribution.

obligation point of view, the extent of natural monopoly, and even factors of production composition (capital intensities, qualifications of the labour force). Therefore, there is not one general accepted EU governance model for all network industries (telecommunications, transport, energy).

Section 15.3 focuses on the telecommunications sector, where the liberalization process is most advanced. It presents the EU model in terms of detailed description and analysis of international competences at both national and EU levels. Section 15.4, again addressing only the telecommunications sector, presents a perspective on the respective responsibilities and capabilities of sector-specific regulation and competition law in the process of the liberalization of the telecommunications sector.

15.2. PRESENT EU GOVERNANCE MODEL FOR NETWORK INDUSTRIES

15.2.1. *Approaches: liberalization v. harmonization*

Liberalization measures are based on Article 86 of the Treaty of Rome. The basic principle of this Article concerns the application of competition law to public undertakings or to undertakings with special or exclusive rights. Member states may not give rights or maintain measures that impede the Treaty's competition rules. Therefore, liberalization has focused on removing the special and exclusive rights, e.g. monopoly status, enjoyed by undertakings in network industries while bearing in mind member state and Community commitments to services of general economic interest. Liberalization measures based on Article 86 are a crucial part of the Community's plan to realize the benefits of full competition. On the basis of competition policy principles, liberalization measures have removed legal entry barriers across member states and set forth general rules for competition in network industries.

This liberalization has to cope with public service obligations that may be imposed by the public authorities on the body rendering the service, such as protecting the environment, economic and social cohesion, land use, and the planning and promotion of consumer interest.[1]

Harmonization is based on Article 95 of the Treaty. The basic principle of this Article is to remove barriers to the construction of a common market. In the context of network industries, harmonization refers to how member states align or 'harmonize' their sector-specific regulatory regimes. The objective of employing a harmonized approach is to create a common denominator of regulatory rules within the common market, to ensure a sense of security (or credible commitment) for private investment, and to encourage the development of a true common market for network industries.

In *telecommunications* liberalization and harmonization have been pursued simultaneously, with liberalization directives opening individual subsectors

---

[1] 'Services of General Interest in Europe', communication from the Commission, Sept. 1996.

complemented by harmonization directives through the open network provision (ONP) framework. The Commission thus adopted a series of directives on the basis of Article 86 of the Treaty asking member states to abolish the exclusive rights and certain special rights that had been granted to their public-sector telecommunications companies. Directives were also necessary to harmonize the legislation of the member states in order to avoid the erection of new barriers between member states.

For the *energy sector*, liberalization (the opening of markets for electricity generation, transmission, and distribution) was begun in 1996 without accompanying harmonization measures. After a first proposal for a directive on common rules for an internal market in 1992, and a very lively debate, the Council of Europe decided in 1996 and 1998 that market opening should entail the selling off of 26 per cent of the electricity sectors and 20 per cent of the gas sectors, increasing gradually over a period of ten years without fixing a date for the full opening of markets.

In *air transport*, liberalization was achieved by the freedom of establishment, with an ending of the exclusive rights of state-owned 'flag carriers' and the introduction of free movement of services, cabotage being now allowed. However, a large number of city-pair routes still feature duopolies of established companies. This is why the control of mergers and alliances is so important in the air transport sector. In contrast to the telecommunications sector, air transport lacks a single unifying theme (such as open network provision) within which harmonization measures can be developed and revised.

15.2.2. *Instruments: legislative initiatives in network industries*

Three main legislative instruments were used in the network industries: regulations, directives, and recommendations. *Regulations* have direct effect in national courts, and so do not require transposition into national law for implementation by member states. Therefore, a regulation as a Community legislative instrument allows less room for variation in application of policy among member states. *Directives* instruct member states to develop and implement national legislation in order to implement policy decisions of the Community. As a Community legislative instrument, directives require transposition into national law in order to be effective. *Recommendations* are not mandatory, but they may be adopted by the Commission and implemented by national authorities within six months, compared with at least three years for directives.

Beginning in 1988, *telecommunications* liberalization directives opened the markets for terminal equipment, advanced telecommunications services, satellite and mobile services, telecommunications services via cable networks, and finally the full array of telecommunications services (including voice telephony) in 1998. Harmonization was also pursued via directives through the unifying programme of open network provision (ONP). As liberalization and harmonization were pursued entirely through directives, much of the programme has required substantial input and accomplishment by member states. Member state implementation of the liberalization directives has been completed by nearly all member states, while transposition of the harmonization directive is proceeding with only a handful of member states behind schedule.

More and more 'soft laws' and recommendations are used in the telecoms sector, since the adoption by the Council and the European Parliament of directives requires at least three years and the technological development in these sectors is quite rapid. Recent recommendations were based on 'benchmarking' exercises as for leased lines or interconnection. These recommendations present the pricing situation for individual member states and recommend that the three lowest prices are benchmarked for all member states.

Energy liberalization has focused on market subsectors (transmission, generation, distribution), although these were opened all at once, in the 1996 Directive on Common rules of the internal market in electricity, rather than sequentially in separate directives. The directive has been transposed into national law in nearly all the member states, and member states have gone beyond the minimum open requirement of the Council when implementing the electricity directive.

15.2.3. *Restructuring of network industries in the USA and the EU*

For the *telecommunications* sector in the United States, which has a long tradition of complex regulatory oversight between the fifty state public utility commissions (PUCs), the Federal Communications Commission (FCC), and the courts, liberalization has proceeded on many jurisdictional fronts. It has advanced subsector by subsector, with challenges from time to time arising from each of the parties having regulatory oversight. First, terminal equipment markets were opened; then international and advanced telecommunications services were liberalized, followed by long-distance services and, finally, voice telephony in 1996. In contrast to the EU, however, this was achieved not through a successive programme of legislation. The 1996 Telecommunications Act bringing full liberalization for telecommunications actually capped nearly twenty years of liberalization at the state level, within the FCC, and in court decisions (most notably with one of the largest antitrust cases in US history, the 1984 AT&T divestiture).

As in the EU, liberalization of the *energy* sector in the USA has only recently begun. Many US states have begun to experiment with allowing competition at the local level for energy transmission, as competition is allowed but not required by federal law.

For *air transport*, liberalization in the USA has involved opening the air carrier market to new entry, and removing price regulation for air fares.

However, unlike in telecommunications or energy, air transport liberalization has culminated in a complete restructuring of regulatory oversight for the industry at the national level. The federal air regulatory agency, the Civil Aeronautics Board (CAB), was abolished entirely; in its place is a new independent agency, the Federal Aviation Administration (FAA), which focuses on air safety. Regulation of ancillary services, such as airport management, is achieved at the state and local level.

In the United States, for industries under the purview of independent sector-specific regulatory agencies, federal legislation traditionally gives the overall framework and powers for oversight of a particular sector, and agency regulations implement the framework through detailed regulations. However, depending upon when the framework statute was written or revised and the general political forces in the environment surrounding regulatory oversight, there may be more or less room for agency interpretation. Finally, in the US judicial system there is an explicit and well developed body of administrative practice which involves the federal courts much more directly in the implementation of regulation, particularly in the form of judicial review.

Regulatory decision-making is far more centralized in the United States (as would be expected), with the FCC especially, since the Telecommunications Act, in charge of developing and administering the full complement of sector-specific regulation required in the transition from monopoly to full competition (e.g. licensing, interconnection). As with the EU, the energy sector has only recently begun to liberalize (and in the USA there is no federal-level legislative measure requiring full competition equivalent to the 1996 directive). With regard to air transport, the United States seems far more aggressive in liberalizing this sector, going so far as to abolish federal-level oversight except for air safety and the full removal of price and entry barriers. In contrast, measures to develop a European-wide air traffic control and safety authority in the EU have languished, while state aid to national carriers was given in order to compensate for some of the effects of competition in air transport.

Table 15.1 sets out the differences in government oversight of network industries in the United States and the European Union.

15.3. INSTITUTIONAL COMPETENCES AT NATIONAL AND EU LEVELS (SUBSIDIARITY) FOR THE TELECOMMUNICATIONS SECTOR

15.3.1. *Overview: institutional division of labour*

The principle of subsidiarity maintains that, if activities can be or should be accomplished at the member state level, they will be. Community-level activities are to be restricted to those functions that involve a Community interest. With regard to the introduction and maintenance of competition in network industries, and particularly the telecommunications sector, the Community

Table 15.1. *Government oversight of network industries in the USA and EU*

	USA	EU
Telecommunications		
Regulation *v.* competition status	No entry restrictions; unbundling for local competition mandated	No entry restrictions; unbundling for local competition not mandated
Decentralization of government oversight	Jurisdiction shared between state PUCs and FCC—all 'independent' regulatory agencies	Jurisdiction shared between EU-level regulator and national sector-specific regulators or government body (e.g. ministry)
Ownership structure	Private	From private to partially privatized
Energy		
Regulation *v.* competition status	No entry restrictions; unbundling for local competition not mandated, but majority of states are experimenting with local competition	Full entry liberalization in process; third-party access regulated by member states
Decentralization of government oversight	Jurisdiction shared between state PUCs and FERC, which are independent agencies	Jurisdiction shared
Ownership structure	Mix of private and some municipal systems at the local level	Seven member states favour public or mixed public–private ownership; eight member states feature public ownership of electricity transmission
Air transport		
Regulation *v.* competition status	No entry restrictions; US competition authorities investigating possible predatory pricing by airlines	No entry restrictions; EU competition authorities have investigated entry via slot allocations and ground-handling services
Decentralization of government oversight	No federal regulatory oversight (CAB abolished); competition rules and air safety regulation at federal level only	Jurisdiction primarily within member states, with EU-level authorities setting general policy
Ownership structure	Private, with some municipal aid for airports	Public or partially privatized, state aid allocated to national airlines for restructuring

interest is in promoting the common market and establishing clear rules of the game for the emerging competitive environment.

According to the economic analysis of institutional incentives (issues of agency), a trade-off exists between the possibility of capture and the information needs of the regulatory authority.[2] Research suggests that, where possible, regulatory oversight should remain as close to the actual players and conduct of the market as possible in order to allow for ease of information-gathering and the development of an accurate perspective on the industry or sector. However, the proximity of the regulator to the regulated industry invites the possibility of capture by the industry or industry segments under regulatory oversight.

While keeping in mind the possibility of capture, which can be overcome by such institutional measures as adequate salaries and arm's-length relationships between regulator and regulated firm, oversight functions have indeed been delegated to the level closest to the industry, e.g. the national level. It is understood by many member states and market players that national-level authorities are best positioned to implement Community policy on telecommunications, based upon their understanding of the unique characteristics of the national environment.[3]

15.3.2. *Regulatory competences*

As liberalization of the sector proceeds, more and more functions are to devolve to the member states. National regulatory authority (NRA) responsibilities include: the drafting or granting of authorizations to enter a market; dispute resolution among market players; universal service and tariff rebalancing; and other aspects of implementation of the ONP and liberalization directives. The results of the public consultation on the 1999 Communication Review present the main elements of the future regulatory framework:

1. introduction of more flexibility into the new regulatory framework via the increased use of recommendations, guidelines, and co-regulatory solutions to problems;
2. more room for subsidiarity in resources areas, since it will make it clear that member states are free to establish auctions and other spectrum pricing mechanisms for the assignment of frequency if they consider them necessary to ensure the optimal use of the radio spectrum;
3. regulation designed primarily to manage the transition to competition, to be imposed on specific undertakings as a function of their market power, and to be removed as competition increases.

---

[2] 'Liberalization of Network Industries: Economic Implications and Policy Issues', *European Economy*, 1996.
[3] COM(1999)537, 11 November 1999, Fifth Report on the Implementation of the Telecommunications Regulatory Package, OJ C 1998/265, 22.8.1998, p. 2.

The concept for imposing *ex ante* obligations related to access and interconnection would be based on the concept of dominant position in particular markets, calculated in a manner consistent with competition law practice. NRAs would be able to designate undertakings on which they could impose *ex ante* obligations where:

- the undertaking has financed infrastructure partly or wholly on the basis of special or exclusive rights which have been abolished, and there are major legal technical or economic barriers to market entry, in particular for construction of network infrastructure; and/or
- the undertaking concerned is an integrated entity and its competitors necessarily require access to some of its facilities to compete with it in a downstream market; and neither national nor EU competition law remedies suffice to ensure effective competition and choice in the market concerned.

The types of obligation that could be imposed on an undertaking will cover non-discrimination and transparency, including accounting separation; pricing of services, including cost orientation; access to, and use of, unbundled network elements and/or associated facilities.

NRAs would draw up the list of organizations for the purposes of implementing the *ex ante* obligations and would notify the Commission of such a list, together with the precise obligations imposed. Thereafter, determinations of the relevant markets, and of the positions of market players on those markets, would be carried out by NRAs on a regular basis, in order to adapt regulatory obligations. Such assessment by NRAs should take place in close coordination with the national competition authority. Guidelines at European level would be necessary to facilitate the correct application of the competition law principles, and to avoid having different market definitions in different member states.

15.3.3. *Commission competences*

Directives
The Commission is in charge of ensuring a correct transposition of directives. Community competition initiatives in the liberalization of telecommunications involved not only the specific liberalization directives, but also the harmonization directives. The Commission has issued decisions relating to the implementation of the liberalization and harmonization directives. It has decided to allow certain member states additional time for the implementation according to their specific national situation.[4] It has also issued decisions on the Licensing Directive, where member states had imposed charges on new entrants in mobile telephony markets which were contrary to Article 86(3).[5]

---

[4] Additional implementation periods for the Full Competition Directive for Ireland, Portugal, Luxembourg, Spain and Greece.   [5] GSM Spain; GSM Italy.

The annual reports on the Implementation of the Telecommunications Regulatory Package focus on the transposition into national law of the key elements of the directives, and in the Fifth Report attention has moved to the effective application of nationally transposed rules. The conclusions of this report underline 'the comparatively low level of harmonization in particular of the Community licensing and interconnection regimes....the lack of a proper national implementation of the regulatory framework for cost accounting in many member states and a lack of competition in the local access market'.

Currently, there are several infringement proceedings open against member states in relation to the rebalancing of voice telephony tariffs. Under the legal monopolies, telecoms operators used to cross-subsidize low line rental with high call charges, especially for long-distance and international calls. According to the Full Competition Directive (90/388/EEC) and the Voice Telephony ONP Directive (98/10/EC), tariffs for voice telephony, when offered by dominant operators, have in principle to be cost-oriented.

The success of the internet in the USA is to a large extent due to the combination of cost-oriented line rental and free local calls—including flat rates—allowing users to benefit more effectively from the economies of scale allowed by a more intensive use of the network.

Tariff rebalancing does not mean that consumers have to pay more, on average. Rebalancing should be a 'zero sum operation', because increases in subscription fees should be compensated by decreases in call charges. Community law requires telephony tariffs to be affordable, and the Commission has promoted the application of social tariffs and low user schemes, to avoid the risk that the weakest consumers will be hit by increases in telephone tariffs.

Competition Policy

The Commission competences in the field of competition policy cover decisions taken under Articles 81, 82, and 86 of the Treaty, including merger control as well as sector inquiries launched for telecommunications in 1999. There were only twelve Commission decisions under Articles 81 and 82 from 1982 to 1997 and seven Commission decisions under Article 86.

Even before any decision is taken, however, Commission investigations on the basis of competition rules have repeatedly resulted in significant reductions in rates. After the Commission carried out an 'own-initiative' (*ex officio*) investigation into the prices of interconnection between fixed and mobile operators, prices decreased significantly in nearly all member states where problems were identified. This rate reduction also occurred following a complaint by MCI Worldcom against termination rates of fixed – mobile operators in three different member states. After the Commission initiated these investigations in late 1999, rates decreased by as much as 50 per cent for many of the operators involved. Experience has proved that operators, when threatened with potential negative decisions, do understand the meaning of competition rules and are very likely to change their behaviour.

The Commission has also launched three sector inquiries on the implementation of Community legislation for liberalization and harmonization: for roaming charges in mobile telephony markets, for international leased lines, and for interconnection charges.

As part of its jurisdiction over joint ventures under Article 81 of the Treaty, the Commission has applied Community competition law to undertakings in the markets for corporate data service,[6] satellite manufacturing and distribution,[7] and mobile services.[8] In general, the Commission has focused on the effect of the concentration on competition in specific markets. It has found that, when the joint venture in question creates new service markets, the concentration is compatible with the Treaty. Where it is judged that the concentration would close off or prevent competition from emerging, particularly in new markets such as next-generation mobile services or media markets, the Commission has imposed conditions (either structural or behavioural) on the undertakings involved, or has found the undertaking to be incompatible with Community law.[9] The Commission has also taken into consideration the level of openness of the member state markets in question, and in some cases has made clearance of the concentrations dependent upon further restructuring or liberalization in these markets.

Finally, the Commission remains responsible for the determination of policy issues in competition law affecting telecommunications markets. For example, in 1998 the Commission issued its Notice on the Application of Competition Rules to Access Agreements in the Telecommunications Sector (e.g. interconnection). This sets out Community policy regarding market definition, the abuse of dominance (including essential facilities), and other relevant aspects of Community competition rules in order to clarify where access agreements might contravene Community law.

Recently the adoption by the Commission of a communication and recommendation on the 'Unbundling of the Local Loop' is a most important initiative. The 'local loop' refers to the physical circuit between the customer's premises and the telecommunications operator's local switch or equivalent facility. Permitting 'unbundled access to the local loop' means allowing other operators to use, partially or fully, the local loops installed by incumbent telephone operators, enabling them to install new cost-effective technologies such as DSL (digital subscriber loops). Under full unbundled access to the local loop, a new entrant has exclusive control of the local loop, and in this way new market entrants can deploy new technologies to provide competitive services to consumers, including new broad-band services and high-speed internet services.

---

[6] BT/MCI, ISPS, Atlas/Phoenix/Global One, Unisource/Uniworld.
[7] Alcatel Espace/ANT, Astra.
[8] Konsortium ECR 900, Iridium.
[9] Astra, Alcatel Espace/ANT; MSG; Nordic Satellite; Telefonica-Sogecable.

In all cases, competition rules apply, and refusals by dominant operators to open the local loop to competitors requesting access may constitute a form of abuse of the dominant position under Article 82 of the Treaty, such as refusals to deal and limitation of production, markets, or technical development to the prejudice of consumers. Where access is granted, fair and non-discriminatory conditions of access are crucial for the successful opening of the local loop and the development of a competitive market telecommunications services, in particular high-speed services. This requires close monitoring of delays, prices, and contractual arrangements between incumbents and new entrants.

15.3.4. *The sharing of responsibilities*

The Commission 'Notice on the Application of Competition Rules to Access Agreements in the Telecommunications Sector'[10] (the 'Access Notice') deals with the relationship between the application of competition rules and sector-specific regulation as well as with procedural issues regarding access agreements in the telecommunications sector. It notably sets out (para. 28) that priority should be given to sector-specific regulation applied by NRAs where applicable, and subject to the rights of companies to complain under the competition rules.

In antitrust cases under Regulation 17 that are clearly national cases,[11] where there are related actions before an NRA and where it has the power to remedy the competition problems at issue, the Commission will generally not initially pursue any investigation as to the existence of an infringement of EU competition rules. In these cases the Commission suspends its own investigation pending the conclusion of the national proceeding. It may then decide to close its own case, if the competition problems have been solved in line with the case law of the Court of Justice. This is however subject to the following points:

1. National proceedings must be concluded in a reasonable period of time, typically not more than six months.
2. Some particular cases may have a substantial Community interest affecting, or likely to affect, competition in a number of member states.

Moreover, the NRAs must ensure that actions taken by them in application of sector-specific rules are consistent with Community competition law. Indeed, on the basis of the case law of the Court of Justice, in particular the Ahmed Saeed judgment[12] and the recent CNSD[13] judgment, they must not encourage, reinforce, or approve anti-competitive behaviour, for example pricing practices contrary to Article 85 or 86.

---

[10] OJ C 265 p 2, 22.08.1998.
[11] Council Regulation No. 17 of 6 February 1962, First Regulation Implementing Articles 85 and 86 of the Treaty, OJ 13/204 (1962), as amended.
[12] Case 66/86, Ahmed Saeed (1989) ECR 838.
[13] C-35/96, Consiglio nazionale degli spedizionieri doganali, 18 June 1998; not yet published.

In competition matters, while NCAs have primary jurisdiction over national matters, the Commission has jurisdiction over cases where it finds a Community interest. NCA responsibilities also involve applying Community law to national cases, in addition to national competition law.

15.4. CONCLUSION

The liberalization of network industries in Europe is a 'success story': it has ensured that technological progress has led to new services, lower prices, and job creation. Operators, financiers, workers, consumers, regulators, governments, and the European institutions have all played a part in this success. But the story is not yet over. Setting the rules of the game for fair competition ensures that the work of the national authorities and of the Commission will continue to be important in the near future.

There are also differences among member states, as well as between one sector and another, in the design, scope, and approaches of general interest services owing to different national traditions. Many member states take the view that general interest services make an important contribution to economic and social cohesion.

16

Alternative Models for Future Regulation

P.A. BUIGUES, O. GUERSENT, AND J.F. PONS

16.1. INTRODUCTION

It was not by chance that Community liberalization policy came into being in the 1980s.

At a time when, following the Single Act, the legislative programme for the creation of the single market on 1 January 1993 was being put in place, the establishment of the single market suddenly made this simple fact obvious: whole sectors of the market would be excluded from the internal market and its anticipated benefits because they were characterized by exclusive rights or a monopoly.

At the same time, the European economies had to face up to a new international environment with four main characteristics: faster technological and scientific progress, a demographic explosion with the corresponding increase in the global working population, an unprecedented increase in the output of goods and services, and greater dependence caused by the liberalization of the movement of goods and capital. In this connection, the two reports submitted to the European Commission by a group of experts set up at its request under the chairmanship of Mr Ciampi highlighted the fact that access to high-quality, low-cost network services (telecommunications, transportations, energy, post) was a vital factor for the competitiveness of European industry as a whole.

This led to the setting up, for most network services, and to varying degrees and by various legal means—whether autonomous directives under Article 86 or Council harmonization directives—of a Community liberalization policy which is based on common general principles but also has characteristics specific to each member state and/or each economic sector.

The views expressed in this paper are those of the authors and are not attributable to the Commission of the European Communities by which they are employed.

16.2. COMMON PRINCIPLES, SPECIFIC REGULATIONS

16.2.1. *Focus on objectives of strict economic efficiency*

All the liberalization policies conducted by the European Union, and consequently all systems of regulation set up in the various liberalized sectors, are based on an intangible fundamental principle, namely that infrastructure management is separate from the provision of services. This principle, whereby production, transport, and distribution activities are treated differently, is based on a simple theoretical observation: only those activities that have the character of a natural monopoly, i.e. activities where yields are increasing sharply and where technical and capital barriers to access are difficult to overcome, are likely to be managed in the form of regulated monopolies.

This concerns two types of regulation that are found in all sectors covered by Community liberalization policy:

1. regulation aimed at ensuring that infrastructure is managed as efficiently as possible: the objective is to avoid on the one hand borrowing, under-investment, and under-innovation and on the other over-investment, which is typical of this type of situation, and which was highlighted in the 1960s in the United States by theorists of the Chicago school, particularly Stigler;
2. regulation of the interface between network management and the service activity.

Beyond the apparent universality of these characteristics, which are common to all sectors in which liberalization has been initiated by Brussels, political requirements, the characteristics of each sector, and the choice of liberalization by means of Council directive, which allows member states considerable room for manoeuvre, have given rise not only to liberalization but also to regulation of variable geometry. Mere observation shows that sometimes systems of regulation are organized differently from one sector to another, sometimes they are similar for different sectors and types of liberalization, and sometimes in a particular sector the type of regulation, and the objectives and instruments of such regulation, are not necessarily the same from one member state to another, even though the Community regulations are identical. This merely reflects the fact that the choice of a given regulation in a given member state for a given market is widely affected by the specific mix between political acceptance and technical considerations.

Thus, as regards regulations aimed at ensuring the efficient management of essential facilities, the regulatory techniques employed are found to vary greatly. In some cases it has been decided to make the market artificially contestable by granting licences of limited duration for the use of scarce resources (Hertzian frequencies for mobile telephony, aircraft frequencies); in other cases the aim has been to facilitate access for competitors through asymmetric regulation (ban on telecommunications companies controlling cable operators); in other cases still the authorities have opted for regulation by objectives (electricity in the UK) or by comparison (regulation of water in the UK). For the same method of regulation, the second choices may vary from one member state to another. For example, as regards the allocation of Hertzian frequencies for mobile telephony, some member states have opted for an auction, and others for a so-called 'beauty contest'. Sometimes, in the same member state and in the same market, the initial licences are granted in the form of a beauty contest and subsequent ones by auction (mobile telephony in the Netherlands); in the case of GSM licences in Italy and Spain, licences were even being granted free of charge to the traditional operator and sold to new entrants, which led the European Commission to intervene.

The same is true as regards the regulation of services and the interface between services and infrastructure. European legislation has not opted to ban those managing essential facilities from also being involved in operating the services that are provided by means of those facilities. In certain cases (energy, postal services), it has even allowed part of the service activity to be allocated to the infrastructure manager. This choice can be explained by an economic analysis in terms of efficiency or a political analysis in terms of acceptability. Be that as it may, a situation in which the most powerful of competitors on the services market is also a mandatory partner for its competitors as regards access to an essential production factor has to be regulated in two ways: by price regulation, where the access charges to be imposed by the infrastructure manager are fixed, and by technical regulation, to ensure that the technical solutions chosen by the infrastructure manager do not in fact make it difficult, or even impossible, for new players to enter the market. Here, too, it can be seen that the member states have opted for different solutions, which have sometimes led the European Commission to intervene.

It can therefore be stated that, although all Community legislation is based on homogeneous fundamental principles, the variants and peculiarities are such that there is no possibility at present of arriving at a single regulatory model in Europe. Some welcome this, observing that this is proof of a laudable pragmatism. Others deplore it, pointing out that systems of regulation in the liberalized sectors have been built up in an empirical way rather than based according to an established theory, in which each structure and each concept has gradually gained ground; there is then, in some ways, a spontaneous organization of regulation.

Both positions are probably correct. The differences in structure and operation of the various systems of regulation in a particular sector, from one member state to another, are moreover even more obvious if the analysis takes account of objectives other than strict economic efficiency which are attributed to the various regulators.

16.3. FOCUS ON OBJECTIVES OTHER THAN THOSE OF STRICT ECONOMIC EFFICIENCY

Article 86(2) of the Treaty of Rome expressly allows national legislators and regulators to take account of objectives other than those of strict economic efficiency. It states:

Undertakings entrusted with the operation of services of general economic interest or having the character of a revenue-producing monopoly shall be subject to the rules contained in this Treaty, in particular to the rules on competition, insofar as the application of such rules does not obstruct the performance, in law or in fact, of the particular tasks assigned to them. The development of trade must not be affected to such an extent as would be contrary to the interests of the Community.

What are these interests other than objectives of strict economic efficiency which can and should be taken into account by the public authority? How does this tie in with economic efficiency objectives? What conclusions can be drawn regarding the architecture and operation of systems of regulation, particularly the links between Community and national level?

These issues open up a wide-ranging debate on the coexistence of a multiplicity of national conceptions of the public service within the European Union and on the conditions governing their compatibility with a body of common rules: the Treaty of Rome. Beyond this, they naturally give rise to the question of the relationships between national and Community levels as regards systems of regulation.

Article 86(2) (like Article 30) is an exception making it possible to derogate from the rules of the Treaty, and thus allowing both the legislator and the regulator to take account of objectives other than strict economic efficiency. However, as it is an exception, (i) it is the object of strict interpretation by the Court of Justice[1] and (ii) it is a matter for the party invoking this exception (enterprise, member state, or regulator) to prove that the conditions for its application have been met.[2]

16.3.1. *The Commission, keystone of the system of regulation within the EU*

The systems of regulation in force in those sectors that have been the subject of liberalization at Community level have, then, a number of characteristics: they pursue a multitude of objectives, some of which are to do purely with economic efficiency, while others are not; the formulation of these objectives and the means used to achieve them may be relatively heterogeneous; finally,

---

[1] Case 127/73 *BRT II* [1974] ECR 318, para. 19.

[2] Judgment in Case 41/83, *Italy v. Commission* [1985] ECR 873, para. 33. Conclusions of Advocate-General DARMON in Case C-393/92, *Almelo v. NV Energiebedriff Ijsselmij* [1994] ECR I-1477, para. 169.

it is the European Commission that is responsible for ensuring that the basic principles of the Treaty or of secondary legislation are respected and that any differences observed are compatible with the functioning of the common market.

This situation reflects the conflict between the need to take account of historical, economic, geographical, political, and cultural differences on the one hand, and the Community objective of establishing a European 'level playing field' allowing proper competition within the internal market on the other. It is, then, the Commission, the guardian of the treaties, that determines, under the supervision of the Court of Justice, the extent to which laws on the one hand and regulatory decisions on the other are compatible with the Treaty. In some ways, the Commission regulates the regulators.

This regulation is carried out in accordance with two principles: the principle of conformity with Community legislation, and the principle of proportionality of the means used to achieve the stated objectives. The European Commission therefore has been led on a number of occasions to take up decisions made by regulators, whether in the search for economic efficiency (including those cases where the Commission contested the decisions of the German regulator on interconnection charges or the conditions for granting mobile telephony licences in Italy and Spain) or in pursuit of other objectives (as is the case in the current dispute between the Commission and France concerning the cost and funding mechanisms for the universal telecommunications service).

The Commission's role, then, is to bring a degree of homogeneity to this diversity by ensuring that common principles are observed and by arbitrating between the Community interest and national interests.

16.4. DEFINING ALTERNATIVE REGULATORY MODELS FOR THE FUTURE

The system described above, which may be termed a 'Community model', is an empirical model in which responsibility for defining objectives is shared between Community and member state (economic efficiency objectives tend to be defined at Community level, while those relating to the general good tend to be defined at national level), and in which the regulatory function in the strict sense of the term is performed at national level, the Commission intervening only indirectly for the purpose of regulating the regulators (by taking an autonomous decision pursuant to Article 86(3) of the Treaty, by initiating infringement proceedings for failure to transpose the Community's legislative framework, or by directly using the powers vested in it by Community competition law).

Can and will this model evolve? If so, in the direction of what type of organization? Defining the outlines of actual and potential regulatory systems means, *inter alia*, exploring the relationship between competition and regulation, between the national level and the Community level, and between economic efficiency objectives and other objectives. These reflections can take the form of a number of questions.

1. From a strictly economic point of view, which 'market failure' problems are solved by opening the sector up to competition? Which are not solved in this way and will continue to require specific regulation other than that deriving from competition law in the long term?

The answers to this first set of questions obviously depend on the economic sector concerned. The problems differ in nature according to whether the area under scrutiny is the postal sector, where the infrastructure consists of manpower rather than cables, as in the electricity or telecommunications sectors, or pipes, as in the gas or water sectors. They also differ according to whether or not the sector concerned is 'technology-driven'. In the postal sector, for example, the instances of liberalization that have occurred—generally without any accompanying regulation, as in Sweden and Finland—have demonstrated that this sector is a particularly favourable target for strategies that concentrate on the most profitable segment of the market ('cherry-picking') and, as a corollary, upset the balance of operators' overall activities. The following finding may also be noted: the distribution and management of scarce resources, such as radio frequencies for mobile telephones or air transport slots or frequencies, are bound to require in the long term public regulation of a technical nature which cannot be replaced by competition law alone. The same is probably true of certain rights of way in the traditional network economies.

2. In what areas is it necessary to introduce or maintain specific legislation, in the short or medium term, in order to allow competition to take root and develop in sectors where the network has long been perceived as a natural monopoly, and where competition law alone is not sufficient to overcome these obstacles and give competitors effective access?

One naturally thinks of networks that cannot be duplicated, or can be duplicated only with difficulty, and of the conditions of access to these networks. In this connection, the question arises whether permanent specific regulation is justified or whether, once competition is firmly established in the future, such regulation could be assumed by competition law.

3. What requirements other than the economically efficient operation of the market in question justify regulation? In these sectors, are restrictions on competition and the continued role of the public authorities in providing an impetus justified by specific factors or by the public interest?

We naturally think of the need to guarantee reasonable economic or social access costs for the consumer or to preserve the universal character of the service, but we also take into account externality effects (e.g. spatial planning aimed at maintaining a dense postal network in sparsely populated areas) or negative externalities, the costs of which are not directly assumed by the firms operating on the market (e.g. taking account of environmental and public health costs in the regulatory system for transport).

4. What have been, are, and will be the economic effects of European integration in these sectors and, in particular, the externality effects on the rest of the economy? What conclusions may be drawn regarding the geographical level at which regulation may be carried out? How is account to be taken of the two-fold requirement of creating a level playing field on the one hand and guaranteeing efficient regulation as close as possible to the market on the other? In other words, should we evolve towards a European regulatory model that is more centralized or more decentralized than at present?

Could the national regulators themselves not carry out the arbitration currently performed by the Commission? Some argue in favour of such a possibility and claim in support of their argument that the case law of the Court of Justice and the Court of First Instance have established the direct effect of the exception contained in Article 86(2) of the Treaty of Rome. The national courts, therefore, can validly apply Article 86(2) to the disputes which they are called upon to settle.[3] Why could the national regulators not do what the judge can do?

The answer must, of course, be in the negative for a number of reasons: first, because, as with state aid control, it is essential that arbitration be conducted by a body that is detached from national interests; second, because the regulator is required, or may be required, to define by means of its decisions a balance between economic efficiency objectives and general interest objectives, and would consequently have to act as its own judge; and, lastly, because it is essential for the future of economic integration in such sectors that the basic principles established by Community law should be applied in a consistent and uniform manner throughout the European Union.

16.5. THREE ALTERNATIVE REGULATORY MODELS IN EUROPE

The answer to these questions determines the scope and methods of any regulatory system, but also the balance between the different geographical levels at which regulation is enforced. Such an analysis must necessarily be carried out on a sector-by-sector basis because the economic features, the degree of integration of the markets, and the nature of the problems that arise vary considerably from one sector to another, and it must comply with the general principles mentioned above.

The broadly empirical 'current Community model', as it was termed above, constitutes one possible means of reconciling a general approach with the need to define, on a case-by-case basis and for each type of public utility, the division of roles between:

- national level and Community level (i.e. and between national interest and Community interest, but also between rule-maker and policy-maker);

---

[3] Case C-393/92, *Almelo v. NV Energiebedrijf Ijsselmij* [1994] ECR I-1477.

- specific regulation and regulation through competition law, i.e. control of the behaviour of monopolists and former monopolists (conduct regulation) and structural regulation;
- objectives geared exclusively towards economic efficiency and broader economic or non-economic objectives in the area of public policy (financing of public network services, taking account of externalities in regulatory systems, balance between safeguarding the interests of consumers and the interests of industry, etc.).

For all that, is it possible to define, on the basis of a single analytical grid, different regulatory models based on general, adaptable principles, taking account of the specific features of the different sectors? Three scenarios may be adopted for future regulation in Europe. They are not necessarily alternatives: they could, to some extent, be cumulative, or could succeed one another in time.

16.6. PERSEVERING WITH THE CURRENT MODEL

The current model was described in detail in Section 16.2. It is based essentially on the co-existence of two authorities, one regulatory and the other concerned with competition. There are also, however, national regulators which apply common standards (i.e., the rule-maker operates at Community level) and a European-level regulator for the regulators, viz. the Commission, whose job it is to ensure a level playing field. This setup has the benefit of clarity: the rule-maker is essentially situated at Community level, while the policy-maker is essentially national.

However, the apparent clarity obscures a number of grey areas. Thus, the Commission, in doing its work of regulating the regulators, itself intervenes occasionally in the process as a prime regulator, sometimes competing with and in opposition to the national regulators, as was the case in Germany over the Deutsche Telekom interconnection charges issue. It is difficult to draw a clear line between Community and national roles, and indeed, the line can be a shifting one. No clear distinction has been drawn between regulatory law and competition law. The assumptions underlying whatever form of arbitration is chosen — more especially between the national interest and the Community interest, but also between economic efficiency and other public interests—are not explicit.

And yet the system works. It gives the national regulatory authorities a great deal of latitude, provided that the way they use this freedom does not contravene the common set of rules and does not upset the internal market. The jumbled roles and the general lack of clarity in defining the objectives for the various players in the regulatory systems in effect give the system the necessary degree of flexibility, while Commission action preserves a minimum measure of overall homogeneity.

It is conceivable that this system will continue in much the same way. On the other hand, there are those who think it unlikely that it can continue in its present state. As liberalized markets come to operate within a competitive system, the likelihood is that competition law will prevail over regulatory law. This is a scenario we shall be examining later.

One other possibility is that the system will simply evolve without shedding any of its essential characteristics. The current 'radial' system, with the Commission at the centre operating a fairly centralist role as guardian of the Treaties, might evolve into a less rigidly centralized and more cooperative 'spider's web' arrangement. This at least seems to be the implication from recent changes on energy regulation under the 'Florence' process, and from the telecommunications practice of periodic meetings between national regulators and the Commission with a view to the exchange of best practice. The recent Commission Green Paper on the 1999 communication review seems to take this line too.

The increasingly frequent use of benchmarking techniques, and the practice of comparing the decisions taken by the regulatory authorities in the various countries, similarly suggest a move towards a more cooperative form of regulation, based increasingly on soft law rather than hard law. What this would mean is a transfer of powers from the policy-maker to the rule-maker. With the rule-maker function under the present system being a Community-level matter, this would be an important element in a shift towards a more decentralized and more cooperative regulatory system.

A cooperative arrangement along these lines might operate according to rules similar to those set out in the Commission's 1999 White Paper on competition policy concerning relations between the Commission and the national competition authorities. The national regulatory authorities and the Commission would operate in a network based on ongoing contacts and periodic meetings, so that all sides were kept informed about problems and could evaluate possible solutions and devise joint action. There would be nothing to prevent the national authorities taking over the proportionality checks that are currently the exclusive preserve of the Commission. The Commission would of course retain the power, in the event of an unresolved dispute, to take the matter to the Court of Justice or to intervene, as it has done in the past, on the strength of the powers vested in it by Article 86(3) of the Treaty of Rome. Ultimately, then, it would be up to the European Court of Justice to rule on any disputes.

16.7. TOWARDS A EUROPEAN REGULATOR

Is it conceivable that the current situation, in which the ground rules are laid down in Brussels but their application is largely decentralized, might evolve towards a centralized form of regulation at European level? There are well-known advantages to the fragmented nature of regulatory bodies, chief among which is the fact that effective regulation is closer to the markets and the perceived problems, respecting the legal traditions of each of the member states. On the other hand, decentralized application of the rules creates a risk of disparity in the way the rules are applied, to the detriment of free competition in an integrated European market.

Clearly, the more marked is the convergence phenomenon (e.g. in the telecommunications sector), the less risk there is of disparities in the way fragmented bodies apply the rules. It is equally clear that the looser the regulatory framework, the greater the risk. But we should be careful not to overestimate the risk. Provided the regulatory framework is sufficiently clear and well defined, there is no basic incompatibility between a fragmented control system and the harmonized application of rules. This, after all, is the case under the current regulatory model, where it is Commission action and the existence of clear common rules that guarantee a level playing field.

At first sight, then, it would seem that the disadvantages of a centralized regulatory system, i.e. a European regulator, outweigh the advantages, and that there are other, more effective and less disadvantageous, means of guaranteeing the uniform application of rules, due consideration for national specificities, and the need for regulation at the closest point possible to the market.

Having said that, however, there are certain sectors and/or segments of the market where the optimum situation might be a little different in terms of the level of centralization. A centralized system might be justified where there are transborder externalities. To take an example, we can reasonably ask ourselves whether Europe should have an air traffic control system that is more centralized than the present one (e.g. by strengthening Eurocontrol's remit). Similar questions are raised by the regulation of trans-European transport networks, particularly from the energy angle.

The recent merger between Vodafone and Mannesmann in the mobile phones sector is a further thought-provoking development, since it opens the way to a truly pan-European mobile phone market. It already seems clear that a number of regulatory issues cannot be addressed properly at national level alone.

To sum up this point, opting for a centralized European regulatory authority might seem logical at first sight, and might have the advantage of putting an end to the ambiguous distribution of roles and overlapping powers (and hence the risk of decision-making conflicts between the various authorities) that characterize the current system. And yet, selecting this option might prove counter-productive in practice—by lowering the level of legitimacy and political acceptability of the regulatory system, by creating too wide a gap between the level of regulation and the concrete problems affecting economic players on the ground, and by shedding the flexibility that characterizes the current system. None the less, in certain specific cases described above, 'European regulation' might prove to be the most effective form of organization.

16.8. THE GRADUAL DEMISE OF SECTORAL REGULATION

It is clear that problems to do with market failures requiring sectoral regulation will persist in a number of markets. As was explained above, the scale and nature of such market failures differ from one market to another; in other words, the need to maintain sectoral regulation will depend on the sector concerned.

On the other hand, and in relation to access to essential infrastructures, it is reasonable to believe that, once the market has been opened up by specific regulation (e.g. giving third parties compulsory access to networks, unbundling the local loop, fixing the price for interconnection charges, etc.), questions of network access will eventually become a matter for competition law alone. This is the view clearly taken by the European Commission in the tele-communications sector under its 1999 review. There are also clear indicators in two Commission communications: concerning the 'access issues' on the one hand, and the application of postal competition rules on the other. These two texts give a detailed explanation of the competition rules governing network access issues. Both communications are based in part on an adapted version of the US 'Essential Facilities Doctrine'.

It is probable, then, that sectoral regulation will gradually give way to the general rule, viz. competition law. At the same time, it seems likely that wide areas of network utilities activity will continue to require specific regulation over the long term.

16.9. CONCLUSION

The current architecture of the European system for regulating network utilities will probably have to change. Generally speaking, this should be in the direction of strengthening the relative position of competition law and reducing the importance of specific regulation. It should also lead to a more decentralized system across the board, based on the current model, as regulators move up the learning curve. Finally, there are a number of sectors or segments that might require more centralized regulation, although in most cases this could be done within a cooperative system of European regulation involving the Commission and the national regulators. Only a small number of highly specific cases might have to move towards a centralized European regulatory model (essentially, the air traffic control regulatory setup).

17

Cooperation between Energy Regulators in the European Union

JORGE VASCONCELOS

17.1. INTRODUCTION

This chapter addresses two basic questions:

1. Why do European energy regulators cooperate?
2. What mechanisms do they use for cooperation?

Ten years ago, these questions would have been nonsensical, for the simple reason that energy regulators did not exist in Europe.[1] Therefore, it seems appropriate to start by explaining why they have been created, what they do, and how they function in institutional terms. To explain the role of energy regulators, however, it is necessary first to describe briefly the structure and development of the energy sector in the European Union.

The chapter is divided into five parts. The following section describes the legal framework and the structure of electricity and natural gas markets in the EU. Section 17.3 explains why energy regulators have been introduced by most member states and why different institutional formats have been adopted. Section 17.4 explains why cooperation among energy regulators is necessary. Section 17.5 indicates the main objectives of the recently created Council of European Energy Regulators. Finally, Section 17.6 briefly considers the role of regulators within the political and institutional framework of the EU.

17.2. ELECTRICITY AND NATURAL GAS MARKETS IN THE EU

Until 1990, electricity and natural gas markets were *de facto* or *de jure* monopolies in all European countries. With just a few exceptions, energy companies were public; i.e., they were state-owned and were controlled either

---

[1] OFFER, the UK electricity regulator, started its activity on 1 September 1989. In other member states energy regulators were appointed some years later, mainly during the second half of the 1990s.

by central government or by regional and/or municipal administrations. In the electricity sector, most companies were vertically integrated, which is to say that they were active in the generation, transmission, distribution, and supply of electricity. Only a few companies sold both electricity and gas. Interaction between the two sectors was very weak since the use of natural gas in power stations was limited by an EC directive dating back to 1975.

During the 1990s, the legal framework of the energy industry changed considerably in Europe, at both national and EU level. The two major key words describing this process are 'liberalization' and 'integration'. Member states decided to liberalize both electricity and natural gas, and they agreed on a common set of rules (unbundling, open network access, etc.) and on some minimum thresholds. At the same time, they decided to increase the degree of integration of their national energy markets, with a view to creating a true single energy market. These agreements were, respectively, translated into the 'electricity directive'[2] and the 'gas directive'.[3] For different reasons, several member states also decided to privatize their energy sectors, selling the existing public energy companies and attracting new private investors. The 1975 EC directive was subsequently revoked and natural gas became the preferred fuel for power generation.

These changes triggered a process of industrial restructuring which has only just begun. Although it is difficult to imagine the future landscape of European energy markets in full detail, some important trends can already be observed which are an indication of what is to come:

- Competition in generation and supply is increasing with time.
- Transmission and distribution remain monopolistic activities.
- Transmission and network operation is becoming a totally independent industry; 'horizontal' interaction among transmission system operators (TSOs) from interconnected networks is crucial and is leading to the establishment of European TSO associations for electricity and gas.
- Organized markets, both physical and financial, are becoming the focal point for electricity trade; such international markets are open to players from several countries.
- Many companies have changed ownership, size, and scope over the last ten years; increasing activity in mergers and acquisitions will further redesign the map of energy companies.
- The political will to speed up liberalization and integration of energy markets is growing, as shown by the conclusions of the Lisbon European Council (23/ 24 March 2000), by the 'Communication from the Commission to the Council and the European Parliament: Recent Progress with Building the

---

[2] 'Directive 96/92/EC of the European Parliament and of the Council of 19 December 1996 concerning Common Rules for the Internal Market in Electricity', published in the OJ No. L 27 of 30 January 1997.

[3] 'Directive 98/30/EC of the European Parliament and of the Council of 22 June 1998 concerning Common Rules for the Internal Market in Natural Gas'.

Internal Electricity Market',[4] by the conclusions of the last Energy Council meeting,[5] by the proposal of a directive amending directives 96/92/EC and 98/30/EC[6] and by several decisions recently taken at national level.

17.3. THE INTRODUCTION OF INDEPENDENT ENERGY REGULATORS IN EU MEMBER STATES

The introduction of some degree of competition in the electricity and gas sectors created the need for appropriate regulation, granting, *inter alia*, non-discriminatory third-party access to networks and efficient dispute settlement mechanisms.

Historically, each member state has introduced energy regulation in different ways, reflecting each individual state's national legal structure, administrative tradition, market structure, and political choice. For the time being, only Germany has decided not to set up a specific energy regulator, sharing supervisory functions between the Federal Anti-trust Authority (Bundeskartellamt), the Federal Ministry of Economic Affairs, and state administrations. Under the new proposal of a directive, all EU member states will be obliged to establish independent energy regulators.

17.4. SOME REASONS FOR COOPERATION AMONG EUROPEAN ENERGY REGULATORS

Cooperation among energy regulators may be justified for two reasons.

1. It improves the performance of individual regulators and therefore has a direct positive impact on the markets regulated by the respective regulators.
2. The lack of cooperation would hinder the development of regulated markets or could harm some market players.

The following examples show how cooperation among regulators can be beneficial. First, the sharing of experiences among regulators, especially in the start-up phase, can improve:

- the management quality of the regulatory authorities;
- the transparency and efficiency of the regulatory process;
- the efficiency of the incentives and of the regulatory formulae adopted, as well as the effectiveness of implemented enforcement and supervision mechanisms.

Second, an exchange of information among energy regulators is important for several reasons, including:

- the supervision of multinational companies, especially in a period of industry restructuring through mergers and acquisitions;
- benchmarking.

---

[4] COM (2000) 297 final of 16 May 2000.   [5] 30 May 2000.
[6] COM (2001) 125 final of 13 March 2001.

Cross-border electricity trade provides a good example of how a lack of cooperation would hinder the development of a single market. In the past, electricity trading within the Western European network was conducted by the operators responsible for high-voltage transmission grids, in line with the technical and economic rules defined by their association.[7] Cross-border transactions were limited to wholesale exchanges among the owners of the high-voltage grids, on either a bilateral or a multilateral (transit) basis; final customers had no access to the interconnections. The Council directive of 29 October 1990 on 'The Transit of Electricity through Transmission Grids'[8] had a limited direct impact on electricity trade between member states, and the share of total exchanges related to consumption of the Western European system was about 10 per cent.

The 'electricity directive' allows member states to shape their energy markets in several ways; in particular, it gives them the possibility of implementing different systems of network access, including access to interconnections. Looking at the way legislators and/or regulators began to make use of this freedom, it was soon recognized that implementation of the 'electricity directive' could lead to incompatible trading arrangements and could block cross-border trade if nothing was done. In fact, parallel liberalization of fifteen energy markets does not ensure the compatibility—let alone the convergence or integration—of these markets. This implies that diversity must be compatible not only with the principles of transparency and non-discrimination, but also with the primary goal of achieving single European markets for electricity and gas.

The need for some degree of institutional coordination was recognized by member states and by the European Commission, which in 1998 decided to set up the European Electricity Regulation Forum. This forum, known as the 'Florence Forum', meets twice a year in Florence and brings together national regulators, member states, and the European Commission, as well as with a large number of interested parties—system operators, market players, consumer associations, power producers, traders, etc.

The first challenge faced by the Florence Forum was to create a simple, low-transaction-cost mechanism for cross-border electricity trade while at the same time maintaining different national market structures. Setting up such a mechanism requires considerable effort. First of all, it is necessary to define some common access and pricing rules and to introduce some degree of harmonization between existing national rules. Subsequently, it is necessary to adapt the existing mechanisms for technical coordination and settlement to the new rules.

The Florence Forum working programme was defined in October 1998 in a paper presented by three regulators.[9] Through voluntary cooperation among

---

[7] UCPTE (Union pour la Coordination de la Production et du Transport de l'Électricité), created in 1951.

[8] Directive 90/547/EEC, published in the OJ No. L 313 of 13 November 1990.

[9] 'Transmission and Trade of Electricity in Europe: Discussion Paper', Autorità per l'energia elettrica e il gas, Comisión Nacional del Sistema Eléctrico, Entidade Reguladora do Sector Eléctrico.

system operators, the European Commission, and national regulators, in dialogue with all interested parties, a solution was reached in March 2000 and ratified in May 2001. Among other things, a mechanism was agreed that grants network users effective access to the full continental European grid (UCTE) as from 1 September 2001. Later, this mechanism will be improved and extended to other EU and non-EU interconnected systems. The new system to be implemented will be put into effect between September 2001 and 30 August 2002. It represents the first step towards the creation of the largest integrated electricity market in the world. Meanwhile, a permanent system to come into effect in September 2002 will be developed by TSOs under the guidance of regulators.

Another important result from the Florence Forum was the stimulus for creating European associations: system operators (ETSO), market operators, and regulators (CEER) have all recognized that representative associations facilitate debate at European level.

17.5. THE COUNCIL OF EUROPEAN ENERGY REGULATORS

The Council of European Energy Regulators (CEER) was created on 7 March 2000 by energy regulators from ten European countries: Belgium, Finland, Ireland, Italy, Netherlands, Norway, Portugal, Spain, Sweden, and United Kingdom. Since then, five more countries have joined the Council: France, Denmark, Greece, Luxembourg, and Austria.

The CEER objectives expressed in the Memorandum of Understanding signed by the European electricity and gas regulators are as follows:

- Promote the development of efficient electricity and gas markets in Europe through the establishment of appropriate mechanisms.
- Co-operate in order to achieve competitive European markets in electricity and gas, in which the principles of transparency and non-discrimination are ensured. The Members will reinforce and follow up the processes of liberalization in the electricity and gas markets.
- Set up co-operation, information exchange and assistance amongst The Members, with a view to establishing expert views for discussion with the institutions of the European Union, and, in particular, with the European Commission, and representative international organisations as other sectors which may be involved.
- Establish coherent and expert knowledge and analysis such that the institutions with which Members wish to hold discussion naturally consult the Members at a formative stage in policy development.
- Provide a framework for the discussion of regulatory issues and exchange of experience.
- Provide the necessary elements for the development of regulation in the fields of electricity and gas.

– Develop joint approaches vis-a-vis transnational energy utilities and companies that operate in separated regulated utility markets (multi-utilities).
– Where possible work to establish common policies among Members towards agreed issues.

CEER is particularly interested in contributing to the achievement of the internal markets in gas and electricity, joining the common efforts of its members with the European institutions, particularly the European Commission, as well as with representative associations of consumers, system operators, market operators, and market players.

CEER's decision-making process is driven by consensus. It meets at least twice a year, and non-members may be invited to attend all or part of these meetings. For the time being, its organization revolves round a rotating presidency, whose first appointment was for two years. The presidency is supported by a local secretariat and coordinates the activities of several working groups.

17.6. INTERACTION OF NATIONAL AND EU REGULATION

The examples given in Section 17.4 of cross-border electricity trade clearly illustrate the need for some kind of institutional cooperation and coordination—not only among national regulators, but also between these and the European Commission.

In the United States, interstate electricity trade is regulated by the federal regulator (FERC), while intrastate trade is regulated by state regulators. In Europe there is no federal energy regulator, although the European Commission has some regulatory functions. Which institutional format will prove to be most appropriate for Europe in the long term—a federal regulator, reinforced cooperation between national regulators and the European Commission, reinforced regulatory powers for the European Commission, or any other scheme? This is one of the critical questions facing the electricity and gas industry as well as energy consumers as we head towards a single energy market in the European Union.

18

Improving Air Traffic Services Performance in Europe: The Economic Regulation Perspective

HERVÉ DUMEZ AND ALAIN JEUNEMAÎTRE

18.1. INTRODUCTION

Until recently, air traffic services (ATS) management has not been a primary focus of EU transport policy. The provision of these services has developed independently from involvement of the European Commission, alongside national cooperative initiatives. In 1960, an attempt was made to transfer air traffic control of the European upper airspace to a single agency, Eurocontrol, but this failed to materialize. Only Belgium, Luxembourg, the Netherlands, and northern Germany agreed on the delegation of air space management to Eurocontrol; the other European member states chose to retain control over their national airspace. Eurocontrol was then left with an advisory role in the air traffic management of European airspace and was given the task of harmonizing national *en route* control systems and fostering cooperation among European states.

Little happened in the years that followed. From 1975 to 1985, the increase in traffic was linear, with delays, if not moderate, at least tolerated by users—i.e. airlines companies—and passengers. In 1986 only 12 per cent of European flights were delayed by more than fifteen minutes for any reason whatever—weather, late departure owing to technical failures or airport congestion, air traffic control problems, etc. Airports and a lack of runways were viewed as the main bottleneck (CEE 1996); air traffic services provision was hardly questioned. Air traffic control, above all, was regarded as a public utility service that should be driven by one and only one objective—ensuring flights' safety—without much consideration of introducing a market perspective.

From the mid-1980s onwards, however, marked increases in traffic (from 5 to 12 per cent per year) radically changed the view of ATS provision. Opening the airways to competition, the 'hubs and spokes' strategy of users,[1] put pressure

---

[1] An airline company uses a particular airport as its connection flights platform. Airplanes land at and take off from all reserved destinations in successive waves at particular times, allowing passengers to transfer for their final destination.

on air traffic control (ATC) systems and made it more difficult to cope with congestion at peak hours. This major shift in traffic patterns was not readily identified by the European states, and resulted in significant increases in delays: 20 per cent of the European flights were delayed by more than fifteen minutes in 1988, 25 per cent in 1989. Unexpectedly, upper airspace appeared a scarce resource; experts began to predict inevitable congestion, with the provision of the ATC service being constrained by a 'capacity wall', i.e. a physical and technical traffic absorption limit (Villiers 1994; Stuchlik 1999).

Not only was the resource scarce, but the limitation of budget deficits and the public-sector borrowing requirement (PSBR) national procedures made it harder for state-owned providers to get proper funding and to make investments in proportion to the growth in demand. The idea of private funding of ATS service provision began to be considered.

In response to the pressure brought to bear by users, air traffic management (ATM) was put on the European political agenda. Ministers of transport of the European Civil Aviation Conference (ECAC)[2] took steps to remedy the situation. First, they looked for technical answers. A foremost decision was to deal with ATC undercapacity in an orderly way which would be non-discriminatory, by sharing out capacity shortages among users. A specialized Centralized Flow Management Unit (CFMU) was set up within Eurocontrol in 1988, in charge of deciding upon take-off slots at congested airports. CFMU became fully operational in 1995. Other short-term technical answers were implemented to facilitate data transfer between national ATC systems and improve the management of cross-border flights. Finally, medium-term harmonized investment and research programmes were launched (EATCHIP, later ATM 2000+), focusing on ATC equipment systems, vertical and horizontal reduction of *en route* airspace separations between airplanes, and VHF frequencies to increase capacity.

All these initiatives had a limited impact on curbing delays, however. Capacity investment did not catch up with traffic growth, and the search for improvements through technological progress proved disappointing. Above all, they failed to address the issue of airspace congestion from an economic angle and did not cover the economic components of ATS provision, particularly the potential for performance improvement through the application of economic principles to the service provision—i.e. better managed investment policies, increased productivity through economic incentives, or the introduction of price mechanisms for supply to meet demand. A European Performance Review Commission was therefore set up in 1998 to review the economic performance of national ATC systems, to propose economic incentives schemes to increase capacity, and in particular to produce guidelines for economic regulation.

---

[2] ECAC (European Civil Aviation Conference) is an enlarged European committee grouping 28 European nations of which 15 are EU member states.

While joint European initiatives were being taken, ministers of transport were also active in dealing with the lack of ATS capacity at national level. European countries split the national administration of ATS into separate entities: the provision of ATS, and the regulation of ATS. National providers were privatized, and the UK went even further in 1999 when it proposed a Public–Private Partnership for its provider and a price-cap regulatory regime for the National Air Traffic Services (NATS) (CAA 2000). In spite of these constructive efforts, however, and even allowing for the Kosovo war, which reduced airspace capacity for civil air traffic, ATC centres experienced their worst delay crisis in history in 1999 and short-term prospects looked rather gloomy.

While not ignoring the potential for capacity increase through technical improvements, which at best would materialize only in the medium term, this paper focuses on institutional and economic arrangements and approaches at European level that might help to reduce the imbalances between ATS demand and supply in the near future. The following section describes the technico-economics of ATS provision. Section 18.3 assesses the current use of market economic principles in the provision of service. Sections 18.4 and 18.5 focus on the Performance Review Commission and its first steps to introduce an economic rationale in the provision of service. Finally, Section 18.6 proposes a regulatory convergence price mechanism in light of the European Commission initiative for a 'single sky' for Europe (European Commission 2000).

18.2. ATS TECHNICO-ECONOMIC CHARACTERISTICS

ATS provision aims at maintaining sufficient vertical and horizontal separation between planes in upper airspace to prevent and avoid collisions.[3] It allows for flights' maximum safety. To ensure safety, the service uses ground radar infrastructure which provides ATC centres with information about airplanes' positions, speed, and direction. Air traffic controllers track plane movements, communicate with pilots through VHF frequencies, and order them to adjust their altitude and speed according to potential trajectory conflicts.

In theory, the control of air traffic movements would not be a cumbersome process if technological progress in air navigation, surveillance, and communication systems enabled a plane to know accurately its own airspace position and those of other planes in its vicinity as well as their intended flight paths. Any plane would then be able to detect potential trajectory conflicts and change its route accordingly. Airspace would not be divided along corridors, and

[3] The ATC service has three components: airport ATC, which deals with planes in landing and take-off phases and runways; approach ATC, which controls planes in ascending and descending phases of flights in airport vicinity; and *en route* ATC, which control planes in the upper airspace above 6000 m at cruising phase. The paper focuses solely on the latter, *en route* control. Nor does it deal with the relationship between civil and military *en route* control constraints, which is a key technical but also economic issue.

planes could choose the most direct and efficient *en route* flight. *En route* control could then be limited, and airspace used to its maximum capacity with flexibility of route flights between destinations. This option is currently being studied in the United States and Europe under the 'free flight' concept (see Chew 1997; Scigliano 1999).[4] However, this is a long-term prospect for dealing with airspace congestion, the operational development of which is scheduled for 2015–20 at best. Moreover, there is little certainty that 'free flights' could be implemented in complex congested airspace portions. In the short and medium term, therefore, airplanes will carry on flying preset routes along airspace corridors.

The upper and part of the lower airspace are sectorized into portions of on average 100–150 km distance, each sector requiring a control unit (a team of two or three controllers) handling simultaneously a maximum of fifteen to twenty flights according to traffic complexity, i.e. the number of crossing-routes at a particular time in a given sector. Each ATC centre manages a certain number of sectors. During low-traffic hours sectors are regrouped; controllers are in reduced number and manage larger airspace portions. Conversely, at peak hours, when airspace is congested, sectors are divided up into smaller units; the number of controllers increases in proportion to the number of sectors opened, and capacity absorption increases. However, under such circumstances coordination problems between sectors and the need to deal with potential conflicts become more complex. So, when dividing an airspace sector by two, the increase in capacity is multiplied by only 1.5. Moreover, after a certain point, increasing the number of sectors by division is no longer workable. Therefore, the capacity of an ATC centre has an upper limit according to air traffic complexity, the number of sectors that an ATC centre can open, and the diminishing returns to sectorization. Daily, ATC centres are assumed to adjust their capacity absorption to traffic fluctuations mainly by regrouping and opening sectors.

From the above overview, it can be seen that air traffic services exhibit particular economic attributes.

- The provision of ATS has network components consisting of 'nodes and links' (Schmalensee 1995), namely sectors and communications between controllers and pilots based on information about ground infrastructure and requiring data transmission and coordination between sectors.
- For a preset route, air traffic control capacity equals the absorption capacity of the weakest node, i.e. the ATC centre that can cope with the smallest number of flights along the set route during a given time interval.
- The ATC network has natural monopoly characteristics. Once the management of an airspace sector has been delegated to an ATC centre, an airplane

---

[4] It is very likely that the 'free-flight' concept would be operational primarily for airspaces that are relatively uncomplicated and uncongested; it would be harder to implement in congested airspace portions with few alternative routes—those that in Europe are the core issue.

cannot choose a competing service provider if it is flying in that particular sector.[5]

- Once a plane is linked to data transmission from ground radar infrastructure, the provision of ATS—i.e. ATC centres—can be set in any geographical location; for example, Maastricht ATC centre handles the ATS of northern German upper airspace.
- Economies of scale are likely to exist in the provision of service.[6] Larger ATC centres would achieve cost savings in management, coordination of control, and rationalization of sectors. But the provision of service is primarily labour-intensive with at present no conceivable big leap in productivity arising from technological progress. The provision of service has not evolved greatly over the past fifty years and still relies on strip bands and VHF frequencies.
- The provision of service cannot instantly meet significant changes in air traffic demand. Adjusting to shifts in traffic patterns implies rationalizing sectors and routes and restructuring airspace management and ATC centres, requiring examination, investment, and a controllers' training period to adapt to new sectorization.[7]

Summing up, ATS appears to be closely related to a network utility even if, in contrast to other utilities, it is difficult to disentangle the monopoly components of its infrastructure. The network characteristic lies in the need for coordination and harmonization in defining routes, sectors, communication between ATC centres, air navigation, communication, and surveillance systems.[8] As for the monopoly components, they prevail in the radar infrastructure and in the provision of service once an airspace portion has been delegated to a provider.

On that basis, economic and institutional developments occurring in other network industries could probably provide useful insights (Vickers and Yarrow 1988; Armstrong *et al.* 1994), and could possibly suggest viable new market arrangements (Mears 1999). Up to now, however, ATSs have been managed according to administrative procedures that ensure high safety levels, without providing for economic incentives to increase performance.

---

[5] A given sector cannot be controlled simultaneously by two or more providers, hence a natural monopoly component.

[6] Currently, there are 42 *en route* ATC centres in Western Europe against 21 in the USA, which handles six times as much traffic.

[7] For instance, the recent transfer of a sector from Reims to Brest required a minimum of 1 year to become effective, and the reorganization of the south airspace London area, $2\frac{1}{2}$ years.

[8] In the past, the European equipment policy of ATC control has developed according to national rationale, giving preference to national industry projects. National industry policies have limited the introduction of economies of scale in equipment ATC production and have increased the cost of service provision. Moreover, they have raised issues on compatibility and coordination between ATC national systems; hence the concept of interoperability put forward by the EU Commission.

18.3. LACK OF ECONOMIC INCENTIVES TO INCREASE THE PERFORMANCE OF ATC SERVICE PROVISION

ATS provision is currently lacking a number of economic incentives to increase performance. These are discussed in turn.

18.3.1. *Lack of a market price mechanism*

In any standard market of goods or services, supply meets demand by means of a market price mechanism. Where the provision of ATS is concerned, that kind of mechanism has not been introduced. Pricing is based instead on collecting *en route* charges through a cost recovery mechanism.

In 1944 the international Convention on International Civil Aviation (also known as the Chicago Convention) organized the use of civil airspace. It put forward two key principles: first, that access to national airspace was to be free for civil aviation; and second, that any country would ensure safety over its national airspace. Nation-states agreed to charge users only enough to cover the costs of delivering safety, thereby preventing them from using their airspace as a financial asset and imposing a surcharge for using their ATS.

In Europe today, *en route* charges are levied in proportion to the flight distance over the national airspace and the square root of the maximum takeoff weight of the airplane.[9] Charges are billed by the Central Route Charges Office (CRCO), the part of Eurocontrol that collects payments on behalf of the European member states. Under the above principles, national *en route* charges are uniform whatever the air traffic density and complexity to be handled in national airspace, and there is no differentiation between ATC centres, or peak *v.* low-traffic hours. So *en route* charges do not reflect the costs of supplying the service at a particular time in a particular airspace. Also, in practice, the costs of providing the service are not related to the weight of the plane. The *en route* charge formula simply introduces a reallocation of expenses among users. It benefits companies using small airplanes and provides a financial bonus to multiple flights between destinations.

At peak hours, when supply cannot meet demand on a set route, airports are regulated. Queuing is organized at airports according to the available capacity of the weakest ATS network node, the most penalizing sector—i.e. the most congested sector along the route, which cannot cope with more than a defined number of flights. Roughly, regulation consists of take-off airport slots being allocated by CFMU in accordance with the available capacity declared by ATC centres a day in advance. Once capacity is known at CFMU, users are allocated slots on a 'first come, first served' basis. An algorithm allows for reactualization in real time to adapt to last-minute reset routing by users.

[9] For a given year, the national unit rate is the ratio of total cost of national ATC service provision (operational costs, capital expenses and investment, contribution to Eurocontrol costs) divided by the number of flights controlled in national airspace expressed in service units. One service unit equals a 100 km flight for a 50-ton airplane.

In summary, airspace congestion is administered in an orderly fashion without regard to users' preferences. Quality of service and costs of delays incurred by users have no impact on ATS national revenues. Thus, whatever the member-state investment in ATS capacity and quality of service (safety, induced delays), costs are fully recovered and are billed to users with no economic incentives for providers to adjust to demand.

18.3.2. *Lack of competition in service provision*

Even if an ATS network has monopoly components, competition could be introduced at various stages. In the first place, although each EU member state has sovereignty over its airspace, bidding for the provision of service over a given airspace portion or for airspace above a given altitude—for example the control of overflights—is conceivable. In so far as geographical de-localization of ATC centres is not an issue, franchises on fixed time periods over particular airspace portions could be delegated to the most competitive bidder. Currently corporatized or state-owned monopolies provide for national ATS without competing. But the issue of national sovereignty—i.e. as relates to military requirements—and the apportionment of the financial revenues arising from the provision of ATS—i.e. as between wages nationwide and wages for air traffic controllers—will make the introduction of competition difficult.

Second, competition could be promoted along preset routes, with airplanes choosing the most cost-effective route by weighing up expected delays, *en route* charges, and fuel costs. Up to 1998, such competition did not exist: whatever the route flown between two destinations, *en route* charges were billed according to the most frequent route used by airplanes. Since then, however, billing is based on the declared route flown by airplanes—which may not be the route flown if a last-minute change in flight plan occurs. Therefore, in theory, users can choose routes according to cost. However, competition can develop only at the fringe, because for most scheduled flights there is no credible alternative route. If choosing an alternative route is possible for some flight (for example choosing to fly over the Netherlands instead of over France between London and Frankfurt), for most cases it is not (e.g. London to Baléares without crossing France). The scope for introducing routes competition is therefore rather limited.

18.3.3. *Lack of monopoly regulation*

Monopoly providers have been said to prevail in ATS provision. But are they regulated?

No credible monopoly regulation has been implemented in the European member states or at EU level. Two regulatory paths are available: the introduction of (1) positive economic incentives to improve performance and capacity—i.e. rewarding incentives; and of (2) negative economic incentives—penalizing incentives, e.g. for lack of service commitment. A combination of rewarding and penalizing incentives is conceivable.

Positive economic incentives could take the form of financial rewards. However, the mechanism of *en route* charges does not provide for this: as mentioned, it is currently based on an automatic cost recovery mechanism, regardless of the fluctuations in air traffic, the performance of ATC national systems, and flight delays. Increases in the productivity of service provision do not translate into additional financial revenues that could be passed on to an investment programme and/or financial bonuses to controllers and managers (or potential shareholders).

In the same way, the mechanism for *en route* charges does not allow providers to be penalized when the provision and quality of service do not meet demand requirements: inefficiencies and lack of productivity that translate into insufficient traffic absorption are not paid for. As costs are fully recovered, under-capacity only causes lower-volume traffic and increases in national unit rates. Similarly, service providers do not incur losses if they make ineffective investment in research and development to improve future performance. Furthermore, delays caused by the mismanagement of national ATC systems are not internalized but externalized: only users bear the costs of delays. From a provider viewpoint, therefore, there is no economic incentive for reducing delays.

18.3.4. *Lack of countervailing power*

Monopolies may be regulated by the emergence of a significant 'countervailing power' (Galbraith 1956) from users. But, except through lobbying and political influence, users cannot bring pressure on national ATC systems; they are not formally involved in the decision-making process on ATC issues. Besides, the *en route* charge mechanism and delays do not introduce a competitive advantage for a particular set of users; therefore any gain secured by an airline company would be passed on to other competing companies. Notwithstanding a divergence of interests among users, an emerging countervailing power would face difficulties in the structuring of collective action (Olson 1965). By contrast, any change in the *en route* formula, or in the allocation of the *en route* slots mechanism, would invite debate among users, as it would increase the competitive opportunities for particular users.

For these reasons, the lack of economic incentives for improving ATC performance has led European ministers of transport to set up the Performance Review Commission.

18.4. THE PERFORMANCE REVIEW COMMISSION (PRC)

The PRC is an independent EU body[10] analysing the performance of ATS provision, formulating ways of improvement, developing performance

[10] Even if its secretariat, the Performance Review Unit, is hosted and its budget managed by Eurocontrol.

indicators and setting up targets, and proposing guidelines for economic regulation.

In a previous research, institutional regulatory models of regulator have been examined in various industries (Dumez and Jeunemaître 1998*a*, 1999*a*). These enable us to comment on the institutional PRC arrangements compared with existing regulatory frameworks in other industries.

1. The PRC has no regulatory coercive powers. The main regulatory tool lies in publicizing its analyses and findings, in defining its performance objectives and targets and illustrating whether or not they are met by ATS providers, and in making recommendations. A provider may risk falling into disrepute before its national counterparts, reputation being the driving force in the system. Moreover, the PRC has the power to investigate any chosen issue. In this respect, it is very similar to what is referred to as 'sunshine or torchlight regulation' (McCraw 1984; Cohen and Henry 1997; Henry 1997).

2. The PRC also has leeway in drawing up economic regulation guidelines and investigating performance issues. Although users and providers are not members of the PRC and do not attend decision meetings, the Commission may decide to seek comments and advice from the ATS 'stakeholders'—i.e. providers and users. In this regard, inasmuch as the PRC may help in the deriving of agreements and consensus on particular items, it shares some characteristics with the 'self-discipline' regulatory model (Jeunemaître 1997).

3. In investigating the scope for ATS regulation, the PRC has to study competition in ATS and the potential competitive market arrangements, and to debate the various ways of introducing economic incentives for performance improvement. In this regard, it has some of the key features of the 'light-handed' regulatory model (Bollard and Pickford 1997), where liberalization and competition take priority over economic regulation. Strictly speaking, the PRC is not a regulator, but it is empowered to issue proposals about airspace management and liberalization in service provision.

4. As the PRC has to draw up and implement guidelines for economic regulation, in particular price regulation—e.g. reflecting on price-cap, peak, and priority pricing—it could move towards a 'sector-based regulator' as for example in the public UK utilities (Beesley 1995, 1997).

5. Finally, the PRC may choose to stick to particular regulatory consultative procedures. It may decide to hold public hearings and to draw stakeholders into its decision-making processes. As such, it may benefit from the experience of US regulatory agencies.

In short, the PRC is a commission of experts and practitioners with no formal regulatory powers, but with the freedom to address issues relating to ATS providers' performance. It could evolve into a powerful commission if it succeeds in gaining legitimacy through the quality of its analysis and its proposals.

It is both an economic review office and an advisory committee on regulatory initiatives and economic regulation principles.[11]

18.5. PERFORMANCE REVIEW REPORTS

The PRC has so far issued three Performance Review Reports.[12] Obviously, an early assessment of the Commission's work is somewhat premature, as gaining legitimacy is a long process (Dumez and Jeunemaître 1998a). The first report gathers and analyses existing data covering the 1998 calendar year. Data are nevertheless fragmented, frequently unreliable, and above all difficult to handle for a detailed review. In fact, one main PRC priority has been to remedy the lack of relevant data in current information systems on ATC service and performance. The latest report, published in May 2000, has made progress in structuring data analysis but still falls short of providing for an operational basis for implementing economic incentives and regulation.

In spite of those drawbacks, however, an embryonic assessment of the Commission is worth attempting as it gives insights into the PRC appraisal system and indications about future developments.

18.5.1. *Focused issues*

The first PRC report (PRC 1999a) was in line with what would have been expected of a network industry review. The lack of efficient service was found to be due to particular airspace portions and time service provisions.

In summer 1998 fifteen controlled airspace sectors (about 3 per cent of the sky sectorization in Europe) were responsible for 45 per cent of delays.[13] Those sectors range across the backbone of European air traffic (mainly, London, Amsterdam, Reims, Karlsruhe, Zurich, Milan, Athens (PRC 1999a: 67)).

Delays were also concentrated at particular times of the day and week, e.g. at peak hours (before 9 am, midday, evening) and at weekends. For instance, Annex 9 of the first PRC report points out that in 1998 Aix en Provence caused few delays at weekdays but bottlenecks at weekends. Finally, delays peaked in the summer, from 4 May to 1 November.[14]

---

[11] A twin independent European Commission has been set up for air traffic safety, the Safety Review Commission.

[12] Performance Review Reports covering the calendar 1998 (PRC 1999a), the calendar year 1999 (PRC 2000), and an interim Special Review Report on delays in 1999 (PRC 1999b).

[13] Delays did not improve the following year. As stressed in PRC (2000), 'the ATC capacity shortfalls identifed in PRR2 still exist... ATFM delays in 1999 increased much faster than traffic. Lack of capacity in some areas caused ATFM delays to increase by 68% compared to 1998, while traffic increased by 6.7%... 20 sectors out of 468 (4.3%) caused more than 40% of the ATFM delays.'

[14] The PRC report reviewing 1999 shows that the difference between weekend and weekday capacities did not change (PRC 2000).

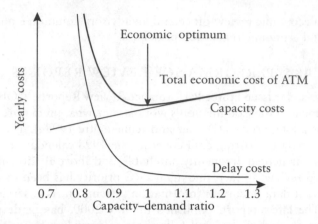

Figure 18.1. *Capacity and Delay Costs: Performance Trade-offs*
Source: PRC (1999a).

18.5.2. *Investment policy*

Poor performance could arise from two separate but non-exclusive factors: technical or network undercapacity, or the mismanagement of existing capacity—or both. Evidence that, at a given capacity, delays are greater at times of *lowest* traffic—summer, weekends—would seem to provide evidence of the latter, in other words of a mismanagement of human resources. However, the first PRC report does not straightforwardly address that issue: it focuses primarily on a lack of investment capacity, without indicating whether this involves a lack of technical investment or suboptimal ATC management. It simply delivers a trade-off characterizing each ATC centre (PRC 1999a: 11 ff.).[15] An optimal capacity–demand equilibrium is found so that marginal cost of increasing capacity—i.e. investing in capacity—equals marginal gains from absorbing additional traffic, the underlying principle being that ATC centres should be neither under- nor over-dimensioned with regard to traffic, as shown in Figure 18.1.

Given that the CFMU provides information on delays that are assigned to airspace sectors, and assuming that capacity cost curves are built into the modelling—i.e. that the cost capacity function is linear—each ATC centre can position itself according to an optimal economic equilibrium and can therefore achieve the required investment to meet demand and traffic forecasts. Such modelling, even if elementary, can provide partial solutions for increasing performance by singling out the necessary improvements to network nodes. However, it will have a limited operational dimension, as ATC centre cost functions are not fully known, and as it is based on average delays, which do

[15] The PRC report takes stock of the Future Air Traffic Management Profile (FAP) methodology developed by the Eurocontrol Experimental Centre (Eurocontrol 1997).

not accurately account for differences at different times of the day, week, or year. Another limitation relates to the use of the ATC centre over ATC sector as the relevant measurement unit. If airspace management rationalization occurs when the boundaries and airspace allocations to ATC centres are modified—for example when a key sector from ATC Reims centre was re-allocated to the ATC Brest centre in 1998—then performance comparisons lose significance. Above all, the issue of what is the true meaning of capacity investment remains open to discussion.

18.5.3. *Member states' responses to review process*

Faced with concentrated inefficiencies in ATS provision, the PRC recommended specific increased capacity investment for ATC centres. Most of the member states' responses, at least as given in the first PRC report (1999: 32), did not live up to expectations. The report cites the 'agreed target capacity', 'achieved capacity', 'forecast traffic variation', 'actual traffic variation', and 'air traffic management delay variation', for each ATC centre. Three comments are worth making.

First, member states were unwilling to commit themselves to capacity investment. Ten out of eighteen of the reviewed ATC centres failed to provide data on capacity planning. The 'agreed target capacity' is therefore misleading, as no clear-cut agreements were really reached. Second, when an increase in investment capacity was agreed upon, it often failed to materialize. For instance, Germany committed itself to increase its Karlsruhe ATC centre capacity by 3 per cent on the basis of a 5.1 per cent forecast increase in traffic. In fact, traffic increased by only 4.4 per cent without any noticeable German commitment to capacity investment, resulting in delays multiplying by 1.5. Finally, and conversely, traffic increases have usually *exceeded* forecasts and therefore the required investments have been underrated. At any rate, capacity investment commitments were in some cases less than the forecast increase in traffic had required.

18.5.4. *The PRC regulatory strategy*

Without coercive regulatory powers, the PRC can only highlight mismanagement in ATS provision and inadequacies in capacity investment, and point out the imbalances between supply and demand. Presumably, it may identify best practices and aid their implementation through benchmarking and the publicizing of its findings. But its recommendations are not legally binding.

To give an account of the dynamics of national ATC systems performance, the PRC has worked out a centralized and detailed information system. This is based on an identification of eight performance components (key performance areas, KPAs): safety, equity, environment, delays, predictability, cost-effectiveness, flexibility, and availability. In the short run, the emphasis is put on three of these, i.e. safety, cost-effectiveness, and delays; the others are medium-term objectives. KPAs are specified by means of accumulating indicators, or key performance indicators (KPIs).

The setting up of a detailed information system invites comment. The diagnostic on ATC service provision performance is clear. The provision of ATS can be assimilated into network production. The network has long been in crisis. It has proved itself unable to cope with air traffic demand. Congestion is concentrated in particular network nodes. Those nodes are already well identified under the current—albeit imperfect—information system. One issue still remains unsettled with regard to the remedies: to what extent, and in what proportion, will an improvement in performance hinge on technical initiatives (control systems, sectorization, military/civil coordination, vertical and horizontal airplane separation, increase in VHF frequencies, etc.), and to what extent on an increase in human resources (number of controllers, etc.) or on the better management of existing capacity and an increase in labour productivity (training, rotation of controllers, etc.) which would allow for flexibility and increase in capacity at peak hours?

Building on that diagnosis, the PRC will then attempt to develop and refine the existing information system under a key principle: 'A system that is not measured can hardly be managed effectively' (PRC 1999: 12). It aims at better identifying key issues in ATC service provision, implementing set performance targets, and reviewing compliance with those targets.

Such regulatory strategy raises two important issues. The first relates to the time scale of the approach. As pointed out in the PRC report (PRC 2000), an investment capacity at time t for a given airspace sector will prove effective only years after being decided. (For example, the training period for a new controller varies from three to five years.) The time required to develop the KPIs information system will be added to the time needed to decide on an investment policy based on the gathering of information and the setting of targets. Therefore, it is very likely that the regulatory approach will bear fruit only in the medium term. Above all, as the report rightly pointed out, the development and implementation of a detailed information system will face technical difficulties (in particular in the definition of disclosure-of-information regime and the harmonization of data) and political obstruction if it is ever anticipated that performance target-setting is going to be linked to financial penalties; then, the less well performing national ATC systems will have interest in concealing information or in using information asymmetries between the PRC and ATC centres. Implementing a detailed information system therefore is likely to be a long process.[16]

---

[16] The PRC report assesses air traffic management performance in Europe during 1999 under three key performance areas—safety, delays, and cost-effectiveness—and develops an initial ATS providers benchmarking. With regard to safety, the report stresses the 'lack of consistency and availability of data at the European level preventing meaningful conclusions being drawn'. It expects harmonized reporting from providers from 2001. Air traffic delays are better identified.

The second issue concerns the relevance of information. It is fair to state that the management of ATS provision requires an accurate knowledge of current practices. However, a core issue is the extent to which the information gathered will be relevant for the purpose of improving network performance. If mismanagement is concentrated on particular nodes, the required relevant information would have to focus on those particular nodes. Will a detailed information system proceeding from the devising of refined indicators help very much to deal with the weakest nodes? The PRC reports have already identified them under the available and current information system. Will a battery of indicators based on average measurements bring forward new insights and provide further guidance for the involved parties? Although the disclosure of information and benchmarking are necessary requirements, it is far from being obvious that such a *modus operandi* will prove effective and sufficient to foster performance. The PRC does have the additional option of carrying out specific investigations, but so far it has not resorted to this.

As time passes before the information system becomes operational and brings noticeable improvements, could other additional regulatory mechanisms be implemented to get maximum results? The following section investigates the potential for introducing a convergence pricing mechanism with incentives for performance that do not exclude other, more ambitious, policies.

18.6. FROM NATIONAL UNIT RATES TO EFFICIENT CONVERGENCE PRICING

Any regulation aiming at short-term effectiveness should take stock of the constraints in which it develops and should abide by general principles. The proposed pricing system seeks to suit those requirements in ATS provision (Dumez and Jeunemaître 1999*b,c*).

18.6.1. *Regulatory constraints*

In the short run, it is likely that member states will wish to retain their ATS provision and not relinquish airspace sovereignty, even if such inroads are conceivable for flights above a certain altitude or in certain sectors. Regulation of ATS provision will therefore concern the regulation of monopolies. Such regulation will have to deal with familiar economic issues raised by monopoly structure and rents: the provision of service at undercapacity levels, suboptimal service quality, and pricing.

1. As there are twenty-eight national members and providers involved in Eurocontrol with divergent views about ATS management, it is very unlikely

---

As for cost-effectiveness, the report identifies 'the lack of economic information as a major impediment in assessing cost-effectiveness'. Like the Safety Commission, the PRC has made proposals for economic information disclosure that should first have to be approved by the provisional council and could not be implemented until 2001.

that a centralized initiative that already failed in 1960 will be workable, or that a European 'hands-on' regulation applied to national ATS providers will easily reach a consensus. Regulation will therefore have to focus on 'light-handed' regulation schemes in respect of national idiosyncrasies and be based on the subsidiarity principle.

2. The pricing of ATS will certainly require the introduction of economic incentives for performance. Even if there is agreement—which is not certain— on a fully commercial approach, it is likely that profits will have to be regulated.

3. Currently, the *en route* charge mechanism provides for non-discrimination towards users. Airline companies that have different business interests and fleets are very set against a billing system that would benefit national dominant users, leading to a potential increase in market power and additional barriers to entry. A radical shift in charging for the use of airspace will therefore prove difficult to enforce.

4. ATS provision is undergoing an irreversible evolution in which the interplay of users and providers is fundamental for devising regulation. At times of capacity shortfalls and delay crises, users will claim their readiness not to buy the service but to pay for it, and will demand to be fully involved in the negotiations with providers and national administrations or regulators. Regulation will then have to put forward a code of best practices for providers and also for users in the management of flight plans and allocation of airspace slots.

5. Another constraint weighing on any regulatory initiative is the need to distinguish between the potential for improvements through new technology implementation and the potential for ATS optimal management.

18.6.2. *A European 'single sky'*

Achieving a 'single sky' for Europe from a user's perspective requires some kind of convergence pricing among the European member states. If similar circumstances—congestion, airspace complexity, safety—obtained throughout the EU, there would be *a priori* no reason for users to pay differently for ATS according to the use of different national airspace portions. Currently, national unit rates for providing the service vary significantly in Europe and bear no relationship to the quality of service—i.e. delays. Airspace complexity and traffic patterns *are* reflected in national unit rates. They vary from 1 to 5 in Europe; the average charge for service per kilometre flown in upper airspace varies from 1 to 7, and the average sector cost from 1 to 4 (Eurocontrol 1999c). Although ATS pricing has to reflect differentiated ATC centre costs, national unit rates and *en route* charges cannot be allowed to deviate on such a scale. Therefore, one regulatory objective would be to seek to a convergence of national unit rates in Europe using the most efficient providers as benchmark.

A 'single sky' for Europe would also assume nondiscriminatory regulation between national providers. At the national level, it is likely that separation between provision and regulation of the service will soon be enforced; in fact, this is already beginning to occur. However the separation is implemented, whether involving the privatization of the provider or not, monopoly components of ATS provision will remain. Those national monopoly components will be nationally regulated. If the service provision and airspace are open to competition, European regulation will have to ensure that national regulations do not introduce a distortion of competition, for example by allowing excess profits in the management of the national provider or by granting investment subsidization. Finally, if national providers are privatized on a commercial footing, so that they are allowed to make profits, then strategic alliances of national providers or even mergers could be foreseeable outcomes, even if these moves are realistic only in the longer term. One issue—as for other regulated industries and utilities—would be the extent to which competition law and policy would apply to ATS alongside regulation.

18.6.3. *Regulatory principles*

European economic regulation of ATS provision has to conform with the previous constraints. Some of these relate to the situation at present, others to medium and long-term prospects. If regulation aims at producing short-term effective results, it should be driven by a few key principles. For example, it should:

- be easy to implement and robust;
- avoid resting on a detailed, complex, and costly information system, which is a medium-term prospect;
- guarantee that the costs of providing the service will be recovered while being performance-driven;
- be forward-looking;
- be non-discriminatory;
- ensure transparency.

18.6.4. *A convergence pricing proposal*

Public utilities have put to the test different regulatory regimes; for example, the price-cap mechanism has been a major tool of UK regulatory policy (electricity, water, telecommunications, etc.) (Littlechild 1983). But none of these regimes have ever been implemented at the EU level, and it is likely that the generalization of a particular member state regulatory regime will not receive consensual agreement. Regulatory regimes are devised according to national idiosyncrasies. On the other hand, the EU has effective experience in policy convergence, particularly in monetary and budgetary policies. Probably a sound mix of policy drawn from national regulatory policies and EU policies can be found.

An interesting feature of the UK price-cap regulation is that it gives managerial autonomy to providers and makes them business-oriented; moreover, it is forward-looking and as far as possible seeks to avoid regulatory risk to investors. The EU budgetary and monetary policies exhibit another appealing feature, which is that national fluctuations of currency rates and budget deficits of member states are kept within narrow bands. This has been achieved by submitting member-states to a general regulatory constraint but not interfering with national policy choices. With regard to a European ATS, a mix of both orientations could probably be worked out.[17] The keystone of a European regulatory regime could then be the *en route* charge mechanism.

National unit rates are currently adjusted on the basis of a full cost recovery mechanism, whatever the fluctuations in chargeable service units volume— i.e. traffic handled by providers. The national unit rates would have to be replaced by national unit prices, of which the fluctuations would be agreed upon for a given period of time (three to five years). National unit prices at the beginning of the period could be estimated according to past national unit rates and CSU volumes trends, for example on data analysis covering the past ten to twenty years. From then on, users and providers would negotiate for increases in traffic in the period, at a national and European level. Prices would then be set in a forward-looking perspective according to a number of positive and negative factors:

- minus X: agreed productivity efforts from providers, taking into account convergence requirements (i.e. defining narrow bands and convergence according to performance providers' benchmarking);
- plus K: remuneration for agreed investment from business plans to meet demand;
- plus C: remunerating efforts in operating and achieving investment arising from air complexity. Similar capacity investments have different performance results according to the complexity of sectors (crossing of preset routes, ascending and descending trajectories of airplanes, interplay of military training sessions);
- minus D: penalizing delays. ATC centres generate delays. In a dynamic perspective, providers would be made accountable for lack of service provision. They would have an incentive to reduce delays. Users would pay for the service and the quality of service. They would pay less if the quality and/or service are not provided; in such case they would benefit from discount pricing. Factor D would therefore compensate for incurring delay and for a lack of providers' service commitment.

---

[17] Institutional arrangements that would be associated with the pricing proposal will not be analysed in this paper. For institutional performance and design, see North (1990), and Horn (1995).

From these general principles, which require data and econometric and simulation analysis, the EU regulatory regime would incorporate features of both a forward-looking and minimized-risk regulatory regime, and convergence. The cost of implementing such a regulatory regime would be minimized. The core of the *en route* charge formula based on weight and distance flown would remain, so that a users' new competitive equilibrium would not have to be negotiated. Only the unit prices rate (determined by X, K, and C) would come in to replace national unit rates. An estimated cost per minute delay would be introduced in the billing for service provided.

Such a pricing proposal would rest on an existing information system sufficiently accurate and robust. Flight and sector delays are already computed by CFMU; it would not require additional information cost, although it would involve a clear and transparent surveillance of *en route* slots allocation to avoid unfair treatment of users and providers. Also, air complexity could in the first instance be estimated according to the proportion of overflights to flights in national airspace. Simulation and statistical analysis would provide for incremental values of the different parameters.

An important benefit of such an incentive pricing scheme would be that European regulation would not have to interfere with national ATS policies and could avoid entangling the European level in debates about estimates of capital costs and rates of return, and providers' profit levels. In this way, the regulatory regime would be based on a subsidiarity principle.

The European regulatory regime would be based on forward-looking negotiations between providers and users first at a national level, the results of which would then be discussed and agreed upon at the European level under contractualized agreements. Such a scheme would include positive incentives (remuneration of productivity efforts and capacity investment, taking air complexity into consideration) and financial penalties according to commitment to service (delays). It would drive service providers to supply full capacity in service provision with regard to weakest nodes in the network and to introduce competition among national providers, which would compete not to be the most delay penalizing provider in order to maximize their revenues. Providers would have the incentive to increase capacity in general, to maximize revenues, to strengthen the weakest network nodes, and to reduce capacity in overmanned ATC centres, thereby providing for efficiency gains and flexibility in Europe-wide ATC service provision.

This would rest on negotiations between users, providers, and national administration or regulators, with disclosure of information being ensured by stakeholders of the air traffic control service. If a provider were to behave in a non-efficient way, not allowing for the recovering of its costs, then the member state would be liable as a payer of last resort. Also, it would not be in the interest of users to minimize traffic forecasts, as they would incur financial losses arising from delays, or to maximize traffic forecasts, as they would pay for higher prices because of the unjustified increases in capacity investments.

Also, in organizing competition for performance, such a scheme would avoid national regulatory distortions through the convergence principle without impeding coordination among member state providers.

In summary, the sketching out of a European economic ATS regulation has been devised according to the constraints and principles stated above: introducing incentives; as far as possible relying on simplicity and robustness without requiring further detailed information system; ensuring costs when committing to service and quality; creating incentives to re-invest profits for improving performance; promoting non-discrimination among users. Obviously, many other regulatory perspectives should be investigated and more ambitious policies could be developed relating to the use of airspace, routing, etc. With regard to economic pricing tools, other credible alternatives should be studied, for example the introduction of congestion pricing (Downs 1992), capacity pricing (Olafsson 1995), the potential for setting up capacity slots brokerage, or peak and priority pricing schemes. Those alternatives would certainly be carefully looked into, not solely from their economic characteristics but also in regard to constraints in the ATM and in the light of their robustness and effectiveness in implementation. If alternatives compete, they should be assessed according to similar criteria.

18.7. CONCLUSION

European ATC is the latest public utility service to witness fundamental managerial change, moving from a state-owned and administrated provision of service to a more commercial approach. European member states have already gone down this path with the separation between regulators—i.e. administration or agency—and operators, i.e. providers. The UK has developed a Public–Private Partnership for NATS and has committed itself to introducing price regulation of the service.

New developments could occur as independent national providers, either corporatized or privatized, behave as business corporations, working out strategic alliances and bidding for airspace management when this is open to competition by member states, or else merging and rationalizing their ATC portfolio assets.

On institutional grounds, it is most likely that the European Commission will intervene with a stronger hand. The 1997 Eurocontrol revised convention scheduled membership of the European Commission in Eurocontrol for 2001. As in other areas, the Commission will push for a clear separation between regulatory functions and ATS provision (Bayart 1995), driving member states, including the most reluctant ones such as France, to modify their administrative arrangements.[18] The European Commission could also make use of directives

---

[18] Logically, separation between regulator and provider should lead to a reorganization of Eurocontrol, the Maastricht ATC Centre having disposed of Eurocontrol: either the Maastricht ATC centre should be made autonomous, or it should be transferred to or merged with a provider.

which would make performance targets legally binding for member states. Penalties imposed on member states for lack of service provision could then be enforced by the European Court of Justice, shifting the process of regulation towards a law-based orientation.

The European ministers of transport expressed their concern about dramatic increases in delays in 1999 and asked the European Commission for review and remedy proposals by the end of that year. A high-level group set up at the European Commission level published its report in November 2000. It remains to be seen whether subsequent institutional proposals will result in increasing the powers and prerogatives of the recently created PRC. It is more likely that a European Regulator independent of Eurocontrol will be set up, with the PRC being left to monitor performance in service provision.

There is no doubt that economic regulation will soon be a major focus in dealing with ATS provision. A suitable regulatory perspective will have to be defined according to ATC characteristics, bearing in mind modesty: 'As regards regulation, it should not be expected to do better than substitute major drawbacks by minor ones' (Henry 1997: 209).

But the real issue probably lies in the available flexibility to implement the new institutional arrangements. The 1997 revised Eurocontrol convention has not yet been ratified by all European member states. The Performance Review Commission, set up barely two years ago and without effective regulatory powers, is already at a crossroads as to whether or not it is a proper regulator. Eurocontrol itself is a mix of ATS provider—i.e. ranging from dealing with such issues as the Maastricht ATC centre, an operator through the *en route* slots allocation by CFMU, and a billing agency through CRCO, to the issue of separation.

The role of the European Commission, speaking on behalf of the EU member states but soon to be sitting alongside them in Eurocontrol, is also a bit of an oddity in the decision-making process for improving European ATM performance. And even if the European Commission were to have effective political tools to implement new policy such as directives and regulation (but binding only to member states), it has neither the resources nor the status to become a regulator itself.

REFERENCES

Armstrong M., Gowan, S. and Vickers, J. (1994). *Regulatory Reform,* MIT Press, Cambridge, Mass.: MIT Press.

Bayart, D. (1995). 'Le Tournant gestionnaire d'un grand système technique: le contrôle de la navigation aérienne fait ses adieux à l'Etat', CRG, École Polytechnique, December.

Beesley, M. (1995). *Utility Regulation: Challenge and Response,* London: Institute of Economic Affairs, no. 42.

Beesley, M. (1997). *Regulating Utilities: Broadening the Debate*, London: Institute of Economic Affairs, no. 46.

Bollard, A. and Pickford, M. (1997). 'Utility regulation in New Zealand', in M. Beesley, *Regulating Utilities: Broadening the Debate*, London: Institute of Economic Affairs, no. 46, pp. 75–131.

CEE (1996). *Air Traffic Management: Freeing Europe's Airspace*, 0055.96/EN, 5 March.

Chew, R. G. (1997). 'Free Flight, Preserving Airline Opportunity', *American Airlines*, 2 September.

Civil Aviation Authority (CAA) (2000). 'National Air Traffic Services Public–Private Partnership', consultative paper, April.

Cohen, E. and Henry, C. (1997). *Service public secteur public*, Rapports du Conseil d'Analyse Économique, La Documentation Française, no. 3.

Department of the Environment, Transport and Regional Affairs Committee (Session 1997/8) (1998). *Air Traffic Control*, House of Commons, 27 March, London: Stationery Office.

Downs, A. (1992). *Stuck in Traffic: Coping with Peak-Hour Congestion*. Washington: Brookings Institution and the Lincoln of Land Policy.

Dumez, H. and Jeunemaître, A. (1998a). 'Regulatory Policies: Institutional Lessons for the Regulation of Air Traffic Control', Paris: École Polytechnique.

—— and —— (1998b). *Évaluer l'action publique: Régulation des marchés financiers et modèle du mandat*, Paris: L'Harmattan.

—— and —— (1999a), 'Les Institutions de la régulation des marchés: étude de quelques modèles de référence', *Revue Internationale de Droit Économique*, no. 1, pp. 11–30.

—— and —— (1999b). 'Towards a Dynamic Incentive System of Pricing in ATM', Economic Regulation Group CAA, London, 20 July 1999, Paris: Centre de Recherche en Gestion, École Polytechnique.

—— and —— (1999c). 'Towards a Dynamic Incentive System of Pricing in ATM: Further Thoughts and Comments, Part 1', Paris: Centre de Recherche en Gestion, École Polytechnique.

Eurocontrol (1997). *Future ATM Profile: Capacity Shortfalls in Europe (1996–2006)*, Brétigny: Eurocontrol Experimental Centre – EEC.

—— (1998). *Annual Performance Review Report (PRR1)*, Brussels: Eurocontrol.

—— (1999a). *Special Performance Review Report on Delays (PRR2)*, Brussels: Eurocontrol.

—— (1999b). *Annual Performance Review Report (PRR3)*, Brussels: Eurocontrol.

—— (1999c). *Cost of the En Route Air Navigation Services in Europe*, EEC Note no. 8/99, Brussels: Eurocontrol Experimental Centre, June.

European Commission (1996). 'Air Traffic Management: Freeing Europe's Airspace', 0055.96/EN, 5 March.

—— (2000). 'Commission Initiative to Reduce Flight Delays in Europe Takes Off', IP/00/585, 7 June.

Fron, X. (1998). 'Evolution du contrôle du trafic aérien en Europe', *La Jaune et la Rouge*, May, pp. 7–18.

Galbraith, J. K. (1956). *The Concept of Countervailing Power*, Boston: Houghton.

Henry, C. (1997). *Concurrence et services publics dans l'Union européenne*, Paris: Presses Universitaires de France.

Horn, M. (1995). *The Political Economy of Public Administration,* Cambridge: Cambridge University Press.

Jeunemaître, A. (ed.) (1997). *Financial Markets Regulation: A Practitioner's Perspective,* Basingstoke: Macmillan.

Littlechild, S. (1983). *Regulation of British Telecommunications Profitability.* London: HMSO.

McCraw, T. K. (1984). *Prophets of Regulation.* Cambridge, Mass.: Harvard University Press.

Mears, T. (1999). 'Getting Optimal ATC Performance: Policy Options and the Role of Economic Regulation', London: CAA, PRC Economic Regulation Group July.

North, D. (1990). *Institutions, Institutional Change and Economic Performance,* Cambridge: Cambridge University Press.

Olafsson, S. (1995). *Pricing Capacity Patterns on Networks: An Approach based on Evolutionary Theory,* London: BT Laboratories, June.

Olson, M. (1965). *The Logic of Collective Action: Public Goods and the Theory of Groups,* Cambridge, Mass.: Harvard University Press.

Performance Review Commission (PRC) (1999a). *Performance Review Report covering the Calendar Year 1998,* Brussels: Eurocontrol, 4 June.

—— (1996b). *Special Performance Review Report on Delays 1999* (PPR2), Brussels: Eurocontrol, December.

—— (2000). *Performance Review Report covering the Calendar Year 1999* (PPR3), Brussels: Eurocontrol, May.

Schmalensee, R. (1995). 'Testimony on Antitrust Issues related to Networks', Federal Trade Commission, 1 December.

Scigliano, E. (1999). 'Delayed Take-Off', *Technology Review,* 102(5): 44–52.

Stuchlik, J.-B. (1999). *De la performance du contrôle aérien en Europe,* doctoral dissertation, Ecole Polytechnique.

Vickers, J. and Yarrow, G. (1988). *Privatization: An Economic Analysis,* Cambridge, Mass.: MIT Press.

Villiers, J. (1994). *Regards sur le transport aérien,* Paris: Institut du Transport Aérien, vol. 34.

19

Transforming Infrastructure in Eastern Europe

DAVID KENNEDY AND NICK STERN

19.1. INTRODUCTION

One of the basic requirements of a properly functioning market economy is a modern, efficient, and user-oriented infrastructure. The infrastructure in eastern Europe inherited from the communist era was poorly suited to a market economy in terms of both physical and organizational makeup. This resulted from the special priorities of the old regime: a focus on heavy goods production; little concern for the consumer; excessive specialization across regions for purposes of political control; limited concern from economic costs; indifference towards the environment. Because of the importance of infrastructure in any economy, and also the heritage in the communist economies, infrastructure restructuring is a major challenge in the economic reform drive of central and eastern European countries.

Specific challenges arise from infrastructure industry organization under communism. Power sectors were operated from inside government ministries, with the objective of providing abundant supplies for use in production and for domestic consumption. Little regard was paid to economic cost, including environmental externalities. High energy consumption[1] was facilitated by tariffs far below levels in western Europe and North America.[2] Price structures were further distorted by a substantial cross-subsidy from large users and businesses to domestic customers. Failure to account for environmental costs when planning investment has resulted in a highly polluting, inefficient power system, with the former communist countries now accounting for over 20 per cent of world total CO_2 emissions compared with a GDP share of less

---

[1] Energy intensity in 1990 in central and eastern Europe was 1,850 tonnes of oil equivalent (toe) per 1990€ mn compared with around 200 toe per 1990€ mn in western Europe; see European Commission (2000).

[2] See EBRD (1998) for evidence on tariffs in former communist countries; even by 1997, tariffs were a maximum of 5 cents per kWh and far lower in most cases; this can be compared with the North American average at the time of 7.5 cents per kWh and the western European average of nearly 15 cents.

than 3 per cent.[3] Telecommunications was not regarded as a priority under communism, with the result that networks were undeveloped and penetration rates very low by western standards.[4] Investment in water and waste water treatment was limited, quality standards were low, and water resources were depleted in the process of supplying heavy industry. As in the case of the power industry, environmental externalities were not factored into water/waste water investment decisions. Rail networks were tailored to the industrial structure; given the preference for heavy industry, rail provided the best means of moving bulky products around. Rail network density is high in the former communist countries by western standards.[5]

Meeting the infrastructure reform challenge—moving to a market-based industry organization—will bring efficiency gains within infrastructure. Introduction of the private sector in a well regulated/competitive setting should result in efficiency gains and in service quality (including environment and safety) improvements.[6] In addition, infrastructure transition should change competitive interactions among firms downstream. Infrastructure investment and reforms that result in lower transaction (e.g. communication, transport, information) costs can result in downstream exit/restructuring of inefficient firms and the entry of new low-cost firms.[7] Moreover, infrastructure reform will facilitate EU accession, planned from 2003 onwards. Consistency with the various market-based EU directives and environmental/safety standards is a necessary condition for accession.

Progress in infrastructure reform has been made since the end of communism. Across infrastructure sectors, public-sector operations have typically been commercialized through, for example, corporatization. Depending on the sector and the country, private operators have been introduced through either asset divestment or some sort of concession arrangement, regulatory frameworks have been developed, and market entry barriers removed.

This chapter reviews advances, and considers remaining challenges, in the power, telecommunications, water, and rail sectors of central and eastern Europe, the Baltics, and the Balkans. The following section focuses on reform progress in the power sector, where there has been significant industry restructuring and regulatory development. Section 19.3 describes advances in the telecommunications sectors, where privatization and liberalization have been key. Section 19.4 analyses water and wastewater, where developments have largely been limited to commercialization within the public sector. This is

---

[3] See European Commission (2000). Average thermal efficiency in generation was around 25% in central and eastern Europe compared with around 45% in western Europe.

[4] Penetration in the former communist countries was around 15 lines per 100 inhabitants as against around 50 lines in western Europe, and waiting times for connection were up to ten years, a figure typical in many of the former communist countries (see EBRD 1996).

[5] For data see EBRD (1996).

[6] Reform paths are specific to sectors and countries. A menu of reform paths is presented in each of the sector-specific sections below.

[7] See Aghion and Shankerman (1998) for analysis and discussion.

also the case for the rail industries of the region, assessed in Section 19.5. The final section concludes.

19.2. POWER SECTOR

At the start of the transition process, power industries in eastern Europe were structured as monolithic enterprises, operated according to plan fulfilment/ ideology as opposed to economic principles. They were characterized by (1) being high-energy-intensity relative to the European Union, the United States, and Japan; (2) having low operational efficiency and plant availability in generation; (3) high losses in transmission and distribution; (4) tariffs well below long-run supply costs; (5) cross-subsidy from large users to residential customers and small businesses; (6) low revenue/cash collection; (7) poor environmental and health and safety records; (8) unsafe and ageing Soviet designed nuclear power; and (9) none of the regulatory or institutional arrangements necessary for operation along commercial lines.

Mapping out an infrastructure reform process for these transition economies requires assumptions regarding the arrangements that will best deliver an efficient and good-quality service (in terms of industry organization, owner-ship, rules of the game, etc.). In what follows, it is the introduction of the private sector in a well regulated and, where feasible, liberalized environment that is held to be the reform objective. Experience in UK infrastructure reform,[8] the widespread private participation in infrastructure around the world,[9] and evidence on private participation from the transition economies[10] suggest that introduction of the private sector in a well regulated and liberalized environ-ment will deliver performance improvements.

Before laying out reform steps, a proviso must be made. There are a number of ways forward. The appropriate reforms are specific to sectors within infrastructure and countries; *a priori*, it is unclear whether a particular country would, for example, benefit from a power pool or some other trading arrange-ments, or from replacing postage stamp pricing with nodal or zonal pricing. The following steps provide broad parameters for infrastructure reform which encompass the alternative forms of implementation:[11]

1. Corporatization of the industry, first through the setting up of a joint stock company wholly owned by the state, then by separating accounts for different parts of the business, next by unbundling this company into

---

[8] See e.g, Newbury and Pollitt (1997) in the case of power sector reform.

[9] Between 1985 and 1995 there were over 900 private infrastructure projects worth US$300 billion of investment in Africa, Latin America, Asia, and the transition economies (World Bank Private Infrastructure Database).

[10] See Commander *et al.* (1999) for a summary. Evidence suggests that privatization and liberalization give the greatest impetus for industry restructuring and productivity increase. The intuition is that such reform replaces rent-seeking insiders and introduces new (commercial) skills.

[11] For a discussion of reform sequencing, see Kennedy (1999).

subsidiaries to form the structure for the introduction of the private sector and liberalization of the market.

2. Setting up of a regulator free from day-to-day political interference to set tariffs for monopoly parts of the industry (i.e. retail tariffs and access charges) and to develop and implement a grid code; also to enforce environmental and health and safety standards, depending on the institutional framework (whether or not separate bodies with these functions exist).

3. Introduction of the private sector, through a limited number of concessions in the early stages of restructuring, divestment of assets, and, eventually, free entry, in order to access commercial expertise and private finance.

4. Raising tariffs to cover long-run costs and eroding cross subsidy while taking care to ensure that affordability constraints are not violated (e.g. through moving from blanket to targeted subsidy).

5. Market liberalization, typically through removing entry barriers to large user markets and allowing third-party network access, where feasible (i.e. depending on data and communications, software, institutional endowment, tariffs, and collection ratios), in conjunction with the setting up of a power pool or contract exchange. This would allow the replacement of high-cost, polluting, and dangerous capacity with more efficient plant; also the rebalancing of transmission prices, depending on network configuration, losses, and congestion, to provide correct signals for consumption and investment decisions.

There have been various drivers of change in the power sectors of central and eastern Europe. One of these has been the need to finance new investments in a context of limited potential for budget finance and highly constrained sovereign debt repayment capacity. A second driver has been the prospect of EU accession—reforms required to bring the region in line with the 1996 Power Directive and conditions relating to environment and nuclear safety (the latter in the case of Bulgaria and Lithuania). Third, there is the need to raise revenue for the central budget (this was the case in Hungary—see below); asset sales can be lucrative where the capital stock is in good condition, where tariffs exceed operating costs, and where a robust regulatory regime is in place. Finally, international financial institutions (IFIs) have pushed reform forward through dialogue with governments, technical assistance, and finance.

One factor that has limited the reform effort is the inherited capital stock. Depending on the state of assets, this can provide a cushion allowing investment and associated structural reform to be delayed, an option that can be attractive given the political effort required to privatize the sector and to rebalance tariffs. Delays have been compounded by the economic crisis in Russia and its fallout, namely the increased price of finance and shortened loan tenors; governments have postponed reform in the hope that the investment climate will improve. In the medium term, however, investments will be required, and radical reform will be needed if these are to be secured at the lowest price.

Table 19.1. *Power Sector Progress in Reform*

Reform stage	Countries
Joint stock company set up	Bosnia, Croatia
Draft law/legal framework in place	Albania, Latvia, Macedonia, Slovak Republic, Slovenia
Radical restructuring under way	Bulgaria, Czech Republic, Estonia, Lithuania, Poland, Romania
Wide-scale privatization complete	Hungary

Reform progress in the power sectors of the region is summarized in Table 19.1. Regarding regulation, in countries where there has been radical reform, the legacy of traditional political interference in the power sector is a reluctance by governments fully to relinquish control through the setting up of independent regulators[12] (see Box 19.1, or Appendix 1 for a detailed country by country account); authorities have chosen to sacrifice privatization revenues or to pay a higher cost of capital in order to keep open the possibility of intervention in the tariff-setting process. Regarding secondary legislation, this tends to be at a very early stage of development with regard to tariff formulas. (Hungary is the exception, where RPI − X regulation is in place.) Having said this, the primary legislation provides scope for the introduction of incentive regulation, typically stating words to the effect that prices should cover costs of an *efficient* company.

Regarding privatization, this has been very limited in central and eastern Europe, southern Europe, and the Baltics. Again the exception is Hungary, where the privatization of distribution and generation to foreign strategic investors has taken place, and where privatization of the national transmission company is slated for 2001. Elsewhere the only private involvement is through a small number of independent power producers (e.g. Bulgaria, Slovak Republic). Many countries in the region have government-approved plans for industry restructuring (accounting separation of different parts of the business, legal separation, privatization), for example Bulgaria and Romania, though these are yet to be implemented in any concrete sense. (See Appendix 19.1 for details by country.)

Regarding liberalization, there is a tension between liberalizing now, resulting in lower prices now for consumers, or liberalizing later, increasing privatization revenues off the back of the higher prices charged consumers from now until the date of future liberalization. Another factor—in addition to budgetary considerations—working against early liberalization in some

---

[12] For a definition of independence see Stern (1997). Independence requires, *inter alia*, a regulatory body that is separate from any ministry, is funded by the industry as opposed to the central budget, and where the appointment of senior staff is for fixed terms. Romania comes closest to this definition of the countries in central and eastern Europe.

Box 19.1. *Regulatory Developments in the Power Sector*

- The Hungarian Energy Office was set up in 1994 under the Act on the Production, Transport, and Supply of Electric Industry. This body is separate from any ministry, but is centrally funded, without fixed terms of appointment for the chairman, and without the power to set prices. Political input in tariff-setting has kept returns on investment below the 8 per cent level promised at privatization.
- In Bulgaria the Energy and Energy Efficiency Act of 1999 established the State Energy Regulatory Commission. This body is separate from any ministry and the chairman has a fixed term of appointment. The secondary legislation is yet to be developed and must be approved by the Council of Ministers.
- In Romania the Emergency Ordinance concerning Electrical and Thermal Energy set up the National Energy Regulatory Commission. This body has key staff appointed for fixed terms with funding through licence fees. It is responsible for tariff-setting and will do so using a methodology currently being developed.
- In Poland the Energy Law of 1997 established the Office of Energy Regulation. This separate body has key members appointed for fixed terms, is funded through licence fees, and is subject to an appeals process. Scope for political input to regulation is through Ministry of Economy approval for tariff-setting guidelines.
- The Energy Market Inspectorate (EMI) of Estonia, set up under the Energy Act of 1997, is less independent than the bodies named above, being within the Ministry of Economy. Although the EMI has a nominal tariff-setting role, there is scope for political input given this lack of independence.

countries is the stranded cost problem (how to finance assets that are not efficient and cannot compete in an open market). There is not a strong impetus in central and eastern Europe for imminent resolution of this problem given that the earliest accession date is still a number of years away. Having said this, liberalization sooner rather than later is required if consumers are to benefit fully from private participation.

19.3. TELECOMMUNICATIONS

As for power, telecommunications industries under communism were owned, operated, and regulated by governments, and objectives were of a non-commercial nature. Network access was low, waiting lists for connection were long, technology was antiquated, and service quality was poor; operating inefficiencies were high, tariffs were below levels of cost recovery, and there was cross-subsidy from business to residential customers. These features, still prevalent today, albeit to a lesser extent, shape the broad reform path as regards commercialization, introduction of the private sector, and liberalization. This includes the following broad steps:

1. *Corporatization of the industry* through the setting up of a joint stock company and separation of telecommunications from postal services.

2. *Private-sector involvement*, through asset sales or concessions.
3. *Development of the regulatory framework*, including tariff-setting mechanisms for retail prices prior to liberalization and interconnection charges in a liberalized market.
4. *Introduction of value added services* (e.g. cellular telephone and data transmission) and advanced services such as satellite phones and the internet.
5. *Tariff re-balancing*, to equate prices and costs for each class of customer.
6. *Liberalization of fixed-line, value added, and advanced services*, not necessarily at the same time; for example, competition in cellular might be allowed first (immediately), followed by competition in fixed line at a later date (through competing networks at the local and national levels).

Reforms have progressed as governments have attempted to cash in on the potentially large sums available through sale of the fixed-line network. These sums relate to the very high suppressed demand at the end of the communist era and thus the need to increase penetration, to be achieved efficiently through the introduction of private-sector expertise and private finance. Introduction of the private sector in this context has political legitimacy in the sense that it caters for excess demand, thus delivering ostensible benefits for consumers (whereas in the power sector, for example, introduction of the private sector is often accompanied by tariff increases). Considerations relating to EU accession, particularly the need to open up markets in line with 1998 Telecoms Directive, and to World Trade Organisation accession, have also spurred the reform process in some countries.

Reform progress in eastern European telecommunications sectors is summarized in Table 19.2. Privatization is moving ahead, with majority stakes in the national telecommunications companies sold to the private sector in Hungary and Lithuania, and minority stakes in the Czech Republic, Estonia, and Latvia. One option for privatization—the method chosen in Lithuania—is through sale to a strategic investor; this should lead to improved corporate governance and new know-how, resulting in better performance. An alternative is to sell shares through an initial public offering (IPO). This method—chosen for Polish telecommunications privatization—is less advantageous when it results in dispersed share ownership and the failure to replace insiders.

Table 19.2. *Telecommunications Sector Progress in Reform*

Reform stage	Country
Joint stock company set up	Albania, Bosnia, Slovenia
Intention to privatize announced	Bulgaria, Croatia, Macedonia
Private sector introduced	Czech Republic, Estonia, Latvia, Lithuania
Private sector introduced and independent regulator set up	Hungary, Romania

Some countries have chosen to privatize both through sale of shares to a strategic investor and through an IPO, thus bringing in private-sector expertise and at the same time mitigating some foreign currency risk by tapping local financial markets: in Hungary, the first and second-stage share sales were to a strategic investor, while the third-stage sale was through an IPO; in Estonia the first-stage sale was through an IPO and the second-stage sale to a strategic investor. Elsewhere in the region, Bulgaria, Croatia, and Macedonia have all announced their intention to privatize.

In contrast to power, the private sector has often been introduced to the telecommunications sectors before fundamental regulatory reform has taken place. Where there have been such developments, these have stopped far short of setting up independent regulators. Privatization has nevertheless been (financially) successful because of the commercial opportunities arising from historically suppressed demand. To the extent that there is regulatory discretion (because at best privatization contracts are far from complete), countries in the region are likely to have sacrificed privatization revenues or paid a higher cost of capital relative to the situation with an independent regulator.

Although there is yet no evidence from the region, lack of independence could also work against the evolution of competition, all the more so when the regulator is also the owner of the incumbent telecommunications company (e.g. where the Ministry of Communications both regulates and owns the national telecommunications company). Then the regulator might aim to influence sector policy so as to delay market liberalization. Alternatively, the regulator might restrict entry by withholding licences from potential competitors, or rule in favour of its own company in disputes over network access.

Liberalization of fixed-line networks has been limited because of the issuing of franchises as part of privatization (with the granting of monopoly power either to raise revenue for the government or to secure funds for investment). Governments have granted monopoly rights both to maximize privatization revenues and to secure the finance necessary for network development (increased coverage and upgrade). Having said this, the telecommunications sector in Hungary will be fully liberalized from 2001 onwards. A consortium of Hungarian companies has formed a company (MKM) with the intention of becoming the country's second fixed network provider. In Poland the national telecommunication company's monopoly over local services has been abolished and a number of operators have started offering alternative services. In the Czech Republic, the public operator—SPT—has a monopoly over long distance and international calls until the end of 2001, and presently faces competition in sixteen out of 160 localities.

Regarding mobile telephony, there are two mobile phone operators in the Czech market, one of which is majority owned by SPT, the Czech telecommunications company. Competition in cellular telephony is deepening in Estonia and Poland, where there are four providers, and in Hungary and Lithuania, each with three providers. Further south, there has been widespread

Box 19.2. *Regulatory Developments in Telecommunications*

- In Latvia the Telecommunications Tariff Council, an independent body, is in charge of setting tariff rates for basic services. The Council does not however have responsibility for licensing or supervising interconnection: these are the remit of the Ministry of Transport.

- In Bulgaria an independent regulator—the State Telecommunications Commission (STC), comprising five members appointed by the prime minister, each with a seven-year term, and funded through licence fees—was set up under the July 1998 Telecommunications Law. The STC has a duty to issue licences, though these must be approved by the Council of Ministers. Drafting of the secondary legislation will be carried out by the STC within a sector policy framework laid out by Council of Ministers. The STC will set tariffs where an operator has a dominant position on basis of rules to be determined in consultation with the Competition Protection Commission.

- In the Czech Republic, the Ministry of Transport and Communications regulates all aspects of the telecommunications industry except tariffs (retail and interconnection), which are the remit of Ministry of Finance. The Czech Telecommunications Office (CTO), directly under the Minister of Transport and Communications, has responsibility for development and implementation of a regulatory framework, e.g. preparation of regulated retail tariffs, access charges. In addition, the CTO has a duty to issue licences. Following an amendment to the Telecommunications Law in September 1999, from May 2000 the CTO will become separate, assuming the features of independent regulator (regarding appointment, etc.) and having comprehensive regulating powers (in addition to licensing, and tariff-setting).

- In Hungary the Ministry of Transport, Communication, and Water Management (KHVM) regulates the telecommunications industry, with support from the Communications Authority (HIF), a separate body whose President reports to the Minister of KHVM. Competition law is enforced by the Hungarian Competition Office; a small number of cases relating to network access have already been referred to the Office (though it is too early yet to make a judgement on the performance of the Office in this respect).

- In Albania the Telecommunications Regulatory Entity was set up under the Law on Regulating the Institution of Telecommunications. This is a body financed through licence fees and staffed by key members with fixed-term appointments. The Entity has a duty to create a legal and transparent regulatory framework that will promote private investments and safeguard public interests. Development of this framework is presently ongoing.

private entry in the cellular telephone market niche. In Bulgaria one Global Telecommunications System (GSM) licence was awarded in 1995 to Mobifon, a consortium of Bulgarian Telecommunications Company (BTC), Cable and Wireless, and Radio Electronic Systems. A second GSM licence will be awarded to purchaser of a stake in BTC. In Slovenia, a second GSM provider—a consortium of Slovene investors with a Swedish partner—entered the market in

June 1998. A memorandum of understanding has been signed in Albania to the effect that a second GSM provider—to compete with the existing state-owned provider—will enter the market soon. In Croatia, in addition to the existing two state-owned mobile companies, a GSM licence has been awarded to a consortium including an international telecoms company.

19.4. WATER

Under communism water and waste water were not operated on the basis of economic decision-making. Prices were below the long-run cost of supply and metering was rare. Consequently heavy industry over-consumed water from an economic point of view, in some cases to the extent that resources were depleted. More recently, owing to a backlog of underinvestment, rates of leakage and equipment failure have increased and are relatively high by western standards. The quality of water and waste water treatment was poor by western standards, not because of the absence of a regulatory framework, but because of a tax enforcement of rules—in practice there was a tendency to ignore environmental externalities, with severe consequences both for health and for pollution. From an institutional perspective, water and waste companies were run from within central and local government departments.

The driver of reform in water and waste water has been the need to unlock private finance and expertise to improve system performance, both as part of EU accession—EU regulations relate to environmental aspects and require the realization of higher-quality standards[13]—and more generally for the economic benefit of local populations, and in a context of limited central or municipal government ability to pay. It is likely that this combination of factors will become more important over time, as assets become more depleted, environmental problems become worse, EU accession draws nearer, and budgets become more strained.

The reform path towards sectors characterized by (textbook) efficient public–private partnerships includes the following elements:

1. *Transfer of company ownership* from the national to the municipal level.
2. *Corporatization of the company* followed by commercialization (raising tariffs to cost recovery levels, introducing international accounting standards and management information systems, developing long-term business plans, passing laws to allow municipal debt finance of investment, competitive tendering in procurement).
3. *Finance of projects based on sub-sovereign rather than sovereign guarantees* with lending directly to the municipal company as opposed to the municipality.

---

[13] EU legislation in water and waste water does not relate to shape and governance of the sector.

4. *Finance of projects based on municipal owned company's cash flows* as opposed to municipal guarantee.
5. *Introduction of the private sector* through competitively tendered management contracts, concessions, build–operate–transfer contracts (BOTs), asset sales, etc., with a transfer of risks to the private sector, particularly those that can be managed by the private sector.
6. *Development of an effective regulatory regime*, usually at the national level, covering tariffs and quality—including environmental—standards. This should be an improvement on local based regulation owing to economies of scale in terms of staff and gathering information, and the lower level of politicization of regulation at the national as opposed to the local level.

Progress in commercialization has been made in all countries except Albania and Bosnia, where there has been little in terms of corporatization and where tariffs are substantially below operating costs; see Box 19.3 for an example of municipal commercialization in Poland. Other countries have moved forward, with wide-scale private-sector involvement through competitive tender or negotiation in Estonia, Hungary, Czech Republic, and Poland. In Slovenia the private sector will be introduced in the Maribor region through a BOT framework for the construction of a waste water treatment plant, and a similar project—replicating the BOT structure—is being developed in Croatia.

Regulation of private-sector operators tends to be on the basis of well specified contracts (laying tariffs and investment levels) with the municipality acting as regulator in areas of contractual incompleteness. One exception is Lithuania, where a national independent regulator has been set up, and another is Poland, where a national regulator is being set up.[14]

Contracts with the private operators typically contain formulas that pass on all exogenous risks (e.g. input price) to consumers. Though there are incentives to reduce costs within given price caps, the absence of periodic reviews (price caps are specified over periods of up to twenty years) means that there is no mechanism for benefit-sharing with consumers. One exception in the Czech Republic is the municipality of Brno, where the private-sector operator is regulated under a sliding scale mechanism, sharing profits above a target level equally with consumers.

On finance, whereas this tended to be backed by sovereign guarantees in the early days of transition, the tendency now is to finance on the basis of either a municipal guarantee, or no guarantee at all, for example in the case of new municipal infrastructure projects in Poland and Romania; this has been supported by tariff increases sufficient to cover debt service. On environment, improved performance has resulted wherever there have been new investments, both directly as a result of the investments, and indirectly as a result of either an IFI loan or EU grant conditionality (see e.g. Box 19.3).

[14] For a detailed assessment of reform progress by country in the municipal sector, see Appendix 19.2.

Box 19.3. *Corporate Development and Environmental Improvement Programme in Bydgoszcz, Poland*

Bydgoszcz, the eighth largest city in Poland, is located in the north of the country and has a population around 390,000. With its water supply and sewerage development programme, it is an example of a municipality where important innovations are being made in terms of regulatory and corporate governance, management, and environmental performance.

The programme is costing €50 million, financed jointly by the European Commission and the European Bank for Reconstruction and Development. The main elements of the programme are modernization of the sewerage network, rehabilitation of the water supply network, modernization of a water treatment plant, and corporate development of the water and sewerage company.

The financial vehicle is a corporate loan to the joint stock water and sewerage company wholly owned by the municipality. The loan will not be guaranteed by either the sovereign or the municipality. This could undermine incentives for the municipality to deviate from the schedule of agreed tariff increases (because it would not have to service debt contingent on failure to increase tariffs). In order to mitigate this regulatory risk, however, there will be a support agreement from the municipality, stipulating circumstances (failure to increase tariffs, failure of municipal owned entities to pay bills) in which it will be liable to cover debt service.

On the regulatory and corporate side, the programme involves a strengthening of the (regulatory) contract between the municipality and the water/joint-stock company. In the longer term, it is envisaged that the private sector will be introduced as part of the programme, probably under some form of concession agreement. On the management side, the programme encompasses a range of measures to improve operational performance, improve service quality, and optimize financial and environmental procedures.

19.5. RAIL

Rail industries under communism were tailored to the needs of the primary and heavy industries. Investment decisions with regard to production and location did not take transport costs into account. As a result, when investments had been made and the industrial structure was in place, demand for transport was high. Rail had a comparative advantage over road in terms of transporting bulky products over long distances. Relative to western countries, rail density with respect to population in former communist countries is high. Regarding tariffs, the inherited structure was distorted with cross-subsidy from freight to passengers (the latter paying less than avoidable cost), though cost recovery was generally high relative to their counterpart public railways in the EU. As for their organization, the railways were typically run as monolithic enterprises inside government ministries.

Reforms that would help first to improve efficiency within the public sector and then to provide a good investment climate for the introduction of the private sector, consistent with the 1991 EU Rail Directive, include the following:

1. Setting the rail industry at arm's length from the state, e.g. through *corporatization*.
2. *Separating the industry* along the lines of business units—e.g. infrastructure, freight, passenger—and contracting out ancillary services.
3. *Rebalancing tariffs, raising prices* for consumers, at least to avoidable cost and possibly higher, depending on the price elasticity of demand in this segment and the extent of competition in freight.
4. Large-scale *introduction of the private sector* through franchises or asset sales.
5. *Liberalization of network access* according to terms and conditions set by an independent regulator.

As a minimum, most countries in the region—including Bulgaria, Hungary, Latvia, Lithuania, and the Slovak Republic—have corporatized their rail industry. In Poland and Romania there has been further separation within the corporatized company. For example, in Romania five railway companies have been created: one each for infrastructure, for freight, for passenger services, for the management of railway assets, and for railway management services. There has been little in the way of large-scale private-sector involvement, for example through the sale of infrastructure assets. The lack of independent incentive-based regulation reflects this fact. One exception is Estonia, where plans to privatize the integrated infrastructure and freight company, and to sell a majority stake in the largest passenger company, are moving ahead. In other countries, the private sector has been introduced to pockets of the industry. In Hungary, a new logistics centre is to be built on the basis of a BOT contract with a private-sector company. In Romania a private-sector company has entered into an agreement to refurbish excess rolling stock.[15]

19.6. OVERVIEW AND REMAINING CHALLENGES

This chapter has focused on infrastructure in transition. Broad industry-specific reform paths were posited, with common elements for each of the infrastructure sectors relating to commercialization and the introduction of the private sector. The assumption was that the introduction of the private sector in a well regulated and liberalized environment should result in efficiency gains relative to the highly inefficient operations across infrastructure inherited from the communist era.

Infrastructure reform in the region is well underway. State companies have been corporatized, the private sector has been introduced, regulatory

---

[15] For a detailed assessment of reform progress by country in the rail sector see Appendix 19.2.

frameworks are developing, and some markets have been opened. There remain however substantial challenges in infrastructure transition. These include:

- implementation of concrete industry restructuring, particularly in rail and power sectors;
- the further distancing of public companies from government and their subjection to commercial pressures / freedom, particularly in municipal and rail sectors;
- the development and de-politicization of regulation, through strengthening independence and the establishment of a track record in implementation in all infrastructure sectors;
- more widespread involvement of the private sector across the infrastructure;
- greater liberalization in power and telecommunications.

The pressure for change is there, as a result of (*a*) EU accession and (*b*) investment requirements combined with the need to finance investments off-budget (i.e. privately). If infrastructure reforms can be successfully implemented, then this could be instrumental in the wider process of transition from a communist to a market economy.

Appendix 19.1. Reform of the power sector, by country

A1.1. *Hungary*

The power sector in Hungary was reformed under the Act on the Production, Transport and Supply of Electric Energy adopted in 1994. Under this Act a regulatory body—the Hungarian Energy Office (HEO)—was set up. This is a separate body (i.e. not part of a ministry) though it does not qualify as independent under various standard criteria: the director of the office is not appointed for a fixed term; conditions for dismissal of the director are not specified; the office does not have an independent revenue source. Perhaps more importantly, although the regulator establishes tariff setting rules, the Minister of Industry actually has the final say over prices, something that has in practice politicized the regulation of the privatized power companies.

The privatized companies were sold with a promise, in the form of a government resolution, that prices would be set so as to yield an 8 per cent return on investments. Although the regulatory framework includes regulatory licences specifying the rights and responsibilities of industry players, the tariff formula is not contained. (Here the regulatory framework differs from, for example, the UK, where a (legally binding) tariff formula is specified in the regulatory licence.) Political input to the process of tariff-setting, based on public opposition to tariff increases, has resulted in electricity prices since privatization that have been insufficient to meet the 8 per cent target. Reaching the target would have required massive (unrealistic) out-performance by the privatized companies under the RPI − X price cap. The main focus of the regulatory review in 1999, whereby price formulas for the next three years were determined, was to erode the cross-subsidy from industrial to residential customers.

Regarding market developments, industry restructuring in Hungary began with a delay after the Industry Act had been passed, motivated by a need to raise money for the central budget late in 1995. At this time there was a vertical unbundling of generation, transmission, and distribution, and a horizontal unbundling in generation and distribution. Seven generation companies, some with investment undertakings, were sold to the private sector, in addition to all power distribution companies and a minority stake in the transmission company.

Given the objective of the government (to raise funds), the industry was privatized on the basis of the single-buyer model[16] with its associated restrictions on competition. The arrangements were that the (state-owned) transmission company (MVM) would have a monopoly on the sale and purchase of electricity and of electricity generating capacity. This was implemented through long-term contracts between generators and the single buyer specifying capacity payments and unit power prices and formulas for price changes (indexing on fuel prices, etc.). Under the terms of the agreements, plant has been dispatched on the basis of a merit order relating to the underlying incremental cost of plant.

In February 1999, a date for the liberalization of large-user markets (2001) was announced. Initially 15 per cent of the market will be open to competition, with further liberalization during 2001 if the first stage proves successful. The intention is to move to fully liberalized markets with open network access for domestic and international producers overseen by a new regulator. (As yet, the arrangements concerning the new regulator have not been developed.) Liberalization should be possible without problems relating to stranded costs that have been present in some parts of western Europe. The reason for this is that the amount of capacity contracted by MVM under power purchase agreements (PPAs) is renegotiable at the start of each year.[17] In addition to allowing the smooth introduction of competition, such a contract structure should improve the prospects for privatization of MVM, recently announced as an objective of the government.

A1.2. *Bulgaria*

In Bulgaria, the Energy and Energy Efficiency Act adopted in mid-1999 provides for radical industry restructuring. The regulatory framework under the Act will be governed by the State Energy Regulatory Commission (SERC), a body separate from any ministry, but under the Council of Ministers. The Commission is in a sense more independent than the Hungarian Energy Office in the sense that Commission members have fixed terms, and circumstances for dismissal are specified in the Act. In common with Hungary, the SERC will be funded from the central budget, and, more importantly, it will not have the power to set prices: the role of SERC will be to propose a tariff-setting methodology that may or may not be adopted by the Council of Ministers.

There is scope under the Act for the proposed methodology to be one that reflects principles of incentive regulation. (*Inter alia*, the Act states that the SERC will 'create stimuli for more efficient operation of energy sector companies subject to price

[16] This is the standard single-buyer model rather than the French variant in the EU Power Directive. Under the standard model all output in the power system must be sold to a single buyer—usually the state-owned transmission company (or trading arm of the transmission company)—which then sells on to downstream users. This is implemented through off-take contracts—'Power Purchase Agreements'(PPAs)—signed between generators and the single buyer.

[17] In effect, the PPAs have reopener clauses.

regulation'.) Once the tariff methodology has been determined, the Act will permit the SERC to set actual tariffs; this could introduce elements of regulatory discretion depending on the chosen tariff methodology (and whether this is price-cap or cost-plus or another variant).

As yet, the secondary legislation remains undeveloped. Part of this will be in the form of regulatory licences listing detailed rights and responsibilities of the various parties, particularly as they relate to service quality, safety, and information for the regulator. Regarding tariffs, the secondary legislation enforcing the general provision under the Act prohibiting cross-subsidy between different producer groups could result in tariff rebalancing with relative prices changing in favour of industrial consumers.

Regarding industrial structure, the Act states that vertically integrated companies will keep separate accounts (in conformity with the EU Power Directive). At present, private-sector involvement is limited to the ongoing development of several brownfield independent power producers. Further legislation is required before full-scale privatization takes place, something that is slated for 2002 at the latest under various IFI loan conditionalities (IMF, World Bank, EBRD). The intention, expressed in the Government of Bulgaria's (GoB) Energy Sector Action Plan, is to divest the industry under the single-buyer model (as in Hungary), allowing some third-party network access by the end of 2003. The date for market liberalization depends on whether Bulgaria is on track for EU accession. There are still some contentious issues regarding the opening of power markets to international competition (the GoB is reluctant to commit to this) and the closure of the unsafe Kozludy nuclear plant[18] (nuclear capacity is 45 per cent of the total in Bulgaria) and replacement with new capacity.

A1.3. *Estonia*

In Estonia, the Energy Act of June 1997 set up the Energy Market Inspectorate (EMI), a government agency within the area of the Ministry of Economy and with its chief appointed by the economy minister. As in Hungary and Bulgaria, the regulating body does not exhibit all the facets of independence. In contrast with Hungary and Bulgaria, nor is the regulating body separate from the government department, though this is likely to have little impact for practical purposes, given the scope for political input to regulation in all three countries. One nominal role of the EMI in Estonia will be to review, approve, and confirm the prices of fuel and energy enterprises dominating the market.

A particularly important aspect of the developing energy market in Estonia, relating to the small size of the domestic market and limited scope for horizontally unbundling installed generating capacity (it may be possible to unbundle into a maximum of only two companies), is the possibility of international competition.[19] In fact, one provision of the Energy Act is that traders will be able to import or export power once they have been granted the relevant licence by the EMI. Under the 1998 Competition Act, access to essential inputs (e.g. power transmission and distribution networks) must be granted under reasonable and non-discriminatory conditions. Though there are no detailed guidelines on network access as yet, this will be regulated by the EMI (a power granted to the body under the Energy Act).

[18] The GoB committed in late 1999 to close units 1 and 2 of Kozludy by 2003 and to make a decision by 2002 on the closure of units 3 and 4.

[19] Having said this, international competition could provide a powerful stimulus for all the countries in the region.

Regarding industry restructuring and privatization in Estonia, two power distribution companies—Laanemaa and Narva—were separated from the integrated state power company (Eesti Energy) and privatized in 1998; five distribution companies remain with the integrated company. The plan is to unbundle the industry vertically, keeping ownership of the transmission company in state hands, completing the privatization of distribution, and privatizing generation. Eesti Energy and the Estonian government are in negotiations with US NRG for sale of the Narva and Balti oil-shale-fired power plants which together comprise the bulk of Estonian generating capacity. It is envisaged that these will be sold together in a package including the Eesti Polevkivi oil shale company (the latter included because a political decision has been taken to protect the oil shale industry). Under present proposals, NRG would be guaranteed a 75 per cent market share for six or seven years, and a 50 per cent share for the following six or seven years; this would be consistent with the market liberalization required for EU accession.

A1.4. *Romania*

In Romania the 1999 Emergency Ordinance Concerning the Electrical and Thermal Energy provided for the setting up of the National Energy Regulating Authority (NERA). As in Hungary and Bulgaria (not Estonia), this is a separate body. The distinguishing factor in the case of Romania is that NERA fits the criteria for independence: the president of the organization is appointed for a fixed (five-year) term; the range of circumstances for dismissal is narrowly defined; and NERA will be financed from licence fees (i.e. not from the central budget). NERA has a duty to establish tariff-setting methods for the sector, within various constraints imposed by the primary legislation, for example encouraging efficient performance, barring cross-subsidy. The fact that the primary legislation is in the form of an emergency ordinance rather than an act of parliament could provide for less investor security in the future (if it is changed), depending on the form of the secondary legislation (whether this has a contractual basis) and/or the specification of privatization contracts. Secondary legislation is in the process of being developed and terms and conditions of privatization are yet to be determined. (There is currently no private-sector involvement in the industry.)

On industry restructuring and liberalization, a Grid Code was developed in 1999 in preparation for vertical and horizontal industry unbundling. The incumbent state-owned vertically integrated company has been made into a holding company with a transmission and dispatch company subsidiary, a subsidiary made up of distribution companies, a hydro-generation subsidiary, and a thermal generation subsidiary.[20] The Government of Romania has committed to privatize eight distribution companies before the end of 2001. The stated intention is to create multiple generators from the existing capacity, starting off with a single-buyer model for an interim period, and moving to third-party network access in tandem with a wholesale pool (i.e. much like the initial model in England and Wales) by 2006.

A1.5. *Croatia*

Croatia is an example of a country that is adopting a more cautious approach to power industry reform. Since 1990, Hrvatska Electroprivreda (HEP)—state-owned and

---

[20] Nuclear power generating capacity has been spun off into a separate company.

vertically integrated—has had a power industry monopoly. In 1994 HEP was corporatized as a joint stock company wholly owned by the Croatian government. The government's long-term aim for the sector is to separate out non-core activities such as heat, distribution, and ancillary technical and civil services, to introduce competition in generation and third-party access to the grid for all market participants, to partially privatize, and to set up a regulator. There has not however been any major legislation relating to radical industry reform.

In the meantime, the private sector has been introduced in a manner typical of first-stage sector reform: Jertovec Power Plant was sold to the international power company Enron with a twenty-year tolling agreement (HEP provides the private operator with fuel and pays a fee for the transformation of this to power) whereby all risks (fuel price, availability, exchange rate, etc.) bar construction are borne either by HEP or the consumer. As there is more privatization, the Croatian government must take care as regards the terms and conditions of privatization agreements (specifically off-take agreements) are to be consistent with optimal risk allocations and market liberalization.

A1.6. *Albania*

Albania is an example of a country where radical restructuring faltered even though enabling legislation was in place. Major legislation relating to the power industry was passed in 1995, but there has been little in the way of reform progress since then. The major problem in Albania is a lack of system financial viability resulting from low revenue collection and theft of power: in these circumstances there is little point in moving to an independent regulator, unbundling, and liberalizing the industry. The present discounted cash flows, particularly when adjusted for sector and country risk, would not attract strategic investors to purchase existing assets, and would not encourage new entry (e.g. in generation). The Government of Albania (GoA) has chosen to move forward by introducing the private sector in the form of a management contract. This contract is designed to maximize incentives for improving revenue collection by rewarding the private-sector managers, to the largest extent feasible given associated risks, according to sector profit.[21] The intention is that strategic investors will be introduced, and the sector radically reformed, as soon as the sector financial viability is improved.

A1.7. *Poland*

Poland is an example of a country in this region in which the problem of how to finance costs stranded in the process of liberalization has arisen (as it has in some of the western European markets). The root of the problem is the fact that plant was built on the basis of dubious least-cost analysis. The PPAs upon which finance for this capacity was secured would not be competitive in an open market. Solution of the problem—deciding who will pay, i.e. banks, customers, producers, or taxpayers will pay, is largely political, rather than economic, in nature, and will be required prior to privatization and liberalization if these two are to be successful. Liberalization is planned for 2001. As for privatization, plans to sell off the thirty-three distribution companies in bundles of three

---

[21] In other words, the GoA pays what it perceives to be the minimum flat fee that will bring in the private sector, and loads up the incentive-based part of the management contract.

D. Kennedy and N. Stern

Table 19.3. *Infrastructure Transition Indicators, 1999*

	Railways	Water and waste water
Albania	2	1+
Bosnia and Herzegovina	2	1
Bulgaria	3	2
Croatia	2+	3+
Czech Republic	2+	4
Estonia	4	4
FYR Macedonia	2	1+
Hungary	3+	4
Latvia	3+	3
Lithuania	2+	3
Poland	3+	4
Romania	4	3
Slovak Republic	2	n.a.
Slovenia	3+	4

Notes: see Appendix for an explanation of the classification system. A + sign following a number indicates an actual figure falling between that number and the next one up.

or four have been announced. Full-scale privatization of generation, where there is presently limited private involvement, is slated for 2001.

The regulatory framework for competitive private-sector involvement was put in place under the Energy Law of 1997. As a result of this Law, the Office of Energy Regulation (OER) was set up. This body is separate, and fits some criteria for independence—(as in Romania, there are (five-year) fixed-term appointments, and the regulator is funded through licence fees), and regulatory discretion is limited through the existence of an appeals process. As in Hungary and Bulgaria, the possibility of political input to regulation remains because, although the OER has responsibility for setting prices, this is within guidelines to be set out by the Ministry of Economy.

Appendix 2: **Infrastructure transition indicators 1999**[22]

The infrastructure transition indicators presented here measure the extent of reform in transition economies in a selected group of infrastructure sectors. Progress is measured in three broadly defined aspects of infrastructure reform identified and discussed in the *Transition Report 1996*: tariff reform, commercialization, and regulatory and institutional development. The infrastructure indicators reported here and in Table 19.3 define a rating (from 1 to 4 +), which is based on the overall reform progress in the three broad areas described above.

[22] The transition indicators were constructed by members of the Office of the Chief Economist at the European Bank for Reconstruction and Development (EBRD). The tables above were published in the *Transition Report 1999* (EBRD 1999).

A2.1. *Classification system*

Railways

1: Monolithic organizational structures still exist. State railways are still effectively operated as government departments. Few commercial freedoms exist to determine prices or investments. There is no private-sector involvement. Cross-subsidization of passenger service obligations with freight service revenues is still undertaken.

2: New laws distance rail operations from the state, but there are weak commercial objectives. There is no budgetary funding of public service obligations in place. Organizational structures are still overly based on geographic or functional areas. Ancillary businesses have been separated but there is little divestment. There has been minimal encouragement of private-sector involvement. Initial business planning has been undertaken, but the targets are general and tentative.

3: New laws have been passed that restructure the railways and introduce commercial orientation. Freight and passenger services have been separated, and marketing groups have been grafted on to traditional structures. Some divestment of ancillary businesses has taken place. Some budgetary compensation is available for passenger services. Business plans have been designed with clear investment and rehabilitation targets, but funding is unsecured. There is some private-sector involvement in rehabilitation and/or maintenance.

4: New laws have been passed to fully commercialize the railways. Separate internal profit centres have been created for passenger and freight (actual or imminent). Extensive market freedoms exist to set tariffs and investments. Medium term business plans are under implementation. Ancillary industries have been divested. Policy has been developed to promote private rail transport operations.

4+: Railway law has been passed allowing for separation of infrastructure from operations, and/or freight from passenger operations, and/or private train operations. There is private sector participation in ancillary services and track maintenance. A rail regulator has been established. Access pricing has been implemented. Plans have been drawn up for a full divestment and transfer of asset ownership, including infrastructure and rolling stock.

Water and waste water

1: There is a minimal degree of decentralization, and no commercialization has taken place. Water and waste water services are operated as a vertically integrated natural monopoly by a government ministry through national or regional subsidiaries or by municipal departments. There is no, or little, financial autonomy and/or management capacity at municipal level. Heavily subsidized tariffs still exist, along with a high degree of cross-subsidization. There is a low level of cash collection. Central or regional government controls tariffs and investment levels. No explicit rules exist in public documents regarding tariffs or quality of service. There is no, or insignificant, private-sector participation.

2: There is a moderate degree of decentralization, and initial steps have been taken towards commercialization. Water and waste water services are provided by municipally owned companies, which operate as joint-stock companies. There is some degree of financial autonomy at the municipal level, but heavy reliance on central government for grants and income transfers. Partial cost recovery is achieved through tariffs, and initial steps have been taken to reduce cross-subsidies. General public guidelines exist regarding tariff-setting and service quality, but these are both still under ministerial control. There is some private-sector participation through service or management contracts or competition to provide ancillary services.

3: A fairly large degree of decentralization and commercialization has taken place. Water and waste water utilities operate with managerial and accounting independence from municipalities, using international accounting standards and management information systems. A Law of Municipal Finance has been approved. Cost recovery is fully operated through tariffs, and there is a minimum level of cross-subsidies. A semi-autonomous regulatory agency has been established to advise on tariffs and service quality but without the power to set either. More detailed rules have been drawn up in contract documents, specifying tariff review formulas and performance standards. There is private-sector participation through the full concession of a major service in at least one city.

4: A large degree of decentralization and commercialization has taken place. Water and waste water utilities are managerially independent, with cash flows—net of municipal budget transfers—that ensure financial viability. A Municipal Finance Law has been implemented, providing municipalities with the opportunity to raise finance. Full cost recovery exists and there are no cross-subsidies. A semi-autonomous regulatory agency has the power to advise and enforce tariffs and service quality. There is substantial private-sector participation through build–operate–transfer concessions, management contracts, or asset sales to service parts of the network or entire networks. A concession of major services has taken place in a city other than the country's capital.

4 +: Water and waste water utilities are fully decentralized and commercialized. Large municipalities enjoy financial autonomy and demonstrate the capability to raise finance. Full cost recovery has been achieved and there are no cross-subsidies. A fully autonomous regulator exists with complete authority to review and enforce tariff levels and performance quality standards. There is widespread private-sector participation via service management/lease contracts, with high-powered performance incentives and/or full concessions and/or divestiture of water and waste water services in major urban areas.

REFERENCES

Aghion, P., and Shankerman, M. (1998). 'Competition, Entry, and the Social Returns to Infrastructure in Transition Economies', European Bank for Reconstruction and Development Working Paper no. 36, EBRD, London.

Commander, S., Dutz, M., and Stern, N. (1999). 'Restructuring in Transition Economies: Ownership, Competition and Regulation', *Annual Bank Conference on Development Economics,* Washington: World Bank.

European Bank for Reconstruction and Development (EBRD) (1996, 1998, 1999). *Transition Reports,* London: EBRD.

European Commission (2000). *Energy in Europe 1999: Annual Energy Review*, Brussels: European Commission.

Kennedy D. (1999). 'Introducing Competition to the Power Sectors of Transition Economies', European Bank for Reconstruction and Development Working Paper no. 41, EBRD, London.

Newbery, D. and Pollitt, M. (1997). 'The Restructuring and Privatising of the CEGB: Was it Worth It?' *Journal of Industrial Economics*, 45(3): 269–303.

Stern, J. (1997). 'What Makes an Independent Regulator Independent?' *Business Strategy Review*, 8(2): 67–74.

20

Regulating the internet?

JACQUES CRÉMER

20.1. INTRODUCTION

My purpose in this chapter is to survey some aspects of the governance of the internet that, as an economic theorist, I find particularly interesting. I will try to reflect on its strengths and weaknesses, and to sketch some ways in which one can begin thinking about the desirability of government intervention.

There are a number of reasons why the problem of the governance of the internet, which is the largest non-regulated network in the history of humanity, is important. First, at least since the Second World War, economists and policy-makers alike have felt that large-network industries needed to be regulated by governments, and even the recent introduction of competition has usually been conducted under the supervision of a regulator. On the other hand, the internet seems to have developed a form of regulation by mutual consent. Could this solution be adapted to other networks?

On a more practical level, the internet is probably the most important new technology of the beginning of the twenty-first century. It is important to know whether its mode of governance is appropriate for the challenges that it will have to face in the next ten years, or whether governments should prepare for more active intervention. Tim Berners-Lee invented the World Wide Web, and is now the director of the World Wide Web Consortium (W3C), one of the two most important governing institutions in the current internet. Yet, even he believes that governmental regulation might be appropriate for some aspects of the network:

More insidiously still, it could also be possible for my ISP to give me a better connectivity to sites that have paid for it, and I would have no way of knowing this: I might think that some stores seemed to have slow servers. It would be great to have some self-regulation or even government regulation in these areas. (Berners-Lee 1999)

I would like to thank my colleagues at IDEI, and specially Claude Crampes, Jean-Jacques Laffont, and Patrick Rey, for their comments. I would also like to thank participants at the 'Economie de l'internet' workshop at the École Nationale Supérieure des Télécommunications de Bretagne (ENSTB), 22 and 23 June 2000, and at the Oxford Conference on the Regulation of Public Services, 3 and 4 July 2000, especially Alain Bravo. I am very grateful to Claude Henry who encouraged me to think about this topic.

The governance of the internet is, as we will see, extremely complex, as there is no one organization responsible for making sure that the different elements meld together. I have therefore chosen some elements of the organization that I find especially interesting, and will discuss how the regulation of this sector differs from that of the other networks. I have restricted my attention to the regulation of the internet itself, and will not discuss how government regulation might be needed to improve the use of the network; hence I will not consider privacy issues, criminal activities on the internet, the tension between freedom of speech and the protection of children from exposure to pornographic material, etc. Basically, I restrict myself to the hardware and the operating system of the internet, rather than its applications or consequences for the 'real world'.

For the purposes of this paper, it is convenient to distinguish two strata in the internet: first, a physical network, composed of many different, privately owned and operated, networks and the standards that are used to manage these networks and their interconnection, and, second, a set of standards used to communicate over these networks. The first stratum is the core of the internet; the second has many components, of which the most prominent is the World Wide Web. I will therefore begin by considering the regulation problems of the internet proper, before turning to the governance of the World Wide Web. Finally, I discuss the problem of universal service in the internet.[1]

20.2. THE NETWORK

20.2.1. Last-mile connection

End-users buy a connection to the internet through an internet service provider (ISP), which provides them with software and support to connect to its network and, usually, with an internet address, such as <u>whyme@nonsensemail.com</u>. However, the connection between their computers and the ISP travels across regulated lines, and the form of the regulation has important consequences for the cost and pattern of use of the internet

For instance, in the United States local telephone calls are unmetered, which implies that the marginal cost of a longer connection is nil. Furthermore, the monthly payment for a line is below cost. Consumers who 'surf the web' stay connected for much longer than the duration of a normal phone conversation, inducing increased costs for 'telcos' (telecommunications companies). On the other hand, in Europe local calls are metered. ISPs have argued that the per-minute charge is higher than the cost for the local phone company, and furthermore that the cost of transmitting data to an ISP is lower than the cost of

---

[1] Readers who want a more fundamental and more complete discussion of the relationship between law and the internet should consult Lessig (1999a,b).

transmitting voice. This is made all the more complicated by the fact that the hourly pattern of use seems to be very different for internet and voice, and that the tariffs are often very far from optimal peak load pricing. In response to these demands, and in order to promote home use of the internet, the French regulator has introduced a special rate for connection to ISPs; but one may wonder if this was not a political response to an economic problem. A complete discussion would also include the distortion created by the vagaries of inter-connection charges in the pricing of ISPs, including the 'free' ISPs who live off payments by the telcos. There is no simple solution to this problem: remember that optimal Ramsey prices would depend not only on costs, but also on the elasticities of demand, which are certainly not measurable with any degree of precision in a market in transition such as internet connectivity.

The development of DSL, which allows faster connection over a regular telephone line, hence bypassing the need for widespread installation of fibre to the home, also creates difficult issues concerning the regulation of 'unbundling'. In addition, it is possible to connect to the internet through the cables laid down for TV, and the United States has seen quite a controversy over the right of the cable company to require connection through its own ISP.

Although the issues mentioned above are crucial for the development of the internet, I will not discuss them further as they require the same type of analysis as traditional telephony regulation.[2]

20.2.2. *The government as an innovator*

Although it is true that the internet is a showcase for the innovative power of free markets, one should not forget that it is first and foremost a child of government-supported research. The story has been told too many times to be repeated in detail here, but the first applied work on the connection of a large number of computers developed out of a research programme at the US Department of Defense centred around a network called the ARPANET. It eventually became desirable to link the ARPANET to other computer net-works, and Robert Kahn enlisted the collaboration of Vincent Cerf, then at Stanford University, to develop protocols that would enable networks of computers to interconnect. During the first half of the 1970s they developed the addressing and forwarding protocol, IP, as well as the two transport protocols, TCP and UDP.[3]

---

[2] There are quite a few other issues over which there is interference between the regulation of traditional telecommunications and the regulation of the internet; for instance, the development of 'IP telephony', or the use of the internet to carry telephone calls, creates competition that telephone companies find unfair.

[3] An interesting history of the development of these technologies, by many of the principal actors, can be found in Leiner *et al.* (2000).

20.2.3. *The basic internet protocols*

In order to understand the discussion that follows, we need to make a detour through a description of the basic technology of the internet. As in many other types of modern telecommunications technology, the internet functions by sending packets. We can think of each packet as a postcard, which contains both an address, useful for the Post Office, and content. It all happens as if, in your computer, there were a factory staffed by gnomes whose job is to send messages on postcards through the internet to other computers.

The simplest situation arises when you send a short e-mail. Your e-mail program (Outlook, Eudora, Netscape Communicator) orders the gnomes to send the message to this or that address. If your message is short enough, it will fit on only one postcard, and the job of the gnomes is to prepare this postcard. The internet Protocol, or IP, gives them instructions on how to do this. The postcard is prepared by adding to the text of the message a 'header'. The most important information on this header is the address of the destination. The gnomes also add the address of your own computer, as well as instructions, for the computers that will carry the postcard, on the way in which the postcard must be handled. When the postcard arrives at the computer of your correspondent, the gnomes in her computer perform the opposite task: they extract from the postcard the information that it needs and hand it over to her e-mail program.

Actually, even in our simple case, the work that the gnomes have to do is a bit more complicated than this. The internet is built by the interconnection of many different networks. You cannot be entirely sure of the reliability of all the networks through which your message is going to transit, but you still want to make sure the message arrives safely. It is the responsibility of another team of gnomes to serve as a liaison between your computer and the networks. The Transmission Control Protocol (TCP) tells them how to do this. In the case of our simple message, their job would be basically to ensure that the computer of your correspondent knows that a message is forthcoming and is ready to receive it. So they would be handed the postcard, but before sending it they will send a message to the recipient computer asking whether it is ready to receive a message, and they will send a postcard only if the answer is positive. The protocol also ensures that the recipient computer acknowledges that the message has been received.

From an organizational viewpoint, it is very important to understand that the TCP gnomes in charge of the transmission and the IP gnomes in charge of the addressing can be in two different 'shops'. Of course, the TCP gnomes need the IP gnomes. For instance, when your TCP gnomes interrogate their correspondents to find out whether they are ready to receive a message, they write a postcard but must ask the IP gnomes to address it. However, the type of action that each shop must take, and the information each must provide to the other, are very precisely specified by the protocols, so that in their day-to-day (or rather, millisecond-by-millisecond) job the gnomes in each shop can organize themselves independently. We will see that this layering of standards on top of one another is typical of the organization of the internet, and in fact determines its organization.

Of course, in general, you want to send more than simple messages, and your latest article does not fit on one postcard. When you ask that the article be sent to a colleague, the TCP gnomes cut it in little pieces and put it on different postcards. It is each of these postcards that the IP gnomes hand over to the network. Then, in order for the recipient TCP gnomes to be able to reconstitute your paper, they need to know in which order to paste the content of the different postcards, in case they did not arrive in the order in which they were sent. Part of the job of the TCP gnomes is to provide 'sequence numbers' that enable this reconstitution, as well as to put a marker on the last piece of data. Furthermore, the protocol provides for methods by which the two TCP shops can communicate with each other in case one of the postcards did not make it.

Remarkably, the same type of strategy is used to send fast-changing content, such as voice or video, over the internet. Assume for instance that you want to make a telephone call over the internet. Your internet telephony software will code your voice, writing down the instructions that the software on your interlocutor's computer must follow in order to reproduce the sounds that you are making ('voicemail'). This stream of code is transmitted to a User Data Protocol (UDP) shop where gnomes prepare postcards to transmit to the IP shop. These gnomes (who must be on steroids, given the very large amount of information they have to treat) do basically the same type of job as the TCP gnomes, except that they are less careful to make sure that every packet makes it—because voice is still understandable even if there are small gaps in the stream of sound. They are interested mainly in ensuring that they all leave fast enough that there is no gap in the transmission: whereas the TCP shop will slow down the rate at which it is sending postcards if it understands that there is congestion in the network, the UDP shop will keep pumping them out. We see here one of the advantages of the layering of standards: two different applications can use the same shop for different functions when this is needed.

20.2.4. *Connecting networks*

Once the data has left your computer, it needs to be transmitted to the computer of the recipient of your message. For this, it travels through a variety of intermediaries, of which it is customary to distinguish two types: ISPs, mentioned above, and internet backbone providers (IBPs), sometimes called top-level ISPs.[4]

---

[4] The discussion that follows is inspired by Crémer *et al.* (1999), which provides many more details.

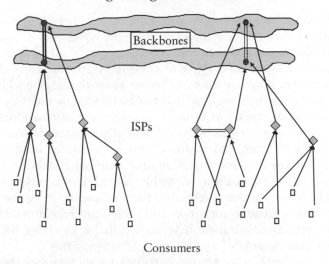

Figure 20.1. *The organization of the internet*

Whereas the ISPs specialize in providing the connection between end-users and the internet, IBPs transmit data over long distances, typically using long-haul fibre. It is quite remarkable that, from any address in the network, one can send messages to almost any other adddress. The basis for this universal connectivity lies in the essentially hierarchical structure of the internet, illustrated in Figure 20.1. The consumers are represented by the boxes at the bottom of the figure, and the ISPs by the diamond shapes. Two local markets are depicted. The data transmitted by customers travels up the hierarchy to the lowest common level. If two clients in the two local markets are indirect clients of the same backbone, the data is transmitted between the two markets by the backbone; on the other hand, if the two clients are indirect clients of different backbones, the backbones need to exchange this information between themselves. Hence, as a first approximation, we find ourselves in front of two hierarchies which communicate only at the top level.

There are two main types of contract in the internet. Transit contracts are represented by arrows in the figure. The supplier, at the tip of the arrow, transmits all data that the client wants to send to the rest of the internet and transmits back to the client all data that is addressed to her. Of course, there is a fee for this service. Note that, although this is not represented in the figure, an ISP can purchase transit from another ISP, and then purchase further transit from a backbone (or from another ISP).

'Peering' contracts are represented by double lines. At present in the internet, these have two characteristics. First, each of the parties accepts from the other all data destined to one of its (direct or indirect) clients. Second, the contracts are of the 'bill and keep' variety, so that no money is exchanged between the parties. The large backbones peer with each other. There is also some 'local peering', where ISPs that are linked to different backbones exchange traffic directly in order to save on their transit bill.

Peering contracts are the subject of controversy. In the early days of the internet they were quite common. In recent years the large backbones have refused to peer with small regional backbones: they argue that this induces an unfair allocation of costs. For instance, consider a major national US back-bone that peers with a regional New England backbone: it will then carry the messages both from and to the clients of the local backbone to San Franscisco, whereas if it peers with another national backbone, the cost of carrying packets over long distances will be shared. On the other hand, small backbones have argued that a refusal to peer represents unfair use of market power.[5] At this juncture competition authorities and regulators have chosen not to intervene, although there have been calls for the large backbones to publish their peering policy.[6]

In this environment, what are the incentives for maintaining the quality of interconnection? Before answering this question, we must define 'quality'. The first dimension of quality is delay. The maintenance of low delays necessitates sufficient capacity, both within the different networks and at the inter-connection points. Current delays are generally acceptable for traditional applications such as file transfer, e-mails, or web browsing, but the develop-ment of real-time services such as internet telephony or video-conferencing require both very low and very uniform delays. It would be very easy for an ISP or a backbone that desired to do so to degrade the quality of interconnection: because of the very rapid growth of internet traffic, even maintaining constant delays requires continuous increases in capacity on both sides of interconnec-tion points, and it would be sufficient to slow down these increases on one side of the connection.

The second dimension of quality is the management of the network. The development of real-time and premium services may call for the development of new protocols that will enable for instance the prioritizing of packets, these new protocols 'sitting on top of' the existing protocols. A dominant provider of connectivity may have the incentive to develop proprietary protocols, and to offer such services only between its own customers, in order to create a com-petitive advantage. I will come back to this point below when discussing the management of standards.

The economics of networks has stressed the strong incentives for firms to limit the quality of interconnection. To see this in the simplest possible setup, consider the case where two perfectly substitutable networks of the same size offer the same service and are perfectly interconnected. If they compete *à la Bertrand*, their profits will be equal to 0. They are better off making their

---

[5] See Milgrom *et al.* (1999) for support for this view.
[6] See Laffont *et al.* (2000) for a study of peering in the internet.

networks incompatible. Consumers will have a tendency to migrate to one of the networks, and, under our assumptions, each of the network has a 50 per cent probability of surviving; but a 50 per cent probability of acquiring monopoly profits is better than a certainty of acquiring no profits. Of course, this example is caricatural, but its basic insights have been confirmed by much of the literature. Furthermore, it has been shown that a larger network has much more incentives to restrict compatibility.

Under these conditions, it is quite remarkable that the internet network has seen such good interconnections up to now. This is probably due to the fact that at each level concentration has not reached a critical point, and furthermore that the rapid growth of the market has deterred connectivity suppliers from offering an inferior service. However, this equilibrium was put to the test by the 1998 merger of MCI and WorldCom, owners of two of the biggest backbones, with a combined market share above 40 per cent.[7] The European Commission felt that the combined backbone would have incentives to restrict connectivity to other backbones, in trying to persuade consumers to migrate to its own network, and it accepted the merger only on the condition that MCI–World-Com agreed to sell the MCI backbone to Cable & Wireless.

This story makes it clear that strong enforcement of competition law will be necessary in order to maintain the connectivity that is enjoyed in the internet today. Whether it will be *sufficient* is not clear. For instance, the time may come when a firm dominates the backbone market sufficiently that only the presence of a regulator, with its ability to move faster, can guarantee universal connectivity.

20.2.5. *Standards*

The fact that degradation of connectivity has been rare does not mean that it has been nonexistent. For instance, one of the most popular applications of the internet has been instant messaging, where groups of users 'chat' in real time by sending messages (basically, text messages similar to e-mail) to each other. AOL, the biggest purveyor of internet connectivity to dial-up users, owns the two largest instant messaging networks: AIM with 91 million users and ICQ, acquired in 1998, with 64 million users, both freely available to non-AOL subscribers. This is the type of application for which there are strong network externalities: the utility of an individual user depends strongly on the number of other users. As a consequence, in 1999 two of AOL's competitors in this market, Microsoft and Tribal Voice, tried to interconnect their own instant messaging services with those of AOL, and numerous others have since tried to do this. AOL has modified its software in order to prevent such

---

[7] The measure of market share in the backbone market is fraught with conceptual difficulties, and hampered by a remarkable lack of data. The figure of 40% is given as illustrative of the more or less general consensus of observers.

interconnection. As a consequence, its rivals have complained to the Federal Communications Commission (FCC) and have tried to persuade the regulator to put pressure on AOL to open up its software. On the other hand, AOL has argued that it has a duty to protect the privacy of the users of its software and the reliability of its system, which were endangered by these actions. It has said that it is willing to permit the interconnection of the different instant messaging systems as soon as a satisfactory standard is available. Because the FCC did not believe that instant messaging is a communications issue, at least not at the beginning of the controversy, it refused to intervene. However, instant messaging services are increasingly allowing the use of voice, and are therefore more and more becoming substitutes for telephone calls. The delimitation between different parts of the industry is becoming more and more complex.

This episode brings to light the double role of standards, and the difficulty of regulating their use. Indeed, it is clear that *ex post* one would wish for a common standard to be implemented, and that full interconnectivity should reign. However, as S. McAteer put it, 'This stuff is on AOL's infrastructure, and it's an application that they built from the ground up. AOL conceived it, executed it and launched it' (Hu 2000). Developing a standard, both technically and commercially, requires significant investment. In the case of new products, the incentives to innovate are provided through the right to temporarily enjoy monopoly profits,[8] protected through patents, technical secrets, or the commercial benefits of being first. On the other hand, the cumulative aspects of dominance in network industries may make even a temporary monopoly in one product extremely powerful, and could create specific problems that need to be addressed, both theoretically and practically.

In the current functioning of the internet, no organization has the authority to impose new standards. On the other hand, a complex of organizations, which I will describe in more detail later but which for the time being I will call the IETF (Internet Engineering Task Force) for one of its components, has a central role in the discussion and approval of new standards. Remember that a standard is useful only if economic agents believe that others will follow it. From an economic viewpoint, the IETF serves as a focal point: a standard approved by it acquires credibility. Coordination games can have inefficient equilibria, but in practice, when there is relatively free entry in the creation of standards, we expect any organization that has shown staying power to be developing efficient standards that correspond to the needs of the public.

The IETF has chosen to do this through a very 'democratic' mode of governance: 'There is not membership in the IETF. Anyone may register for and attend any meeting' (see IETF n.d.). Anybody can propose a standard, although in practice most standards seem to be proposed by IETF working groups. Once

---

[8] Like ICQ and AIM, all the instant messaging servicing services of which I am aware are freely distributed, the owners deriving revenues from advertising or the sale of complementary software. Market power in this case yields benefits in forms different from textbook monopoly profits.

again, anyone can propose the creation of a working group, which will be approved if it has a 'charter' that guarantees that it will be able to do its work and will not conflict with the work of other working groups. Furthermore, 'Essentially all work in the IETF is done by volunteers. ... Everyone has a different reason for volunteering, but the majority of the people do so because they want the internet to operate better ... Most participants have day jobs, and many have to cajole their employers to let them participate as much as they do on company time' (Hoffman n.d.).

Of course, as professional cynics, economists will be less enthused by such a totally volunteer effort, wondering about the incentives of the participants.[9] A quick check on a small number of working groups reveals directors who are either academics or employees of large corporations, and both academics and employees of large corporations can certainly have agendas that are not necessarily aligned with the maximization of social welfare. On the other hand, the type of issues and the extremely open nature of the process probably limit, without eliminating, the possibilities of capture: 'as soon as you propose that your protocol become an IETF standard, you must fully relinquish control for the protocol. If there is general agreement, parts of the protocol can be completely changed, whole sections can be ripped out, new things can be added and the name can be changed' (Hoffman n.d.). It seems to me that there is scope for theoretically interesting as well as practically important research on the way in which firms can use this process, and the limits that it implies. It should probably focus on identifying the circumstances under which an agreement between producers would not be too detrimental to consumers.

The way in which the IETF functions also provides interesting topics for reflection. The IETF *stricto sensu* is part of a constellation of four groups. The *Internet Society* is a professional society, open to individuals and to organizations, which, apart from different activities in support of the diffusion of the internet, partly finances the IETF and also approves the appointments to the *Internet Architecture Board* (IAB) which are submitted by the IETF nominating committee. The IAB provides oversight of the general structure of the internet and serves as an appeals board for the decisions taken by the *Internet Engineering Steering Group* (IESG) and the IETF. It also approves the nominations submitted by the IETF nominating committee to the IESG. The IESG is composed of a chair and the directors of the eight functional areas of the IETF. These directors are in charge of overseeing the working groups in their areas of expertise; as a group, they approve new standards.

The outcome of all these activities is formalized in documents called RFCs.[10] Some RFCs describe Internet Standards, Proposed Standards, and Draft

---

[9] For instance, Lerner and Tirole (2000) critically examine the motives of programmers that freely contribute to open-source software.

[10] RFC is the acronym of 'request for comments', but this is misleading as they are in fact final documents.

Standards, while others are Informational, Experimental, or Historical RFCs. Interestingly, the management and the relationships between the four groups that compose the IETF are also detailed in RFCs.

The functioning of all these organizations seems to balance the need for broad participation and for the provision of incentives in ways that are reminiscent of the free software movement.[11] Apart from the defence of the interests of their employers that we discussed above, one can only assume that the same type of career concerns that motivate contributors to open-source software motivates them during the discussion of internet standards. The role of the leaders, and in particular of the working group chairs, is extremely important. There seem to be very explicit criteria by which they are judged, in particular the appropriate end of the task of the group. It is interesting to note that the documents oriented to new members describe very explicity what to an economist looks very much like an equilibrium of the repeated game[12] that all these rules determine.

20.3. THE WORLD WIDE WEB

One of the most important applications of the internet is the World Wide Web, which has become so important that it is hard to believe that the internet started its existence before the Web was invented, with its main applications being e-mail and file transfers.

Tim Berners-Lee, a physicist employed at CERN, developed the web in order to enable users of computers connected to different networks to share information easily. A file transfer protocol enables me to send you a PostScript file that contains this paper, or enables you to come and fetch it from my computer and to see it using your version of GSView on your computer. A totally different type of interaction is possible if I make a .html file and allow you to see it through your browser. By clicking, you can reach any other documents that I quote; in some sense, whatever extra information I have provided is integrated to the vast store of information already allocated on computers all over the world.[13]

Three interrelated innovations were required. The first was to find a way in which computers could refer to the documents they needed to transfer to each other. This is the URL, the strange address of the type www.walras.edu/economics.great, which tells us that on the server (the computer that provides

---

[11] A discussion of the IETF that stresses the parallel to the open-source movement can be found at http://www.editions-oreilly.fr/divers/tribune-libre/fr-ch03.html [27 Feb. 2001].

[12] A more proper model may be a model of corporate culture, as in Crémer (1986).

[13] A hypertext is a text that is designed not to be read linearly. For instance, in a microeconomics textbook, the phrase 'as **Walras** first discussed' would provide a link to a biography of Walras, which would be reached by clicking with the mouse on the box **Walras**. The basic idea of the web is to transform the entire set of documents that are available into a large hypertext-like repertory; hence the prefix 'HT' in the name of the protocols 'http' and 'html'.

the document) called 'www.walras.edu' the client can obtain the document 'economics.great'. The basic idea of the web is that the browser, i.e. the program that serves as a window on the documents that are called, must be able to understand documents in many different formats. For instance, your browser should be able to display pictures, in formats called .gif or .jpg, but also Acrobat Reader files. A way had to be found for a browser to ask the server for a file, and to explain the types of file it could accept. This was the 'http' protocol, which was also designed to ensure that the dialogue between the computers is rapid. Finally, Berners-Lee created a new file format, 'html'. This format has three important special features: it enables the description of a simple page very efficiently and in a small file; it enables the inclusion of other files, and in particular graphics, within the document; and, most importantly, it provides for the possibility of links to other documents.

Berners-Lee sold the development of the web to CERN as a way of connecting the many computers, which used very diverse systems on very different networks, of the high-energy physicists who worked and visited CERN. Like the internet, the web is the result of publicly funded research; however, whereas the internet was the intended result of a long-run programme, the web was the result of the vision of one person, who was able to scrape together resources in an environment not intended for the end-result to which he put it.

Developing protocols is not sufficient. They are useful, and can be demonstrated to be useful, only when they are implemented in programs that actually run. The next stage was to persuade programmers to build browsers, and a browser per type of machine was needed. Berners-Lee and Fishetti (1999) describes the work that Berners-Lee had to do to 'evangelize' and find such programmers. Remarkably, it was only at the end of 1990 that the first implementation of the World Wide Web began to function. It was limited to one server, with one browser which functioned only on NEXT computers. Ten years later, this technology was changing the world!

From a regulatory viewpoint, the story becomes interesting after this beginning. For a number of reasons, including the fear that Netscape and its predecessor Mosaic would implement proprietary standards, Berners-Lee decided that he should set a body standard. Michael Dertouzos, director of the Laboratory for Computer Science at MIT, agreed to help him, and it was decided that the new body should be managed jointly by MIT and CERN. Eventually, CERN decided that it was not within its mission to manage the development of computer standards and decided to bow out. The INRIA, a French research group in computer science, became the European home of the new group, the World Wide Web Consortium (abbreviated W3C), although its intellectual centre is in the United States. It is quite remarkable that Tim Berners-Lee, a European working in Europe, developed the World Wide Web in Europe but eventually felt that he had to move to the United States. In part his decision was based on the fact that the centre of the development of networks was based in the USA. It is difficult, however, not to feel that the much more entrepreneurial nature of the American academic sector provides it with a substantial advantage in managing tasks such as the running of a large consortium, and also makes it more aggressive in pursuing those opportunities. This is an important policy issue, both for Europe and more generally for the management of standards-based communications networks.

The W3C is run on a very different model from the IETF. Membership is restricted to organizations, with relatively high membership fees[14]—$50,000 is the normal fee, which is reduced to $5,000 for non-profit organizations, government agencies, and small firms (those with less than $50 million of gross revenues). On 14 June 2000 it had 426 members. Only members participate in the development of standards, and only they have access to work in progress.

The W3C describes its mission very broadly.[15] 'By promoting interoperability and encouraging an open forum for discussion, W3C commits to leading the technical evolution of the web'. Also, however, 'W3C must guide the web's development with careful consideration for the novel legal, commercial, and social issues raised by this technology.' This very large role is very clear in the general organization of the consortium: 'There are three qualities an individual must possess in order to join the W3C Team or participate in a W3C Activity (e.g., act as a chair, editor, etc.): technical competence in one's role, the ability to act fairly, social competence in one's role.'

Unlike the IETF, the W3C has a very top-down structure. For instance, the rules state that it is the director who proposes the development of new activities; members of working groups must put forward nominations and the director may reject a nomination. The evidence suggests that the circumstances of the creation of the W3C explain, at least in part, this hierarchical model. Berners-Lee had been somewhat perturbed that the creators of Mosaic seemed to want to control the development of the Web (Berners-Lee and Fishetti 1999: 81-8), and a fast-moving organization was required to counteract such plans. One wonders whether an IETF-type structure would have been able to deal with the threat to the standardization of HTML that occurred in 1995–7 (see Garfinkel 1998: 42 for a brief discussion).

The main task of the W3C is the development of technical standards. In recent years it has been very active in the development and promotion of XML, the successor of HTML. It also has an agenda for the development of the web. For instance, Berners-Lee has argued forcefully over the years that a browser should also be an editor, so that the web is not just another way of publishing documents, but rather a facilitator of 'intercreativity', where users could not only acquire knowledge, but also contribute to its development. Research programmes are conducted within the W3C to pursue this objective; for

[14] As a consequence the W3C has lots of resources, and, unlike the IETF, people who do the work are salaried. In June 2000 the W3C had 58 employees.

[15] The following citations are taken from the 'World Wide Web Consortium Process Document', which can be found http://www.w3c.org.

instance, a free source browser-cum-editor, Amaya, has been built as a demonstration project.

It seems clear to me that no government regulator could have done the work that the W3C has done. However, its success itself raises a number of issues. First, as in the case of the IETF, a private group whose membership includes all the major companies in the industry yields enormous power, and one cannot assume *a priori* that this power will be used in the best interest of society. Of course, nor can we assume that society would be better off if this group did not exist, or that any other solution would be better. However, we cannot assume *a priori* that no problem will ever necessitate intervention either by a regulator or by competition authorities. Furthermore, a number of critiques have expressed reservations about the fact that a private group yields so much power over matters that are not only technical, but also societal. To put it in more polemical terms: economists agree that profit-maximizing firms should be entitled to rents from their innovations, but they expect such rents to be monetary. How do we deal with an individual who has invented a remarkable new technology and whose rents are taken in the form of induced societal change? Here again, what is important is not so much what the W3C has done up to now, as the need to understand the issues involved before any problem arises.

At a more mundane level, a comparative study of the top-down and bottom-up approaches to the organization of standard-setting groups could be very instructive. The work of Sah and Stiglitz (1986) could provide a starting point for that reflection.

20.4. UNIVERSAL SERVICE

Politicians, like academics, are fireflies that converge around anything that shines. Academics claim they understand the internet and try to predict its development. Politicians claim credit for its existence and try to control its future. This paper provides an example of the behaviour of academics. Readers will find in their own countries examples of politicians who claim credit for inventing the internet or being in at the beginning of its rapid growth. They will also easily find examples of politicians who justify an extension of its control by the need to provide universal service; they talk about the 'digital divide' that separates those with access to electronic communication from those without, both within developed countries and between developed and developing countries. In the United States, the federal government's universal service policy has been focused mostly on ensuring connection to the internet for all schools and hospitals. There have also been a few local attempts to provide connection to the internet for all or a substantial proportion of a community. For instance, in March 2000 the town of Lagrange, Georgia, announced that it would connect every household to the internet through cable television. The town of Blacksburg, Virginia, has provided very cheap connection to all members of the community, and about 80 per cent of the population now has access to the internet. A program called NetSchools provides for the distribution of a laptop to every student in a school and access to the internet both from home and during the day[16] through an infrared, wireless network.[17] It claims great success in the number of students meeting reading, writing, and mathematics standards in some low-income communities.

Because 'universal service' is such a popular term, it is used to defend many policies, and we should be somewhat more careful in our own use. First, if computers and internet access substantially increase the quality of education, we should make use of these technologies, simply because government has taken on the responsibility to provide education, and should do so efficiently. If this has something to do with universal service, it is with the universal service of education, not the universal service of the internet. Second, it is clear that a new technology diffuses first among the wealthiest and most educated parts of the population. The fact that in 2000 about 50 per cent of the population is connected in the countries with the greatest connection rate should not be taken as any indication of the steady-state situation. Furthermore, even if it was found in the long run that a substantial proportion of the population did not connect to the internet, this would not necessarily be cause for alarm. There are many goods that are not consumed by parts of the population: although increasing the income of the poorest segment of the population should be part of the goal of government, this need not be done by providing subsidized access.[18]

The third reason for universal access is the existence of network externalities. There are some types of communications that the sender wants to reach all the members of a group. For instance, before an election the French government sends to the house of every voter an envelope that contains advertisements provided by each of the candidates. A school may want some announcements to be sent to all parents.[19] We will call such communications 'broadcasting communications'. At the present time, the postal service is by far the cheapest method for broadcasting this information; the internet is a potential alternative. The situation is complicated by the fact that, among the recipients, there are some people who prefer one mode of communication over the other, and that there are increasing returns to scale in sending messages through any of the two technologies.

In Crémer (2000), I built a model that tries to represent these trade-offs.[20] I showed that there exist circumstances under which the marginal social value of another subscriber to the internet increases as the proportion of subscribers

[16] According to the netschools.com web site, the total cost, without home access to the internet, in around $750 per year.

[17] Of course, appropriate teaching material is also provided.

[18] Of course, economic theory shows that giving away some goods can be the optimal way in which to redistribute income, but I know of no evidence that, absent other considerations, internet access is a better candidate for such giving away than, let us say, food.

[19] The NetSchools program allows for communicating with the parents through e-mail.

[20] Interested reader might also want to consult Crémer and Laffont (2000).

becomes important, allowing the use of the internet as a broadcasting technology. Under these conditions, it may be efficient to subsidize the use of the internet, and I showed that this is done more efficiently by subsidizing the providers of information. I doubt that in most OECD countries we find ourselves in a situation where the time has come for general subsidy of access to the internet, except perhaps for the school-age population. However, the time when this is the case may be fast approaching.

20.5. CONCLUSION

There is a strong current of anti-regulation and anti-government feelings in the internet community. For instance, Barlow (1996) states: 'Governments of the Industrial World, you weary giant of flesh and steel, I come from Cyberspace, the new home of Mind. On behalf of the future, I ask you of the past to leave us alone. You are not welcome among us. You have no sovereignty where we gather.'[21] He calls explicitly for the autonomy of the regulation of Cyberspace: 'Where there are real conflicts, where there are wrongs, we will identify them and address them by our means. We are forming our own Social Contract. The governance will arise according to the conditions of our world, not yours.'

However passionate these appeals, governments will intervene. Furthermore, they have the legitimacy to intervene. The electronic world is becoming more and more an integral part of our lives and is interacting with all human activities; the 'voluntary' organizations that regulate it hold monopoly power over an important industry, and their behaviour should be scrutinized with the same intensity as that of any other organization holding monopoly power. This scrutiny should be conducted by institutions who have democratic credentials. Of course, the intervention of governments will bring its own baggage of inefficiencies, pettiness, over-regulation, and self-serving policies, but this is the trade-off with which we all live, and we have not yet found a better solution.

Stating that the governments have the legitimacy to intervene does not mean that I believe that they *should* intervene, and I do not see any reason to believe that the future of XML, or of the IP protocol would be better served by governmental intervention. In any case, we need to think much more about the consequences of this self-regulation by interested parties. I have mentioned some lines of enquiry that seem promising. I would now like to suggest another one. The internet is regulated not only by the ITEF and the W3C, on which I have focused, but by a number of other organizations. The overall architecture of this regulation, and the relationship between different standard organizations, should be an interesting topic of theoretical and applied economic research.

---

[21] Although Barlow's view might be extreme, he is a widely recognized and respected member of the internet community. Since writing this text, he has been named a fellow of the Berkman Center at the Harvard Law School.

REFERENCES

Barlow, J. P. (1996). 'A Declaration of the Independence of Cyberspace', http://www.eff.org/barlow/Declaration-Final.html.

Berners-Lee, T. with Fishetti, M. (1999). 'Weaving the Web', San Francisco: Harper-SanFrancisco.

Crémer, J. (1986). 'Cooperation in On-going Organizations', *Quarterly Journal of Economics*, 51 (1): 33–50.

——(2000). 'Network Externalities and Universal Service Obligation in the Internet', *European Economic Review*, 44: 1021–31.

——Rey, P., and Tirole, J. (1999). 'Connectivity in the Commercial Internet', unpublished manuscript, IDEI, Université de Toulouse I.

Cremer, H. and Laffont, J.-J. (2000). 'Public Goods with Access Costs', IDEI Working Paper, Toulouse; http://www.idei.asso.fr.

Garfinkel, S. L. (1998). 'The Web's Unelected Government', *Technology Review*, 38–46.

Hoffman, P. (n.d.). 'A Novice's Guide to the IETF', URL http://www.imc.org/novice-ietf.html.

Hu, J. (2000). 'Instant Messaging Battle Goes to Washington', CNET.com, URL: http//cnet.com/newx/0-1005-200-2033664.html/tag = st.

IETF (n.d.). *The Tao of the IETF: A Guide for New Attendees of the Internet Engineering Task Force*, IETF Secretariat; URL: http://www.ietf.org/tao.html, accessed 27 February 2001.

Laffont, J.-J., Marcus, S., Rey, P., and Tirole, J. (2000). 'Internet Interconnection and the Off-Net Pricing Principle' unpublished paper, IDEI, Toulouse.

Leiner, B. M., Cerf, V. G., Clark, D. D., Kahn, R. E., Kleinrock, L., Lynch, D. C., Postel J., and Wolff, S. (2000). 'A Brief History of the Internet', Internet Society; URL: http://www.isoc.org/history/brief.html.

Lerner, J. and Tirole, J. (2000). 'The Simple Economics of Open Source' unpublished paper; http://www.people.hbs.edu/jlerner.

Lessig, L. (1999a). *Code and Other Laws of Cyberspace*, New York: Basic Books.

——(1999b). 'The Law of the Horse: What Cyberlaw Might Teach', *Harvard Law Review*, 113 (2): 501–46.

Milgrom, P., Michell, B., and Srinagesh, P. (1999). 'Competitive Effects of Internet Pricing', Technical Report, Stanford University and Charles River Associates.

Sah, R. and Stiglitz, J. E. (1986). 'The Architecture of Economics Systems: Hierarchies and Polyarchies', *American Economic Review*, 76 (4): 716–27.

Index